Ma, He Sold Me for a Few Cigarettes

*To my most precious gifts,
my children Fabian and MarieClaire*

Ma, He Sold Me for a Few Cigarettes

A heart-rending memoir that will both horrify and inspire

MARTHA LONG

MAINSTREAM
PUBLISHING

EDINBURGH AND LONDON

This edition, 2008, 2009

Copyright © Martha Long, 2007
All rights reserved
The moral right of the author has been asserted

First published in Great Britain in 2007 by
MAINSTREAM PUBLISHING COMPANY
(EDINBURGH) LTD
7 Albany Street
Edinburgh EH1 3UG

ISBN 9781845963132

A catalogue record for this book is available
from the British Library

Typeset in Caslon and Sabon

Printed in Great Britain by
Cox and Wyman Ltd, Reading

Acknowledgements

With thanks to my children Fabian and MarieClaire. Both of you a joy. Both, every mother's dream, and I am the mother! Wonders will never cease. How lucky can I get?

To my firstborn Tina, always a special bond, and to her two little beauties, Charlie and William, my adorable grandchildren.

To Ailsa, my editor. Thank you for your extraordinary patience and most of all your warmth and your kindness.

To Bill, a very astute man. Thank you, Bill, I feel very privileged to have your faith in me.

A special thank you to Mary Dunne for tirelessly poring over my handwritten script and managing to type it all. Not an easy task. Take a bow, Mary!

Last but not least, to Helen Scully. Thanks, Helen, for all your encouragement. Without you this would not be in the public domain. Thanks, friend!

Author's Note

This is the true story of my early childhood. Originally, I did not write it for publication. Instead, my intention was to rid myself of the voice of the little girl I had once been. For many years, I had tried to leave her behind and bury her in the deep, dark recesses of my mind. I tried to pretend she had never existed and went on to become someone she wouldn't recognise. But she was always there in the background, haunting me and waiting for her chance to burst back into life and give voice to the pain she endured. I got old and tired before my time as I struggled to escape her, and, finally, the effort of suppressing her became too much. As I started to write, she exploded back into life, and I let her tell the story in her own voice.

1

The ma an me, an me mother's sister, Nelly, an her son, Barney – he's only three, I'm bigger, I'm nearly four – live together in one room in a tenement house in the Liberties of Dublin. We were all born here. Me aunts an uncles were born in this room, all ten of them, but most of them now live away in England, so it's just Nelly an me ma left.

Me ma, Sally, had only just passed her sixteenth birthday when I arrived in the world. It was a shock te everyone, they said, though how her growin belly was not noticed was a mystery. The hawk-eyed women missed tha one! When her brothers an sisters arrived over te find out wha was goin on, she wouldn't tell anyone who the father was, an the local parish priest said me ma would have te go inta a Magdalen laundry te stop her getting inta more trouble. 'The baby can go into a convent as well. The nuns are very good in these homes, they'll take care of it.' But Nelly said she would take care of us an told the rest of them te go back te England.

Me granny was a dealer in the Iveagh Market. She sold second-hand clothes, an on Sundays she'd have me grandfather take her apples, an oranges, an chocolate, an things on his horse an cart, an drive out te Booterstown at the seaside, where she sold them te the city people comin off the train te get the fresh air an let their childre play in the sand an get a good wash at the same time, runnin in an out of the water. Me granny worked very hard, gettin up at four o'clock in the mornin te be at the market in time te get her fruit an vegetables, or fish on Fridays.

Me grandfather was a baker. He was a terrible man for the drink.

9

An he was always angry. He didn't make me granny's life easy. He fought in the First World War, an he brought home a huge big paintin from a bombed church in Belgium. I don't know how he managed te get away with tha an bring it all the way back te Dublin, but he did, an it used te hang in the back room (we don't go inta tha room for some reason), takin up the whole wall. Now the paintin's gone, cos Nelly sold it for drink.

Me poor granny lost four of her childre, one after another, an then me grandfather, within nine months. A three-year-old boy, he fell off a low wall an was killed. A little girl, she was only nine years old. A twelve-year-old girl, who died of pneumonia. She was late for school, an the doors were locked, so she sat on the cold steps of the school in the pourin rain, too frightened te go home. A neighbour saw her sittin there an told me granny. She ran down an found her still sittin there an soaked te the skin. Me granny took the shawl from aroun her head an put it on Delia, who was now shiverin like mad. But me granny couldn't save her, an she died.

The next girl te die was Molly, who was eighteen years old. They say she was a real beauty. Gorgeous long wavy hair, down past her waist. She was very religious an probably would have joined the nuns, but she died of consumption. Then me grandfather died, all in nine months. Soon after, me granny got very sick an she was taken inta the Union. Me ma was still only young when she died. The Union used te be called the workhouse. It was a place where sick an destitute people went when there was no hope left.

Me granny left six childre behind te fend fer themselves. Me granny's maiden sister – she never married – lived close by, an she kept an eye on them. One by one, they took the boat te England, each bringin over the next. Me ma even went at fourteen years old.

There was loads of work for everyone. Because England was tryin te rebuild her cities, after the war with Hitler, who nearly blew them te Kingdom Come. Anyway, for some reason, her brother Larry brought her back te Dublin just before I was born an dumped her with Nelly. So here we are – me, the ma, her sister, Nelly, an Barney.

We all sleep in the one big bed. Me an the ma at one end, an Nelly an Barney at the other. Me aunt Nelly is a real hard chaw – I heard tha word from a neighbour. I suppose it means roarin an laughin one minute, an screamin she'll kill ye the next. It wouldn't be a good idea te have a fight with her! One day she sent me fer a Woodbine, an on the way back, I saw tha gobshite Tommy Weaver. I hate him, I do! He thinks he's so big cos he says he's five. He doesn't look it! Anyways, I decided te look like Nelly an put the cigarette in me mouth, I was suckin away like goodo, an yer man was ragin. But by the time I tried te hand it te Nelly, it was all mashed in me mouth, an I was spittin out gobs a tobacca.

Nelly went red as a tomato an then the colour of green grapes. She was gummin fer a cigarette. 'Gimme me coat!' she roared, an leapt out the door, screamin at me te come on! She was up in the shop an had managed te browbeat the aul one inta givin her another cigarette by the time I got there. 'An another thing!' she was sayin. 'We were all well reared! If the babby says she didn't get the cigarette, then she didn't! We don't tell lies! An we're not beggars, we pay our way. So don't act high an mighty wit me, or I'll swing for ye! Com on, you!' she roared at me, an I galloped out behind her, shoutin back at the aul one, 'Yeah! Tha's right!'

2

The ma gave me a brush an told me te sweep down the stairs. I was delighted. I was sweepin an hammerin the brush against the aul wooden banister an back te the wall again. The brush was makin an awful noise altogether. Dust was flyin everywhere, an I stopped te watch it swirlin an risin inta the air, caught in the rays of light comin in from the street. Lovely! I went back te me work.

Suddenly the holy priest came up the stairs. He was on his way up te see old Mrs Coleman, who was ailin. I carried on wit me work, an he stopped te stare.

'You're a grand girl,' he said.

'Yes, Father! I'm helpin me mammy, an I'm nearly kilt tryin te get them clean, so I am.'

The priest had a big red face an a big belly. Me ma says tha's a sign of the good feedin the priests get. He threw back his head an gave a big laugh, then he patted the top of me head.

I was workin so hard when the priest came back down. He could tell, cos I was bangin an hammerin. An ye couldn't see a thing, cos I had risen so much dust. An I nearly put his eye out, cos I was wavin the brush so much. I was red in the face meself. The priest admired me so much he put his hand in his pockets an took out a load of coppers an gave them te me. I never saw this much money in me life. I dropped the brush on the stairs an flew down te the shops.

I stood lookin in the shop winda, gazin at the gorgeous cakes, tryin te decide if I'll have a hornpipe cream first, an then back te me coppers te see if they were real. Me head was spinnin! I had te hold

12

me pocket up wit both hands, cos me pocket was torn an the weight of them was great.

Nelly came up behind me, an I said, 'Look, Nelly! Lookit wha the priest gave me fer sweepin down the stairs.'

Nelly's eyes lit up. 'Ah! Will ye give tha te me te buy the dinner?'

'No! It's mine!'

'I'll buy you a lovely dinner.'

'What'll ye get?'

'Cabbage an potatoes an a bit of bacon. I promise I'll cook it fer ye's all. Just think – a lovely dinner!'

I gave her the money, an she went off in great humour. I ran straight home te tell me ma the great news. She sat there lookin an listenin te me until I got te the bit about Nelly.

'Ah! Did ye give her the money?'

'Yeah, Ma, she's gone te get the dinner.'

'No, she's not! She's gone te the pub. She'll drink it.'

'But, Ma, she said she'll be back wit the dinner.'

'No! She won't be back till the money's gone. Why'd ye give her the money? Why didn't ye hide it an bring it straight up te me?'

'She wanted it, Ma, fer the dinner.'

'Ah, stop annoyin me! You an yer dinner. What am I goin te do fer bread an milk? An lookit! The fire's gone out. I've no coal left te boil the kettle.'

I sat down te listen te the silence of the room. Me ma went back te twitchin her mouth an runnin her fingers through her hair, lookin fer lice. So Nelly was only foolin me!

13

3

I started school today, cos I'm now four. I'm goin te be a scholar. I'm lookin forward te tha. All the big people said they wished they could go back te school, an these are goin te be the best years of me life!

There's loads of us sittin at desks, tha's wha they're called. We have things called inkwells – tha's wha ye dip yer pen inta an write on a copybook. But we won't be doin tha now, cos we're not real scholars yet.

The teacher shouts down at the young fella sittin beside me, cos he's eatin his chunk of bread an drippin. We're not supposed te do tha until we get out te the yard at playtime. She bangs this big long stick on the blackboard. 'Now, pay attention and sit up straight. No! You can't go to the toilet, you have to learn to ask in Irish,' she told a young one who was joggin up an down wit her legs crossed. The pooley streamed down her legs, an the young one was roarin her head off. The teacher had te take her out. We could hear her shoes squelchin, cos they were filled wit piss, an her nose was drippin wit snots. When she got back, the teacher went straight te the blackboard. 'Now!' she said. 'We are going to draw a . . .' an when she was finished, she pointed her stick at a young one an said, 'What is this?' pointin at the blackboard.

'A cup an saucer, Teacher,' squeaked the young one in a hoarse voice.

'Yes! Good. And all together now . . .'

We all shouted up, 'A cup an saucer!'

14

But it was dawnin on me slowly I didn't like this school business at all. I wouldn't be able te draw a cup an saucer. School was too hard, an I don't want te be a scholar. When I got home, I raced up the stairs te tell me ma I was now a scholar. I'd learnt everythin an didn't need te go back te school any more. She was sittin by the fire an looked a bit lonely without me. She had a cup of tea an a saucer sittin on top, wit a slice of Swiss roll on it, warmin by the fire fer me dinner. In honour of the occasion.

Me ma says I have te go te school. She holds me hand an keeps tellin me I'll be grand. The school's only a few doors down, an I'm back in the school yard before I know wha's happened. All the childre are millin aroun, waitin fer the door te open. Me ma asks a big young one te mind me, an Tessa who lives across the road takes me hand. Me ma goes off smilin an wavin, an Tessa tells me I'm a big girl now I'm started school, an isn't it great!

At playtime when they let us out, I try te escape, but the gate is locked. I look te see if the big young one who is supposed te be minding us is watchin, but she's too busy tryin te placate all the other childre who are cryin fer their mammies. I try te squeeze meself out through the bars, but I can't get me head out, an I can't get it back in either! Panic erupts in me. I give a piercin scream, an the other kids come runnin over. They just stand there gapin at me, an some are even laughin. I've made a holy show of meself, but I don't care. A neighbour, Mrs Scally, sees me an rushes over.

'What ails ye, child?'

'I want me mammy! Let me out, I want te go home!'

'Here, don't struggle. You'll only make it worse.'

She pushes me, but me head is tightly wedged between the big black bars, an she's pullin the ears offa me. There's a big crowd aroun me now, but I can't see them cos Mrs Scally is suffocatin me wit her shawl. The smell of snuff an porter an sour milk pourin up me nostrils is makin me dizzy.

'Here, Teacher! I'll let youse take over. We're only makin it worse. Maybe we'll have te get the Fire Brigade. I'll run an get her mammy.'

15

'The bars will have to be cut, or maybe we could grease her head,' another teacher said.

I lost me mind. 'No! No! Don't let them cut me head off! I'll be good. I won't do this again! Just let me out!'

The Fire Brigade arrived, an they had te cut the bars te free me. I kept screamin, cos I thought they were goin te cut me head off. The ma brought me home, but she stopped first te talk te the crowd, an the woman from the vegebale shop gave me a banana. She said it was good fer shock. The ma told them all I put the heart crossways in her an I'll be the death of her yet, cos I was very wild.

4

Me ma an me are rushin down te meet Dickser. Or she is. I'm not, I don't want te go.

'Come on, will ya! I'll be late!' She grabs me hand, an she sorts of bounces up in the air, but we're not movin any faster. I want te watch our shadows, hers long an skinny, mine small wit hair stickin out, chasin beside us. They glide up the old tenement houses as we hurry past the street lamp an then swoop down again, dancin before us on the ground as we leave the light behind us. The cobblestones are black an shiny on the road from the cold mist comin in from the Liffey. The chip shop across the road from Fishamble Street is still open. The smell plunges up me nose before we get there. As we hit the shop, I stop te look in at the bright lights. The Italian man wit the big black whiskers an the dirty white apron hands over a newspaper burstin wit chips an a big ray. 'One an one,' he shouts happily at the woman rootin in her purse fer the money. Me belly turns te water, an the shop is screamin at me te come in.

'Ma, Ma! Buy me chips.'

'No, I can't. Wha do ye think I am? Made a money?'

We rush on, an Dickser is waitin fer us at the Ha'penny Bridge.

'There ye are! I thought I'd never get here,' me ma said, laughin.

'I was just about te go. It's freezin here,' he said, diggin his hands deeper inta the pockets of his old overcoat. It was raggy an torn, an ye could see his hairy legs, cos his trousers was at half mast an held up wit twine.

'Have ye any money?' he said te me ma.

'No, I spent the last of it on milk.'

17

'Lend us a shillin. I'll need tha fer the back lane hostel tonight.'

'No! I've nothin.'

'Ah, Jaysus! Come on, then, let's get movin,' he said.

We wandered along the dark streets, me ma talkin an yer man busy walkin along the edge of the footpath, pickin up cigarette butts. We walked down laneways, an as we turned down a very dark alleyway, Dickser said, 'Leave her here.'

Me ma said she'd be back in a minute, but I didn't want te be left behind in the dark, an I started te cry. Dickser came back as I started te run after them. He lifted me off the ground by the scruff of me neck, stranglin me, an carried me back up the alleyway.

'Stay there! Don't make a sound. Don't move,' he said as he threw me down onta the ground. I hit the back of me head. I tried te get up, but I was spinnin like mad. The ground was goin faster an faster, an me hands couldn't find the ground te lift meself up. I rolled over on me belly an got up slowly on me hands an knees, an the roarin in me ears slowly stopped. I staggered over te the wall an looked aroun me. Everythin was quiet, an I looked up an down the dark lane, but I couldn't see anythin.

'Me ma's gone an the monsters'll get me! Ma! Ma! Mammyee! Don't leave me! Where are ye?' I croaked in a whisper. I didn't want Dickser te hear me. Then I went quiet. Very, very still. The big lump in me chest tha wanted te erupt outa me mouth was pushed down inta me belly, an I went limp. I shut meself up tight an just waited. When I'm still, nothin will happen te me. I'll be safe. Nobody will see me.

5

Me aunt Cissy is over from England. She says she's gettin married! She bought me a lovely pair of white kid-leather boots wit laces in them – I can smell the kid leather when I press them te me nose – an a gorgeous white linen frock. I'm te wear them fer her weddin, but she seems a bit upset wit the ma.

'How long has this been goin on, Sally?'

'Ah, I'm not bothered about him any more,' me ma says.

'Here, Martha love,' says me aunt Cissy. 'There's a bun fer you. You go on outside an sit in the sunshine, an I'll keep an eye out fer you. Now don't go too far, I'll be watchin ye from the winda.'

I wanted te be very good fer me aunt Cissy, so I didn't gallop across the road, cos me ma says I'll get kilt doin tha, even though I think ye'll get kilt if ye don't run. Anyway, I sit meself down an stretch me legs out te get comfortable, an Cissy is sittin on the windasill, watchin me an drinkin a cup a tea.

I look te examine me bun. Wha's these black things in it? I take a bite an spit it out. Yuk! I can't eat tha!

'Ah, eat yer bun, it's good fer ye!' Cissy shouts across. 'Them currants will clean ye out!'

I put the bun behind me back an started te pull the currants out, watchin her at the same time. I couldn't move, cos I had a pile of currants behind me.

Suddenly, there's great excitement when a horse an cab comes aroun the corner carryin me aunt Biddy an me aunt Nelly an me cousin Barney. The women are roarin an laughin at somethin the jarvey said te them.

19

'Whoa there, Jinny! Easy girl. Now, ladies, who's first?'

'She is.' Biddy points te Nelly, laughin. 'She's the desperate one. I'm already landed wit me own fella back in England.'

'Ah, no. I'm very particular,' Nelly says. 'Ye'd have te have plenty a money te get me.'

'Right, girls! Hop down, an I'll give ye's a hand up wit the suitcases.'

I ran across the road, an Biddy swooped me up.

'Lookit you, ye got very big since I saw ye last.'

'Yeah, Auntie Biddy! I'm four now, so I am.'

I looked at me cousin, an he was wearin eyeglasses.

'Look! Lookit, Martha,' Barney said, an he showed me a load a money. 'Come on, I'll buy ye somethin,' an we bought ice-cream cornets, an broken biscuits wrapped in paper, an bull's eye sweets.

They opened up the back room, an me an me ma slept in there. Tha night me an me cousin Barney took it in turns te vomit up our guts inta the bucket. Our mas laughed an said it was all the sweets we'd eaten, an tomorrow they'd get us a wormin powder te clean us out.

We went te the park beside St Audoen's Church an sat in the grass. Me ma an Dickser made plans te go te England.

'I'm savin every penny I can get me hands on,' me ma said.

'How much have ye now?' Dickser asked, an me ma told him.

'That'll do,' he said. He seemed very happy an even grinned at me, but I turned me head. I didn't want anythin te do wit him.

They arranged te meet tha night, an the ma would give him her money. She was all excited on the way home. 'We're goin te England, Martha! An Dickser's goin te find us a place te live. We'll be grand!' I was delighted te see her so happy an forgot about Dickser.

When we got home, the aunts were waitin.

'Where were you?' asked Biddy.

'Out!' me ma said.

'Look at the condition you're in, ye should be ashamed of yourself. You're seein tha Dickser fella, aren't ye?'

'No, I'm not.'

20

'Ye are! I'm tellin ye's all. She should be put away. Ye're bringin shame on this family an destroyin our good name!'

Cissy came over te me an asked me gently, 'Is she seein Dickser?'

Biddy joined in an shouted, 'Look! Here's a penny, tell us the truth, an we'll give you this.' An Nelly waved a half-crown in me face.

The ma shouted, 'No! Don't tell them anythin, Martha,' an they were all shoutin at once. Me eyes swivelled from the penny te the half-crown an back again. I wanted the money.

'Yeah, she is,' I said, an reached out fer the money.

'No! No! Don't tell them anythin.'

'No, she isn't.'

The money was whipped back, an there was some more shoutin.

'Yes, she is!' I said, reachin out fer the money, but they put it back in their pockets!

The hooley was goin on upstairs. Old Mrs Coleman had died; she lived in the room above us wit her grandson Neddy. We heard the bang on the ceilin, an me ma shouted te Nelly, 'It's Mrs Coleman, quick! We'd better run up, there's somethin wrong.'

Neddy came runnin down the stairs, an he was white as a sheet. 'Me granny collapsed when she was tyin her boots te get ready fer Mass. Come up quick!'

'You stay there,' me ma said te me. An they ran up the stairs, leavin me behind wonderin wha was goin on.

Now the house was crowded wit people. All me aunts were upstairs keepin the wake when me ma sneaked outa the house. 'Come on,' she said te me. 'Quick! Before they miss us.'

We went up aroun High Street an met Dickser at the Corn Market. She gave him the money, an he asked her if she wanted a walk. She said, no, she had te hurry back. They'd have plenty of time fer tha when they got te England, an they both laughed. Dickser gave me a penny, an when I examined it, it was all bent an black. I didn't think they would take it in the shop, an I was disgusted.

On the way home, the ma asked me if I wanted a single, an we went inta the chip shop. We ate the chips comin home in the dark, an they were lovely an hot. When we got te our hall door, there were people spillin out onta the street. There was a coupla young ones an young fellas loungin against the walls. The young fellas hid the bottle of porter they were drinkin under their coats, an they stopped laughin an pushin each other when they saw us comin. 'G'night, missus,' they said te me ma.

We walked on inta the dark hall. We could hear the singin an the buzz of voices comin from upstairs. Me ma fell over a body lyin at the bottom of the stairs. She gave an awful scream, an the mound of coats moved te show a head wit bloodshot eyes starin up at us in confusion. 'Jaysus, it's Hairy Lemon! Get out, ye dirty aul sod,' me ma shouted at him.

The young fellas rushed in, an when they saw me ma was all right, they laughed an said, 'He won't harm ye, missus. We'll put him out fer ye, if ye want.'

'Ah, leave him. So long as he doesn't come up an murder me in me bed, I don't care.'

The door opened on the landin, an Cissy came out. 'Who's that? Who's down there?' she shouted.

'It's only me, Cissy. Hairy Lemon gave me an awful fright. He's sleepin at the bottom of the stairs.'

I dashed inta the room, an it was lovely an warm. The fire was roarin red, an the fryin pan was on top of the fire wit sausages an rashers sizzlin away. The lamp had a new wick, an it was burnin brightly, throwin shadows on the walls. Me cousin's head shot up from the pilla, an he was delighted te see me. 'Cissy told me a story,' he said. 'An I saw Mrs Coleman. She was dead! An I got lemonade, an biscuits, an cake. Me ma's up there, an Cissy is mindin me. You should a been here, ye've missed it all. I got everythin!'

I was lost fer words an started te cry. I was not goin te be outdone.

'Ma, bring us up te the wake, Ma. I want te go te see Mrs Coleman.'

'No! Ye're goin te bed, it's too late.'

'Ma, I want te.'

22

'If ye don't stop tha keenin, I'll leave ye down wit Hairy Lemon!'

Then Cissy said te me ma she'd take me up fer just a minute, an Barney was outa the bed in a flash. 'I'm comin, too. Me too, Cissy!'

So we banged up the stairs ahead of Cissy, an the landin was crowded. Nelly was draped over two old women sittin wit black shawls draped aroun them, their noses blocked tight wit the free snuff they were shovin up. They had bottles of stout lined up an were shovellin ham sambidges, an cake, an pig's cheek inta their mouths like there was no tomorrow. Nelly was dozin wit the bottle of porter in her hand but stirred herself when she saw us comin.

'Ah, me beauties! Me lovely childre! The light a me life, come here an give us a kiss.'

She dribbled all over Barney an tried te catch me. Barney was tryin te climb up on her lap at the same time she reached out fer me, an the chair toppled over. Nelly went backwards, takin Barney an the old women wit her, cos she grabbed a hold a them. The pig's cheek an the porter spilt over them, an they all ended up in a heap on the floor.

Nelly said, 'Fer the love a Jaysus!' An the old women screamed, 'Help! I'm kilt!' An Biddy, who was wrapped aroun two old men an a woman, stopped singin an squinted over te see wha was happenin an said, 'Ah, nobody's hurt; it's only Nelly enjoyin herself.'

I went inta the back room where the corpse was laid out on the bed. Chairs were lined up against the wall, an people were sittin suppin porter an eatin an talkin in hushed whispers.

'Come in, babbies, come in,' they said te me an Barney. 'Go over an say a little prayer. Little childre are always very welcome. Yer prayers are mighty. Holy God always listens te the prayers of little childre. Kitty! Will ye lift up there the little craturs te see the corpse.'

Barney sped outa the door, screamin fer his mammy. But I'm not a babby. He is, he's only three. I'm four. I held me breath, an Kitty, the daughter of the corpse, lifted me up. The corpse was like a marble statue. She was in a brown habit, an her hands was wrapped in rosary beads.

'Tha's right, chicken. You say a little prayer te our blessed Lord,

23

an he'll take poor aul Mrs Coleman straight te heaven,' Kitty said te me as she began te swing me closer te the corpse.

I started te squeak, cos I could see up the corpse's nose, an I thought she was goin te suddenly wake up an grab me. I was gone like lightnin an didn't wait fer lemonade an biscuits an cake.

6

Me ma is very busy in the back room, sortin out all our things. She has the suitcase opened up on the bed. She's puttin things in an takin things out again. 'Jaysus Christ!' she mutters te herself. 'I can't get anythin in this suitcase, it's like herself.'

She means Aunt Biddy, who left it behind when Cissy an herself went back te England. Me ma tries te squeeze in me granny's two china dogs, but they won't fit.

'What'll I do? I can't leave them behind or tha Nelly one will pawn them if she gets her hands near them. Ah, fuck it, she can have them.'

'Ma! Mind me weddin frock, don't crease it!'

'Wha weddin frock are ye talkin about?'

'The one Cissy bought me fer the weddin she's havin. Is it at the bottom of the suitcase, Ma? An me boots?'

'Ah, don't be mindin them an their weddin, they can keep it.'

'But what about me frock an boots, Ma? I want te see them. Let me see them, Ma!'

'No! Gerraway from tha case. If ye toss them things, I'll swing fer ye.'

'I only want te see me frock, Ma! Let me!'

'Lookit! I had te pawn them te get the few bob. We're takin the boat tonight, an I'll need every penny I can get me hands on. Now come on! I have te rush aroun an get me hair permed.'

I roared me way up Thomas Street, me ma pullin an draggin me an threatenin she'll be hanged fer me if I didn't stop me carry on. Aul ones stopped te chastise me, an one aul one bent down te tell

25

me Johnny Forty Coats was on his way down te take me away cos he could hear me roarin. Me ma laughed. Then the aul one put her hand inside her shawl an gave me a penny. So I went inta the shop an bought meself an ice pop. Me contentment lasted as long as me ice pop, an when we got te the hairdresser's, I started again.

Me ma pushed open the door, an the bell on top of the door rang out.

'How're ye, Sally? Haven't seen you in a long while?'

'I'm grand, Ivy! I'm lookin te get me hair done.'

'Lovely! Sit down over there. I'm just takin these outa Mrs' hair here, an I'll be wit ye in a minute. What are ye havin done, Sally?'

'Ah, I'll have a cold wave.'

'Yeah, that'll suit ye. Is this the little un? God! She got very big, God bless her.'

'Ah, me heart is scalded wit her, she's tormentin me no end.'

'Ah, now, ye have te be good fer yer mammy. Ye'll be very good, won't ye? And do wha yer mammy says.'

I got very annoyed, the cheek of the ma sayin tha about me when I'd stopped cryin! So I started again.

'Ma! I want te go home, bring me home, Ma!'

'Will ye stop interruptin me when I'm tryin te talk! Ye see what I mean, Ivy?'

'Right!' Ivy said te me. 'I'm goin te put ye out in the back yard wit the Banshee.' But I knew she was only kiddin, cos the Banshee only comes at night te sit on yer winda an keen te warn ye someone was goin te die. So tha didn't frighten me.

I was enjoyin meself playin wit the door, openin an shuttin it te make the bell ring. But the aul ones said it was drivin them crazy. Aul Mrs Rafters, the wida, called me over an asked me te pick up her bag, an she took out her purse an handed me a thruppeny bit. I was gone fer ages, cos I wanted te take me time decidin on wha te spend me money on. When I got back, me ma was ready. Her hair was flat on her head wit waves. I didn't get a chance te get a good look, cos she covered it wit a scarf in case the wind blew out her perm. She was all excited. 'Come on, Martha! It's gettin late. We'd better hurry.'

26

The ma put on her frock an coat, an washed me face, an combed me hair, an put on me other clean frock, an buttoned up me coat. An then she took the suitcase from the bed an checked her handbag te see if she had everythin. She put her door key on the mantelpiece an looked aroun the room an said, 'Have I got everythin? Let's go, then.'

She closed the door behind her an banged the suitcase down the stairs. I ran through the hall an out inta the street. I was all excited. I looked up an down, but there was no one te see me goin. I was hopin Tommy Weaver might see me an be ragin, but there was no sign of anyone, it was very quiet. We went down the hill past me old school. The bars were still gone, an they'd covered up the hole wit chicken wire. I never went back there. I don't know why, an I didn't ask.

I was askin me ma about the boat an wha would we do if it sinks, but she wasn't listenin te me. She was chewin her lip an lookin inta the distance, tryin te hurry wit the heavy suitcase.

We walked down along the quays an waited at the Ha'penny Bridge. There was no sign of Dickser. Me ma looked very anxious. 'We'll wait,' she said, chewin her lip. She looked up an down an said, 'He'll come, he has te come!'

We waited. 'He's not here, Martha. He's gone. Oh, sweet Jaysus, he's gone, an he's taken all me money! The whole six pounds I was puttin by fer months. I gave it te him te mind fer me. We've nothin, it's all gone! What'll I do? Wha can I do now?'

I said nothin, nothin at all. Me ma's pain went inta me belly, an me chest was very tight. It was lovely te be happy, but it didn't last. Me ma looks lost, an I'm afraid.

We go up te St Kevin's Hospital in James's Street. It used te be called the Union. The porter lets us in te the waitin room. We're hopin te get a bed fer the night. We wait a long time, but nobody comes te talk te us. Me ma gets restless, an I'm tired. The wooden bench is too hard te sleep on. She goes off te find out wha's happenin, an I mind the suitcase. When she gets back, we have te leave, cos it's too late fer a bed.

27

She drags the suitcase down past the Guinness Brewery, an I can smell the hops. 'What'll we do?' she mutters te herself. 'We've nowhere te go.'

We pass Frawley's in Thomas Street, an a cat leaps outa an alleyway. It's covered in rotten vegebales. It screeches an runs fer its life, knockin over the dustbin lid. It's bein chased by a skinny dog tryin te protect its territory. There isn't a sinner about, an all the shops are locked up wit the big grids pulled down te protect the windas an stop people breakin the glass an robbin the stuff. We turn down inta Francis Street an very slowly cross the road, the only noise made by our footsteps an me ma trailin the suitcase along the cobblestones on the road. I'm too tired te walk any further. An me ma is miles ahead of me. We pass the Iveagh Market, an I stop te look up at the buildin. Me granny used te sell here. But I never knew her.

As I turn te move on, I'm suddenly lifted outa my body, an I'm wit me granny. We're like air, the two of us! She wraps me up inside her shawl, an we don't speak. I can see she has lovely blue eyes an long brown hair. I feel her holdin me tightly. She whispers in me ear, 'Shush, child. I'll always be mindin ye,' an then it was over. I looked all aroun me, but there was no one there. I thought maybe I'd fallen asleep, but I was still standin in the same spot at the Iveagh Market, an me ma was passin the St Myra's an Nicholas Church. I moved on, still feelin the warmth of me granny's arms. We went inta Cork Street an sat behind the door in the hallway of a tenement house. There was a fight goin on in one of the rooms upstairs. A man was shoutin, an I could hear the woman cryin, tellin him not te wake the childre. We could hear him beatin her up, an furniture an dishes gettin smashed, an the childre were screamin. Me ma jumped up an said, 'Come on, we'd be better off on the streets than listenin te this.'

I wanted te lie down on the bench we passed in Camden Street, but me ma said, 'No, we'd be arrested fer bein on the streets this time of night.' We fell down exhausted under the stairs in the hallway of another old tenement house.

We went over te Brunswick Street te stay at the Regina Ceoli hostel fer women, run by the Legion of Mary. But we were too early, the hostel doesn't open until evenin. We had hours te kill, but we just sat on the steps, too exhausted te move. The men's hostel is just next door. Tha's called the Morning Star. By five o'clock we were stiff an cold. We hadn't had any tea or bread since yesterday. But I was beyond carin an just wanted te lie down in a warm bed. We hadn't said a word fer hours until a man came over te me ma an asked fer a match te light his cigarette butt. Me ma said, no, she doesn't smoke.

'It's a long aul wait,' he said, 'but it shouldn't be too long now till they open.'

Me ma said nothin, an he wandered off te talk te other men who were arrivin an congregatin aroun the men's part, smokin, an coughin, an spittin, an laughin, an throwin the eye at me ma. She pretended she didn't see them.

When we finally got in, we had te go te the office te talk te the sister in charge. Tha's wha they call themselves! The woman was fat an had a tight perm tha looked like a roll of steel wool on her head. She had little glasses on her nose an asked me ma loads a questions. Me ma gave her a wrong name an said she was just back from England an was lookin fer somewhere te stay. Me ma said she had te come home cos England wasn't a Catholic country, an she was glad te be back among her own. The woman seemed satisfied an then looked at me. 'How old are you?' she snapped.

'Four, Mrs,' I said.

'Sister! You call me Sister.'

'Yes, Sister Mrs,' I said, confused, cos she looked like a woman te me.

'Do you wet the bed?' she asked me.

'No!' I said, terrified, cos I do.

She picked up a big walkin stick, an she said, 'If you wet the bed, I'll break this on your back. Do you hear me?'

I didn't answer, an me ma said nothin either.

We slept in a very big room wit lots of other women all sleepin in

29

single iron beds. I slept wit me ma, an there was one other child in the room. He slept in a cot, cos he was only two years old. His mammy didn't sleep there, she slept somewhere else. I don't know where. But every mornin he wakes up cryin, an his ma comes clatterin in on her high heels. An he's standin up in the cot, holdin on te the bars an roarin his head off. His ma gets very annoyed when she sees the child has shit himself an the blankets are destroyed. So she wipes his arse wit the blanket an dresses him. Then she yanks him outa the cot an onta the floor. Then she says te her other two little girls, who are about five an six years old, 'Right! Take him an get him outa me sight.' An the little child goes off wit his sisters, one holdin each hand. An the little babby laughs happily, then the mammy marches off about her own business.

We get ready an leave fer the day. Me ma collects a tin mug a tea an a chunk a bread an margarine. They don't give anythin fer the childre, me ma says, so I share her bread an try te sup the tea from the tin mug, but it's too hot an burns me lips. So I go without. We have te leave the hostel by nine o'clock. The doors are locked after us, an we aren't allowed back in until night. We walk aroun, goin nowhere. If the weather is nice, we sit in the park. If me ma has the price of a cup a tea, then we'll sit in a café an try te make the tea last. If it's rainin, we go inta a church. But mostly we just wander aroun the streets waitin fer the time te go back te the hostel.

This mornin I opened me eyes an was surprised I was awake first. The babby was still asleep an wasn't standin up cryin. His cot was next te our bed. I watched him te see if he would wake, but he didn't, an I was happy he was quiet cos when his mammy came in te collect him she would tell him he's a very good boy an he wouldn't get inta trouble. Everyone was now gettin up an beginnin te move aroun, but he was still asleep. Me ma was gettin me dressed when his mammy came in. She went over te the cot an shook him, but he didn't move! She shook him again an then felt him. 'He's stone cold,' she muttered. Then she screamed, 'He's dead! Oh, Christ Almighty, he's dead! Me little boy is dead.'

She started te shake the bars of the cot an scream. Then she started te pull her hair out. Me ma grabbed me an pulled me out the door, not botherin te wait fer her tea an bread. 'Oh, God bless tha poor woman,' me ma said. We left the hostel in an awful hurry.

Me ma went down te collect her money from the relievin officer. I think it's five shillin fer a week. The waitin room was crowded wit people, all sittin on long wooden benches behind each other an everybody starin inta space. Nobody talkin or lookin at each other. They were all smokin their Woodbines, an the place was thick wit blue smoke. I was beginnin te get a terrible headache, an me stomach felt very sick.

When we got inta the relievin officer, he asked me ma an awful lot of questions. He asked her if she had any valuables she could pawn or sell. She said no. Finally, he said he would come up te the house te check, so she had te tell him she was now homeless, an we were stayin at the Regina Ceoli hostel. 'If that's so,' he said, 'then you'll have to bring me a letter from the people in charge, and until you so do this, I won't be giving you any money. Now, send in the next one.'

'But . . . excuse me, Sir, when will I get me money? I've nothin te even buy the child a bit of bread or a drop a milk.'

'You're wastin my valuable time,' he barked at me ma. 'I've already explained that to you. Bring the letter to me next week, and then we'll see. Now get out of here and stop wasting my time. I've nothing more to say.'

We trailed out the door like two snails. Me ma was shocked. She didn't think he'd find out an make trouble. 'Tha's it, then, we're well an truly bet! What'll we do now?' I wasn't listenin te her mutterins. I was too busy tryin te get sick. Me stomach is heavin an heavin, but there's nothin comin out. Oh, me head, the pain is so bad. I just want te lie down, an I'm so thirsty. I need a drink a water. I drag behind her an start te cry. She whirls aroun an snaps at me, 'What ails ye? Stop yer fuckin whingin, I can't hear meself think.' So I keep quiet an just follow behind.

She wanders up te Thomas Street, lookin fer her aunt who is a dealer an sells fruit an vegebales. 'Well! Wha do you want?' Lizzie asks me ma. Me ma gives a little cough an chews her mouth while she tries te think of the best way te ask Lizzie fer somethin te keep us goin.

'Eh, Lizzie, would ye ever be able te lend me somethin fer a few days? I'll pay ye back when I get me money.'

'An why would I do tha? Do ye take me fer an eejit? It's lockin up you need! Lookit the state you're in again. This is yer third time te get yerself in tha condition. You're bleedin populatin Dublin all by yerself! Well, this time ye've gone too far. Enough is enough! I'm now goin te take steps meself te have ye put away. I'm gettin ye put inta the Magdalen Asylum in Gloucester Street. That'll put a stop te yer gallop! So it's money ye want, if ye wouldn't be mindin! Is there anythin else ye'd like? Go on, be off wit ye. I've no time fer you.'

'I'm sorry I asked ye!' me ma said, an turned te go.

As I turned te follow, Lizzie took me arm an put a half-crown in me hand, an she closed me hand over it. 'Lookit you,' she said, 'you poor cratur. Are ye not well? What ails ye?'

'I have a headache, Aunt Lizzie, an I feel sick.'

'Bad cess te tha one. May God forgive her fer the way she's carryin on. She'll roast in Hell an the sooner the better. Bringin disgrace on everyone, she is. Here, eat this, it'll build ye up.' An she gave me an apple an a banana. 'Go on, get after her,' she said.

I rushed after me ma, who was now miles up the road an just turnin down onta Meath Street. When I got up behind her, I shouted, 'Ma! Ma! Wait fer me.'

She half turned an then her head shot aroun when she saw me holdin up the money. Her face lit up, an she said happily, 'Did Lizzie give ye tha?'

'Yeah, Ma, an she gave me these.'

Me ma started te laugh happily, 'Oh, thank God fer tha,' she said. 'I thought we were goin te have te go without.'

We spent another week at the hostel an made another visit te the office te talk te the aul one wit the steel-wool hair.

'Make sure you come straight back here with the money you

owe me. You won't get in this door if you don't pay it all. Do you understand this?'

'Yes, Sister. Very well. I'll be back here straight away wit yer money. There'll be no hesitation about tha,' me ma said. So we set off fer the relievin officer, me ma holdin on tightly te the letter in her pocket fer yer man. An he gave us two weeks' money, cos Steel Wool told him te. She said she wanted te be paid fer the two weeks. So we were loaded wit money! He gave me ma a big ten bob note, it's red!

'Come on,' me ma said, grabbin me an laughin.

'Are we goin back now te the hostel, Ma, te pay the woman?'

'Like hell we are! I'm not goin back te tha hell hole. No, we're goin home.'

'Home, Ma? But Nelly won't let us in.'

'She can't stop us. It's my home, too.'

We stopped in Thomas Street te get the messages. We went inta the Maypole an got Marigold margarine, the good stuff. An two ounces of tea, an half a pound a sugar, an me ma asked me if I wanted Marietta biscuits, an I said yeah. Then we went te St Catherine's Bakery an got two fresh loaves, an we got a packet of cheese an two bottles a milk. The ma gave me the milk te hold while she fixed the messages in the bag. An I forgot I was holdin the milk, an I let me arm go, an the milk smashed te the ground! Me ma was very annoyed, an she said, 'I told ye te hold them! What am I goin te do now? Tha's the last of me money.'

I started te cry, but a very nice young woman, who was dressed lovely, came over te see wha happened, an she smiled at me an said te me ma, 'Don't worry! Here's one and six, go and buy some more milk,' an me ma an me was happy again.

Nelly opened the door an stood lookin at us when we got there. But she let us in when me ma said she had the messages.

Me ma took me aroun te John's Lane Church te light a penny candle. Then she knelt down te say a prayer. I loved lookin at all the little candles burnin an the smoke curlin from them. An the grease drippin offa them when they melted. I was squeezin an feelin them, an gettin me fingers burnt, chewin on the bits a wax an tryin te put me fingers in the little hole where ye put the money, wonderin how ye got the money out. An then me ma hissed at me an told me te go away from them. So I wandered aroun the church an stopped in front of a box. I'd seen people go in an out before, an I decided te have a look. I went in an closed the door, an it was very dark. I was afraid, but I decided te sit down on the kneeler an wait, but nothin happened. So I decided te make whisperin noises like I'd heard other people do. But nothin happened. So I tried te get out, an the door wouldn't open! I was locked in the dark!

Well, I nearly lost me mind. I banged me fists on the door, an I screamed fer all I was worth. I heard feet runnin, an an aul one wit a black shawl wrapped aroun her head whips open the door. The light hurt me eyes, but as soon as I had me senses back I shot out the door, an the woman grabbed me. 'Tha's not for playin in,' she snorted at me. I looked up at her. I was red-faced an pumpin sweat. 'There now, ye gorra fright, but ye'll be OK. Come on wit me an we'll say a prayer.' Me ma was on the other side of the chapel an was pretendin she didn't know me. She doesn't like me te make a show a her.

The aul one tightened the shawl aroun her chin an pulled me down te the statue. 'Now!' she explained, 'This here is the statue of St Jude. He's the saint fer hopeless causes.' She joined her hands an held them high in the air, an lifted her eyes up te the statue, an started te pray in a loud voice. I was sittin beside her on the kneeler, an she told me te hold me hands together an pray.

I didn't know wha te say, so I just made it up. I was sayin, 'Hally, Mally, Vecha, a do,' an the aul one smiled an nodded at me, an said I was great. Then the ma came down the chapel, an we went out inta the sunshine. I felt a very good girl.

34

7

The noise woke me up, an I sat up in the bed wonderin wha was happenin. Me ma was standin at the side of the bed, shiverin an moanin. Nelly told me an Barney te get up an put our clothes on. I saw blood on the floor an blood streamin down me ma's legs. Nelly threw her coat over her shoulders an shot outa the door. She was back in a minute, an a load of aul women streamed in behind her. They started fussin aroun the ma. One aul one picked me ma's only frock up from the chair an swooped down te wipe up the blood from the floor. I didn't think tha was a good idea, cos what is me ma goin te wear now? Another aul one grabbed me an said, 'Here!' handin me a shoppin bag. 'Go down an get the potatoes an messages fer the dinner.'

I'd never been sent fer messages, an we didn't get potatoes, but I thought this was a great idea. So I held onta the bag an looked up at the aul one, waitin fer her te give me the money. But all she did was roar at me an say, 'Go on! Go down te the vegebale shop, yer mammy needs the messages.'

So I set off confused. I thought ye needed money te buy the potatoes. When I got te the shop, I handed up the bag te the woman behind the counter. I knew what I wanted now. I'd heard me ma an Nelly talk often enough about it. 'Ye can give me a bit a bacon an cabbage, an potatoes, an a load a good butter, an two loaves a bread, an a bottle a milk,' I said. 'An a bit a tea an sugar. An gimme a nice big cake fer the tea.'

'Grand,' yer woman said. 'Now where's your note wit the money in it?'

35

'I haven't gorrit,' I said.

She stared at me an said, 'Where's yer mammy?'

'At home,' I said. 'They sent me fer the messages.'

'Who did?'

'Granny Rafters did.'

'Well, you can go home an tell tha aul Granny Rafters I'm not behind this counter fer the good a me health. Ye need money if ye want te eat!'

When I got home, they wouldn't let me inta the room. 'Go off an play!' An they slammed the door shut! I called fer Tommy Weaver, an we came back an sat outside our room on the landin. We watched the commotion, wit aul ones runnin up an down the stairs. 'Wha's wrong?' I asked. 'Why's me ma sick?'

Then one aul one said, 'We're busy. Ye're te keep outa the way. Why don't ye look out fer the doctor, he's comin wit a new babby fer ye!'

I was delighted. Tommy Weaver was ragin an then said te me, 'Anyways, I'm bigger than you! I'm six, you're only five.' So then I was ragin. So I snatched the pencil an copybook from his hands an said, 'Lookit! I can write.' I did lovely wavy lines. He said I was a liar an I didn't even go te school like him – tha he was goin te be a scholar. So I asked him how did the doctor bring the babby, an he said the doctor brought the babbies in his bag. We went off te sit on the street an wait fer the doctor. But he never came. So Tommy went in fer his dinner, an I went off collectin ice-pop sticks along the streets on me own.

When I got back hours later, the room was very quiet. There was only Nelly an Barney. 'Where's me mammy?'

'She's gone,' Nelly said. 'They took her away in an ambulance te hospital.' I said nothin, just looked out the winda, quietly wonderin wha would happen te me ma an would I ever see her again. 'Now,' Nelly laughed at Barney. 'See! Martha doesn't cry when her mammy leaves her, not like you! I can't even go te the tilet without you holdin on te me skirts.' Then Nelly went off te the pub, takin Barney wit her. He wouldn't stay wit me. He's nine months younger than me, an he's a real babby. I continued te stare outa the winda until it got too dark te see, an eventually I fell asleep on the bed waitin fer Nelly te come home.

I was all excited. Me ma was comin home wit the new babby! We walked up the steps of the Coombe Hospital, an Nelly told me te wait outside while she went in te collect me ma. When me ma came out carryin a bundle a blankets, she looked very tired. She was too tired te talk te me an barely looked at me. Everyone was very quiet as we made our way up Meath Street. An we went inta the chapel an sat down an waited quietly fer the priest te come an baptise the new babby boy, called Charlie. Tha was the first look I got of him. They took all the blankets offa him, an Nelly held him over the font filled wit water. Charlie stiffened an gasped an shot his tiny hands out as the priest poured the jug of water over his head. The babby screamed, an me an Barney watched, wonderin if the priest was goin te try an drown us in the font, too, cos we didn't like gettin ourselves wet.

Me ma took straight te the bed when we got home. Nelly took out a drawer from the press an put it on the table at the end of the bed, an tha's where Charlie slept.

The next day, the district nurse arrived te wash an clean the babby's belly button. It looked very yucky. I watched very closely as she stripped Charlie. He smelled terrible an his poo was yella! An he lay in his box, naked an screamin. The nurse turned aroun te get the box of borax powder, so I leaned in closer te get a better look, an the nurse roared at me. She said I was te keep me filthy hands offa the babby. Well, I'd had enough! I didn't like him anyway. When she was all ready, an Charlie was sleepin peacefully in his drawer, an the nurse was packin her bag, I sneaked over an looked inta the drawer. He was all washed an polished, an smelled lovely, but the nurse shouted, 'Get away from that baby.' So I pinched his cheek, an she gave me an unmerciful slap on the ear. The babby was roarin, an me ma was threatenin te kill me. The nurse picked up her bag an galloped out the door. I started roarin, too. I wanted me ma te get up outa the bed.

37

'If I have te get up outa this bed, I'll be done fer ya!' she kept sayin. 'Give tha babby his soother.' But I wouldn't. I wanted te see if she still had legs, cos she was walkin in a queer way when she came home from the hospital. So she dragged herself from the bed. First one leg, then the other, all the time grindin her teeth an starin at me like she was goin te tear me from limb te limb. When she finally stood up, holdin onta the bed an the press, I stared at her legs. She had them miles apart, an she couldn't walk properly. I was very worried she might not get better, an on top of tha she didn't seem te like me any more. She wouldn't talk te me.

'Get tha babby's soother an put it in his mouth!' but I just kept starin. I wanted her te move some more an be me mammy again. 'I'm warnin ye, Martha, if ye keep on tormentin me, I'll throw this at ye,' an she picked up the bread knife. I ran te look after the babby.

I walked past the pub on the corner, an me cousin Barney was standin outside, eatin a bag of grapes. Nelly was inside drinkin porter an roarin her head laughin. I said te Barney, 'Wha's them ye're eatin?' An he said, 'Grapes.'

'Give us one.'

'No!'

'Ye're very mean!' I said.

'Don't care, ye're not gettin any.'

'Right, I'm not playin wit ye no more!' an I ran home te tell me ma. She was sittin by the fire lookin very annoyed when I dashed in te tell her about Nelly an Barney havin money an grapes an he wouldn't share wit me. 'Ah! Don't be botherin me about them,' she said. 'They're not bothered about us any more. Tha Nelly one is goin off te England tonight, an she won't be back.'

I went runnin back out te stare at Barney. Yeah! He had his face washed an his hair combed, an he was wearin a lovely coat. Nelly must have picked up tha in the Iveagh Market.

When I got home, the fire was out, an me ma was sittin in the dark, starin at nothin.

We're on our own now. There's just me, the ma an me babby brother, Charlie. Me ma doesn't talk much except te say, 'Shut tha babby up!

Give him his soother.' He cries a lot. I think it's cos he's hungry. Sometimes me ma can't light the fire, cos we've no coal. So she can't boil the water te make the babby's bottle or make a drop a tea. I'm always hungry, but the babby hasn't learnt te get used te it yet. He won't shut up! He just keeps on screamin. I'm worn out, rockin him up an down on me knee. Sometimes he'll nod off fer me when I give him me finger te suck.

Last night when me ma was givin him his bottle, she suddenly jumped up an said, 'Run, Martha, run,' an she was gone like the wind out the door wit the babby in her arms. I turned te ask her wha's wrong, but she was already down the stairs an flyin through the hall. I banged the door behind me an galloped after her. She was up the hill an aroun the corner before I knew wha was happenin. I pushed meself fer all I was worth, tryin te catch up, but she was halfway up Thomas Street.

'Ma!' I screamed. 'Wait fer me, Ma! Wait fer me!' But no, she just kept runnin, like Ronnie Delaney. Me chest was poundin, an me legs were seizin up, an I still didn't know wha was wrong. I shouted at the top of me lungs, 'No! I'm not comin, I'm not movin any more!'

Me ma half turned an shouted back, 'The hospital! We have te get te the hospital! Don't stop, keep goin.'

It's the middle of the night, an there isn't a soul on the streets. We fly off James's Street an turn right down the hill, past the mad house, St Patrick's Hospital. Me ma bursts through the doors of Dr Steevens' Hospital an inta the out-patients. 'He's not breathin!' she shouts. 'The babby's not breathin.' She's still runnin when she slams the babby inta the arms of a doctor.

'He took a convulsion when I was feedin him. He turned blue, an I couldn't get him te breathe.'

The doctors an nurses rushed aroun the babby, an we were put outside te wait. They told me ma te go home; they're keepin the babby in. She went te take a look at him, an when she came out she said we have te pray he'll be all right.

* * *

39

We went te the hospital te collect the babby. He looks lovely, like a little china doll wit big blue eyes an white curly hair. His eyes are like saucers starin out at ye from his tiny white face. I can't squeeze him yet, cos me ma says he's delicate. So I just keep lookin at him an makin faces, tryin te make him laugh.

8

Me ma says I have te go back te school now, cos I'm nearly six. So she brings me up te Francis Street, an I start straight away. I'm in the First Holy Communion class, an today they told us all about St Patrick. He's the saint fer Ireland. He was kidnapped by the English an brought here te mind the sheep on a very lonely mountain, an he was only a child! I felt very sorry fer tha poor young fella, so I did. All by himself an no mammy te mind him. The teacher was very impressed wit me when I repeated the story back fer her, an she said I can make me Communion!

Me ma's all excited. She said the nuns sorted me Communion clothes an we can go te the shop in Francis Street an pick them out. I picked out a lovely red coat, an me ma said, 'No! It has te be blue fer Our Lady.' Then I saw a gorgeous pink one. I'd look lovely in tha, but me ma said ye can only wear blue. So I said I wouldn't wear it, an the aul one in the shop said Our Lady was watchin me, an I'd made her cry. Then I picked out a lovely Italian frock. Ye'd think I was gettin married in tha! But me ma said, 'No!' If I got tha I couldn't afford the coat. Tha sounded grand, an me mind was made up. I'd take the Italian frock. So then me ma started te lose her rag, an she was grindin her teeth. The aul one said I couldn't make the collection fer the money if I didn't have a blue coat fer Our Lady, cos I wouldn't be dressed properly. An me ma wouldn't get any money. So we ended up wit the blue coat. I hate it, I do! It has no style.

The mornin of me Communion is here. Me ma's friend Tessie turned up te get me ready. Last night they washed me hair an scrubbed

41

me in a tin bath belongin te Tessie. They dragged up buckets a water from the tap in the back yard an then boiled the water over the fire. I'd never seen so much water in me life! Me ma held me down while Tessie covered me in Sunlight soap. I couldn't breathe, an I was screamin an roarin an tryin te escape from the bath. Me ma was pushin an slappin me back down inta the water, an I thought me last hour had come. I never want te see a bath of water again fer as long as I live. Then they put pipe cleaners in me hair te make me hair curl. But I couldn't sleep, an me ma wouldn't take them out. An just as I got te sleep, now they've woken me up again.

'Come on, Martha! It's time te wake up. We've te get ye ready.'

'No, Ma! I'm tired. I don't want te make me Communion. I want te go back te sleep.'

'There's a good girl, ye'll be grand! I'll just give yer face an hands a wash before I dress ye.'

'Ma! I want a bit a bread.'

'No! Ye can't eat anythin, ye have te fast.'

'I'm hungry.'

'Lookit! Ye'll get yer lovely breakfast of jelly an ice cream after ye receive Holy God!'

'I don't want Holy God, I want a bit a bread,' I whined.

Tessie took out the pipe cleaners, an me ma put me in me frock an me shoes an socks. Tessie fixed me veil on me head, an I'm all ready now.

Charlie is sittin in his go-car, in his new romper suit, an he has a lovely blue pixie hat sittin on top of his mop of white curly hair. He gorra wash, too, after me. He's after bangin his teeth wit the new rattler Tessie gave him. An he thinks it's my fault, cos he gave me a smack of it when I leaned in te give him a squeeze.

Me ma finished her tea, an now we can all get movin te the church.

'She looks like an angel, Sally. She's a picture of beauty!'

'Yeah, she turned out well, didn't she? Listen, Tessie. Will you take the babby, just in case he starts in the chapel?'

'Right, Sally, I'll mind him. How old is he now, Sally?'

'Eh, he'll be ten months soon. Martha was six three days ago.'

'Tha was lucky, or she wouldn't be makin the Communion now.'

We arrived at the chapel in Meath Street, an all the mammies took their places in the seats. We were lined up outside on the street. We formed a procession of girl an boy, wit the priests an altar boys carryin lighted candles at the top of the procession. We slowly made our way along Meath Street an up the steps an inta the brightly lit chapel, singin hymns. As the last of us filed in, the great black doors slammed shut behind us, an we broke inta 'Ave Maria'. I looked aroun, startled by the thuddin doors, an saw crowds of old women in their black shawls linin the back of the chapel. They were all cryin an dryin their eyes wit their shawls.

We sat in the benches at the top of the chapel, an I listened te the hushed drone of the priests murmurin the Latin an swingin the big incense box, an the whispered prayers of the old women at the back. I smelled the lilies from the altar an heard the expensive sound of starch an crinkle comin from our frocks as we shifted ourselves fer more comfort. The bright lights came from all aroun us. Every statue had its lights burnin, an candles was lit fer every one of us by our mammies. I looked aroun at the others, an they had white faces an shiny curly hair under the snowy-white veils, an the tiaras glinted against their faces. An they were very quiet an still. I looked down at me baby-blue coat an me starched white frock, an me white gloves coverin me hands tha I had joined together an wrapped aroun me mother o pearl rosary beads tha Tessie gave me, an I felt in me senses tha we were all precious. Heaven must be somethin like this. An I wanted me mammy te be happy, too. I asked the angels te whisper te God's mammy, Our Lady, te send me mammy enough money so she won't have te worry about coal, an we could have dinners, an she could pay the rent. An maybe a bit more te buy the babby a few more romper suits, an a teddy fer him. An maybe a doll fer me. An enough so she can go te the pictures, cos she loves tha, an take me wit her. An she'd laugh all the time, an she wouldn't be lonely, sittin starin inta nothin. An then I wouldn't be worried, cos me ma is me whole world.

43

We stood now in front of the altar rail, waitin our turn te kneel at the marble steps. But the little girl in front of me has gorra fright. She doesn't want te take Holy God! The priest is annoyed, an he barks at the altar boy te hold the brass shovel under the child's chin while he grabs her face an tries te squeeze Holy God down her throat. But she twists an fights an tries te get sick, an they drag her away. We stare, hopin nothin happens te us. The priest is very angry an his face is roarin red. 'Hold it under! Don't let them drop it!' he keeps sayin te the altar boy. I was glad when I went back te me bench an concentrated on tryin te swallow down Holy God.

We walked down the aisle in twos, singin 'The Bells o the Angelus', an the doors were thrown open. The church bells rang, an our mammies looked at us wit stars in their eyes. The old women cried an blew their noses in the corner of their shawls. An the traffic was held back while we sang our way across Meath Street from the chapel te the Little Flower dinner house te get our breakfast.

We sat on benches along a big table covered in a white tablecloth, an we were given a big bowl of jelly an ice cream. They put cloths on over our dresses te keep us clean. Then the nun an the teachers came aroun te admire us. The nun smiled an spoke te each child, an admired them an told them their mammies were very good. An then it was my turn. I turned aroun te show her me dress, but the teacher said somethin te her, an she nodded te the teacher, looked at me, an kept goin on te the next child. She smiled an admired the other child's dress, but she didn't look at me. I looked down at me jelly an ice cream, an I knew I shouldn't be havin it. I wasn't supposed te be here wit the others. I'm just like Hairy Lemon, an people are afraid te go near dirty tramps. I held me head down in shame. I didn't want people lookin at me the way the nun did.

Me ma brought me te make the collection an visit all her friends. We went all aroun the Liberties, down te the Oliver Bond flats an up te Keogh Square. The babby's new romper suit was covered in chocolate, an he kept smilin at everybody, cos they were kissin an squeezin him, an tellin him he was gorgeous, an givin him crusts a bread dipped in sugar te chew on. I was admired an patted, an told te twirl te show off me frock. Me ma drank tea an ate cake, an I drank lemonade an ate cake an biscuits. An we did the same thing the next day after the Mass on Sunday. Me ma kept this up fer a week, until me frock was filthy an I was sick of the sight of me veil, which kept fallin offa me head, an then I wouldn't wear them any more.

9

We're leavin our house, cos it's condemned. We're movin up te James's Street. We pass St Patrick's Hospital down the hill an then turn right inta a row of flats wit a wall at the end.

The horse an cart arrives te move our furniture. We don't have much, me ma says, cos it's all gone over the years te feed Nelly's drink. All me granny's lovely antique furniture, which she got from her mother an father who were French Huguenots an tha had been in the family fer hundreds of years. Me granny had been a Protestant until she married a Catholic.

We have two rooms in our new flat an a separate scullery an bathroom an tilet. We share a landin wit another flat, an an old woman lives in there on her own. Our flat looks a bit bare. We put the wardrobe an bed in the bedroom, an the table an one chair in the sittin room along wit the chest a drawers. We put the chair by the fire, but we don't light the fire. So me ma sits there until it gets dark an just stares over at the winda, which looks over onta another row of flats. We have gas fer cookin on, but we can't, cos we don't have a cooker.

A man from the St Vincent de Paul brought us a cooker. An he gave me a shillin. Me ma told me te go down te the shop on the corner an buy a bottle of milk. So I ran down an left the man talkin te me ma. When I came back, I went te the wrong flat an opened the door. The people were strangers, an I didn't know where I was. They explained it must be in the next block, but I was worried, cos they all looked the same te me, an it was gettin dark now. So I rushed inta the next block an hurried up the stairs, but I was afraid te turn

46

the handle of the door in case I was in the wrong room again. So I opened the door quietly an saw two people lyin on the floor. I got a shock an ran back down the stairs an onta the street. I was beginnin te cry an felt the fear risin up in me chest, cos I was lost an I'd never find me mammy again. So I went back te the room where the two people were lyin on the floor te ask them where me mammy was. I was sure we were livin there, so I couldn't understand it. I knocked on the door, but they didn't answer. So I opened the door an put me head in. They both saw me an jumped up laughin, an then I saw it was me mammy. They told me te go out an play, but I said it was pitch black out. The man was annoyed, an me ma chewed her lip an looked anxious, an then he left in a hurry. The room seemed empty, cos earlier we had been happy.

We have te put a shillin in the gas meter if we want te use the cooker. Tha's a lot of money, so me ma spares the gas an only uses it te boil the milk fer the babby's bottle or make a drop a tea. We don't turn on the light, cos tha costs money, too, so we go te bed when it gets dark.

I look after the babby now an give him his bottle. Me ma doesn't give me anythin te eat these days, so I share the babby's bottle wit him. I take a coupla sucks fer meself an give him a coupla sucks. He used te scream an buck himself in me lap, sometimes nearly fallin off. But now he just sits quietly lookin up at me while I have me turn.

Me ma went in te visit the old woman on our landin. She invited us in. Me ma sat aroun the roarin red fire an talked an listened te the old woman, whose name is Mrs Enright. I stood watchin the flames lickin up the chimney an enjoyin the heat. She had lovely old pictures on the walls of her childre, all grown up now an gone te the four corners of the earth, she said. Her husband, God rest him, was gone te his reward. He'd worked fer Guinness an drove the horses pullin the barges up an down the canal. She had nine childre livin an lost four young. She turned te me ma an said Charlie, our babby, was not thrivin. Me ma ought te be givin him solid food offa the table. She said the ma should start him on rusks mashed in boiled milk. Me ma told her she can't get out te get the bit of shoppin, tha

47

the shops were too far down in Thomas Street. An Mrs Enright said me ma could give me the bag wit a note an put me on the bus next te the conductor an tell me where te get off in Thomas Street. It was only two stops down, an I was six years old, an I'd manage. I listened carefully an began te work out in me own mind the problems I might come up against an how I would work them out. But me ma wasn't interested.

Me ma didn't bother te send me back te school after me Communion. I wasn't there long anyway. There's nothin much te do, cos me ma just sits starin inta nothin. If I try te say somethin, then she'll notice I'm there an start askin me te look fer lice in her hair. So I just take the babby out onta the street in his go-car. There's nobody aroun, cos all the childre are in school. So we sit outside the shop on the corner an watch the people goin in an out.

The babby's cryin in me ear, an rockin him up an down doesn't do much good. So I stick me finger in his mouth, an after a few sucks he gets inta a rage an bites me, cos it's not his bottle. It hurt me, so I roared at him, 'Ye're bold.' An he went red in his face an got inta an even worser rage. A woman comin outa the shop ate the head off me an looked at the babby an said he was starvin. 'Get him up an take him home an feed him,' she said. I brought him home an asked me ma te boil him a bottle, but she said we'd no shillin fer the gas. The babby was hysterical now, so I looked aroun fer somethin te appease him. I dipped a bit a bread in water an gave it te him an put him in the cot the St Vincents man gave us. He smelled terrible, an when I looked, his rompers was covered in shit. I told me ma, an she said, 'Ah, just leave me alone an clean it up.' An she went on chewin her lip an starin an runnin her fingers through her hair, lookin fer lice.

I went back te the cot an pulled the bars down. I tried te hold him while I got the rompers off, but he kicked an bucked, an the shit was flyin everywhere. I was destroyed, I needn't tell ye. I wiped the biggest bits offa his arse wit the rompers an got his vest off. I put him on the floor naked, an he sat lookin up at me an then lookin at himself, an I was glad of the peace te get on an clean the blankets.

I'd nothin te wipe them wit, so I used his vest an looked aroun fer somethin else. The best I could find was an aul pair of me ma's knickers. They did grand. So when I had the cot cleaned, I tried te put the babby back in, but he was ragin an wouldn't let me lift him. I was in an awful sweat by the time I got him back in the cot.

There was nothin te put on him. So I found an old frock belongin te me, an I put tha on him. It was miles too short fer me an miles too big fer him. He kept losin his arms an tryin te strangle himself. So I took it off him an took off me jumper tha I hadn't had off fer months. It was too small fer me an was so hard an tight I was cryin from the strain of tryin te get outa it. At last it was off, an I put it on the babby. It nearly fitted him, an he sat there lookin at himself. I felt very draughty now, cos I had no knickers an no vest or socks – only the frock tha was too short fer me, an it was very light an torn under the arm. Ye could see I was naked, but there was nothin else I could wear.

The other childre won't play wit me. They laugh an call me names, cos me frock was torn an I had no knickers. But now they run when they see me, cos me head is covered in sores, an me ma had te cut off all me hair. The lice are crawlin aroun me head, an it's very itchy, so I scratch it. An it bleeds an gets huge scabs, an now pus is oozin from the sores, an I look terrible. So the childre stand a mile away from me, cos their mammies said they'll catch it. An they call me terrible names, 'Scabby Head', 'Pauper', 'Baldy Head', an loads of other names. An they say me ma is a whore. Tha's very insultin te call me ma tha. It means she's no good, an tha makes me want te cry. But I pretend I'm not bothered, an I think up names te call them. But I have te fight the whole gang on me own. An I'm ashamed I'm not like them. I'd love te play piggybeds an swing on the lamp posts wit a rope, an play chasin an have me friends. But I'm not like them, an they don't want te have anythin te do wit me.

49

10

We didn't stay long in this flat. Me ma has a friend who lives in the Benburb Street flats, an she wants te move inta our flat an we move inta hers. It's down on the quays, next te Arbour Hill Army Barracks. It's a big aul Victorian row of about ten blocks of flats, an it's about eight storeys high. We have one room, an we share the landin wit about eight other families.

I went down on te the street te play. There are lots a shops aroun, an the road in front is very busy wit traffic. There's lots a cars an delivery vans an horses an carts flyin up an down. I'm not used te it yet, an it's taken me a long time te cross the road. I want te get over te the sweet shop an meet all the childre millin aroun outside.

Other childre are crossin the road now. Some are smaller than me, an they step out as soon as there's a little break in the traffic an dash inta the middle of the road, makin the cars swerve an brake an blow their horns. I do the same thing, an a car swerves at me. I dash back towards the footpath, right under the wheels of another car comin in the opposite direction. I can smell burnin rubber, an big puffs of smoke come outa the tyres when the man brakes an nearly swerves inta the other car.

I decide te go up an see wha's happenin in the shoe-repair shop. The man wears a leather apron, an he has a hammer, an nails stickin outa his mouth. An he has a shoe stuck onta an iron bar wit a big lip on it. An he's bangin the nails inta the shoe. There's a smell of glue comin outa the shop. At first I thought it was nice, but now it's beginnin te give me a headache. So I move off towards me own block.

I'm standin there an a big fight starts out between about six dogs in the next block. Then I see an old man comin past me. He's wearin a hugh boot, cos one of his legs is much shorter than the other one. An he swings along, throwin out the big boot in front of him, cos it's very heavy te lift. Suddenly the dogs jump on him an knock him over. They all start te savage him, an there's blood beginnin te pour from his head an face. He can't do much te save himself, an he tries te cover his head. I see the weakness in his face, an he seems te let go an stop strugglin. An I watch quietly, but I'm screamin inside meself, cos the dogs are killin him, an I don't know wha te do. I start te run up an down, lookin fer someone te help, but nobody sees wha's happenin. A winda opens up in a flat, an a woman shouts down at the dogs. An then suddenly people appear outa the flats an start te beat the dogs off. But the dogs won't let go, an it seems a long time before they drag the dogs away. The man lay white as a sheet, covered in blood, an his eyes kept flutterin open an shut. The people chased away us childre, an the man waited a long time on the ground wit a coat thrown over him before the ambulance arrived te take him away.

Me ma doesn't stay in the flat any more. She goes off fer the day, an I stay in te mind the babby. I can't bring him out, cos he has no go-car. It's broken an gone. An I can't get him down the stone stairs, cos we're far too far up in the top floor, an he's not walkin yet. So even if I managed te carry him down, wha would I do wit him? So we lie on the bed. He cries an cries, cos he's hungry an there's no bottle te give him an not even a bit a bread we could eat. There's nothin! Not even in the bins – I looked.

It's night time now, an she's still not back. As long as I keep me fingers in his mouth, he'll suck it an be quiet. We have a bit a comfort, lyin wit our heads together, lookin inta each other's faces an watchin him suck me finger. He'll only cry now if I take me finger back.

The sun was shinin outside, an I could hear all the childre playin on the street. Me ma was all excited. She was goin out. She had herself

51

all done up. She said she had te meet a man. She asked me te go te bed early wit the babby, but I said no! It was the middle of the day, an I wanted te go out an play. So she went across the road te the shop an bought me a little ball fer sixpence. Now I could play handball against the wall when I got out te play. This was me own, an now I could get childre te play wit me. I could play this game, but ye need two balls fer this. Maybe we'd share. I could get a young one who has a ball. It goes like this – ye throw the balls against the wall, an ye say, 'My muther an yer muther were hangin out the clothes, my muther gev yer muther a bang on the nose, wha colour was the blood, R.E.D.', an if ye drop the ball ye're out.

There was a dog shiverin in a box outside one of the blocks. We went down te gerra look. There was an old woman sittin on a chair outside, an she was mindin the dog. It had no hair, an its skin was all red an bleedin. 'Wha's wrong wit it, Missus?' we asked.

'It has the mange! Now gerra way an don't be touchin it. Ye's'll catch it! I'm waitin fer the animal-cruelty man te come.'

Suddenly there was a roar from the end of the street, an a load a cattle came stampedin down. 'Hold er! Ho there! Easy now!' An we could see young fellas wit sticks runnin in an outa the cattle, scatterin them everywhere. The drover was screamin up behind them wit his arms held wide an a big stick in his hand, wellington boots covered in green shit, an an aul coat tied wit string. His hat blew offa his head, an he didn't stop te pick it up. More young fellas came roarin outa the flats te give the drover a hand. 'Feck ye's all, ye's little feckers. Ye's are losin me, me animals.'

'I'm not, Mister! I'm helpin ye!' one young fella said. 'Lookit, them young fellas are robbin a cow. They whooshed it up the alley, an they'll sell it te Mickey the Butchers.'

'Where are they? Bring it back fer me, son, an I'll see ye right!'

'OK, Mister! Wha's it worth? Half a crown?'

'No!'

'Ten bob, Mister.'

'Five bob an get a fuckin move on.'

An he was off te tell his pals they were in the money. An then the aul one grabbed up her chair an screamed, 'Mind the dog!' An she ran inta the hall, sayin, 'We'll be all kilt! Is a body te get no rest?'

We grabbed the box an tumbled the dog inta the hall, outa the way of a mad cow tha was rushin towards us. We could see the white of its eyes an the steam pourin up from it an the shit caked on its back – it was huge! The dogs came from everywhere, an they went bananas, bitin the legs of the cows. An the mad cow changed direction at the last minute an decided he wasn't comin inta the hall. He skidded an slipped, an the drover whacked him on the arse an whacked out at the dogs an looked at us te see if we should be whacked as well.

The cars were all chopper blocked. An we ran out an jumped on the back of a horse an cart, an the horse was rearin an snortin wit all the cars blowin their horns an the cows an childre an dogs flyin everywhere. An the man wit the horse lost his rag an turned aroun an lashed at us wit his whip. A black dog ran under the legs of the horse, an a young fella said, 'Go on, Nero! Get them!' an the horse reared up from the fright of the dog. The man jumped down te quieten the horse, but the horse was foamin at the mouth, an the man was in an awful state. An the woman from the shop came out te see wha was happenin, an she still had her fork in her hand, cos she musta been eatin her dinner. An the men came over from the flats te help steady the horse an said it was a terrible conster de nation altogether. An I thought it was like the cowboy fillums! Only they left plenty a shit behind them – even the horse was shittin wit fright.

I had te sleep in the end of the bed last night, cos me ma had a man in the bed wit her. I didn't like tha at all, cos they were very noisy, an he was tormentin her all night, an they kept kickin me, an I couldn't sleep properly. His name's Anto, an he sells newspapers on the street corner. He got up outa bed this mornin, an he left in a hurry. Me ma looked at me an said, 'He didn't leave me any money! I was goin te ask him fer a few bob. I've no milk or bread! Run after him an ask him fer the loan of one an six.'

Tha's a shillin an sixpence. So I ran down an shouted, 'Anto!'

53

But he wouldn't answer me, so I caught up wit him on the street. An he said he had nothin. But I said, 'Me ma needs it te buy bread an milk,' an he gave me a shillin, but he was very annoyed.

Me ma was disappointed an said, 'Is tha all he gave ye?'

'Yeah, Ma! An he wasn't goin te give me anythin!'

Today, me ma went down te see a neighbour, an she said te me, as she was rushin out the door, 'You stay here an mind the babby!'

But I said, 'No! I'm goin out te play,' an I rushed out behind her an down the stairs. When I got onta the street, I saw all the people lookin up at a winda an screamin. They were pointin an shoutin an coverin their faces wit their hands. An some were gettin weak. When I looked up te see wha was causin all the bother, I saw me babby brother Charlie sittin on the windasill lookin down. I rushed inta the hall an up the stairs. I couldn't move fast enough – there were too many stairs, an it was an awful long way up. A door opened, an me ma shot out. She roared at me as she galloped up the stairs, 'I told you te mind the babby!' I came rushin in behind her as she grabbed me babby brother from the windasill. The cot was in the corner, right beside the winda, an the winda was open. So the babby climbed outa his cot an crawled onta the windasill an was kneelin there lookin down at everyone. He's barely twelve months old, an we nearly lost him.

11

Me ma got te know the neighbours. An two of them are her friends. They dye their hair white an wear lots a lipstick an powder. They gave their childre te another woman te mind, an now we're all gone down te the North Wall Quay, where the boat te Liverpool docks. Me an the babby an me ma an her two friends wait outside a pub just opposite the boat. They wait fer someone, but he doesn't turn up, an it's gettin late. Then a man comes along, an he's wearin a blue blazer, an his black hair is shiny an combed back wit Brylcreem. He has a black moustache, but he's very small an has a big belly. The women say te each other, 'He's probably a sailor, go on over an ask him.'

The man sees them lookin at him an shouts, 'Ay, ye's all right, girls?' an smiles. The women smile back an shout, 'Is there any chance of a passage?' An the man comes over te talk te them. Then he goes off an we wait. After a while, he comes back again an brings us up the gangplank an onta the ship. The two women go off wit some sailors, an the man takes me an the ma an the babby down te a room wit seats all along the walls. He tells me ma te put us on the seats, an we'll be fine there. Then he tells her te go wit him. She turns te us an says, 'You stay there, Martha. I'll be back in a minute!' An then she goes off. I was a bit worried about bein left alone in a strange place, but I didn't follow her, cos I couldn't leave the babby. I sat there waitin, an people started te come inta the room wit their suitcases an sit themselves down. They were givin me odd looks, but nobody said anythin. I wanted te ask someone te find me mammy, but now they were just ignorin me. The babby was curled up beside

55

me, an he was fast asleep. I kept puttin me hand on him te mind him, an I was very frightened.

It was now in the middle of the night, an the other people were sleepin. I kept creepin out an up the stairs te see if I could find her. But I was afraid of gettin lost, an I wouldn't find me babby. So I kept lookin back te make sure I knew where I was. An when I got te the top of the stairs an turned right, there were crowds an crowds of people, all drinkin an laughin. I couldn't see anythin, an I was just walkin through people's legs. They were knockin me down, cos they couldn't see me, an I was panickin an shovin people's legs outa the way. I wanted te get back down again te me babby brother an me seat, an I started roarin, cos I lost me way fer a minute. I was runnin aroun tryin te find me way, but nobody would listen te me, cos they were all drunk. I did find me way back down the stairs an found the babby. An I never moved again.

The next mornin, people started te get ready te leave the ship. An when we docked, the people started te leave the room. I started te shake wit fright, cos me ma didn't come back, an we were goin te be left here. When everyone was gone, I rushed out the door an up the stairs an started screamin, cos everyone was gone an only a man was sweepin up. I ran aroun shoutin fer me mammy, an the man wit the brush came over an asked me where she'd gone. I said she'd gone wit the sailor an she didn't come back. He took me back te the babby an told me te wait. Then me ma came, an she didn't look too happy. She gave us nothin te eat or drink. I was hungry an thirsty, an the babby was starvin. But she didn't bother. We left the ship an walked inta the city. The women went inta a shop an came out wit a bar a chocolate, an they were laughin. I don't know why, but I didn't see anyone give money fer the chocolate. Me ma went te Social Assistance, an they gave her the boat ticket te go back te Ireland or they'd put us in a home. So we came home on the next boat.

When we got te our flat, the door was broken, an our stuff was gone. Me ma's handbag wit all her papers was thrown aroun the room. An some were missin.

'All me stuff is gone! Me papers are missin!' An she was in a terrible shock. Any bits an pieces we had left from me granny was all gone. Our clothes were gone, even the babby's stuff. They took his cot an smashed up our bed. The spring, wit all the spokes stickin up, was thrown against the wall. The teapot an cups an plates were gone. We had nothin left, nothin!

I took the babby an carried him outside, an we sat on the landin. I didn't know wha we could do. I heard me ma crunchin aroun on the broken china an talkin te herself. 'I know who's fuckin responsible fer this,' she said. An then she marched outa the room. She went past me an down the stairs. I didn't get a chance te ask her where she was goin, so I picked up the babby an dragged him down the stairs. He was too heavy fer me te carry. I didn't know where she'd gone, so I kept on goin down, draggin the babby's legs down the stairs after me. I was afraid I'd drop him on the stone stairs, cos they were very steep, an it was an awful long way down. So I held him tight under his arms, an he was afraid, too. He kept a tight hold on me arms, an he was holdin his breath, afraid te cry.

When we came onta a landin, we could hear shoutin an screamin. It was comin from downstairs, so I tried te hurry. We nearly fell backwards, but I landed against the banisters, an I was still holdin onta the babby. When I got on te the next landin, me ma was screamin at the two neighbours she'd been friendly wit. One of the women looked at me an shouted, 'Go on, ye whore! There's yer bastards now!' An before she could finish, me ma lunged at her, grabbin her hair. The other woman joined in, an they started tearin me ma te pieces. I screamed an tried te drag the babby away. But they toppled over us, sendin the babby flyin te bang his head on the concrete floor an stampin on him. Me forehead hit the ground, an I was kicked in the head an me back. An me nose started te pump blood. I was tryin te reach out fer the babby, but everythin was spinnin. The babby was tryin te reach his hands in the air te turn himself, an he was blue an he was makin gaspin sounds.

The women were still draggin me ma along the landin by the hair an punchin her. I crawled over te the babby, an me nose was pumpin blood away like a tap. Everythin was still like a merry-go-round.

57

Blood was pourin onta him, but I grabbed him an started te slap his back te get him te breathe properly, an I was chokin meself in me blood. People came runnin when a man came down the stairs an shouted, 'There's kids hurted here! Help me, someone!' An then doors opened an a woman rushed te pick up the babby, who was white as a sheet an gone very quiet. He was covered, soakin wet, in me blood. They carried us inside the room while the man went te break up the fight.

We were taken by the ambulance te hospital. An I was put in a ward wit a load of other childre. Me ma didn't come te the ward wit me, an they didn't put the babby in wit me. I don't know wha happened te him, an I'm afraid te ask, cos the nurse is very strict. We have te lie very still in the bed under the white sheets an black blankets, cos the nurse doesn't like ye te crease the sheets. An we have te keep our arms by our sides, under the blankets. A little child in a cot has knocked down the bars, an he's whimperin wit fright, cos he can't get the bars up. He doesn't look three years old te me. The nurse comes stampin down the ward, grabs him outa the cot an swings him aroun the ward by his arm. She says she'll teach him a lesson. An she's screamin an hittin him somethin terrible. I don't move or breathe; I'm afraid of me life.

We can only have visitors on a Sunday from three p.m. te four p.m. The doors open, an the visitors rush in. I'm lookin te see if me mammy's comin. But she's not here yet. The little girl beside me in the next bed has her mammy an daddy an her granny. An they're brushin her lovely long curly hair, an fixin her, an pettin her, an makin sure her pillows are fluffed up. An they keep askin her is she all right. But she's afraid te say anythin, an just buries her head in her mammy's chest an keeps whisperin, 'Take me home, Mammy! Take me home.'

The mammies are all busy, emptyin shoppin bags filled wit Lucozade, an biscuits, an sweets, an washcloths, an towels, an clean nightdresses, an pyjamas fer the boys. I keep watchin the door, but there's no sign of me mammy, an I feel me heart begin te empty. She's not comin, an it's nearly all over. Then the nurse crashes in, wavin the big bell, an announces te everyone, 'Visitors' time up,' an then the childre panic, grabbin their mammies. An some leap inta their arms an won't let go. 'No, Mammy! Take me wit ye. Don't leave me here,' an they flood inta tears. But the mammies have te pull themselves away. The nurse arrives te stand guard at the door, an there's sudden quiet. As soon as the last mammy leaves, the doors are shut, an the nurse gets very annoyed. She stamps from locker te locker, takin the childre's sweets an tellin them they're very greedy, an they're not goin te eat them all. She gets te me, an I've no sweets. I'm very lucky, cos she didn't roar at me. An then she says they have te be shared. So she put an orange in my locker an a box a Smarties. She left everyone wit a bit a somethin an took away the rest.

12

I was sittin at the table wit the other childre finishin me dinner. It was lovely! Mashed white potatoes an mincemeat an turnip. I wanted te lick the plate, but the other childre didn't do tha, an I didn't want te make a show a meself. But I didn't like the custard. It was all lumpy an me stomach was turnin. So I was tryin te get at the jelly underneath an wonderin what I'd do wit the custard, cos we're supposed te eat it all up. Suddenly the door opened an the nurse appeared wit me mammy. She had a brown package under her arm, an the nurse said te me, 'Your mammy's here to take you home.'

Me heart jumped, an I was delighted. She put me inta a long brown frock. It was a bit big fer me, but it felt lovely an warm. I was well covered, an it had sleeves, an the shoes were grand. Then me ma shoved tilet paper down the toes te stop them fallin offa me. An the coat was green wit a bit a fur aroun the collar an sleeves. I even had a vest an thermal navy-blue knickers! But I had te hold them up, cos they were a bit big fer me, an the elastic in the legs was gone. The only thing I need now is a pair a socks an a hat, cos it's rainin out. But me ma said we were goin on the bus. I asked her where we were goin an where was the babby, but she just said, 'Stop askin questions an moidierin me!' an then she went back te herself. So I kept quiet, cos I didn't want te annoy her.

When we got off the bus, we walked along a road wit a high wall an huge trees. An then we came te big gates, an me ma went in. We went up a dark road wit big trees keenin in the wind. I didn't like the look of it, an I was afraid. I held onta me ma's hand tight an hoped nothin was goin te happen. 'Ma! Where are we goin?' I croaked, but she didn't answer me.

When we rounded the bend, I could see a big house wit a chapel, an there was white pebble stones all round the front, an it made crunchin noises when we walked on it. Me ma pressed the big roundy bell, an a woman wit a hairy chin an a man's haircut opened the door. Me ma said the Reverend Mother was expectin her, an the woman brought us in an told us te sit down. She left us in the hall, an me ma sat down on a wooden priest's chair tha kept creakin when she moved. Tha was the only sound we heard. The hall smelled of polish, an ye could see yer face in the shiny black an white floor tiles. There was a big statue of Our Lady holdin the Babby Jesus standin up on a wooden stand, an holy pictures on the walls.

The nun appeared, an me ma jumped up. Me ma smiled at her an said, 'This is Martha, Sister,' an the nun said, 'Good! Follow me.' We went inta a parlour, an there was a tray wit a pot a tea, an a plate wit ham an tomatoes, an another plate wit bread an butter. Then the nun left an said she'd be back later when we'd finished eatin. Me ma said, 'Eat tha up,' an I wondered why it was only fer me.

'You eat it, Ma! I don't want it.' I was feelin sick. 'Wha's happenin, Ma? Why're we here?'

'Go on! Eat it up before the nun gets back.'

I tried te eat, but I kept lookin at me ma's face. Her eyes were starin at me, an then she'd look te the door waitin fer the nun te come back. I knew me ma was gone from me. An there was nothin te do but wait. The nun came in an took me hand, an we walked off down the passage. Then the nun stopped an said te me, 'Wave goodbye to your mammy!' But I didn't look aroun, an I didn't say anythin. I just walked on, holdin on te the nun's hand. An the life went outa me, an I just shut down. Cos now I was empty.

The nun brought me inta a tiled room wit a big bath tha looked the size of a barge. There were pipes along the walls an sinks. She put the plug in the bath an turned on the tap, an then she told me te take off me clothes. I looked at the steamin water pourin inta the bath, an I got an awful fright. I knew I was goin te drown in tha.

'Come along, now. Hurry up, get undressed, I haven't all day,' the nun said. I was shakin an tryin te get me clothes off, an she went out. I was in me skin, lookin at the water in the bath an shiverin an wonderin how I was supposed te get in when the door opened an the nun came back wit two childre an a big bar a scrubbin soap an a washcloth an towel.

'This is Josephine and Rose, and they're going to give you your bath, Martha. Now, these are very nice girls, and you be good for them,' the nun said te me.

I had me doubts when I looked at them. One looked a bit older than me, about seven, an the other one looked younger than me, about five. As soon as the nun left, I started te cry. But Josephine told me I would be grand an started te cover me in soap. But I pushed away the cloth, an Josephine said, 'It won't hurt you. Rose always gets her hair washed, an she loves it. She never cries, do you, Rosie?' An Rosie nodded her head up an down an agreed wit everythin Josephine said. An they kept smilin, an Josephine kept tellin me I was great altogether. An then we had another long talk, an a fight, before I lay back an let Josephine pour the jug a water over me head te rinse it. An then it was all over. They dressed me in a warm woolly vest, an thick warm knickers, an long brown woolly socks, an a lovely warm frock wit an apron tha went over me head an covered me back. An then the nun trimmed me hair an gave me a fringe, an looked back te admire me. I smelled lovely, an I was gorgeous an warm an squeaky clean, an me brown leather shoes fitted me.

I bounced along when I walked wit the nun out te the yard, an she left me there an shut the door behind me. I was left lookin at a high wall wit a concrete ground an a load a childre runnin aroun chasin each other. I stood rooted te the spot, afraid te move. I kept lookin at the height of the wall an the other childre playin an laughin. An I wondered would I ever be like them. Could I laugh an play wit them an everythin be all right? An me heart'd stop painin me.

A big young one rang the bell, an we lined up an marched outa the yard an down long passages te a big room wit long tables an benches. We sat down an drank mugs a cocoa an ate chunks a bread. Then we said prayers an left the room. We marched again, down more passages an up onta landins, an there were more stairs an statues everywhere. An then we arrived in a very long room filled wit beds. It was a bit like the hospital ward, only the beds were pushed together more. They said it was six o'clock, an the sun was shinin in the winda. The nun put me in a big warm nightdress an inta an iron bed wit white sheets an black blankets, just like the hospital. But I knew, in the hospital, I was goin te get out sometime. Here, I was goin te be locked up fer ever. I pined fer me mammy, an I worried about wha happened te me babby brother. I missed him wrappin himself aroun me neck an me kissin him an squeezin him. An I knew he'd be missin me an me mammy, too.

The bell woke me up. The nun was marchin up an down the dormitory – tha's where we sleep – bangin the big bell up an down. It's the middle of the night – well, it must be, cos it's still pitch black outside! The big ones come in te help us get dressed an make our beds. Mine is wet as usual. But so is a lot a other childre's. The big ones quickly strip the beds an throw the wet sheets in a mound in the middle of the floor. Then they put new sheets on the beds an make them up. Then we're all dressed an go down te the chapel an pray. All the dormitories come together on the chapel passage. The biggest are up the front of the line. An we're nearly the last lot te go inta the chapel, wit the big young ones herdin us in an keepin order, an the nun leadin the way.

There was a big fight outside the refectory at tea time last night. The nuns were up gettin their prayers, an the big ones were left in charge. The big ones can be very vicious. If a nun goes fer a big one who's been lazy or sloppy or didn't polish a floor properly, then the big one can take her spite out on a little one an punch an kick her an pull the hair outa her fer maybe wettin the bed or maybe she didn't like the way the little one looked at her. If ye have a big sister te look out fer ye, then maybe ye'll be all right.

These two big ones were tearin each other up an down the passage cos one of them hit a little young one te get back at the big one who loves mindin the little one. She's her favourite, an she won't let anyone near her. The two of them are left standin outside the refectory this mornin, an they got no breakfast.

Rosie an Josie an me are the bestest of friends. They think I'm great, an I think they're great. We always hold hands, an we play chasin, an we talk, an they always ask me what it's like on the outside. I tell them they're not missin much. If I could have me babby wit me, an me mammy could stay here – sure, wha more could a body want? But they tell me she'd have te be a nun te get in here or a child, an then I'm back te square one.

Rosie doesn't remember comin here – she was only a babby. But Josie remembers comin in a Black Maria from the court, an her mammy tellin her she was goin te England te find a place, an she'd be back te take her. Her mammy was cryin when they took her away. She was three at the time. Now she's seven, an she doesn't think her mammy will be back. I said tha me ma put me away lots of times when I was younger, even when I was a babby, but she always takes me back. If we be patient an just wait, they'll come an get us. Then Rosie smiled an said, 'Do you think my mammy might be famous?'

An I thought about this an then it hit me. 'Yeah! They're fillum stars! They're gone off te America, an when they come back te collect ye's, they'll stand up in the parlour wit all the nuns talkin te them, an smilin, an admirin their lovely fur coats, an lookin at their high heels, an smellin their perfume. An the mammies will say, "I've come te collect my childre! Me big car's outside," an all the nuns will rush te the winda te get a look. An a man wearin a lovely suit an a big cigar in his mouth will wave at them. An then Josie's mammy will say, "He is me new husband." An Rosie's mammy will say, "My new husband is a very important man. Too important te meet youse nuns. An Josie's mammy here is givin me a lift te take me back te me airplane where I'm goin te America an takin me Rosie wit me, so I am."'

Then the door of our playroom opened, an a big young one came over te me. 'Martha, come on, come wit me,' she said, an she took me hand. 'Sister wants you. I'm te take ye over te her.'

'Why?' I whispered. 'I didn't do anythin. Am I goin te get inta trouble?'

'No! Why would you get inta trouble? Wha did you do?'

'Nothin!' But I tried te think. Maybe cos I wet me bed, I thought.

We arrived over at the shoe room, an the nun was in there rummagin among the shoes. 'Good girl! Try these on!' An she put me sittin on the stool, an we tried several pairs until she found a pair tha suited me. 'Now, let's get you changed.' An she put me in a lovely warm woollen dress wit a blue cardigan an brown woollen socks te me knees. Then a lovely tan coat tha went past me knees wit a velvet collar an a matchin velvet hat, an woollen gloves wit the string through the sleeves so I wouldn't lose them. I was lookin lovely altogether, an then she brought me up te the parlour, an me ma was there.

'Now, we'll expect to see you this evening. Before five o'clock,' the nun said te me mammy.

'Yes, Sister! I'll be back before then. I'll have her back on time. Don't worry, she won't be late!' me ma said.

'Very well, then. Be good now for your mother!' the nun said te me. An she slammed the door after us.

Me ma looked at the shut door an said, 'Go fuck yerself, Sister!' an she grabbed me hand an laughed an said, 'Run, Martha! Let's get outa this place. We're not fuckin comin back here!'

I didn't know wha was happenin, an me ma said, 'I had an awful time tryin te talk the nun inta lettin me take ye. I'm supposed te be in court today te sign you away!'

Me heart leapt wit fright! 'Ma, wha's happenin?'

'Nothin!' me ma said. 'I'm not goin te turn up.'

'Where's the babby, Ma? Where is he? Is he all right? Can we go now an collect him?'

'I will when I'm ready,' she said. Then she went quiet.

We went over te the Liberties, an me ma hung aroun her aunt's house. She was walkin up an down but keepin a safe distance so we wouldn't be seen. 'What are we waitin for, Ma? Can we not go te collect the babby now, Ma?'

'Wait! Wait! I'm lookin te see if Lizzie's aroun.' An sure enough the door opened, an me aunt Lizzie came out in her shawl an shut the door behind her. Me ma took off an shouted, 'Run, Martha! Quick, before she sees us,' an shot aroun the corner.

Aunt Lizzie roared, 'Come back here, you! I saw you.'

An me ma put her head aroun the corner an shouted, 'Come on, Martha. Don't let her catch ye!'

'Come over here, Martha!' Aunt Lizzie said. 'I want ye!'

I looked at the corner where me ma vanished, an I looked at me aunt Lizzie rushin over te me. An I stayed where I was.

'Wha's tha one been up to? I've been lookin everywhere fer her.'

'I don't know, Aunt Lizzie,' I said.

'Where'd ye get the style? Ye're lookin the picture of health.'

'I gorrit in a convent, Aunt Lizzie.'

'Wha convent? Wha's goin on? What in the name of Jaysus is tha one up te now, may I ask ye? Wait till I get her.'

Me ma came back aroun the corner an stopped. Then she smiled an came down te Aunt Lizzie. 'I'm in an awful hurry. I have te rush.'

'Is tha right, now? Well, I have the authorities out lookin fer you. You're bein put inta a home. An when the parish priest catches ye, the only place you'll be rushin te is Gloucester Street Convent. That'll put a stop te yer gallup.'

'Ah, Auntie Lizzie! Don't do me any harm. Sure I'm lookin after everythin grand! Lookit Martha! Amn't I keepin her lovely?'

'Bad cess te ye, ye dangerous liar. I don't know where you've been keepin yerself, but ye weren't mindin tha child. She told me ye had her in a home.'

'I'll catch up wit ye again, Aunt Lizzie. I'd better rush,' an me ma grabbed me hand an took off in an awful hurry. 'I'd better not let tha one find me,' she said. 'We'd better clear outa here.'

Me ma took me on the bus an handed the conductor a ten bob note. 'Nothin smaller, Mrs?' he asked.

'No, I didn't get a chance te change it in the shop.'

So the conductor gave it back an said he was only startin out an he hadn't any change. 'Don't spend it all in the one shop!'

'Don't worry, I won't,' me ma said, an laughed.

'I'll meet ye outside the Tivoli at eight o'clock,' he shouted after me ma when we stepped off the bus.

'You'll be lucky,' me ma shouted back.

We arrived at the home where me babby brother was kept. There was trees all aroun an high steps up te the big door. I stood on the iron thing fer cleanin yer shoes an looked in the coloured glass at the side a the winda. There was another door inside an a big pot holdin umbrellas. Me ma rang the bell, an me heart was poundin up an down. I fixed me hat te make meself look respectable, an hoped nothin would go wrong. A nun opened the door, an me ma said, 'Good afternoon, Sister. I'm here te pick up me babby.'

'And you are?' the nun said. Me ma told her, an the nun brought us in. Me ma went inta another room, an I was told te wait in the hall. I sat on a big black chair, an me heart was flutterin in case they kept me here or they wouldn't give us back our babby. Or maybe they'd call the police, cos me aunt Lizzie told them, an they'd take away me ma an lock her up. An I'd never get a chance te see me babby brother or me ma again.

A big clock suddenly bonged, an I wet me new knickers wit the fright! I crossed me legs an dragged meself across the hall, lookin fer someone te take me te the tilet. I opened the door where me ma went, an said, 'I need te go te the tilet.' She was talkin te the nun, an she said I'd have te wait. I was jiggin up an down an tryin te reverse out the door, but me face was red, an I was sayin, 'Ah! Ah! I'm wettin me knickers.' I didn't care any more about the nun, an I shouted wit me head in the door, 'Ma, Ma! Me pooley's comin.' Me ma chewed her lip, an the nun jumped up, grabbed me by the arm an rushed me down the hall. She kept sayin, 'Don't soil the floor. You're a very naughty girl.' I was sloshin piss down me legs an inta me new shoes, an keepin me legs apart so I wouldn't destroy me new dress. An leavin a trail of piss behind me. I couldn't see where I was goin, cos me hat was knocked over me eyes, an I was holdin me frock an coat wit me free hand te stop them gettin full a piss.

When we got te the tilet, I didn't need te go, cos I'd pissed meself all the way down the passage. I was soppin wet, so I took off me shoes an me socks an me knickers, which were swimmin. An I put them on the floor, wettin the floor. An I wondered wha te do now. So I emptied me shoes of all the piss an put them back on again. Then I looked at me knickers an socks an decided te leave them there, they were destroyed.

I came back out an looked fer the hall, an I went in the wrong direction. I seemed te be walkin fer miles, an I couldn't find the hall. So I opened a door, cos I heard voices inside. An there was a load a nuns wit white veils an black veils an white aprons. Some were laughin an talkin, an some were knittin, an two young ones wit all their hair an a lace on their heads were doin a jigsaw. They all looked up, an I said, 'Excuse me, can any of youse tell me where the hall is?' An they looked at me, from me hat down te me shoes, an they burst out laughin. 'I'm lost,' I said. 'I went te the tilet, an I can't find me way back. I left ye's a pair a knickers an me socks, they're in the tilet. They're no good te me, cos they're soppin wet! But youse can wash them an put them on the childre.'

The young ones asked me where I came outa an gave me a box of chocolates, te help meself, they said. Then they asked me loads a questions, an every time I opened me mouth they roared laughin. 'An tell me now!' they said, blowin their noses an wipin their eyes. Then one of the nuns said they'd better get me back te the parlour, an they gave me the rest of the chocolates in the box.

When I got back, me ma said, 'Where were you? The nun's lookin everywhere fer you!'

An the nun who brought me back said I was a tonic. They hadn't enjoyed themselves so much fer a long time. An she was still laughin when she said, 'Come and see us again some time.'

The nurse brought in our babby. He looked different. His face was fatter, an he looks gorgeous. He had a mop a white curls, an his skin was so white. They must have washed him te nothin! He had a lovely red suit wit glitter buttons an a lovely blue furry coat. He stared at us, an me ma laughed an put her arms out te take him. 'Ah, come on te me,' she said. But he turned his head inta the nurse's neck an cried. I jumped up an ran aroun te see his face, but he

68

slapped me away. The nurse laughed an said he was makin strange cos he hadn't seen us fer two months.

Me ma asked the nurse fer a bottle fer the babby an maybe a few nappies, cos she hadn't anythin left fer him. An maybe a few extra clothes, an she'd be very grateful. The nurse said she'd have te check wit Sister. She said the babby was twelve months old an was eatin solids, an the bottle was only te give him a drink when he was thirsty. Me ma was smilin an chewin her lip, an shakin her head up an down, an sayin, 'Is tha right now? God, he's gettin big, isn't he!' An then she said, 'Wha do you feed him?'

The nurse said, 'Oh, mashed potatoes and mashed vegetables and mince and custard and ice cream and mashed banana. He has a great appetite and will eat anything you give him. You can give him the same food you cook for yourself, and cut down the Cow and Gate powder, he doesn't need it now. You just put a couple of spoons in his bottle, particularly at night when you put him down to sleep, otherwise give him orange juice. He loves that.' The nurse danced him up an down on her lap, an he roared laughin. I joined in wit the nurse an wrapped meself round him an kissed an sucked his face. He held on te me hair an squealed wit delight an tried te bite me chin. I was in heaven!

The nun gave us a big bundle a clothes fer the babby an me. She wrapped them in a sheet an tied the bundle in four corners. Me ma carried the babby, an I carried the bundle. I was glad when we arrived at the bus stop. Me arms was achin me from carryin the weight. 'Where are we goin, Ma? Are we goin home te Benburb Street?'

'No! We're not. I gave tha place up. We couldn't stay there. They're all animals, livin in tha place!'

'So where are we goin, Ma?'

'We'll have te stay in the hostel.'

'The Regina Ceoli, Ma?'

'Yeah!'

I said nothin, an I just looked at the babby. He was dozin off on me ma's shoulder.

It was gettin dark now an the street lamps had come on. It was cold an drizzlin, an the wind was beginnin te blow. I looked at a woman puttin up her umbrella, she was rushin home, I suppose. An I saw her in me mind, goin inta a room wit a roarin fire an a big round table wit a heavy cloth. An the lamp would be lighted, an she'd take off her coat an rush te the fire te warm her hands, an she'd ask the childre, 'Do ye's want a big bowl a stew fer yer tea an some lovely brown bread I made meself, wit lots of good butter?' An the daddy sits at the fire wit his pipe an wearin his slippers. An afterwards, the daughter sits in his lap at the fire while the boy does his schoolwork at the table. An the mammy sews, an they all listen te the wireless. Tha's what it's like in the pictures, anyway. Tha's what I'll be like when I grow up. I'll be respectable!

Every mornin, we have te leave the hostel by nine a.m., an we can't come back until night. The doors shut at eight p.m., an after tha ye're locked out! At night when we go up the avenue, men an women are leanin against trees, hidden by the bushes. Me ma tells me not te look. We walk the streets day after day. Me ma carries the babby, an I carry our bundle. Cos me ma won't leave our clothes in the hostel, cos she says they'll be robbed. She worries a lot tha people might rob our things. So I have te carry them. Sometimes we can go inta a café an buy a cup a tea. An when they ask us te move on, we buy another cup if we have the money. Today, we have no money, an me ma keeps worryin, cos we've no milk fer the babby. 'What are we goin te do, Martha? I've no money an I need te get milk fer the babby. Will we sell our clothes? What are we goin te do?'

I say nothin, an we keep walkin nowhere, lookin fer somethin! I'm thinkin, if we sell the bundle, we'll have nothin te put on the babby, an everythin will be gone. But the bundle is heavy, an I can't manage it. I'm tired, an me arms is painin me. I don't want te sell our clothes, an I don't want te carry them every day. The babby has te have his milk, an we have te get money. 'I don't know, Ma. We'll sell the clothes!'

'But what'll we do, Martha? They're the good clothes, an we'll have nothin te put on the babby.'

'Ma, it's too heavy fer me te carry.'

'Wha? I don't know what I'm goin te do!' an me ma kept chewin her lip an worryin, an we kept walkin nowhere.

'Ma! Let's sell them, we need the money.' I had an empty feelin in me stomach. We would have nothin left, but we needed the money.

We walked down te Henrietta Street an went down the lane te the rag an bone man. The Jew man threw our bundle up onta the scales an weighed it. 'One shillin an sixpence,' he said.

'Ah, no, Mister! Them's good clothes. They're not rags, ye know!'

'That doesn't matter, it's the weight I go by.'

'But they're worth more than one an six! They're the childre's good clothes, an the babby's blanket is worth more than tha!'

'That doesn't matter te me,' he said. 'We only go by the weight.'

I understood. 'Ma! He's not bothered about the clothes, they could be rags ...'

'But they're not rags!' she said.

'I know, Ma! But the man doesn't care. The weight of them is only worth one an six.'

We all went quiet, an I watched me ma chewin on her lip an flutterin her eyelids an givin short coughs, tryin te decide wha te do. She slowly said, 'We'll take the money.' An I watched him hand over the shillin an two thrupenny bits. An I felt bad, cos I told me ma te sell them, an we had been robbed!

71

13

We were walkin through the church at Church Street one night, on our way back te the hostel. Me ma said hello te a man walkin wit a bicycle. 'There ye are again!' she said te him.

'Ah, hello there!' he said, an they stopped te talk.

'I was only up visitin someone in the Mornin Star,' he said. 'I'm on me way home. I have a place now of me own, an it's grand te get outa tha kip.'

'Have ye?' me ma said. 'Tha's lovely! Wha have ye got?'

'Ah, it's only one room,' he said, 'but it'll do me. It's grand te be able te go in an shut yer door an have nobody botherin ye. So how are you? Are ye still in the Regina Ceoli?'

'Ah, indeed I am,' she said.

I stopped listenin an jumped on the man's bike. I was hoppin up an down, tryin te get it te move. 'Hey, Mister! Will ye give us a lift, will ye, Mister?' But they weren't listenin. Me ma was happy an talkin away, an the man was laughin an talkin away te me ma. An they were at it fer hours. I was dyin te go te the tilet, but me ma showed no sign of movin. An I was so busy jumpin up an down on the bike an hopin the man might give me a lift, tha in all the excitement I pissed all over his saddle. It poured down te the ground, an they never noticed!

Me ma was very excited when she finally left him. They had arranged te meet on the Wednesday, after she collected her money from the relievin officer. An as soon as she collected her pound, we went off te meet Jackser.

'I hope he'll be there! Suppose he doesn't turn up, Martha . . .

72

Jaysus, tha'd be terrible,' she said. 'I hope he's not makin a fool a me!'

We met him outside the bird shop on Parnell Street. 'Ah, there he is,' she said te me, an she started laughin wit excitement. 'Come on, hurry over te him.' I was lookin at his bike an wonderin if I'd get a lift. But now they were gone a bit quiet an just kept smilin at each other.

'So . . . will we go, then?' he said te me ma.

We walked on, up Summerhill, an me ma said, 'Wait here a minute!' an she dashed inta a shop. I waited outside wit the man, keepin me eyes on the bike. When me ma came out, she had bread, an tea, an sugar, an even a quarter-pound a good butter! An Jackser said, 'Ah, ye shouldn't a done tha, there was no need te bother. I have plenty up in the room.'

'Ah, sure ye'll need it,' me ma said.

We turned left onta Rutland Street, an we passed old houses wit steps up te them. They had two storeys an a basement. We went inta the hall, an there were rooms there wit families livin in them. An then we went up the stairs onta a little landin wit a big sink an a tap fer water. Then we went up more stairs an came onta the landin wit two doors. We went in the first door, an there was a winda facin out onta the back yard. The other room faced onta the street, an a family lived there. I looked at the big bed beside the winda, an there was a chest a drawers an a wardrobe, an a table wit two chairs. An there was a fireplace fer doin the cookin on, an a big paraffin lamp fer givin the light at night time. Me ma put the babby on the bed.

'Are we stayin here, Jackser?' I asked.

'Yeah! But ye don't have te call me Jackser. Yeah, ye can call me Daddy!'

'But ye're not me daddy, Jackser! I don't have a daddy.'

'No, but ye will now. I'll be yer daddy.'

I didn't think much of this. I looked at him, an I felt very uneasy. I looked at the bed, an I was wonderin wha will I do when he finds out I wet the bed?

* * *

73

Me ma was upset, cos Jackser said he was goin up te the Mornin Star te see someone. She wanted me te go wit him. When we got there, he parked his bike at the end of the road, outside the shop opposite the Richmond Hospital. He told me te mind his bike, an if I didn't move away from the bike, he would buy me a Halloween mask in the shop winda when he got back. I stood lookin in the shop winda, tryin te decide which mask I would buy, all the time lookin te keep an eye on his bike parked at the kerb.

He was an awful long time comin, an the shop was beginnin te close. Then the shop closed, an it was very dark now, but there was still no sign of him. I wanted te go up te the corner, te see if he was comin, but I was afraid te leave the bike. There wasn't a soul on the streets, an I was freezin cold. I wondered if he would ever come back.

At last I saw him comin, an I said, 'The shop is closed, wha will I do about me mask?'

'Never mind the mask, get on the fuckin bike,' he said.

So I kept quiet. I felt really let down. No mask after all tha!

When we got back, me ma was sittin up in the bed, waitin. Jackser went down te get paraffin fer the lamp, an me ma was ragin. 'Wha kept him? Who was he wit?'

'I don't know, Ma. I was mindin the bike.'

'What! Ye didn't go up wit him?'

'No, Ma, he left me te mind his bike.'

'He was wit another woman, tha's wha he was doin!' she said. 'Why didn't ye watch him?'

'I couldn't, Ma, an he didn't buy me a mask. He said he would!'

'Was he lookin at dyed blondes?'

'No, Ma!'

'He was!' she said.

'No, Ma! He wasn't lookin at any dyed blondes.'

'Tell me the truth an I'll give ye a penny.'

'Will ye give it te me now, Ma?'

'When you tell me the truth, I will.'

'Where is it, Ma? Give me the penny now an I'll tell ye.'

'Here!' an she gave me a penny. 'Now, wha was he up to? Why was he gone all this time?'

'I don't know where he went. He left me te mind the bike.'

'So tha's it! He didn't want you te see wha he was up te, cos he knew I'd find out. Was he lookin at women?'

'Yeah, Ma! Dyed blondes.'

'Are ye sure? Ye told me he wasn't!'

'He was, Ma.'

'An did he say anythin te them?'

'No! He was jus lookin.'

'Ye're not tellin me everythin tha he was up te.'

'I am, Ma! He was whistlin at two dyed blondes in high heels.'

'I knew it! Ye never told me tha.'

'Will ye buy me a mask, Ma, if I tell ye the rest?'

'Ye're makin a fuckin eejit of me. I want te fuckin know wha he was up te.'

'He wasn't up te anythin, Ma.'

When he got back, me ma roared at him he'd been wit another woman. He said she's only in the place five days, an he'll do wha he likes. An she'd better not talk, cos she had two bastards from different men, an no other man would take in a woman wit two bastards an give them a home. An if she kept this up, she can take her two bastards an get the fuck back on the streets where he found her.

Me ma wouldn't let go an asked him why he didn't take me up te see wha he was doin. Why did he leave me well outa the way? He lunged at her, draggin her from the bed an throwin her on the floor. I ran te the corner an hid behind the chest a drawers. I watched as he punched an kicked her, an she kept tryin te get up. The babby woke up an started cryin wit the fright. I wanted te get over te him, but I couldn't move.

Jackser stopped killin me ma an looked up at the babby. I was terribly afraid. Jackser's eyes were bulgin, an he was dribblin from his mouth. I was ready te grab me babby, an I was watchin Jackser's eyes when suddenly he plunged the babby from the bed an charged out the door onta the landin. 'I'll fuckin show you, ye whore.'

Me ma jumped up, an I raced out after him. He held the babby by one leg over the banisters an was threatenin te drop him down inta the hall. Me ma was screamin, an I was screamin, an the babby was givin piercin screams. He was frightened outa his life. Me ma was tellin him not te drop the babby, an the people from downstairs came out an were lookin up. Jackser was foamin at the mouth an tellin everyone she was a whore an these were her bastards – she expected him te take another man's leavins. I was creepin down the stairs, hopin te find somethin te catch the babby in an tryin te think of a way te stop Jackser from killin me babby brother. The man from downstairs was talkin up te Jackser an tellin him it wasn't worth doin time fer. 'An you a good man. It's not many that'd take in another man's childre. Fer the love of God, give the child back te his mother.'

Jackser asked the people te tell me ma how lucky she was an not be drivin him te have te chastise her. Me ma put out her arms fer the babby an said, 'No! I won't be tormentin ye again. Just give me the babby.'

'Here, take it,' he said. 'An count yersel lucky he's not splattered in the hall.'

Me ma won't leave Jackser, she won't hear of it. The woman next door told her te leave him quickly. 'Get away from him, he's an animal!' she said. But me ma won't listen.

Jackser put bread an sugar in a bowl an poured hot milk. He told me te give it te the babby. I sat on the floor wit the babby an gave him a spoonful. He loves it. Then I took a spoonful. It's gorgeous! Jackser said the babby will thrive on it. Tha's wha his mother gave te her childre when they were small, an now Jackser is thirty-five.

He was standin behind me watchin, an I moved me back, then he moved te see what I was doin. He saw me take a spoonful of the babby's bread an milk, an he gave me a punch in the side of me head. I was sent flyin, an the bowl upended over the babby. Then he gave me a kick an lifted me by the hair of me head. He roared inta me face, spittin all over me. I was not te be eatin the babby's bread an milk. It was fer him, not me.

I was not te know tha, cos I'd always shared the babby's bottle when there was nothin else te eat. Me ma said nothin.

Jackser took me down te the relief office, an he had a whispered talk wit the man there. When we got back, he said te me ma, 'The only way I can collect the labour money fer you an yer two kids is te get them put inta my name. Now, I'm told, if we go te a solicitor an we say I'm the father of the kids, we just have te sign a sworn affidavit in front of a commissioner fer oaths. We'll get a solicitor who's a commissioner, an Bob's yer uncle, we'll get elected, on the pig's back. The kids'll be in my name, an we'll go after the Corporation. They'll have te house us.'

'Right, Sally! Let's get movin. You stay here an mind him. Don't let tha fire go out an don't use too much coal, go easy on it!' The door banged behind them, an the babby lifted his head from the bed. He looked aroun, beginnin te fret, an I went over te him an stroked his head an hushed him. An he put his head back down an went back te sleep. I got off the bed an went over te sit on the floor in front of the fire, te make sure it didn't go out.

The noise woke me, an I felt a sharp pain in me head from the bang Jackser gave me. Then I was dragged te me feet. Jackser was shakin me by the neck. 'Ye stupid bastard! Ye let the fire go out. I fuckin told ye te watch the fire. Now there's no fuckin tea.' I looked aroun, dazed, wonderin wha was happenin. The room was dark, an the fire was out, an Jackser was roarin inta me face.

I was shakin. 'I'm sorry, Jackser! I won't do it again. Don't hit me, Jackser. I'll be good. I'll do what I'm told.'

I looked te me ma. She was chewin her lip an lookin at me nervously. 'Don't hit her, ye'll hurt her,' she said.

Jackser ran at her an started stabbin her chest wit his fingers. 'She's yer bastard, Mrs! If ye's don't do wha ye're told, ye can get back out on the streets where I found ye's. Now, do I make meself clear?'

'I hear ye!' me ma said.

***

77

Jackser took me wit him aroun te Mountjoy Square. We went down a lane an stopped at the stables. 'Gerrup outa tha,' Jackser roared at the two fellas backin a horse out. An then he laughed.

'How's it goin, Jackser? Wha's happenin?'

'By Jaysus, I've landed on me feet!' Jackser said. 'I've got meself a mot. This is her young one. Go on over there, you, an play.'

I kept outa the way. I wandered up an down the lane, lost in me own thoughts, keepin a wary watch on the stables in case Jackser was callin me. I could hear them laughin, an then Jackser shot up the lane, runnin wit a horse. At the top of the lane, he turned an came runnin back. The horse lifted its legs high in the air an was beginnin te break away from him. I broke away from the wall I was pressed against an dashed inta the stables. Jackser skidded te a stop outside, pullin on the horse's head. 'Whoa! Easy! Easy!' he said, an petted the horse. 'She's a lovely mare, ye'd know she'd been a racin horse,' he said te the men.

'Ye would at tha!' one man said, squintin through the smoke of a Woodbine an suppin his mug a tea. I was sittin on the sacks of oats, watchin the other man sweepin out the horse manure an the wet hay. He swept it all up inta a corner of the lane, an when he was satisfied it was all clean, he put the brush away an started te put down new hay.

I had a bad headache now, an it was gettin worse. The man wit the Woodbine noticed an said, 'I don't think tha young one is lookin too well. Maybe ye should get her home.'

Jackser looked at me an said, 'Wha's wrong wit ye?'

'Me head is painin me. I feel sick!'

'Yeah, OK. I'll get ye back in a minute.'

When we got back, Jackser told me ma I wasn't well. But she wasn't listenin. 'Go down te the shop an get me an onion. I'm goin te fry it fer his tea. An get me a bottle a milk.'

'Ma, me head is painin me. I don't feel well.'

'Go on! Hurry up, then, he's waitin on his tea! I don't want him te start.'

I took the money an went down the street, an then me stomach started heavin. I was bringin up the tea an bread I'd had tha mornin, an it was all water now. I couldn't bring up any more, but me stomach continued te heave. I held on te the railins an then had te sit down on the step. Me head was burstin, an I knew I'd have te move. Jackser would be down after me, an he'd kill me if I took me time. He'd be waitin fer me te get back.

The next mornin, he woke me te get up. I was sittin on the side of the bed an couldn't move. The room was spinnin, an me head was worse. Jackser came over an said, 'Come on! Get dressed.' I made a move te get me shoes offa the floor an keeled over. Jackser picked me up an put me sittin back on the bed. 'Wha's wrong wit ye?'

'Me head is painin me bad,' I said.

'Right! Go down te the dispensary an ask tha doctor te come up an see ye,' he said. I slowly left the room an headed down the street. But instead of goin down te Summerhill, I sat down on the steps of a house an waited. I was six years old, an I knew it was foolish te ask the doctor te come up te the room te see me when I was the sick one.

When I got back, I said the doctor would be up, an they put me te bed. I lay at the head of the big bed on me own. I must have dozed, cos when me eyes fluttered open I saw Eddie, Jackser's brother, lookin down at me. I closed me eyes again. It hurt te open them.

'Ah, the poor young one looks bad! Do ye think she'll be all right?' Eddie asked.

'Ah, she's in the best place. She can't go wrong there. As long as she gets plenty a rest, she'll be fine,' Jackser said.

I don't know how many days have passed. But this evenin I'm feelin better. Jackser put me in a cot shoved over inta the corner. We've moved inta the front room, which faces out onta the street. This room is bigger, an the family who lived here moved out, leavin this cot behind. I can't stretch me legs an am all doubled up, but it's better than sleepin wit them. Now Jackser can't kick me any more, tellin me te move over when I was sleepin at the end of the bed an draggin me from me sleep when I was wettin the bed.

79

The two of them are gettin ready te go out. Me ma is wearin the new red coat she bought fer thirty bob when she collected the childre's allowance an he collected the labour money. He bought himself a Crombie coat an a pair of fawn trousers an brown ankle-length horsey boots. All the horsey people wear them. An Jackser an me ma were all delighted wit their new style. 'We're goin out,' he says te me, lyin in the cot. 'We're headin up towards the convent where the nuns give us the bread. I saw a doll fer you, lyin in the bin. An we're goin te go up an get it. So don't move from the cot. An don't mind the babby, he's asleep. If he wakes up, just ignore him. He'll go back te sleep when he sees it's dark an nobody's mindin him. An if anyone knocks, don't answer the door.'

I lay in the cot, watchin the shadows thrown in from the street lamp dancin up an down on the wallpaper, an I imagined the doll. I worried it might be gone – someone else might get it. Maybe it might have a broken leg. But tha wouldn't matter. I could brush its hair an wash it. An wrap it in one of the babby's blankets an bring it te bed wit me.

Time passed. I'd nodded off, but they weren't back yet. I waited wit longin fer the doll. But I enjoyed the peace of the room an was content tha Jackser was happy an excited, an me ma was laughin when they went out.

The next day, there was no sign of the doll. I didn't say anythin, but I wondered wha happened. Me ma an Jackser were talkin an laughin. 'Tha was a great fillum, Jaysus, *Shake Hands With the Devil*. Did ye see the way he was runnin wit the coffin, an the fuckin thing broke open when they dropped it? I nearly kilt meself laughin, Sally! Did you like it?'

'Yeah!' me ma said.

'By God, tha was a great night last night. I really enjoyed meself, I did.'

'Yeah,' me ma said.

The Legion of Mary turned up this mornin an knocked on the door. They wanted te talk about religion. 'Youse are not gettin in here,' Jackser said te them. 'I've no time fer religion.' An he started roarin,

'Them Antichrists, the priests, wit their thick red necks from all the best feedin of steak an the best food money can buy. Wit their motor cars, an it's all in the name of religion! When they're only gettin rich on the backs of the poor!'

When he stopped fer a minute te get his breath back, one of the two women said, 'Do you pray? It's a great comfort to the soul. I don't suppose you go to Mass, then? You are living in terrible sin. If you were to drop dead today, you'd go straight to Hell!'

Jackser got his breath back an shouted, 'I went through fuckin hell when I was locked away in Artane Industrial School fer nine years! An them so-called Christian Brothers beat the shite outa me wit a leather strap an made me plant fuckin potatoes an work out in all weathers, out in the farm. An they put me in hobnail boots tha were too small fer me, so I couldn't walk, an now lookit me!' An he stood back te show them. 'Me legs are fuckin bandy! They destroyed me!' he roared.

The women peered inta the room an spotted me. 'Ah, could we take the child to one of our club meetings? We're having one today. It's for the children, and our club is just around the corner. We hold them on a Sunday.'

'No!' Jackser roared.

'Well, could we come in and maybe say a little decade of the rosary?'

'Youse have had all the time I'm givin youse. Now gerraway from me door.'

He went te bang it shut, but the woman put her foot in the door an said, 'I implore you to see it in your heart to let the child come around to the club. It's only for an hour, and we'll bring her back.'

'Youse are not gettin yer hands on her te corrupt her wit yer religion. I'm havin no religion in my house. An furthermore, it'd suit ye better if ye were te offer te feed the childre. They're starved fer the want of a bit a food. I can't work any more, I had te give it up. I was a night watchman on a buildin site in England, an the coke fire te keep me warm at night destroyed me lungs. I used te sit hunched over the fire, tryin te keep meself warm, an only a hut

81

over me te keep out the elements. I'm destroyed, I'll never be able te work again. Now fuck off wit yerselves.' An he slammed the door.

They were back the next Sunday. 'We offered our prayers for you,' they said te Jackser when he opened the door. 'We prayed to our Blessed Mother to intercede with Our Lord, you would open your heart to God's love and mercy. Please let us take the child around to our club.'

Me ma said, 'Maybe ye should let her go. Tha way we'd get a bit a peace!'

'Right!' Jackser said. 'But after this no more! Ye's are comin the hound wit me, an I'm master in me own home. Me word is law.'

Me an the Legion women went aroun the corner te an old church. I was all excited, cos I was gettin outa the room an goin somewhere. The club was a big room wit a table an benches. There were about four women runnin in an outa the kitchen, makin sambidges an tea. An I could see plates of fluffy pink an white biscuits. Young ones were sittin along the benches an had copybooks an pencils in front of them. I thought we were all goin te school when I saw this. The young ones looked very important te me. One said, 'Sister! Will ya be readin out the *Maria Legionis* te us? I have all me good deeds fer the week wrote out. Me big sister helped me. Look at all I done, Sister!' an she slapped the copybook down in front of the woman an started makin a big noise suckin on her pencil.

'Lookit what I done, Sister! I done a lot more than her.'

'I was kilt helpin me mammy all week, so I was.'

'No, ye wasn't,' another one shouted. 'I saw ye out on the streets, day an night, playin an havin a great time!'

'How would you know?' Sucky Pencil roared back. 'You musta bein doin nothin yerself, then!'

'I saw ye from the winda. I was helpin me mammy polish the oil cloth on the floor wit me ma's lavender polish. I was waitin fer the tin te be emptied so I could get it an play piggybeds on the street.'

'Ye're a liar! Youse don't have oil cloth on yer floor.'

'Children!' said the sister. 'No fighting! Our Lady's watching.' Then the two women arrived from the kitchen carryin trays wit sambidges an biscuits, an another woman came in wit a big kettle an white tea cups wit matchin saucers. The woman poured out the tea, an it had milk an sugar already poured inta it. I was handed a plate wit sambidges, an I helped meself te a ham sambidge. The plate was put in front of me, an I supped the tea an took a bite of the sambidge. It was good butter, an the ham was gorgeous. I kept me eye on the plate of sambidges, an I tried not te guzzle down what I was eatin. But as I reached out te take another one, hands came from nowhere an cleaned out the plate. I looked an saw the young one beside me. She had a sambidge in each hand, an she'd put two more under her, an she was sittin on them. I swallied me spit an decided te ask her fer one.

'No! They're mine.'

'But I only got one,' I said.

'Well, ye won't be so dopey next time, will ye?' she said.

I lost me rag an said, 'Aw, fuck off! Stick them up yer arse! I hope they poison ye!'

An yer woman roared up at the woman, 'Sister! Sister! Tha new young one is after tellin me te fuck off, so she is!'

'Mary Cissy! That's not nice language in front of the Statue of Our Lady.'

'She did, Miss, Sister! We heard her, too. She told her te fuck off,' they all roared.

'Yeah, an she told me te fuck off as well!' another young one said.

'That's enough now,' the woman said, slappin her hand on the table.

Yer one beside me slid off down the bench, takin her copybook an chewed pencil. 'I'm not sittin beside ye, ye fuckin eejit!'

'An fuck you, too!' I said back. An then we all said prayers, an the women brought me back.

I started school again this mornin, round in Gardiner Street. It's down a lane, an it's run by the nuns. The classroom is very big. We have first an second class in the room. I'm sittin at the back, an the nun walks up an down between the rows of desks an talks an checks te see wha the childre are doin. She writes things on a blackboard. But I don't know wha's goin on, so I just sit there lookin aroun me, an I'm dazed. All the other childre are busy doin somethin, but I do nothin. At lunch time, the sister calls me over an says me mammy is waitin fer me in the lane. When I get there, me ma hands me a billy can an says I'm te go inta the dinner house an get a can of stew. The sister will give it te me, cos me ma already spoke te her.

I collect the stew from the women servin behind the counter, an I don't have te pay the penny. I don't have te queue long behind the other poor people, cos the nun comes in an takes the can offa me an gives it te the woman te fill. An then I run home wit it an then rush back te school. The bell is ringin just as I arrive, an I find me line an go back inta class.

I'm feelin tired now, an me head is beginnin te ache. The watery sun is comin in the winda an shows all the dust floatin aroun the room. It feels hot an stuffy, an I can't make out wha people are sayin. It's just a buzzin noise in me head, an I give up tryin te understand what I'm supposed te be doin an put me head down in me hands an fall asleep on the desk.

Today, they sent a big young one te come over an sit beside me. She has a blackboard an chalk. 'Now,' she says, an starts te write. 'One plus one equals?' an looks at me an waits. I don't know wha she's talkin about, so I just look. 'Equals two,' she says. 'Now again,' but I still don't know, an after a while she gets fed up an says, 'Do ye not know any sums?'

'No!' I say.

'OK,' she says. 'Do ye know the alphabet?'

'Wha's tha?' I ask.

'Jaysus, ye don't know anythin, then! Can ye count yer money?' she asks. 'Wha do ye do when yer mammy sends ye te the shop?'

'I get the messages,' I said, hopin she'd think I was grand, but she didn't.

'Ah, ye're too stupid,' she said. An then she ignored me an started te draw.

'Wha's that?' I asked.

84

'It's a cat.'

'No, it's not! A cat doesn't look like tha,' I said. 'You can't draw, ye're pure stupid,' an she gave me a slap of the blackboard.

The nun came runnin down an waved her stick at her. 'I'm shocked!' the nun said. 'I thought you were a responsible girl. That's why I put you in charge of Martha. You were supposed to help her, not hit her!'

'But I was helpin her, Sister, an cos she doesn't know anythin she started te call me names!'

'I didn't, Sister,' I said. 'She said I was pure stupid!'

'No, I didn't, you said tha,' the young one said, an then she started te cry.

The whole class turned on me then an said I was terrible. So the nun turned te the class an put her fingers up te her mouth an said, 'The next one who speaks will be kept back after school.' Then she told the blackboard one te go out te the tilet an blow her nose. An she looked at me an smiled, an put her hand on me head an said in a whisper, 'Be a good little girl for Sister, won't you, Martha?'

An I said in a whisper, 'Yes, Sister, I'll be very good fer ye.' An I sat there fer the rest of the day lookin up at her an wishin she was me mammy!

This mornin, when we were gettin ready te go out te our break, everyone was shoutin. So Sister said we were te be very quiet. We all stood up an someone gave their seat an unmerciful bang. Sister asked, 'Who did that?' An nobody answered. So she said we were goin te wait until the person responsible owned up on their honour. But nobody owned up on their honour. So we waited. The young one in the next row beside me is always annoyin me. She has a Cleopatra hairstyle an she always stares over at me until I look at her, then she makes a face at me an flicks her hair wit her hand an turns away. I can't flick me hair back at her, cos it's too short an stands up like straw. Me hair is still growin back from when I had the sores an me ma had te cut it. 'I'm tellin it was you,' she whispers.

'No, it wasn't!' I said.

An I'm tryin te think wha name te call her when Sister asks me gently, 'Was it you, Martha?'

'No, Sister!' I said.

An then a young one owned up an suddenly said, 'It was me, Sister, an I'm sorry, Sister, an I'm on me honour, Sister.' An we all went out te the playground. It was freezin cold in the yard, an I didn't run aroun. I was too cold an stood in a corner outa the wind. I didn't bother te play wit the other childre, cos they wouldn't play wit me anyway. The nun appeared an told us te gather up in two lines. Cleopatra was tormentin me in the other line. She kept flickin her hair an sayin she was goin te tell on me. I was ragin an tryin te think how I'd get me own back when suddenly Sister called me outa the line. As I passed Cleopatra, she cackled at me. 'Now, I told ye I was goin te get ye inta trouble. Ye're fer it!'

Sister brought me inta a little room off the school yard an it had shelves of clothes. She put me sittin up on the table an took off me rags an put a lovely warm frock on me an a snowy-white soft cardigan wit pearl buttons, an a pair of white knee socks an a pair of red sandals. Then she combed me hair an lifted me down an stood back te admire me. Then she rushed over te the sink an dipped a corner of the towel under the tap an wiped me face an damped me hair down. I walked out the door wit springs on me feet, an I was lovely an warm. The childre were still lined up an were very quiet when we appeared. An they all looked me up an down. I bounced past Cleopatra, an her jaw was hangin down te her belly. Then she tightened her mouth an squinted her eyes at me. I threw back me head an flicked me hair, an patted me new cardigan an marched past her.

When I got home, Charlie was sittin outside in a big pram wit springs an a hood. It was lovely. I ran up te the room an asked, 'Can I take him fer a walk?'

'No!' me ma said. 'Have yer tea an bread an go out an watch the pram.'

I was outside sittin on the steps an fed up lookin at the pram. The babby was asleep. I wouldn't have been able te get the pram down the steps, cos it was too heavy, so I couldn't push the pram off an take him fer a walk. A young one from school was passin an asked me te go wit her fer a message down te Summerhill. I said, 'No, I can't. I have te mind the babby.' But she wouldn't believe me an kept on askin. I was dyin te go, so I said, 'Yeah, OK.'

We were on our way back up Summerhill when suddenly I got an awful blow tha sent me flyin out onta the road an nearly under a car. I didn't know wha hit me until Jackser picked me up by me neck an kicked me back onta the footpath. I didn't get time te get me wind back before he had me offa the ground again an was shakin me. 'I told ye! I told ye!' he said as he boxed me. 'Not te leave the child alone. Ye were told te mind the pram.' I was convulsin up an down, me whole body was shakin, an great sobs were comin outa me. Loads a people were aroun, but nobody bothered te interfere. He kicked me again, sendin me flyin te the ground, an roared, 'Get up! Get movin, cos I'm goin te kick ye all the way back te tha pram.'

87

14

Jackser took me off on his bike te collect the bread from the convents. I sat up on the crossbar an held on te the handlebars. Jackser was gettin ready te jump onta the bike, but first he had te do his habits. 'Now! Well . . .' an then he started te suck air up inta his nose very fast an at the same time stretch an shake his right arm inta the air while bendin his head te the ground. He can't help it, he does tha after he gets an idea or before he does somethin interestin. He bursts the arse offa all his trousers doin that, an he always has te sew his coat under the arms. But this time he was tryin te hold the bike wit me on it an do his habits at the same time. The bike started te see-saw out onta the road, till me feet were touchin the ground, an then back te Jackser, faster an faster. I started te squeal an went, 'Ah, Mammy, help!'

Jackser stopped suddenly an said, 'What! Wha the fuck is tha about?' I jumped offa the bike at the same time as he went back te his snortin an salutin an bendin, an he lost his balance, toppled over the bike an rolled onta the road. He lay there lookin very white, an he said, 'I'm done fer! Run in an get Sally. Tell her te get the ambulance. I'm damaged!' I kept lookin at him, not knowin wha te do, an a man came along on a bicycle an picked him up an said, 'There now, you'll be all right. Ye just gorra fright.'

Jackser held onta the railins, an I went up te tell me ma. 'Ma! Ma!' I said, 'Jackser fell off his bike an ye're te come down.'

'Is he hurt?' she asked.

'No, Ma, he's just shocked. But he thinks he's near te death.'

Me ma laughed an said, 'It's a pity he's not!'

'Yeah, Ma, it serves him right.'

Then I heard him comin up the stairs, an he was moanin, 'Sally! Sally! Are ye there, Sally?'

The man was helpin him up an sayin, 'Ye need a strong sup a tea, very sweet, wit lots a sugar fer the shock. Don't underestimate shock, it can kill ye!'

I started te laugh, an me ma was pinchin me te stop, but she was laughin, too. An I started laughin harder, an I was afraid, cos I knew he'd kill me. But I laughed even more. An when his head appeared aroun the banisters wit the man helpin him, he was annoyed cos we hadn't rushed down. Tears were comin down me ma's face, an Jackser said, 'Are ye's fuckin laughin?'

'No, Jackser!' I shouted. 'We were cryin! An we were afraid te come down in case ye were dead.' Me ma snorted an ran back inta the room, an I ran after her.

Jackser looked very suspicious, but he sat at the fire, suppin his tea an smokin his Woodbine, an talkin te me ma about death. 'Ye never know the hour or the day,' he kept sayin. 'I've an awful fear about dyin, I have, Sally. Jaysus, I have te take care of meself!'

Me ma sat the other side of the fire. Her eyes were closin an she was dozin off. She just kept murmurin, 'Hm, Hm,' te keep him quiet. I lay on the bed wit Charlie's head in me lap, an I was strokin his long curls. His eyes were open, but he was relaxin an enjoyin the peace. Just listenin te Jackser talkin quietly.

The next day we took off fer the convents. Jackser had a lump on the back of his head, an he kept gettin me te feel it. 'Is it big? Can ye feel it?' he kept askin me.

'Yeah, it's huge, Jackser!' I kept sayin.

'I coulda been kilt, ya know! Tha was a close call.'

'Yeah, ye coulda been kilt,' I kept sayin. An was very disappointed he wasn't. I was thinkin, me ma was right, the bad live longer.

We got goin without any fuss this time. Jackser pedalled us up te Drumcondra, an as we flew past the Bishop's Palace, he said, 'There's no point in goin in there. Them rich bastards would give ye nothin.'

'But he's a bishop, Jackser! He's a very holy man,' I said. 'He's supposed te give te the poor!'

'Wha have they ever given you?' he said. 'It took someone like me te take youse in an give ye's a home! Listen te me an ye won't go wrong. I'll teach ye everythin there is te know about life.'

We pedalled up the back entrance te the convent. We came along a dark road surrounded by a high wall, wit trees on our right an green fields on the other side, wit vegebales growin in some parts an cows grazin in others. There was a little lodge house fer the farmer an his family. I could see the childre from the convent playin in the fields. They were wearin pinnies over their frocks, an I wondered if they'd like te swap places wit me. We cycled past the childre's buildin an came aroun te the women's part. Here the women worked in the laundry an never saw the light of day. We saw a coupla them comin outa the big buildin an goin inta the yard. They were carryin buckets an wore wellingtons, an berets on their heads. Their hair was cut very short an was stone grey. They stopped te stare at us.

'Yer mammy nearly ended up as one of them,' Jackser said. 'An you'd a been put away like them childre round the corner. Ye should remember how lucky ye are!' he said te me. I felt me heart begin te ache an wondered why God doesn't listen te me. If me ma was in here an I was wit the childre, then Jackser couldn't get his hands on us. Then I looked at the women fer a long time, an I pitied them. They were locked up, an I wondered why we went on livin. I was feelin old, even though six is not supposed te be old.

When we got aroun te the front of the convent, we walked down te the grotto, where there was a statue of St Bernadette prayin te Our Lady. Jackser took off his cap an held it between his hands. 'Get down on yer knees an say a prayer,' he said te me. 'Let the nuns see ye prayin. They might even give us a drop a soup if ye impress them. Ye never know,' he said, 'we could strike lucky an even get a bit a dinner.'

I was prayin hard wit me eyes closed, hopin we'd get a bit a dinner an Jackser would stay in good form, when suddenly he shouted,

'Fuck me! Wha's tha?' an a tramp came outa the bushes behind us an crept up te Jackser.

'Have ye got an aul smoke?' he said te Jackser. An the man was weighed down wit coats an trousers an jumpers, an he was wearin three hats. An he was holdin everythin together wit a rope tied aroun his waist.

'No, I just smoked me last butt,' Jackser said, an we went up an rang the bell.

A woman came out wearin a blue smock like they usually wear in shops. She had men's laced shoes, an her hair was very short an grey. She had hairy legs an no stockins, an a beard on her chin. She looked at us an said nothin, then went back in an closed the door. We waited. 'That's "Hairy",' Jackser said. 'She's been here fer years, an the nuns trust her. Can ye see why? Wha man would have her?' Jackser walked over te the grass an sat down wit his back restin against a statue of the Sacred Heart. 'Ah, it's lovely here. Can ye smell the fresh air?' I looked aroun at all the green grass an the daisies growin in it. An all the lovely flowers an the big trees. 'There isn't a sound te be heard,' Jackser said. 'I grew up in a place like this. I was only seven an me brother was eight when they took us away from me poor mother. She's dead now, God rest her, an it's all my fault. I kilt her. I broke her heart. It was the drink, ye see! The aul drink ruined me. I could've made somethin of meself, but I threw it all away. I'm married ye know!'

I said nothin, I just listened. 'Oh, yeah! I married a dealer from Moore Street. She was a fine-lookin woman, blonde, she was. But it didn't last. Three weeks is all she stayed, then she left me.'

'Why'd she leave ye, Jackser?' I asked.

'Ah, we had a bit of a row. I was drunk, she was givin me too much lip, an I gave her a smack. But she was stone fuckin mad! I woke up tied te the fuckin bed, an she was on top of me chest wit a big fuckin bread knife held te me throat. "Ye're not touchin me again. Cos I'm not stayin. If I ever see ye again, I won't hesitate te cut yer throat. Do ye get that?" she says, then she was gone out the door, leavin me in tha state. I was one lucky man. Well rid a her,

I can tell ya! I'm still not the better of it. Ye'd never believe it, but there's mad bastards out there, Martha, I'm tellin ye!'

'I know, Jackser.' An I thought te meself, I'm never goin te be like me ma. I thought the dealer in Moore Street was great, I'd love te meet her.

The door opened an Jackser rushed over, whippin his cap offa his head, but he put it back on when he saw it was only Hairy. She handed him two stale loaves, an he asked her fer a drop a tea. 'The kitchen's closed,' she said.

'Well, I'll have te see the nun,' he said. 'This child is fallin from the hunger. So will ye go an send her out.'

'She's in the chapel getting her prayers, and she won't be out for a while.'

'We'll wait,' Jackser said gruffly, an Hairy slammed the door.

'Dried up aul fucker!' Jackser said te the door. 'I hate the Church. Them fuckers are the ruination of this country. Them bastards destroyed me an poor Eddie in Artane. I was out sowin potatoes when I was only your age. Workin in all weather. Me boots were too small fer me feet, an they crippled me. Them Christian Brothers were very vicious. They'd wait until yer back was turned, then they'd suddenly run at ye an punch the head off ye. But I learnt tailorin. Yeah, I'm a tailor, they gave me good trainin. They always made sure everyone left wit a trade. I coulda made somethin of meself. But I sold the key of me mother's house. The day we buried her, when me brothers an sisters came home tha night, they'd no home te go te. I drank the money in the pub. They had te get the money saved an take the boat te England. They never set foot in this country again, an they never forgave me fer it. An I don't deserve it. I put me mother in her grave. I tormented her wit the drink, ye see. I was mad fer the drink. I try now te keep away from it, but it's very hard when it gets a grip on ye.'

Jackser went up an rang the bell, an the nun came out. Jackser blessed himself te the nun an bowed his head an said things are hard fer him at the moment. If she could see her way te maybe givin him a bit a food te take home te the childre, he'd get us all te pray fer her. She said she'd see wha she could do, an she went in an closed the door. 'Say a prayer she'll give us somethin,' Jackser said. 'Otherwise, we'll have te move fast. It's gettin late, an I want te do a few more before we mosey home.'

By the time we arrived back in Rutland Street, it was nine o'clock at night. Jackser had te peel me hands off the bars of the bike, an I couldn't straighten up. I was frozen solid. We had two pillacases of food, though, an Jackser had more wrapped up in his jumper. Me ma had the fire goin an the lamp lit on the table when we arrived in. She turned up the wick te give us more light, an I could smell the paraffin. Charlie was rockin up an down in the bed wit excitement when he saw me comin in. An me ma's eyes lit up when she saw the bags of food. 'The kettle is boiled,' she said, laughin an followin Jackser's hands takin out the tinfoil filled wit roast meat. We had lumps a beef drippin fer the bread an fer fryin, strings a sausages an lumps a cooked bacon, loads a bread, an loose tea, an bags a sugar. An we didn't break the eggs wrapped up in Jackser's socks. He robbed them from the hen house at the back of the home fer the blind off Drumcondra.

I was out on the street playin, but there was no one aroun te play wit. I was standin there, leanin against the railins, mindin me own business when a young fella came along an gave me a shove. Then he started laughin at me an callin me names. 'Eh! Skinny, smelly, ye can't catch me!' I was ragin, an I looked at him. He was bigger than me. Then he started throwin stones at me. I could feel me heart poundin, but I waited. I'm not lettin him get away wit tha.

As soon as his back was turned an he bent down te pick up somethin from the ground, I charged. I grabbed him by the jumper an knocked him down. He rolled over an started te lash out wit his legs, still callin me smelly. But I dropped me knees on his stomach an grabbed his hair. Then I stood up, still holdin tight te his hair. 'Do ye give up?' I shouted.

'No! I'm goin te get ye fer this,' he roared, so I pulled his hair tighter te the ground, an he couldn't get a hold a me. 'Ah, let go!' he shouted.

'Do ye give in?'

'Let go! Lemme go! Ma! Ma! Mammy! I give in, I give in!'

Then a man came along, an I let go. The young fella ran off. I was lookin at the man te see if he would roar at me fer fightin, but he just laughed. He was all dressed up, an he must be back from England, I thought. He called me over, an he was still laughin, but I hesimitated, ye never know ... Then he put his hand in his pocket, an I shot across the road. He handed me two shillins, an he said, 'Ye're a little topper, tha young fella won't be back fer more.' An he looked down at me. 'Jaysus, them eyes a yours are spittin!' An he bent down te me. 'Listen, you remind me of meself when I was your age. Only fight when ye have to. There's other ways of beatin them.'

'How, Mister?' I asked.

'Work hard an get away from them. Be yer own man. Don't look down on anyone, but don't look up te anyone either.'

'Where do ye live, Mister?' I asked him.

'I'm livin in England, an I have me own buildin business now. I never looked back.'

'Do ye have childre?'

'No! I'm not married,' then he laughed an said I'd be grand. 'I'd better hurry,' he said. 'I'm meetin me brothers. Go on down an get a few sweets, an don't spend the money all at once.' Then he was gone. I watched him go, hurryin down Summer Street, an I wanted te run after him an ask him will he take me back te England wit him. But I knew I'd have te take me mammy an me little brother. An somehow I knew me mammy wouldn't suit him. She's too quiet fer someone like him. Or maybe he wouldn't like her hairy legs. I felt I'd lost somethin, an I turned aroun an started te walk home. I was lookin at the shiny two shillins, an I started te run. I'll bring this up te me ma an watch her face break inta a laugh. Me world is grand an everythin is lovely when I see me ma laugh, cos it means everythin is OK.

I ran up the stairs an rattled the doorknob an banged the door. 'Ma! Ma!' I shouted. 'Open the door.'

Jackser shouted, 'Wha do ye want? Get out an play.'

94

'I have money, I got money, Jackser! I have two shillins!'

I heard Jackser laugh, an then me ma laughed an said, 'Jaysus, I wonder where she got tha!' Then I heard the bedsprings creak, an Jackser got up an opened the door. He was holdin his hand over the front of his shirt, an his legs was bare. I dashed inta the room an flew over te me ma in the bed. An I handed her the money.

Jackser was strugglin wit the leg of his trousers, an he started snufflin. His arm shot up in the air a few times, an his head went down te the ground, an he lost his trousers, exposin his hairy arse. 'Oh, fuck me,' he said, an pulled them up an started snufflin again. When he was finished, he said, 'Sally! Send the young one down an get me five Woodbines. I'm dyin fer a smoke!'

'Right,' she said. 'An get me a bottle of milk. An make sure ye bring back the right change.'

'OK, Ma. An can I have a penny fer meself?'

'Yeah, go on, then.'

On me way out the door, I knocked on me friend te ask her if she wanted any messages doin. 'Come on in, Martha, she said. 'How are ye?'

'Do ye want anythin at the shop, Maizie?' I asked.

'Ah, no. Paddy's bringin me back fish an chips on his way back from the pub later. How's yer mammy?'

'She's grand, Maizie.'

'An how's the babby? I haven't seen him out recently. The pram's gone outa the hall. I suppose tha Jackser fella pawned it, did he?'

I said nothin, an I went over te play wit Chrissie. She's gorgeous. She's nearly three, an she has fat cheeks an her mammy dresses her lovely. She always has standy-out frilly frocks an lovely big bows in her hair. Her mammy makes ringlets when she washes her hair, an they curl down her back. She showed me her new doll her granny Kelly bought her. I wanted te sit down on the floor in front of the fire an help Chrissie te dress the doll, but Jackser will kill me. I have te go an get his Woodbines.

'Listen, Martha. Do ye want te come te the zoo wit us on Sunday? Go an ask yer mammy.'

Me heart leapt. 'Is tha where they have all the animals from the jungle, Maizie?'

'Yeah,' she laughed. 'Let me know wha she says, OK, Martha?'

'Yeah, OK, Maizie.' I shot out the door an down the street an galloped as fast as I could. The aul one behind the counter wasn't in a hurry te serve me. She was leanin on her elbows wit her face in her hands, close te the other aul one who was stretched out on the counter wit her big milkers spread over her arms. An they were whisperin te each other. The shopkeeper threw her head back an roared, 'Tha's a terrible carry on!'

An the customer said, 'I'm not tellin ye a word of a lie! As true as I'm standin here. Stark naked, he was!'

'No!' the shopkeeper said, an her eyes was bulgin. 'Go on, tell us more!' An they pressed their heads together.

'Mrs,' I said. 'I'm te get five Woodbines an a bottle of milk.'

'Hold yer horses!' the shopkeeper roared at me. 'Bloody kids.' An she shook herself te get more comfortable an said, 'Go on, Nelly, keep goin. I'm listenin!'

But the customer looked down at me, an her jaw was hangin. 'Tha young one is listenin te everythin.'

'I want me messages, Mrs,' I said. 'Me ma is waitin.'

'Ah, serve her then an get rid of her. We've no comfort wit big ears here.'

When I got me Woodbines an milk, I checked me change. 'It's all there!' the shopkeeper roared. 'Nobody's robbin ye!' An the two of them watched me.

'Thanks, Mrs,' I said, an ran like the wind.

When I got back, they were waitin fer me. 'Wha kept ye?' Jackser roared.

'The shop was crowded, Jackser,' I said, an handed him his Woodbines. He snatched them an whipped open the packet an started snufflin. I let out me breath an let go of me shoulders. I put the milk on the table an gave me ma the change.

'Where'd ye get the money?' she asked. An I told them the story, leavin out wha the man said te me.

'Tha's the stuff!' roared Jackser. 'Never let them get the better of ye!'

I looked at Charlie, who was sittin on the floor eatin the cinders. 'Them's hot,' I said, snatchin the cinders from his mouth. The babby's mouth dropped open, an he started te cry. I picked him up te give him a kiss, an he gave me a wallop on the nose. I laughed.

'Put him down!' Jackser roared. 'He was quiet until you came in.'

'He'll get burnt, Jackser!' I said. 'He's eatin the hot cinders!'

'No, he's not, he got them from the bucket.'

I felt his arse an it was cold. So I carried him over te me ma an put him beside her in the bed. 'Put him in the cot,' she said. I looked over te the cot, an I could see she hadn't aired his blankets. I went over an lifted his blankets, an they were soppin wet.

'Ma, the babby's blankets are all wet,' I said.

'Leave them! Just put him in,' she said.

'But they're wet.'

'Do as ye're fuckin told,' Jackser said te me. Then he went te the cot an whipped out the blankets. 'Holy Jaysus, Mrs, she's right, the young fella's bed is soppin wet!'

'Ah, he'll be all right,' me ma said.

Jackser started te put more coal on the fire te dry the blankets. An me ma said, 'What are we goin te do fer more coal fer tomorrow? Tha's the last of it.'

I looked at me ma an whispered, 'Don't start him off, Ma! Don't say anythin.'

But she glared at me an roared, 'This is all yer fault! Ye're always causin trouble.'

I took the babby an went over te me own corner where me mattress was. It was a cot mattress, an it was lyin on the floor. An I sat down wit the babby in case Jackser went fer me ma, then we could dive under the bed outa harm's way.

On Sunday, Jackser let me go te the zoo. 'Go on, then,' he said. 'Yer mammy needs the rest anyway.' An he winked at her an laughed. An she laughed back. I didn't know wha was funny, but I was glad they were happy.

I clattered off down the stairs, cos me shoes were too big fer me an I kept leavin them behind. I couldn't believe me luck! I was goin somewhere! An te the zoo. The only animals I'd seen were dogs an cats an horses an cows up in the convent.

I waited on the steps fer them te come out, cos when I'd rattled the knob an shouted in, 'It's me! I'm here!' Maizie said they were gettin ready an would be out in a minute. When they came down, they looked lovely. All done up. Paddy was wearin a blue suit an a red shirt wit a white tie an Elvis Presley blue suede shoes. An his black wavy hair was combed back wit Brylcreem. He looked lovely an handsome. Maizie had her blonde hair curled an parted at the side an fallin over one eye in waves. An she had lipstick on an powder, an black pencil on her eyes. Her frock was white wit little red roses, an it had a belt at the waist, an then it stood out. She was wearin black high heels an stockins, an carried a white cardigan an handbag. They were holdin Chrissie's hand. When I looked down at Chrissie, she was like a fairy ye'd see on top of a Christmas tree down on Henry Street. They put her in a pink satin frock wit pink lace an tiny ribbons, an it stood out so ye could see the layers of underskirts. An she had a wide ribbon, white satin it is, tied aroun her stomach, an a big bow hangin down at the back. Her jet-black shiny ringlets were tied up at the front wit a big white ribbon.

I was tongue-tied, an I couldn't say anythin. Paddy looked at me an then looked at Maizie, an I could see she was disappointed. I was in me rags. I felt very ashamed when I looked down at meself. Me frock was too small fer me, an it was torn an filthy. An me shoes weren't modern, I think someone left them behind in the famine! An they were huge. I was thinkin how I coulda made meself look better. I'd washed me face an flattened me hair down wit water. But I forgot te wash me knees, they were black. An me feet were all red an dirty from carryin me shoes when I got fed up runnin back te pick them up when they fell off. I'd no cardigan, an me arms were a holy show, dirty an skinny. I wouldn't win a beauty contest, tha's fer sure.

Maizie said, 'Are we ready?' An I said, 'Yeah!' an off we went. I could hear Paddy mutterin te Maizie, an I was sure he was ragin wit her fer bringin me. Poor Maizie, I pitied her. I was makin a holy show of her. An I'm sure she was worried people would think I belonged te her.

I decided te keep well back from them. When we got on the bus, I sat in a seat opposite them. But I didn't pretend I was wit them until the conductor came up an rattled his money bag in me face. 'Fares now, please!'

I didn't know wha te say, an Maizie tapped him on the shoulder an said quietly, 'I'll get this.'

The conductor whirled aroun an shouted fer everyone, pointin at me, 'Is this child wit youse?'

'I told ye she was, didn't I?' Maizie roared, very annoyed. An everyone was gapin. They were all lookin at me, an then at the style of them, an tryin te figure this out.

'Right, ye's are grand. I didn't think, tha's all!' an he gave Maizie the tickets an went off, hummin a tune. Paddy looked after the conductor an said te Maizie, 'I'll give tha fuckin red-necked culchie a dig in a minute if he doesn't watch his step.'

Maizie said, 'Don't mind him, we'll be gettin off in a minute.'

When we got te the Phoenix Park, there was crowds of people strollin in the gate. They were all dressed up in their Sunday clothes, an I didn't see anyone like meself. I was lookin at the ducks in the pond an forgot te keep me eye on Maizie, an then I started te panic. I couldn't see them in the crowd. I'm lost! Then I picked them out, turnin the corner, an I ran like hell.

We got inta the zoo, an I couldn't believe me eyes. There were big birds on long legs struttin aroun like they owned the place. I pushed me way through the crowd at the gorillas, an when people looked down at me, they all moved away an gave me plenty of room. Maizie followed me, holdin Chrissie, an laughed. I looked at a gorilla scratchin his arse an thinkin, an I said te Maizie, 'Tha's like Jackser when he has no smokes.'

Paddy an Maizie laughed, an Maizie said, 'Yeah, but tha gorilla has more sense, an he's better lookin!'

On the way home, Paddy tickled me on me ribs an said, 'Come on!

Let's go in an get fish an chips, an ye can have a big knickerbocker glory. It'll put meat on yer bones.' An we went inta Cafolla's in O'Connell Street. Me belly was burstin from the food, an I was tryin te get all me ice cream down me, cos I knew this was me only chance. I wouldn't see the like of this again fer many a day te come. An I was thinkin how I could get Maizie an Paddy te let me come an live wit them. I'd have te bring Charlie, too, of course. Me ma could stay wit Jackser. But I knew they wouldn't let me do that. They need me te look after things, an I knew they wouldn't look after everythin themselves.

I was outside playin when I spotted the two Legion of Mary women comin down the street. There was a gang a kids trailin them. Then I saw the young one who ate all the sambidges at the club. She was linkin arms wit another one. 'Where ye's goin?' I asked, but she ignored me, an they went up the steps of the house next door.

'We're goin te Matt Talbot's room te pray,' roared one of the young ones at me.

'Can I come, too?' I shouted te the women.

'No!' the sambidge one roared. 'Ye have te be holy te get in there, an you said fuck off te me.'

'Well!' I roared back. 'Ye're not holy either, ye just said fuck off te me!'

'Children! Children! No fighting. You can all come up but two of you at one time. We don't want you to wreck the place.' An they all charged in the door an up the stairs, knockin the women outa the way. There was terrible fightin over who was goin te be first, an the women couldn't get near the door te open the room, cos they were all squashed against it, tryin te get in first.

I didn't bother me head. Ah, let them have it, I thought. An I went back out onta the street. I saw Mr Wills from the house a coupla doors down standin on the step talkin te a man. I dashed down an waited till he was ready. Mr Wills is not married an has no childre, an if ye catch him after work he'll give ye money fer doin his messages. I was waitin an waitin an hoppin up an down from one foot te me other, waitin. Then another young one saw him an came rushin over. 'I'm here first,' I screamed at her. 'Ye're not gettin him! I saw him first.'

'Ye don't own him!' tha one screamed back at me.

Mr Wills stopped talkin an looked at us. 'Take it easy, childre. Wha's wrong wit ye's?'

'Do ye want any messages, Mr Wills? I was here first, an I'll get them fer ye,' I said.

The other one roared, 'No, Mr Wills, she'll take all day! I'm faster!'

'No, ye're not!' I roared. 'I'm faster than you!'

'OK,' Mr Wills said. 'If ye don't stop fightin, none of ye's will go. I'll go meself!'

So we both shut up an just stood there watchin him quietly. He turned aroun an leaned on the railins. 'Ah, look!' I said. 'He has a big tear in the arse of his trousers.' An the two of us stood starin at his arse an wonderin if he knew his trousers was torn an everybody could see up his arse. I felt sorry fer him, cos he didn't have much money after all.

He gave me thruppence fer doin his messages, an I bought meself a Flash bar – tha's toffee covered in chocolate, an it's very dear. It cost me tuppence, an I bought a hapeworth of black jacks an the jelly babies fer me brother.

I was comin along the street lickin me Flash bar when I saw them young ones comin outa Matt Talbot's. 'Where'd ye get that?' they asked, starin at me Flash bar.

'Give us a lick, will ya?' Sambidge asked.

'Fuck off!' I said, lickin me Flash bar.

'I'm tellin! Ye won't get inta the club again. The sisters will bar ye!' Sambidge roared.

'I don't care, cos I'm not let go anyway,' I said.

'Listen, I'll be yer friend if ye give us a bite!'

'No!' I said. 'Ye're too mean. I don't want te know ye.'

Then the woman came down. 'Sister! Sister! Can I see Matt Talbot's Room?' I asked. They brought me up, an I knelt at the side of the bed, but I forgot me prayers, cos I didn't go back te school after the nice nun put the lovely clothes on me. Jackser got me ma te pawn the lot. I was lookin at how clean the room was an wondered if Matt Talbot kept it this clean or did the Legion women clean it themselves after he died.

I was talkin te Annie, me friend from the next house. She's bigger than me, she's eight. She wears lovely clothes. She was wearin a wool pleated skirt an long socks, an brown leather shoes wit straps, an a jumper wit animals on it. An she has lovely long hair. Anyway, I asked Annie where she got her doll from, an she let me hold it fer a minute. 'I got it from Santa Claus,' she said.

'Who's tha?' I asked.

'It's a man. He has a long white beard, an he wears a red suit an wellington boots. He comes down the chimney at Christmas.'

'I never heard of him,' I said, wonderin. 'How do you get him te come te ye?'

'Well,' she said, 'ye leave a letter out on the mantelpiece, an if ye're good, he'll give ye toys.'

'Will he come te me if I write a letter fer him?' I asked.

'Yeah, course he will, just write him a letter!'

'OK, I will,' I said, eyein her doll. But I had a feelin Santa would never find me. Some things just don't happen. Like the doll in the dustbin. They were makin a fool of me. They'd gone te the pictures. They were only liars!

We were still standin against her hall door, an it was beginnin te get dark an very cold, when a man stopped on a bicycle an asked us fer directions. He asked me te come over, cos he couldn't hear us. I went over te him an was pointin in the direction he should go when he put his hand under me frock, an I had no knickers on. I looked at his face in shock. An I was very afraid. He was tryin te get a hold of me an lift me up on te the bike, an tryin te pedal off at the same time. 'Let me go! I want te get down! Mammy!' I shouted.

'Keep quiet! I only want you te show me where the place is. Then I'll bring you back,' he said.

'Annie! Help me!'

He had one arm aroun me waist an was tryin te stop me gettin off the bike, wit his other arm holdin the handlebars. I hit him in the face wit the back of me head, an his glasses flew off. Then I stretched meself rigid an dropped te the ground. He landed on top of me an was lashin out, hurtin me. He was tryin te keep a hold of me an find his glasses. I was not even screamin, I was too intent on tryin te loosen his grip on me. I scrambled off as he was gettin up, an he grabbed me foot, holdin me by me ankle as he looked aroun fer his glasses. 'I'll snap yer fuckin neck if ye move again,' he said.

I immediately went quiet. 'There's yer glasses, Mister,' I said. His nose was bleedin a little.

'Where?'

'There, over there!' I pointed.

He let go of me fer a minute, an I rolled away an was up an runnin. Annie hadn't moved from the door; she was watchin everythin. 'Help me! Help, Annie!' I yelled.

Annie dashed in her front door an banged on the door of her room, screamin fer her mammy te let her in. She said te me, 'Tha's the Bogeyman,' as I raced in the hall door, then she slammed the door of her room. I stood lookin at the closed door, not knowin wha te do. I was afraid te say anythin, an I was nearly suffocatin from the poundin in me chest. I looked out the door, an the man was pedallin back slowly. What'll I do? I can't run te me ma, Jackser would kill me. He'd say it was my fault fer talkin te the man, but I didn't know he was the Bogeyman come te take me away an kill me! I sat wit me back against Annie's door. It was dark, an nobody'd see me here if I'm quiet. If the Bogeyman comes in here, I'll kick at Annie's door an scream me head off. I won't give him a chance te get a hold of me, an Annie's mammy will save me. She's a nice woman. Tha's what I'll do so.

So I sat an listened an waited. Then I dozed sittin in the cold. The wind was comin in under the front door, an I couldn't hear any more sounds comin from Annie's room. I must have been there fer hours. I tried te move, but I was frozen solid. Then I slowly opened the front door, listenin, but I couldn't hear a sound. I put me head out the door an looked up an down the street. It was pitch black, an there wasn't a sinner about. Then me heart started te rattle again. Jackser will kill me! It's very dark. Tha must mean it's late. I started te run. When I got up the stairs, Jackser whipped open the door, an he was wearin his coat, an so was me ma. 'Where the fuck have ye been till now?' he roared. He was marchin up an down wit his fists clenched.

'Where did ye get te?' me ma asked.

'First thing tomorrow, Mrs, you get tha young one inta a home,' Jackser said. Then he ran at me an punched me in me head. He kept batterin me wit his fists. Me ears was bleedin, an he picked me up an threw me across the room. I hit me face against the fireplace. Then he came runnin fer me as soon as I hit the ground.

I tried te roll meself inta a ball te protect me head. He was kickin me an punchin me. I was screamin all the time, 'Don't hit me, Jackser! I'll be good, I promise I'll never do tha again.' Jackser doesn't like te hear me screamin when he's killin me. An he's kickin me an tellin me not te cry!

'No, Jackser, I'm not cryin! Ye see, Jackser! I'm not cryin now, just don't hurt me any more, Jackser!'

He picked me up an threw me again, an then ran te the winda. He whipped open the winda an ran fer me. Me ma screamed, 'Stop! Ye're goin te kill her!' But Jackser hauled me over te the winda an dropped me out, hangin me upside down by me ankles. The terror in me is like nothin on earth. I'm goin te be kilt! I try te grab on te somethin, but there's nothin te grab on to. Everythin is spinnin. Ah! Ah! I can't breathe, everythin is black. Me eyes are closed. When will it end? I can't shout, Ah, Jaysus, don't let me die!

I'm hauled through the air an swung inta the room. Me ma grabs me, an I'm suffocated between the two of them. Jackser won't let me go, an me ma has me by the head. 'Let her go! Harm her an ye won't see me again!' me ma screams. Jackser drops me, an me ma grabs me. I don't even feel any pain. I can't hear anythin, an everythin seems far away, like I'm lookin at somethin from a distance. Me mouth feels twisted, an me eyes can only see through slits. I can feel the blood tricklin down me throat, then I realise I'm chokin – there's blood everywhere.

These two are pullin an draggin me, an he has a spoon an he's puttin it down me back. They're lyin me down on the bed an liftin me back down again wit me head onta the floor. There's an awful lot of blood. It doesn't bother me. I'm just takin it all in, tha's all. Jackser's eyes are bulgin, an me ma is fussin an shoutin, an they're pullin an draggin me. But I can't hear wha they're sayin, an I'm not bothered anyway. I'm just glad I'm not still hangin out the winda an Jackser's not killin me any more. I think they're tryin te stop the bleedin, cos it's pumpin from me nose.

Jackser doesn't let me out te play much any more. I mostly stay in an mind Charlie an keep the fire goin. Tha always worries me, cos if I put too much coal on, he kills me fer usin up all the coal, an if I don't put enough on, he kills me fer lettin the fire go out. If he does let me go out, it's only fer the messages. An he times me. Sometimes he follows me down te the shop. He'll sneak behind me an ducks inta shops so I won't see him. So I always have te run everywhere. An he won't allow me te talk te anyone, cos tha's wastin time, an he wants me back in a hurry. He wants me te call him Da. But he's not me da, an I don't want him. He tells people I'm belongin te him. But the people who know him knows I'm not. So then he always calls me 'Sally's young one'.

One day, he brought me off on his bike, an he was in very bad humour. He kept givin out, cos people were starin at him, he thought. He has a terrible habit of goin up te people in the street an askin them wha the fuck they're starin at. Sometimes he will stand an stare at people an say te me, 'Do ye see tha fucker over there starin at me?' I say nothin, cos I know they're not even lookin at him. Then he goes after them, tryin te start a fight. He stopped the bike in Drumcondra one time an told me te get off. 'Walk up there,' he said te me. 'I want te see if tha fella follows ye.' I didn't know wha he was talkin about. I couldn't see anyone lookin at him, but I walked up the road anyway an then back te Jackser sittin on the bike. 'Get up there, stand at the end of the road an don't come back till I say ye can. I'm watchin this fella across the road te see wha he's up to.' I went back up the road an waited. An I saw Jackser starin across the road, but people were comin an goin an mindin their own business. Jackser's always doin this. He waved his arm at me te come back, an he put me back on the bike. 'He knew I was watchin him! The bastard knew I was wide te him, tha's why he didn't come after you,' Jackser said. I got terribly afraid an wondered how Jackser found out the Bogeyman had tried te take me away. I held on tight te the handlebars, not knowin wha te think. Was it the same one? Or was it another one, or was Jackser just his usual self, thinkin everyone was starin at him an talkin about him behind his back? I knew tha was only his imagination. People don't really be mindin him. It's himself tha causes all the trouble. Accusin them in the wrong.

We'd left the shops an houses behind us, an we were now out in the country. 'This is where ye can take the airplane from. It will take ye te England, or America, or anywhere ye want te go to.' I wanted te go te England, but I'd have te be fourteen, an I'm still only six. I wouldn't be able te get a job an mind meself yet. All I want te do is escape by meself an not have anyone killin me. An never have te see Jackser again.

We stopped in a laneway, an Jackser climbed over a gate. He hid his bike in a hedge an lifted me over. We walked through a field fer miles it seemed. An then Jackser stopped. There was nothin aroun fer miles. Just fields an hedges an trees. There wasn't even a cow te be seen. 'Right!' Jackser said. 'Ye're stayin here, don't look aroun, don't move, I'll be watchin ye te see if ye look or even move. So do nothin! Just stay.' An then he was gone!

I stood rooted te me spot, starin straight ahead. Doin exactly as I was told te do, an I waited. I waited a long time, but Jackser didn't come back. The sounds aroun me changed, an I knew it was gettin late. I started te turn aroun now in panic. I'd kept up this position all mornin, an it was now comin inta evenin. Me legs were like two iron bars from not movin them, an I had the feelin Jackser wasn't comin back fer me. I started te cry an look aroun me, but there was nothin te be seen except miles an miles of fields wit hedges an trees separatin them. I couldn't hear any traffic, or people, or animals, or anythin. I must be in the country, miles from me mammy an me brother. What'll I do? I started te run up an down, screamin, then I stopped te listen. Nobody will find me, me best bet is te stay here. Jackser's the only one who knows I'm here. If he comes back fer me, he'll know where te find me.

I didn't sit down, even though I was tired. Jackser said not te move, an, anyway, he might not see me sittin down in the grass. Suddenly I heard a sound behind me, an Jackser appeared outa nowhere. He wasn't comin a few minutes ago, I would've seen him. I don't know how he did tha, but I'm glad te see him. 'Come on,' he says, wit the same look on his face he gets when a dog he's tried te stray turns back up at the door. An he says, 'I can't get rid of tha fuckin dog! It's back again.'

107

15

All the people have left the house, an we're the only ones left. Jackser says the house is condemned, an me ma says it's cos of him. Jackser roars an shouts now, an there's no one te bang up on the ceilin wit a brush or run in an bang the door an tell Jackser if he doesn't stop roarin an fightin, they'll knock the head off him, cos he's drivin them mad.

We move, too. The Corporation gives us two rooms in a tenement house down in Sean McDermott Street. I sleep in the bedroom wit Charlie, an me ma an Jackser sleep in the sittin room. They said it's warmer in the sittin room, cos the gas cooker's in there. We have no chairs, cos Jackser broke up all the furniture when he was drunk. So everybody sits on the bed. Our bedroom is big, an we have a winda high up in the wall, so we can't look out. If we could see out, we'd be lookin at waste ground, cos the Corpo demolished the old Georgian tenement houses tha stood there. The room is freezin cold, an the glass is broken in the winda. When I'm in me bed an I look aroun, there's nothin te look at, cos me room is bare. An I'm lookin at the bare walls. But I don't care. I snuggle under the hairy blanket an wrap the coats aroun me an Charlie, an I'm delighted. Jackser can't get his hands on us. An I can peek me nose up from under the coats an look at the sky an wonder what it would be like te be a bird an shit on Jackser's head an fly back up onta the roof an torment him until he wears himself out, screamin curses at me an threatenin te kill me. Then, when he's tired, I'll fly back down again an give him another good shit all over him. Yeah, I'd love tha!

* * *

Jackser let me out te play, an I dashed across the road te a gang of childre who were standin aroun a door in one of the houses opposite. They took one look at me an told me te get lost. I didn't move, cos I hoped they'd change their minds. But instead, they all jumped on me an hit me. So I got up an ran fer the safety of me own hall. After a few minutes, I put me head out the door, an they were still there, watchin over an waitin fer me te come out again. No fear! I rushed up the stairs an in the door, an Jackser was waitin fer me. I thought he'd agree wit me, them childre was very treacherous! But instead, he gave me a box an lifted me offa the floor, roarin, 'I saw ye! Runnin from them kids when they hit ye! Get back over there an pick out the leader. Beat the fuck outa him an the rest will leave ye alone. Now go! Remember, I'll be watchin ye from this winda. An ye'll have me te reckon wit if ye don't do as I say.'

I shot out the door an down the stairs, an flew through the hall, thinkin, they're all big young fellas, they'll kill me. But Jackser would kill me more. If I put up a good fight, then tha's me only chance. Jackser might not kill me then. I whipped open the front door, an, still runnin, I leapt across the road. I could see they all had their backs te me an their heads close together. They were busy lookin at somethin a young fella had in his hand. I leapt on them, bangin two of their heads together an lashin out wit me foot at the same time at the other fella, who looked up in surprise. I was all legs an arms, lashin out, the fear in me drivin me on. The young fellas were too surprised an shocked tha a squirt of a young one like me would come back at them. An before they had a chance te come te their senses, I was gone! Back te Jackser te report tha I'd carried out his orders.

Me brother Charlie is two now, an he's walkin by himself. I'm very annoyed, though, cos me ma tells me I was only seven a coupla months ago. I've been tellin people I'm seven fer ages. Tha means now I have te wait years before I'm grown up te wear stockins an high heels, an have a big fat purse wit loads a money te buy all the sweets I want. An go te England te get away from Jackser.

Every mornin I have te get up an get Charlie dressed an take him out on the street. It's still dark, an nobody is outa their beds yet. An we walk up an down the street, me holdin tight onta Charlie's hand, an I don't know why we do this every mornin. Me ma stays snug in her bed as we leave the room, an I wonder when we can come back. It's dark an freezin cold out here as we walk up an down, an I'm thinkin it must be cos Jackser wants te pretend we don't live wit him. He's always shoutin at me ma tha he doesn't want other men's bastards aroun an she has te get rid of us. Ma looks at us like she's very annoyed wit us, but she doesn't know wha te do, so she looks away. She's stopped botherin about us now, an if I try te talk te her like I used te, she's not bothered. She'll only talk te Jackser. The only time she wants te talk te me is if I bring her back money or somethin she wants.

The ma makes sure I go everywhere wit Jackser an then tell her if he was lookin at women or talkin te his friends about them, or maybe if he was seein one. I always tell her he was doin nothin. I learnt me lesson good an proper when he nearly threw Charlie over the banisters. So I'm not tellin them anythin tha will start a row. I tell them nothin about anythin, an Jackser beats inta me tha I'm never te tell anyone wha happens at home. So I don't answer questions people ask me, like, where'd ye get the black eyes, or, wha's them zig-zag blue marks on yer legs an arms an back? I say nothin.

This mornin I was walkin up an down the street, holdin Charlie's hand. An it was very cold. It was beginnin te get light, an a few cars were movin up an down, an people were startin te go te work. A man came over te us an asked me te show him where someone lived in one of the houses. I ignored him an tried te walk on, but he took me arm an pulled me along the street an inta one of the houses. I was holdin tight te Charlie's hand, an I couldn't run away, cos Charlie could only take little steps. He brought us up the stairs an lifted up Charlie, cos we weren't fast enough. An he hurried up the stairs, wit me still holdin tight te Charlie's hand an rushin te keep up. Then he stopped an put Charlie down an lifted me up. I wouldn't let go of me brother's hand, an he was bein lifted inta the air, too. So the man lay down on the stairs an tried te put me lyin on top of him. I was afraid te do or say anythin, cos the man might get upset an hurt me, or, even worse, hurt me brother, who's very small. He didn't notice or care or even see me poor little brother, who was tryin te grip me from the man wit his free hand. I was bein tugged inta the air te get me te release me brother's hand. 'Let him go an come wit me an I'll buy ye sweets!' he kept sayin. But I started te cry, an me brother started te cry. An the man couldn't get me on top of him. Then the man put his hand over me brother's mouth te quieten him. An I panicked, cos he'd smother him. I shouted, 'Let him go! Jackser's comin! An ye won't get down the stairs, cos he'll kill ya. Gerraway from him!' I was jumpin up an down on the stairs, screamin me lungs out in fright. An the man heard a noise comin from one of the rooms an dropped Charlie an ran off.

I picked me brother up, an he was screamin, too. An old man put his head out the door an said, 'Wha's wrong wit ye's?' I just sobbed me chest up an down an held onta me brother, an looked at him, not knowin wha te do or which way te run. The man said, 'Get back te where ye's came from an do yer screamin there.' An he banged the door shut. I hurried down onta the next landin an stopped. I told Charlie we were all right, the man's gone, but we'd better be quiet an listen te make sure he's gone. So we sat down on the stairs, wit Charlie snuggled beside me, an we listened te the quiet. Me chest was slowly easin of the pain, an I wasn't shakin so much now. Charlie would give a sob now an then, but otherwise everythin was quiet. An then, as we were beginnin te doze off from the peace, another thought hit me. Jackser could be lookin fer us. When it's time fer us te go back in, he opens the winda an shouts down. I'd better hurry, an me heart began te pound again. An Charlie started te cry, cos I gave him a fright when I moved off wit him so fast.

Jackser took me down te Bachelors Walk, an we crossed over the Liffey te the toy wholesalers an bought a box of balloons an windmills an whistles. The next mornin, we were up when it was still dark, an we made our way up te the stables off Mountjoy Square an harnessed up the horse te the cart. Jackser promised te pay his friend, the owner of the horse an cart, a few bob when he makes money on the rags an the bottles we get fer givin out the toys, mostly te childre. We give the horse his oats, an when he's fed an watered, we set off.

'Right!' Jackser says te me. 'We'll head out te Ballybough, an from there we'll see.' So we clipclopped outa the lane an turned right onta Mountjoy Square. I saw some of me old friends hangin aroun the square. 'Look, Jackser! There's childre, we might get somethin if we stop here.'

'Not at all!' Jackser said. 'The only rags them beggars have is on them. We'll keep on movin.' So we trotted on an stopped at the traffic lights at Gardiner Street before turnin right on te Dorset Street. When we arrived at Ballybough, we clipclopped inta the narra archway an inta the flats. Jackser pulled the horse up. 'Toys fer rags!' he shouted, an the kids playin aroun the pram sheds came runnin over.

'What've ye got, Mister? Wha will ye give us?'

'Get blowin them balloons,' Jackser said te me, 'an we'll tie them onta these sticks.'

The childre came runnin out wit old clothes an porter bottles an jam jars. I handed them the balloons. 'No! I want the one on the stick, like he got!' I was puffed out from blowin up balloons an tried te get them te do it themselves. They started roarin an shoutin, an tried te grab the toy box. 'Give us tha one!', 'Give us the windmill!', 'Gimme the red balloon on a stick!' The childre were mobbin me, an Jackser didn't notice, he was busy admirin a man's suit an fittin it up te himself until there was a scream from one of the doors.

'Eh, you! Don't move. I'm comin down!' a woman shouted te Jackser. An she came runnin over wit a child she was draggin behind her holdin onta a windmill. 'Tha's me husband's good suit!' she roared, an she snatched it back from Jackser. 'I had it out, ready te bring it te the pawn. An ye took it offa the child knowin its worth, ye aul toerag, ye!'

Jackser jumped off the cart an snatched the suit back from the woman. 'How do I know tha's yours?' he said.

'Right! Get up them stairs an get yer father outa the bed an tell him te get down here quick,' she said te her child. I watched as about half a dozen childre raced off te get the father. 'Mickey! Da! Mickey!' they were all shoutin as they ran up the stairs.

'Now!' the woman said te Jackser. 'We'll see how ye get on when ye're faced wit me Mickey! He'll sort ye out quick an proper!' She was white-faced an stood in front of Jackser wit her arms folded. Jackser was even whiter, an I was lookin forward te meetin Mickey.

But Jackser had a change of heart an handed the woman back her suit an said he was sorry fer the misunderstandin, anyone can make a mistake! Then he said, 'There's no need fer any more trouble!' An he slapped the horse wit the whip an said, 'Go on, Daisy! Get movin.'

The horse neighed an threw her head up, an Jackser gave her another crack of the whip. We took off, throwin me flat on me back inta the rags an sendin the sack of jam jars an porter bottles crashin aroun the cart. We galloped inta the bend an raced down the arch just as Mickey appeared in his bare feet an still tyin up his trousers. We came te a screechin stop before we hit the main road, an the horse was snortin wit fright. I was lookin back, an Jackser was lookin back, an we could see Mickey wavin his fists at Jackser. 'Jaysus, tha was close!' Jackser said, still white as a sheet.

'Yeah!' I said, all delighted an excited. An tryin te look sad.

'Fuck this!' Jackser said. 'I'm goin up te the respectable parts, where they don't all act like animals!'

I felt as tired as the horse looked, draggin herself down Capel Street. She was probably thinkin about her warm stables an a nice bag of oats before she rested. I'd buried meself in a mound of rags sittin in the middle of the cart, an I'd be glad when we got these sold te the aul Jew man at Henrietta Street. 'Oh, yeah,' Jackser was sayin. 'I used te work fer the circus. I looked after the horses. I was wit them all – Chipperfields, Billy Smart's, the lot. An I was good, I may tell ye! I could be doin this more often, makin a few bob. But yer mammy stops me. She doesn't like me goin out an leavin her on her own. Wit you helpin me, I could probably do a coal round. Then we'd be on the pig's back. We'd be flyin!'

Jackser sorted the clothes out as we waited our turn te be weighed. 'Here! Put tha up te ye an see if it fits ye!' I looked at the coat, an

113

it went down te me toes. Then it was our turn. Jackser carried the clothes off the cart an threw them on the scales. Then he backed Daisy down the lane an left me holdin the reins.

I was holdin her head too close te the ground, cos I couldn't reach up further, an she didn't like this. She snorted an threw her head back, an nearly pulled me arms from the sockets. I was raised off the ground, but I wouldn't let the reins go. I was afraid of me life she'd hurt me or turn aroun an bite me. 'There, there, Daisy,' I kept sayin te her. Then Daisy moved forward, an I pulled tight on the reins. So she decided te move backward. 'Ah, Mammy! She's runnin off wit me!' I said in a quiet panic.

Jackser didn't look down. He was too busy arguin wit the Jew man. But another horse an cart came up behind me, an the man jumped down an came over te Daisy an pulled her over te the side, sayin te me, 'Leave her be, chicken! She'll wait there, she's a quiet one!'

Jackser collected his money an he whipped me offa the ground, plonkin me down beside him on the cart. 'Right! We're off,' he said, snufflin an raisin his arm in the air an shovin his head down towards the ground. He roared, 'Go on, Daisy! I'm takin ye home,' an we hurried outa the lane. When we arrived back at Mountjoy Square, Daisy's ears picked up, an she lifted her head an took off inta a gallop. She was delighted now she was home. I sat on the bales of hay, watchin an waitin as Jackser unharnessed Daisy from the cart an walked her inta the stables. When he had all the harness on the cart put away, an the hay was put down fer Daisy's bed, an she was fed an watered, we locked up. Jackser jumped up on his bike an lifted me on te the crossbar. I was stiff an cold, an couldn't wait te get home fer a hot sup of tea an bread, an maybe somethin else, cos Jackser had a few bob now.

It was dark now, an the street lamps was on. I held tight te the handlebars, feelin the cold wind whip away me breath, an I tried te keep me head down. Jackser was pedallin like mad, an he was in good form. 'We'll be home in no time,' he said. 'Yer mammy will be glad te see us.' Then we hit Marlborough Street. 'We're just aroun the corner now from home,' Jackser said. 'I'll just stop in here fer a minute,' an he pulled the bike over an left it at the side of the footpath. 'I'm only havin one, so mind me bike, an I'll be out in a minute,' an he disappeared inta the pub. Me mouth fell open, an me heart fell down inta me belly. Me ma's voice came inta me head. 'Why didn't ye stop him?'

Jackser came reelin outa the pub at closin time. I was sittin on the footpath next te his bike, an I was frozen solid. The damp night air an the cold footpath had gone right through me bones, an me legs was blue. I only had a thin frock an a light coat on me tha was too short. I had no socks, an me shoes had no soles, only big holes. Jackser couldn't manage the bike, he was too drunk. An the bike was too big an heavy fer me te manage it. So Jackser said, 'Ah, fuck it!' an he left it there.

Jackser couldn't make it either! He staggered from the footpath an smashed inta the wall an back again out inta the middle of the road. When he made it back te the wall again, he gave up an dug out his heels an plonked himself against the wall. Then he spent ages tryin te find his Woodbines in his pocket. When he did get one inta his mouth, he couldn't light it, cos his eyes kept crossin an the wind was blowin out the match. We were never goin te get home, an he's probably drank all the money. Me ma will go mad! An now we've nothin. If only me ma would leave him! We'd be better off on the streets, I thought. I was playin wit the idea of runnin home te me ma, an leavin him. He's so drunk, he might forget he had me wit him. I looked at him, he was spittin an great big snots was comin outa his nose. 'I love yer mammy!' he was sayin. 'I love Sally, I do! I'd do anythin fer her. An ye're a great young one, you'll go far, any flies on you is payin rent! I took youse in when no one else wanted ye's, so I'm not at all bad, wouldn't ye agree wit me?'

'Yeah, Jackser, I would!'

Then Jackser slid down the wall an went off te sleep, still mutterin. I started te cry. I was cold, tired an hungry, an I was afraid te move in case he'd wake up an find me missin.

I was sittin on the edge of the footpath, thinkin this would never end, when an aul one wit a shawl wrapped aroun her head came aroun the corner an stopped. 'What ails ye, love? Will he not take ye home?' An she ran at him. 'Get up, ye drunken aul sod, an take the child home. Do ye hear me talkin te ye?' An she gave him a kick wit her boot. Jackser stirred himself an looked up at her. But he didn't see her, an he curled himself up inta a ball an went back te sleep.

'Where's yer mammy? Where do ye live? Did she send ye te find him? Ye shouldn't be out on yer own at this time a night. Come on! I'll take ye home.'

'I can't leave Jackser,' I said. 'He'll not want me te go!'

'Ye can't stay here, daughter! Te hell wit him. The Devil takes care of his own! Come on, I'm takin ye home. Let yer poor mammy worry about him.'

I cried on the way home, worryin about wha Jackser was goin te do te me when he woke up. 'Ye'll be all right! Yer mammy shouldn't be sendin a little one like you out this time a night.'

The woman left me at the hall door, an I went up the pitch-black stairs. Me heart was heavy. I hoped maybe the fire was still lightin an I'd get a sup of hot tea. I hoped she didn't need a shillin fer the gas meter. An maybe she wouldn't take it so bad, Jackser drinkin all the money we made.

I knocked on the door an then harder. I could hear noise inside, but she wasn't openin the door. I tried lookin in the keyhole, but it was too dark. 'Ma! It's me! Open the door. Let me in, Ma. Ma, Mammy! Will ye let me in?' I was shoutin at the top of me lungs, an then I stopped te listen. Me ma was comin.

'Wait!' I heard her say. An I waited. Then I heard her shufflin an pantin, an I wondered wha was wrong.

'Open the door, Ma!' I knew somethin was wrong.

I rattled the doorknob, an I heard her cryin, 'Fuckin wait!'

When the door opened, me ma was holdin her big belly an sayin, 'Where's he?'

'He's not here, Ma!'

'Where is he, fer fuck sake! Get him!' An she collapsed against the wall, moanin. 'Martha, get him te get an ambulance. Tell him the babby's nearly here!'

I looked at her. 'Wha babby, Ma? Jackser's drunk! He's asleep outside the pub, Ma!'

'Ah, Jaysus Christ. The whore's melt! Go te a phone box an get someone te ring fer an ambulance. Hurry, hurry, Martha, fer God's sake. Then wait fer them outside, bring them up here, the door's open.' Then she went very white an slid down on her hunkers wit her back te the wall an gave a terrible scream. I started te cry, not wantin te leave her an wantin te get someone te help at the same time.

I came te me senses an turned, plungin meself down the stairs in the dark, holdin onta the banisters te stop meself breakin me neck. I was out the front door, down the steps an on the street runnin, headin towards the lights on O'Connell Street. There's nobody aroun. I need a phone box. No! Don't stop te ask fer help. Wastin time. Have te get a phone box. Me chest is crushin me. A man passes by me, but I don't stop. I need the phone box! I round the corner onta O'Connell Street, an I see a man comin outa the Gresham Hotel. 'Mister! Mister! Call an ambulance fer me mammy. She's lyin on the floor very sick, an she says the babby's comin. She's all on her own! Will ye help me, Mister? Will ye get the ambulance?'

He stared at me fer a moment, his jaw hangin open. 'Right! Come with me! Where do you live?' An he rushed back te the hotel door an called, 'Paddy! Quickly! Call an ambulance. It appears a woman is about to deliver a baby.'

Paddy, who was the porter, was on the phone. 'What's the address?' he asked me, an I gave it te him. 'Right! It's on the way,' Paddy said.

'Thanks very much, Mister!' An I dashed off, tryin te race back te me ma as hard as I could. I wanted te see her again. Prayin she was all right. What ails her? As I neared home, the ambulance flew past me, bells ringin, an then slowed down, lookin fer the number of the house. It stopped at the house before mine, an a man jumped out te look at the numbers. He waved his arm at the driver, an they stopped outside my house. The driver jumped out, an they opened the ambulance doors an took out the stretcher an the red blankets.

Just then, Jackser staggered aroun the corner an stopped, holdin on te the railins. Me heart gave an awful jump, an I stopped dead in me tracks, ready te run in the other direction. But instead I ran on te help the ambulance men find the room up the stairs an help me mammy.

'She's up here, Mister! I'll show ye's.' An I shot past Jackser, tryin te make his way up the steps.

'Ah, it's fuckin you, ye sleevin, ye! Wait till I get me hands on ye! I'll teach ye te go runnin off like tha.'

I said te the ambulance men, 'Hurry! Me ma's on her own.' An they followed me up the stairs, shinin a big torch. Jackser was still in the hall, roarin an shoutin somethin, but we ignored him.

When we got te me ma, the door was open, an me ma was on her knees, pantin very fast. 'It's here! Fer the love of Jaysus help me!' The ambulance men pushed me outa the way an told me te go back downstairs. I could see Charlie standin in the doorway of our bedroom. He only had his vest on, an he was cryin. But they wouldn't let me inta the room te get Charlie. So I sat on the landin fer a minute an then thought I'd be better down at the ambulance. Tha's wha the man told me te do.

I was just about te move when I heard Jackser comin up the stairs. 'Sally! It's me,' he was sayin. 'Open the door te throw out a bit of light. I'm breakin me fuckin neck here.'

Me heart was leapin wit fright! I turned aroun an crept back onta the landin an went onta the next landin at the top of the house. An I sat down, keepin very quiet, not makin a sound. I could look over the banisters an see down when they opened the door. Then I'd know wha te do. But right now I'm not goin te let Jackser get his hands on me.

He was bangin an hammerin on the door, impatient te be let in. 'Who're you?' I heard him roar. The man muttered somethin, an I heard Jackser say, 'Oh! I'm sorry. I'm sorry! Are ye all right, Sally? Poor Sally. Ah, ye'll be grand, Sally! These gentlemen will look after ye.' Then I heard me ma give an almighty scream, an me heart stopped. I wanted te run down, but they'd kill me. I started te cry again. Not knowin wha's goin on. She must be dyin! I stopped cryin te think. If me ma dies, I'll wait till Jackser goes out, then I'll take me brother an I'll go over te the Liberties. I'll find someone te take us in. Now tha me mind was made up, I was at peace. I wasn't afraid any more of Jackser.

I must have dozed off on the landin, cos I heard Jackser callin me. I was afraid, but then I remembered, I'm not stayin wit him. So I came down, an Jackser said te me, 'Yer mammy's gone te hospital. I'm goin te leave now an walk up there. I have te go te James's Street, St Kevin's Hospital, tha's where they've taken her. You get in an mind the other fella, an don't move outa this room until I get back.' An he pushed me in the door an slammed it shut behind me. I went inta the other room, an Charlie was fast asleep in bed. I stepped outa me shoes, threw off me coat an fell inta the bed beside me brother. I was out like a light, sleepin the sleep of the dead.

Charlie was cryin an slappin at me te wake up. I shot up in the bed. I looked at him an then all round me. Quiet! I could hear only the quiet. I whispered out, 'Mammy?' an listened. No! It wasn't a dream after all. Me mammy is really gone. Charlie started cryin again. He wanted somethin te eat. I went inta the sittin room an looked aroun the sink. No! The bread is all gone. We've nothin te eat. There's a small sup of milk in the end of the bottle, but Jackser might want tha fer his tea. Better not touch it.

'There's no bread, Charlie. I'll get ye somethin te eat in a minute, when me ma gets back.' I tried te lift him then te give him a kiss, but he slapped me away an then started te tear his hands through his hair an cry louder. 'Oh, look! There's a bird in the sky!' An he stopped cryin te look up towards the winda. But when he saw no bird, he was really ragin an started te cry even louder. The winda was too high fer me te get a look out, an we'd no chairs, so there was nothin te stand on.

'Come on, Charlie! I'll put yer trousers on,' an he followed me inta the bedroom, still whingin. 'Ah! They're all wet, an there's nothin else! I'll spread them on the floor till they dry. Come on! We'll go te the sittin room.' He followed me in, still cryin. I couldn't think of anythin else te do. So I sat him up on the bed an sat down beside him. He was cryin an scratchin his head, an lookin aroun him fer me mammy. There was nothin I could do. I looked over at the gas cooker. I wouldn't be able te work tha. Ye need matches when the fire's not lightin. An anyway, we'd be blown up. It wasn't worth it fer the sake of a cup a tea. Then I thought of Jackser's milk. Maybe he won't know there was any in the bottle! I jumped up, givin Charlie a fright. 'It's all right! Ye're all right. Look what I have fer ye!' An I put the drop of milk inta a jam jar an gave it te him. The cups were all smashed. Jackser does tha when he's drunk. He smashes up everythin. I took the jam jar from Charlie, an he screamed. He wanted me te get him more. 'All gone!' I said, holdin me arms out wide. I put the jar in the sink an climbed back on the bed. Charlie was quiet now, an I took his head an put him on me lap an stroked his hair. I was afraid te think of anythin. The worst could happen now if me ma is gone! So me mind just went blank.

120

16

I woke up an it was pitch black. The room was freezin cold, an there was only a strip of blue light comin in through the winda. Me heart was hammerin in me chest. Somethin woke me up. I tried te hold me breathin te listen. There it is! Jackser's footsteps on the landin. An he's tryin te get the key in the door. Holy Mother, grant tha he doesn't kill us. I promise, if ye do this fer us, I'll never be bold again. Me whole body was shakin. He fell in the door. 'I've got a son! I'm a father!' he roared. 'Yer mammy has a lovely new babby. He's jet black an as brown as a nigger. He's fuckin lovely.' He fell aroun the room, an I was up on me knees in the bed, ready te spring. I didn't care about him an his babby. I wanted te know if me mammy was all right. I couldn't understand wha was goin on. But I had a feelin him an his babby were behind me ma nearly dyin. I knew now she wasn't dead, or he would have said. But I still didn't know if she was goin te get better an come home te us.

'Here!' Jackser says. 'I brought back bread. You get down te the shop an get me a bit of black an white puddin. An hurry! Don't be there till ye're back!' he roared.

'OK, Jackser. I'll get me coat,' an tha's when I grabbed Charlie an put him on his feet, still half asleep, an rushed him inta the bedroom. It was freezin, but he'd be safer in here, outa harm's way. I put him inta the bed an covered him up te his neck. 'Now, you stay there an go back te sleep, an don't make a sound until I come inta ye. Then ye'll be grand.' I put me coat on an looked fer me shoes.

'Get a fuckin move on! Wha's keepin ye?'

I rushed out, closin the door behind me.

121

'Right! Here's the money. I'm warnin ye! Don't be long!'

'No, Jackser! I'll run all the way.'

I was back in a flash! Jackser took one look at the puddin an screamed, 'Tha's the fuckin dear stuff. It's wrapped! Where's me change?'

'There's none, Jackser.'

He picked up the heavy fryin pan an whacked me. I ducked me head, an he brought it down on me back. The pain sent me crashin down te the floor, an before I could get me breath he yanked me back on me feet by me hair. I was doubled up.

'Get back te the shop an get the ordinary stuff.'

I was winded an couldn't straighten up. 'Yes, Jackser!' I tried te straighten an control the big sobs in me. Jackser hates ye te show pain or cry when he hurts ye. It makes him worse.

I could hardly walk, me stomach was heavin from the pain. Jesus! Jesus, help me! The aul one in the shop looked very annoyed, but she didn't fight me. She gave me the puddin an change. Jackser was satisfied an gave me a ha'penny an told me te go back te the shop an buy sweets. 'An make sure ye bring back sweets fer tha child in there!'

'OK, Jackser,' I said. I got three jelly babies an brought them back te share wit me brother. There'll be two fer me an one fer him, I was thinkin as I came up the dark stairs. Then I dropped two. Jaysus! Where are they? I couldn't see. I spread me hand along the stairs but I couldn't find them. I searched an searched. But they were gone in the dark. Ah, well, tha's me bad luck. Lucky I still have one fer Charlie or Jackser would go mad.

When I got back in Jackser said, 'Where's the sweets?'

'Here, Jackser! I kept one fer me brother.'

'Where's the rest of them, eh?'

'I dropped the other two on the stairs! They're lost.'

'Ye fuckin lyin bastard.' An he lifted me off me feet wit a kick, sendin me sprawlin. I was doubled up in agony an screamed wit pain. He came chargin at me, an I rolled inta a ball te protect me head. He lifted me off the ground, tearin me coat, then he grabbed

122

me from the front, tearin the frock off me. I was naked. He whirled aroun an went over te the press an pulled out a rag. It was a coat at one time, but now it had no sleeves, just two big holes in the armpits, an the linin was gone, an it had been cut off at the end. He threw it at me an said, 'Here, put this rag on. No bastards are stayin under my roof. I want no other man's leavins! Get back on the street where I found ye.'

I put the coat on me, an it went down te me shoes. Then he lifted me by the neck, opened the door, an roared, 'Get back on the streets. An if I see ye aroun, ye're fuckin dead!'

I went down the stairs an out onta the street. I pulled the coat aroun me, but the armpits was too big an left me all exposed te the cold night air on me bare skin. The coat was trippin me up, an I looked down at meself. An I was so ashamed. I was walkin up an down outside the house not knowin wha te do. People will laugh at me if they see me like this. What am I goin te do? I looked up at the winda, an I could see the flickerin from the candle. But he was not goin te call me back. Me head was full of lumps an painin me. An me hair was all gone in a big bald patch. It came out in me hand when I touched me head. Holy God! Are ye listenin te me? Make Jackser stop hittin me, an don't let him hurt me brother. Help me te find a way te put him in good form. An make me mammy better, an let her come back te me. An maybe Jackser will fall off his bike under a lorry an get mashed, so he can't come back. An I promise, Holy God, I'll be good fer the rest of me life.

Ah, Jaysus! I'll have te sit down on them steps. The pain is killin me. It's cuttin right through me, an me breath is hurtin me in me chest. I don't want anyone te see me. They'll think I'm a tramp an be afraid of me. They'll be thinkin, look at her, she's a dirty little nobody, move away quick before ye catch a disease. An they'll be afraid te come near me. I need te hide. I know what I'll do. I'll creep up te the top of the house an hide on the landin up there. Then I'll be outa the cold, an I can see wha happens. Oh, me head. I'm goin te get sick! But there's nothin comin up. I drag meself up the stairs. Me head is swimmin from all the pain. If I could lie down in a warm bed, tha'd be heaven. But I'll settle fer tha landin. Oh, tha's better! I can lie down now at last.

I'm curled inta a ball te ease the pain, an it's nice an quiet. An I'm outa the freezin wind. All I need is somethin te wrap aroun me. Holy God! Are ye there? Listen! I have somethin te say te ye! I'm very annoyed wit me ma! While she's off gettin herself sick an collectin babbies fer Jackser, she's not bothered about me an me brother any more. I think she's sidin wit Jackser now, an she's finished wit us. I heard tha Jackser fella say they'd lose the money if they get rid of me an Charlie. So this is what I'm askin ye, Holy God. If ye don't want te mash Jackser inta nothin, then will ye make me grow faster so I can take Charlie an meself an get away from Jackser. I want te be able te manage on me own, in peace an quiet. I've been watchin people, an I know how they do it. Ye see, I'm only seven, an people wouldn't take me seriously. I wouldn't be able te wear nylons an high heels an work. An have money an be very busy lookin after everythin. An be terribly respectable. An I'd look well an have a fat purse wit loads a green pound notes. An people would say te me, 'Yes, Mam! Certainly, Mam!' I'd be different, God, from me mammy. Me ma doesn't seem te know anythin! So will ye let me get a move on? Even if I was nine or ten, tha'd do. Is tha OK, God? An I promise not te curse any more.

I woke up, an it was light. Jackser was slammin the door shut on his way out. I jumped up without thinkin an came down the stairs. 'What're ye doin there?' Jackser roared. 'Where were you?'

'I was here, Jackser!'

He stared at me an said nothin. 'Right!' he said, openin the door. 'Get in there an mind tha young fella. An remember! You're on borrowed time in this place. Look crooked at me an ye're out tha door. You fuckin bastards will be out soon enough. Ye're not wanted here.'

'OK, Jackser!' I said, not lookin at him.

Charlie was sittin on the floor in the sittin room. When he saw me, he lifted his arms an started te whinge. I was happy te see him an wrapped meself aroun him on the floor. He went quiet an was content te leave his head in me lap. But I was stiff an cold, an needed te get a bit of heat an somethin te drink an eat. I got up an pulled Charlie te his feet. 'Let's see wha there's left te eat.'

There was a chunk of loaf, an I got the knife an sawed it in half, an gave the other half te Charlie. There was no margarine te put on it. There was nearly a quarter pint of milk left in the bottle, so I poured a little fer Charlie in the jar an gave it te him. An then carefully took mouthfuls from the bottle. Jackser would know how much he left, so I put water in the milk te make it look more. 'Come on an we'll go te bed!' I said te Charlie, an he slapped me away. No! He didn't want tha. 'OK!' I said. 'Day! Day! I'm goin!' An he ran after me, roarin. I laughed an whooshed him inta the bed, an then he laughed, an I put the hairy blanket an coats over us, an I was out like a light.

We were in the sittin room, sittin up on the bed, when Jackser came in. 'Right!' he said. 'Get him dressed an put yer coats on.' I was flyin te get ready, but it was only me heart hammerin in me chest tha was goin fast. Charlie was puttin his two legs in the one leg of his trousers, an I was shakin so much I couldn't get him ready. 'Gerra a move on, Mrs!' Jackser roared at me. 'I haven't got all fuckin day!'

'OK, Jackser! I'm just ready,' I squeaked.

Charlie was happy, an he was tryin te help me. He knew we must be goin somewhere. But he got all tangled up again. I couldn't turn aroun, but I was expectin a punch in me head or a kick any minute. So I pushed Charlie down on the bed an whipped the trousers off him. Charlie saw the look on me face an lay still. I was very silent, but he could tell we'd better be quiet, this was no time te mess. I put his shoes an coat on him, an looked at me own coat. It was ripped, but so was me frock. I wish I had a pin. I'd better put it on anyway. I can't go out in me skin. He'll go mad now when he sees this, an we won't go out. I held the coat together an clamped me right arm down tight over it an put Charlie standin in close beside me, so he mightn't notice.

'Right!' he said, downin the last of his tea. 'Follow me.' An we were out on the street, clatterin after him aroun onta the hill. It used

125

te be called the stones, long ago, by the old people. Every Saturday mornin it's a market where people sell old clothes an furniture, an everythin cheap. We went on te Parnell Street an turned right on te Gardiner Street, then left up the hill. I was makin sure te look as if I was runnin. But I couldn't go fast wit Charlie, he'd only started te walk not long ago. I was jumpin up an down in me big shoes, tryin te keep them on me. An they were makin an awful noise altogether. When Jackser looks back, he'll see we're hurryin.

Two young fellas were sittin on the path, throwin stones on te the road an hittin cars an horses tha was passin. Then they'd run off. They came back an were sittin down again. As we neared them on the hill, they looked aroun as me an Charlie were comin, an they watched us until we were passin them. Then one of the young fellas said te me, 'Hey, young one! If ye're thinkin of enterin fer the Irish dancin, they won't let ye in, cos ye're too smelly an scabby!'

I looked at him an forgot about Jackser. 'Go on over an drag yer aul one from the pub an tell her te bring ye home an give ye a good feedin. Cos ye'd need tha before ye take me on!'

Yer man leapt out in front of me. 'I'm goin te fuckin mill ye fer tha!'

Jackser looked back at tha minute, 'Come the fuckin on!' he roared, wavin his fist at me.

'Lookit!' I shouted te the young fella. 'He'll kill ye if ye don't let us pass!'

'I'm not afraid of yer aul fella!' yer man roared. Then he roared up at Jackser, 'Me da's a docker, an he's a boxer as well!'

Jackser came walkin back, an the young fella moved himself well back outa Jackser's way, ready te run. 'She called me ma names, Mister! Ye should chastise her fer tha. There was no call fer it, so there wasn't! We said nothin te her, we were just mindin our own business, so we were! Isn't tha right, Madser?'

'Yeah, Mister, ye should put manners on her,' tha Madser said.

Jackser looked at me. 'I'll fuckin down ye fer causin trouble,' he said, an he was clenchin his fists an openin them again.

I looked in fear at the young fellas. Their faces were alive wit excitement. 'No, Jackser! They laughed at ye an said terrible things about ye. They said ye were bandy! "Lookit the bandy little fucker!" they said, when ye passed them. I wouldn't let them get away wit tha. Wasn't I right, Jackser?'

'Yeah!' Jackser said. 'Go on, ye little bastards, before I fuck ye's under a car,' an they ran off, callin him bandy midget, Jew nose, whore master. 'We know where ye live. An we'll send me da te get ye!'

We went aroun the corner an inta an arch an came inta the flats. Jackser went inta a ground-floor flat. He knocked at the door an said te me, 'This woman is a friend of mine. She'll mind ye until yer mammy gets outa the hospital.' The door opened an a woman came out wit an apron aroun her an slippers on her feet. She had her dyed blonde hair in curlers an a Woodbine hangin in her mouth, an she looked down at us wit one eye closed, cos smoke got in her eye. She took a big drag of her cigarette an took it outa her mouth an said, 'Is this them, then? I suppose ye'd better come in.' An she dragged herself off up the hall, cos she was very fat, an the weight was too much fer her. Jackser shut the door, an we followed him inta the sittin room.

There was a gang of kids, some were millin each other under the table, an a big young one, she was about nine, was holdin a babby on her knee an tryin te feed it somethin on a spoon from a bowl. She stopped wit the spoon halfway te the babby's mouth te get a good look at me. I don't think she liked wha she saw, cos she clamped her mouth shut, which was gapin open, an at tha minute the babby got fed up waitin fer his feed an gave the spoon a clout, sendin the mushy food splatterin all over the young one's hair an face. 'Ah, Mammy! Lookit wha he done!' she roared.

'Mind wha ye're doin,' the mammy roared back, 'an he wouldn't a done it. Here! Give him over te me.'

A young fella who was stretched out on the floor playin wit a kitten got up an came over te me. 'Lookit! He's mine,' an he showed me the newborn kitten.

'Ah, can I hold him? Lookit, Charlie! Isn't he gorgeous?' I said.

127

The mammy looked over an said, 'I told ye. Tha's not stayin! When yer father gets in, he's goin te drown it!'

The young fella started roarin, 'Ye're not drownin me kitten, ye cow, ye!'

The mammy looked as if she was goin te make a run at him, an I backed meself an Charlie outa the way. But she just went red in the face an ground her teeth, an said te the young one, 'Get up an put them all outside te play. Before I'm hung fer murderin the lot of them.'

I opened the door an took meself an Charlie outside. Then the young fella wit the kitten came chargin out an knocked inta us an sent Charlie flyin te the ground. He kept runnin an looked back an laughed when he saw me pick Charlie up from the ground cryin. I kissed Charlie. This was all very strange fer him, an I knew he wanted me mammy.

The young fella was tormentin me now. 'Ye're not stayin in me house. Me ma said ye're poxy bastards!'

'Ye're a liar!' I shouted back. 'She didn't say tha, an we are stayin here! So why is she lettin us stay, then, if she didn't want us?'

'Cos yer man Jackser promised her a few bob. Tha's why!' he said.

'Right, so we're stayin, an ye're not stoppin us!'

Wit tha, he threw the kitten at me, hittin me smack in the face. I felt the warmth of the kitten's belly in me mouth an then the thud as it smacked the ground. I looked down in fright, an the kitten jerked an blood came outa its nose. I looked up at the young fella, who started te laugh. Me body went rigid, an then a hot fire hit me belly. I lunged at him, sendin him flyin flat on his back. Then I jumped on him. 'Come on, I'll show ye wha Jackser taught me! I'm goin te stand on yer belly an rip yer tongue outa yer mouth!' I was just like Jackser, an the young fella, who was older, he was eight, was screamin fer his life. I was roarin an shoutin, an standin on yer man's belly, an tryin te catch his tongue, an tellin him all the horrible things I was goin te do te him, when a crowd of aul ones came runnin outa their doors an dragged me offa the young fella.

They were shoutin at me an blessin themselves an sayin, tha was a terrible carry on, an they'd never seen the like of it in their lives! An they were holdin the young fella te their chests an lookin at him, an fixin his hair, an wipin his snots wit their shawls, an holdin him again. An tellin me I should be locked up! I looked up at them, an I couldn't understand why they were so annoyed, cos I thought tha tha's wha ye're supposed te do! I looked at the young fella, an, yeah, he did get an awful fright, but's tha's wha Jackser does te me all the time, I thought! ... So ... I wasn't supposed te do tha!

I'm after gettin an awful fright, too, cos the mammy came runnin out, an she was terrible annoyed as well. An ye could see the look on her face, like she couldn't understand how I could be so vicious. 'I'm not keepin ye's. Jackser can come an take ye's away,' she said te me.

So now I know not everyone is like Jackser. Ye're not supposed te go mad an hurt people. An not everyone is like me ma. Other mammies don't let other people hurt their childre. I'll never copy Jackser again. An I'll never be like me ma. I'll be somebody when I grow up. People will respect me.

Jackser came te collect us. He gave me a dirty look an just said, 'Well, tha's it then. There's nothin more I can do fer ye. Go on! Get movin.' An we stayed in the room, sittin on the bed, waitin fer night an slept. An Jackser came in at night an fell inta his bed drunk. We didn't see him, we'd only hear him movin aroun. An tha's the way it is until me mammy comes outa hospital.

17

The new babby is inchy whinchy tiny. Charlie stands beside me, lookin over at him wit his mouth open. He doesn't know what it is. We watch me ma givin him his bottle. He's in a little white nightgown, an me ma has him sittin on her lap. An his head an neck is held in me ma's hand, an she's rubbin his back. Jackser told us te get away from him, cos we were breathin on him, he said.

The babby brings up a little white stuff from his neck, an Jackser is very worried. 'Ah, look, Sally!' he says. 'Me son is gettin sick. Is he all right, Sally? Do ye think we should get him looked at? He's lookin a bit dozy, don't ye think? Will he not drink all tha bottle fer ye? Them hospitals don't know wha they're doin. Maybe we should get ourselves a good doctor? Sally! I'm talkin te ye! Are ye fuckin listenin at all?'

'Will ye stop moidierin me!' me ma says. 'Tha's only wind! Get me tha nappy an borax powder, will ye. I'm tormented wit ye!' she says te Jackser.

'You, Mrs!' Jackser turns on me. 'Ye heard yer mammy. Run an get wha she wants.'

I dash over te the press an bring the stuff.

'Where's the pins I asked ye te get?'

'Wha pins, Ma?'

'The pins fer the nappy!'

'I don't know where ye put them, Ma.'

'They were wit the dirty nappy I gave ye.'

'No, ye didn't, Ma. Jackser took tha.'

'Ask him where he put them pins!'

Jackser comes runnin over from the sink an grabs the back of me neck an pushes me head down te the floor. 'Do ye see them, Mrs? Do ye see them now?'

'Yeah, Jackser. I have them, they were on the floor beside me ma's chair.'

He releases me head from the floor, an I hand the pins te me ma. She takes them an looks away from me, an she looks far away. Then the little babby gave a jerk an kicked his legs out an squealed. He was fed up in this position. An me ma remembered him an looked down at him as much as te say, are ye still here? Then she looked away again, gone te her own world. An I knew then I was never goin te have me mammy ever again.

I looked over at Charlie, an he was still gapin at the little babby. His mouth was open, an his eyes were starin. An every time the babby moved his tiny hands an head an made a noise, me little Charlie lifted his hands in a fist an looked at me like he wanted te get a better look. An maybe he could play wit it. But there was nothin I could do fer him, we had te stay away from Jackser's babby.

The little babby is called Teddy, an Jackser has a photograph of the three of them. He calls it the family photograph, an his babby is in the middle of them. It sits in a frame on the mantelpiece, an Jackser can't stop lookin at it an admirin it.

I have te be sent back te school, so I'm sent te Rutland Street School. When all the childre get inta school, they lock the doors. Tha's te stop us escapin. There's a lot of other kids, an they look a bit like me. So they'll talk te me, but I have te be tested before they will decide if I'm one of them. There's a few who are put sittin in the back of the class. I'd prefer te be wit the ones who behave themselves. They are not as hard as the dunces at the back. But I don't know anythin, an I don't know me letters or numbers or about anythin te do wit school. The teacher just asked everyone a question. But I don't know wha she's talkin about. A few of the childre are jumpin up an down wit their hands in the air, an one young one is holdin up the leg of her knickers an hoppin off the desk, an she's lickin her snots comin outa her nose. 'Miss! Miss! I know! I know!' she shouts.

The teacher finally asks her, an she takes a big gulp of air, an then a big lick of her drippin snot, an shouts out the answer. The teacher is satisfied an says, 'Now, you lot! Pay attention. Good girl, Lilly! You were the only one listening.' Lilly looked aroun at the rest of us an made a face an gave a big sigh of breath, an we were ragin. The dunces at the back called her names an said they were goin te get her, an they were laughin. The teacher heard them an roared at them te, 'Come up here, you ignoramuses!' An she made them all line up an hold out their hands high in the air, an she brought the cane back an it came flyin down on their hands wit a whoosh through the air an a whack on the hand. She watched their eyes te see if they showed fear, but the brazen ones were like a block of ice. She put all her mighty strength inta the cane, but she didn't get the better of them. When the five of them went back te their seats wit their hands roastin, they had a smirk on their faces, an everyone looked te see if there was any giveaway signs of softness. But they held their ground, an not one of them gave a sniffle. I could see tha's how ye got te be tops an had everyone afraid of ye. Then ye'd have people admirin ye, no one would fight ye, an ye'd have lots a friends.

I was in the yard eatin me bun. On Friday, ye get a currant bun an a little bottle of milk. I prefer the other days, when ye get a sambidge, cos I don't like currants. But I'm hungry. So I'm sittin on the ground wit me back te the wall an tryin te keep me legs in, cos the other kids are goin mad, tearin aroun an pullin an draggin each other. An I don't want te get kicked, cos me legs are always painin me. I'm sortin the currants outa the bun, an Lilly comes over. 'Do ye not want yer bun? I'll take it if ye don't want it!' Lilly says.

'Ah, yeah! I'm eatin it meself, but ye can have me currants.'

'Lovely!' Lilly says, an sits down beside me. 'Ye're new,' she says. 'Where were ye at school before here?'

'Gardiner Street,' I says. 'What's it like here? Them young ones who was hit by the teacher look vicious.'

'Ah, I don't mind them. I have me big sister. She'd tear them alive!'

'Ye're great in class!' I said. 'Do ye know yer letters an can ye do sums?'

'Yeah, I know me letters. I watch me sister an she learnt me.'

'Ye're lucky,' I said. 'Look! Will ye learn me a few letters, cos I'd love te be able te write me name. An then maybe sometime I'd be able te learn te read. Will ye help me? Will ya? An I'll give ye me currants on a Friday.'

'Yeah, course I will, Martha,' an the bell rang. I felt lovely an warm inside me, an Lilly linked her arm wit me. An we stuck together, laughin an duckin outa the way at the slaughter tha was goin on, te get first in the line.

The teacher gave me a new copybook an pencil when I was goin home. 'Now!' she said. 'Don't lose these, and you are to bring them to school in the morning with your homework done and clean. No rubbing out, please! I've written down what you are to do. Now run along and be here before the bell rings, or you will be locked out and marked absent, and the school inspector is keeping his eye on you! That's all!'

'Yes, Miss! No, Miss! Thank ye, Miss!' an I flew out the door, happy wit school, afraid of her, an wishin I could do me homework, an she'd smile at me an I'd be one of her good girls.

When I got down onta the street, Lilly was waitin fer me. 'Wha kept ya?' An I told her about the teacher. 'Ah, don't be mindin her, her bark's worse than her bite. She'll be all right when ye get te know her,' Lilly said. An we linked arms until we got across the Diamond an on te Sean McDermott Street. Then she turned right back up te Summerhill, an I turned left, draggin meself home.

Me heart was down in me belly now, an the fear was back in me chest. I started te run, an I was wonderin where te hide me copybook an pencil. Jackser tore the pages outa the last one, an me brother scribbled an chewed wha was left of it.

When I got back, I knocked on the door, but there was no answer. I knocked a bit harder an listened. It was all quiet. They must be all gone out. I sat on the stairs fer a minute te think. I know what I'll do, I'll sit on the steps out on the street. Maybe I might get someone passin who'll give me a hand te do me sums an show me wha the letters are. Ye never know yer luck! I'm goin te be like Lilly an get tha teacher te think I'm great!

I sat there waitin. A few aul biddies passed me, tellin each other a pack of lies. 'I'm not tellin ye a word of a lie, may I be struck stone dead,' one aul one said. 'An the smell of porter offa her, this hour of the day.' The other one said, 'An was it enjoyable, after all tha?' An then the two of them stopped fer a rest, hangin onta the railins beside me.

'Ah, lookit tha young one wit the mouth gapin open, listenin an takin in everythin!'

The other one looked at me, annoyed her story was interrupted. 'Shut yer mouth, you, before ye catch flies!' Then she shook herself an fixed the bottle of porter she had hidden in her shawl. 'Come on, Nellie, I need te do me piss.' An they moved past me, leanin in an outa each other te keep themselves movin. The smell offa them was like how me an Charlie smell first thing in the mornin after pissin the bed. An it only eases when we've been in the fresh air fer a while.

I looked up an down. There's nobody aroun. I didn't think I was goin te get anyone te stop an talk, an I don't think they'll be back fer a while. I know what I'll do! I'll go up an see Lilly! Yeah, great idea. No, I won't bother bringin me copybook, cos I'll be worryin about losin it, an I won't be able te play. I dashed up the stairs an looked fer some place te hide it. It'll be grand on the top landin. Nobody goes up there, an the aul woman who lives there won't rob it.

I ran up the hill onta Parnell Street, turned right an crossed Gardiner Street, an up Summerhill. I didn't know where she lives, but it should be easy te ask someone. As I came up Summerhill, a gang of young fellas – they were all about six, seven an eight years old – were playin cowboys an injuns. There was about six of them. 'Hey, lookit her!' they roared. 'Let's get her!'

I stopped fer a minute te think which way I'd run. An before I knew it they were chargin aroun me doin an injun war dance. 'I'm lookin fer Lilly!' I squeaked, pretendin I wasn't afraid. 'Do ye's know where she lives?'

They stopped, an the bigger young fella, he was about nine, stabbed me in the chest wit his finger an said, 'Where do ye come from? Ye're not allowed up here!'

'I'm lookin fer Lilly!' I said. 'She's me friend!'

'Ye're not gettin te see no Lilly up here!'

'I'm from Sean McDermott Street,' I said.

'Well, go back there an stay there. Who do ye think ye are? Who told ye ye can come up here?'

'Let's mill her,' a little young fella said.

I knew I was outnumbered, so I decided te talk me way outa it. 'Listen, if ye let me go, an tell me where Lilly lives, I'll let ye's play on me big brother's bike. It's a lovely new three-wheeler. Me uncle brought it over from America. He's a millionaire!'

They all stopped te think. 'Ye're a liar!' the big young fella said.

'No, we don't believe ye!' they all shouted. 'Show us the bike an show us yer money if ye're a millionaire!' An they were lookin at me rags an no shoes on me feet. 'Get her!'

I screamed, 'No! Wait! Wait, I can prove it.' An they all stopped again. 'Get me Lilly an she'll tell ye! She was there when me rich uncle was puttin all his suitcases inta the big black motor car, an he had a suit on an a big belly from loads a feedin. An a ten-gallon hat on his head wit a big fat cigar in his mouth. An he gave me a red ten bob note. I was supposed te buy meself a new pair a shoes, but I didn't bother. I spent it on sweets an the pictures instead.'

They all nodded their heads an agreed tha was the best thing te do. 'An did he give ye anythin else?' the big young fella asked.

'Yeah! The big three-wheeler bike fer me brother an a fur coat fer me ma. She's in great style now.'

'An did ye get anythin else?' they asked me.

'Yeah! A pair of rollerskates.'

'Jaysus, I'd love tha!' they said.

Then the big fella said, 'Why're not wearin them an flyin up an down then if ye got them? I don't believe ye! Ye're tellin us a pack a lies!'

'No!' I said. 'I can't wear them, cos I haven't got me shoes.'

'Oh, yeah,' they said. 'Tha's true!'

'Come on, then,' the big young fella said. 'We'll take ye te where Lilly lives.'

On the way, one fella asked me wha's me uncle's name.

'Eh!' I was tryin te think, an I said, 'Roy Rogers.'

'Who?' they all screamed, an they stopped wit their mouths open. 'Roy Rogers an his horse Trigger? We know him, he's a cowboy in the pictures! Ye were makin a dirty eejit of us. Get her, Gang! We're goin te mill ye te mash!'

I shot off, straight onta the road, makin cars screech te a stop. I raced up Summerhill, an when I looked back, the cars an vans an horses an carts were pulled out in front of each other, an the people were hangin out, wavin their fists an callin them all the names under the sun. The young fellas were caught between the traffic, an a hackney cab driver was lashin out wit his whip at them. But the young fella an another one behind him was tearin after me, an I was tryin te lose them by turnin onta Rutland Street an shootin in one of the hall doors an slammin it behind me.

I stayed in the middle of the hall, waitin, wit me heart poundin, an tryin te get me breath back. If they come in, I'm not backed inta a corner. I'll duck past them an out onta the street again. I crept out an looked up an down. They were gone! I won't go back tha way again. I dashed across the road an down past Rutland Street School.

By the time I got home it was tea time, an I went up te the landin an got me copybook an pencil. It was still where I'd left it. I came down onta me landin an knocked on the door, no answer. Good job fer me. They won't know I was missin. So I went back up te the old woman's landin an sat down te rest meself. I can wait here an listen fer them. I like this place best, cos it's quiet an I feel safe up here, an nobody bothers me. It would be great if I had a doll. I could sit here an dress her, an I could hold her in me arms an mind her, an I'd have company. I'm thinkin, if I could find somewhere like this place, I could get away from Jackser an everyone, an no one would be able te bother me. All I'd need is somethin te eat an somethin te wrap meself in te keep me warm at night. An then I could wait until I'm old enough, an start workin an find a place fer meself te live. Then I wouldn't be at the mercy of anyone. But how would I get the food? An even if I found somewhere safe, people would ask questions. They wouldn't let me be. There's nowhere te go. I'll just have te wait. An I'd be worried about me mammy an Charlie.

I heard them comin up the stairs, an me heart jumped. Me head started te fly. Right! Have I done anythin wrong? Is there somethin I might have forgotten te do? I'll stay here until I see which way the wind blows. If he's in a mood, I'll have te think up somethin te put him in good form. Pity I didn't get any money, maybe fer doin people's messages. Then I coulda bought him five Woodbines, tha'd stop him hittin me. Pity I wasted tha time. Me ma arrived on the landin holdin the little babby. An I watched Jackser puffin up the stairs, carryin the big folded-up pram. It was a silver carriage walker wit big springs! An it was very deep inside wit a lovely big hood an apron. 'Nothin but the best fer me son,' Jackser said when he bought it second-hand wit the Childre's Allowance money an the week's labour money. He put the pram down an put the key in the door.

I heard Charlie comin up the stairs a long way down. I looked over the banisters, an he was comin up on his hands an knees. He was lookin up, an he saw me lookin down. An he gave a little whine an tried te come up faster. Me heart leapt at the sight of him, an I forgot Jackser an rushed down te help Charlie up an give him a big kiss. He was tired, an he put out his arms fer me te carry him.

'Ah, where were ye?' I said te him. 'Did ye have a great time? Ye're home now! Come on, I'll help ye.' An I held onta the banister an held his hand an pulled him up. Jackser was startin te light the fire, an me ma was lightin the gas te put on the water fer the tea. The babby was lyin in the middle of bed, wrapped in his blue frilly shawl. He was kickin his legs an screamin. Me ma told me te give him his soother, an I looked at Jackser te see if he'd say somethin, cos he might not want me near his babby. But instead, Jackser turned aroun, an snufflin, said te me ma, 'Jaysus, tell Martha, didn't we have a great day, Sally! Man alive! Ye should a seen the dinner we got, it was fuckin lovely. Wasn't it, Sally! An pipin hot, an a big bowl of soup wit hunks of bread, an a pot of tea. It was a new convent we went te, an she gave yer mammy ten bob. A really nice nun, we struck lucky meetin her. An then we went inta a shop an bought a pipin-hot apple tart. An we all sat down on a bench an ate it. I thought of ye, an I said te yer mammy, "Poor Martha, she's missin this!" So, here, go down te the chip shop an get yerself a bag of chips.'

I took the shillin he gave me, an I looked aroun me. Me ma was smilin an agreein wit Jackser, an I gave the babby his soother an took the chance of givin the babby a kiss on his face. His tiny face was soft an brown, an he was lookin at me wit his lovely blue eyes. Jackser's is brown! An he sucked on the soother an was lookin aroun him fer me ma, an he was sayin, 'Golly, Golly, Golly.' I wanted te pick him up an kiss him te nothin. But Jackser likes me te keep away from him. An Charlie was still standin in the middle of the room wit his coat on, waitin fer someone te look after him. An he was very tired. I took his coat off an brought him inta bed, an took off his trousers an shoes an covered him up. I left the door open in case he wanted te get up an come te me ma. Then I was out the door an down the street fer me chips, an I was jumpin inta the air wit bein so happy.

Me an Jackser are sittin at the kitchen table. It's grand, the bit of comfort since we got the table an two chairs. He's tinkerin aroun wit a big radio, it's called a 'Bush'. He came in the door wit it today an I couldn't believe it. 'Will we be havin music from it, Jackser?' I said.

'I hope so, if I can find out wha's wrong wit it.'

I sat waitin patiently, rememberin te let me breath out, cos it's hurtin me stomach. I gave meself a big shake an crossed me legs an me arms. An I put me head down on the table. I was tryin not te fall asleep, cos I didn't want te miss anythin. Me ma was dozin in the bed. She had the babby under her arm, an he was wide awake. He was enjoyin suckin away on his soother, makin big sucky noises an lookin me ma up an down, an wonderin why she had her eyes closed. Then he'd lose the soother an wriggle his head, tryin te catch it in his mouth, an say, 'Ah! Ah! Grr! Grr!' an me ma would open her eyes an shove the soother back in his mouth an hold it wit her finger. An the babby would go back te his big sucky noises an slap away at me ma's chest wit his tiny hand, enjoyin himself. Charlie was fast asleep in the bedroom, an the lovely fire we had earlier was settled down te a red glow. An I couldn't believe we were really goin te get music.

But Jackser says, 'I have it! There's the problem, this valve here was loose.' He switched it on an there was a cracklin noise, an then he turned the big knob fer a while, an suddenly a beautiful, melodious man's voice burst inta the room wit, 'This is the BBC.' I shot up in me chair, me back goin rigid wit excitement. An then we heard this music! 'Radio Luxembourg. Radio Luxembourg,' an Jackser shot up an lit the gas an put the water on te boil. He made a pot of tea an went over te me ma in the bed, an said, 'Sally! Do ye want a sup of tea?'

Me ma stirred an opened her eyes, an the babby stopped suckin an shot his little head aroun te look at Jackser. Me ma said, 'I won't bother,' an the babby shot his head back te mooch fer his soother. Me ma put it in his mouth an closed her eyes again, an the babby went back te the contentment of suckin his soother an slappin me ma's chest. Jackser poured me a sup of tea an one fer himself. An he moved his chair quietly over beside the fire an lit up a Woodbine. An we sat listenin. Then I heard the most beautiful music, an suddenly I was outa me body an flyin. An I wanted te cry inside meself. I wasn't dead any more, I was lifted away, far away. I can do anythin. I can be somebody, I can be beautiful, I can be gentle, I can be rich, I can smell good. The world is waitin fer me. I can be what I want. Then it ended. An I was back in the room. I opened me eyes slowly an took in everythin aroun me. One day I'll be able te stop this. Nobody will keep me down. I'll work hard, an I'll be at the top, cos I don't want anyone lookin down on me. I want te be in a position, if someone treats me like dirt, cos they think they're better than me, I'll be able te say, 'Ye're not comin te me cocktail party!' An the best bit is, they didn't know I was rich, cos braggin about it is no good, they have te be friends wit me cos they like me. Tha's the only way they'll know.

I heard Jackser say, 'Ah, tha's lovely, tha's real music. Wha did the man say it was?' An cos I was easy in meself, I was able te tell him.

'He said it was written by a man called Greig. It's called "Morning", an he wrote it the mornin he woke up after his weddin!'

Jackser looked at me an shook his head. 'By Jaysus, Martha, ye're a smart young one. Ye'll go places.'

But I was thinkin, I'm not always like tha. In school I don't understand anythin. I don't hear the teachers talkin. It's like me head is under water, an it's like tha all the time if I know I have te learn somethin. When I'm easy in meself, ye can tell me a story or talk fer hours an I'll be able te repeat it word fer word.

Jackser likes ye te know things, an he wants ye te explain things te him. He takes me te the pictures wit him now, sometimes, if he doesn't stop at the pub first, an he even gives me the tuppence te go on me own. But it's no good, cos he's waitin fer me as soon as I get in the door. 'Right! Wha was the fillum all about?' he asks. An tha's OK. I can tell him all about the fillum, but then he asks who was in it. An I don't know the names, an he goes mad an calls me terrible names, an loses his head an kicks me aroun fer wastin his money. This is happenin now every time he sends me te the pictures. An I'm afraid of me life. So then he gave me tuppence an sent me off te the pictures again. 'Right!' he said. 'This time make sure ye find out who the actors are! An don't come back here tellin me ye don't know!'

'Yeah, I will, Jackser! I'll make sure, don't worry. I'll let ye know everythin tha happens.'

I got te the cinema on Talbot Street an joined in on the huge queue. The childre were millin aroun wit big bags of sweets, an a lot of them had their babby sisters an brothers wit them. The usher said he'd kill the lot of us if we didn't shut up shoutin an fightin. Some of the bigger young fellas were fightin each other, cos their little sisters an brothers were gettin mashed. Then the usher said, 'Right! Ye's can come in now,' an he put his arms out te stop us all rushin in at the same time. An we knocked him down in the rush, an there was an awful lot of screamin an roarin, cos the babbies were flattened an stretchered in the stampede. The usher shouted, 'Ye's fuckin shower a beggars, there's no talkin te ye's! Ye's all should a been drownded at birth.' An he lashed out at the bigger young fellas' heads wit his gloves. They just ducked an laughed.

When I got me ticket at the winda – ye have te pay, cos they're wise te us, an they check the ticket; if ye manage te get past one of them, there's six more of them waitin at the door inta the seat, te catch ye – we made our way inta the long wooden benches an charged fer a place up the front, cos if ye get stuck at the back, the young fellas up in the balconies piss down on ye! The noise is like the end of the world has come. Childre stand on the benches an shout fer their lost brothers an sisters. Babbies cry fer their mammies. Young fellas fight each other over robbed sweets. Others piss on the benches, cos they don't want te miss the start of the fillum. An then the lights go out an the blue an white smoky beams from the two holes in the wall high up behind us tells us the fillum is startin. There's a big roar an cheer goes up from the crowd. An everyone is screamin at everyone else te shut up an listen. An then we're quiet an watchin wit our mouths open. Then everyone is shoutin advice te the chap in the fillum. 'Look out! He's behind ye!' an the baddie is called all sorts of names. An we're all hopin he gets kilt, an we can't wait! 'Get him! Mash him!' An I'm very nervous, cos I want te know their names. I can't be easy an enjoy the fillum. 'Wha's his name? Wha's her name?' an they tell me te shut up. 'Fuck off! Don't be annoyin me!' But I have te find out, an when I do, I keep repeatin it over an over te meself.

I ran home still repeatin it. An when I get in the door, Jackser is waitin fer me. 'Well! Wha was the name of the fillum?'

'*Oklahoma*, Jackser!'

'Right! An wha was the actor's name?'

'Dan Duryea, Jackser.'

'Ah, fuck it! I can't stand tha swine! I don't want te hear any more!'

The next time I went te the pictures, Jackser asked me who was in it. I couldn't remember, so I said, 'Dan Duryea, Jackser!' an he said, 'Again?'

I said, 'Yeah! The fillum was a waste of money!' So now I just find out who he doesn't like an then I tell him they were in it. An now he doesn't ask me any more!

18

I told me ma the sores was back in me head, an she had a look. 'Tha's from pickin up dirty hair clips from the ground an puttin them in yer hair!' she roared.

'No, Ma! I didn't, it's not! They just came back by themselves.'

She just looked at me an started chewin her lip, an then turned away from me. It got worse an started te spread all over me head. So I told her again. 'Ah, leave me alone,' she said. 'I warned ye not te be puttin other people's clips in yer hair.'

'Nobody gives me clips, Ma, it just happened!'

Jackser heard us an roared over, 'Wha's goin on? Wha's tha young one up te now?'

An me ma said, hopin te get me inta trouble, 'She has her head full of sores from pickin up dirty clips! An now she's complainin te me! What am I supposed te do?'

I looked over at Jackser. I was expectin him te run at me an give me a dig. But instead, Jackser roared at me ma an said, 'Well! Get up off yer arse, Mrs, an bring the child te the doctor! She's ye're young one, an she needs te be seen! Now, get movin, ye'll catch the dispensary doctor if ye go now!' An then he pointed te Charlie, 'An take him wit ye! He's very chesty. Tell tha doctor te give ye somethin te build him up.'

Charlie laughed an rushed aroun lookin fer his shoes an coat. An I got him ready while me ma dragged herself up from the chair, givin out te herself cos no one was listenin, an Jackser told her te shift herself, cos the doctor wouldn't wait fer her.

We sat in the dispensary, waitin our turn te see the doctor. An me

143

an Charlie climbed on the back of the benches, chasin each other, while me ma had a great time, complainin te aul ones sittin beside her about how hard it was te rear childre. An men were no good, an if she had her time over again, she'd have no childre. An have nothin te do wit men, cos they were all a curse. An childre would break yer heart! People sat an smoked, an coughed an wheezed, an thumped their chests, an said they were done fer this world. They said the doctor was no good. He didn't know his arse from his elbow, tha ye'd know more yerself! An tha he didn't even look at ye, never mind give ye a chance te say what ails ye! An then an aul man asked the lot of us, 'What did I fight fer in the First World War? Who gives a care?' Everyone shook their heads in agreement an murmured, 'True fer ye! The poor will always be downtrodden an them rich get richer on our backs.' An then there was a roar, 'Who's bloody well next? The doctor's waitin in there!' Me ma jumped up, laughin an wipin the corner of her eye – she always does tha when she feels foolish – an me an Charlie clattered off the benches an charged inta the doctor's room. An waited fer me mammy te tell him.

The doctor ordered ointment fer me head, an me ma's te bring me back if it doesn't work. Then he looked over his glasses at Charlie an said he was malnourished fer a two-an-a-half year old, an I was, too. An he asked me ma wha she was feedin us. Me ma chewed her lip fer ages an coughed, tryin te think of the right answer, an then she said, 'Eh, the usual – potatoes an things like tha.' An I looked at her, very annoyed at her fer tellin lies. The only potatoes I saw was sittin on Jackser's plate!

The doctor, who had been starin at her from over his glasses an waitin patiently fer her answer, sniffed an said, 'Indeed,' an ordered Radio Emulsion an malt te be given te us after our meals, three times daily. The emulsion was yella, an I couldn't stomach it. An the malt looked like toffee. Me ma dug in the spoon an wrapped the gooey malt aroun it, but I wouldn't open me mouth, an Charlie ended up gettin the lot fer himself. He loved it! We picked up a box of DDT te get rid of the fleas – tha's wha the doctor calls them, we call them hoppers! Anyway, I covered meself an Charlie in the white powder an shook it all over the bed, hopin we'd get a good night's sleep fer once without bein eaten alive wit the hoppers.

Me ma kept puttin the ointment on me head, but it doesn't work. The sores are coverin me whole head, an me ma cut me hair off. But it's no good. Jackser said I'm not te go outside the door in tha state, cos I'd make a show of them. So now I'm stuck in, at the mercy of him an her. Me ma has te go fer the messages herself, an she's ragin. She keeps givin out over me gettin meself a scabby head, an he keeps tellin her if she doesn't stop her naggin, he'll do time fer her. I pretend te be busy, rushin up an down the room doin nothin. They say te me, give me this, get me tha – slap! wallop! Not tha, ye fuckin eejit, an then Jackser roared at me ma again, 'Get tha young one back te the doctor, Mrs.' Cos me head was bleedin an oozin yella pus, an I was scratchin an cryin, cos the lice was eatin me head alive. The doctor shook his head an jumped back. 'Take this child to St Kevin's Hospital today. They will admit her,' an he wrote out a note an gave it te me ma.

We walked up te St Kevin's Hospital in James's Street. It used te be fer paupers an was called the Union. People went in there te die. I don't suppose people die there any more, cos they changed the name. I said tha te me ma as we walked up. But she wasn't listenin, an she just shouted, 'Ah, don't be annoyin me. I've more things on me mind!'

When we got te the hospital, we passed in the gate, leavin behind the porter's lodge gate. We walked along windy paths, wit big buildins on our left an a huge high old wall on our right. We walked aroun this big wall fer miles. All the buildins were different hospital wards fer different diseases. Me ma knew her way aroun.

'Wha's tha buildin over there fer, Ma?' I asked her, pointin.

'Tha's the dead house!'

'Yeah! I knew I could smell death,' I whispered te her.

'Ah, shut up outa tha!' me ma roared.

'OK, Ma,' I said. I forgot she hates anythin te do wit death.

Me ma was upset, an I knew she was wonderin how she'd manage without me, but I was upset meself. I wasn't happy te be left in a place not knowin wha they were goin te do te me. An I'd miss me ma an me brother an the babby, who was always waitin fer me te tickle him, an he'd roar laughin an dribble all over me when I stuck me chin in his mouth an managed not te let him bite me wit his two teeth. I was glad when me ma finally headed inta a buildin an said, 'We're here.' Me legs were painin me, an I was tired. Me ma left me wit the sister in charge of the ward an said, 'Right, Martha! I'd better go, he'll be waitin an wonderin where I am.' An then she left.

The sister took me down te the bathroom an stripped me clothes off. Then she put a box on the chair an got me te climb up an kneel on it. Then she turned on the hot tap an filled the sink an put me head inta it. I was screamin an she was puttin stuff on me head, an tryin te pull the loose scabs an soften the sores, an clean the oozin stuff out. An then she gently put a towel on me head an had me stand down. Then she got a little scissors an started te cut away the hair still stuck te me head. I was cryin, cos it was hurtin me, an the sister said, 'I know, pet. Your head is walkin with lice, and I have to clean your scabs out. This is a dreadful mess. But if you bear with me, it will be over soon.' It took an awful long time, washin an cleanin wit swabs, an cuttin an dabbin. Me head was screamin in agony, an I was so tired.

When it was finally over, the sister bandaged me head. An I couldn't see me head any more, it was completely covered in white bandages. I had nothin te wear fer bed, an the sister said she had nothin, but she finally found me a shift tha was miles too small fer me, an it barely covered me arse. I think it must have belonged te a babby! I had no slippers, so the sister put me shoes back on me an threw me clothes inta the bin fer burnin. Me shoes were miles too big fer me, an the sister threw out the rags I used te stuff them. 'Right, pet! Come along, and I'll get you into a nice warm bed.' She took me hand, an I dug in me toes te hang on te me shoes, an I clattered along wit her. I was lookin forward now te seein me bed. I could dive under the blankets an hide, an no one would get me, cos I was still afraid in this strange place.

We went inta a little ward wit a big winda on the right an only two beds. One bed te the right, behind the door, an another bed on the opposite wall down under the winda. The winda was much too high fer me te see out. There was a grown-up girl wit red hair in the other bed, an her skin was completely yella. There was another door leadin inta a very big ward, an it was filled wit women. The sister put me inta the bed behind the door an tucked me under the lovely white sheets. An I had te adjust me bandaged head on the lovely white pillas, tryin te find a spot tha didn't hurt me. An then I was out like a light.

The next night, I woke up an it was the middle of the night, an me head was so itchy it was killin me. I was tearin an tearin, but I couldn't stop the itch, an eventually I managed te lift the bandage in one piece off me head – it looked like a turban. The inside was crawlin wit lice, an pus, an scabs, an blood. An I had a good scratch on me head an put the turban back on, so the sister wouldn't know, an went back te sleep.

This mornin, the nurse, her name is Philomena, changed me bandages. She got the scissors an started cuttin the old ones away. I didn't tell her all she had te do was lift it off me head. I'm wonderin now if this new one will be easy te lift off when I need te scratch. When she was finished, she said I could pretend I was Napoleon wit me war wound. Then she took me hand, an said, 'Come on, Napoleon, I'm taking you for your bath.'

I pulled me hand back an said, 'Ah, no, Nurse! I only just had me bath.'

An she said, 'That was yesterday! This is today and now you need to be fresh.'

I said, 'Ah, Nurse! I'm fresh enough. You'll give me a cold if ye wash me too often, tha's wha me ma says.'

'OK,' the nurse says. 'We'll only dip your toes in. We don't want you catchin cold now, do we?'

'Right so,' I said, an I took her hand. We were walkin down the corridor, an me shoes was makin a slappin noise on the floor. They kept fallin off me, an Philomena said, 'I'll try to find you some socks.' An these two porters were pullin a trolley along, an they stopped te let us pass. 'Mornin, Nurse. Howa ye, titch?' they said te me. I asked the nurse wha tha means, an she said it means tiny. I pulled back on the nurse's hand an stopped. I opened me mouth te roar somethin back, an then I said, after thinkin about it fer a minute, cos I was ragin, 'Youse are not worth the milk yer mothers fed ye's! Don't youse call me titch. I'm big! I'm nearly eight, so I am!' An I turned back an walked on wit the nurse. She was screamin laughin an crossin her legs. An them porters thought it was a joke, too! But I wasn't laughin. The cheek! I'm gettin bigger all the time!

The red-haired one I'm sharin the room wit is called Kathleen. She doesn't talk much, she's very quiet. Kathleen is fifteen years old, she's grown up. But there's no one else. The rest of the patients is aul ones, an most of them is very cranky. I'm the only child here. I asked Kathleen how she got her skin all yella, an she said it was jaundice. Whatever tha is! 'Ye must have been eatin too many oranges,' I told her. 'Ye should stay away from them oranges.' She's always eatin them. But she won't listen te me!

I was sittin on me bed, examinin me toes an remarkin te Kathleen how clean they were, but she wasn't listenin. She was readin a book an dippin her hand inta the bag of sweets she had hidden under her sheets. I felt like sayin, give us one! But I knew she wouldn't, an I wasn't goin te make a show of meself! I got fed up when I'd nothin left te look at, so I wandered over te Kathleen an climbed on te her bed. 'Ah, get offa me bed!' she said. 'Ye'll crease it.'

'Ah, I won't. I'll be good. Read us a story, an if ye give us one of yer sweets, I'll get yer messages fer ye! OK?' an I looked at her, cos she put her face back inta the book.

'No! Now get offa me bed or I'll shout fer the nurse,' an she hooshed me off. 'Go on!' she said. 'Scram!'

So I jumped off the bed before she landed me on the floor. 'Will ye not even give us a sweet?'

'No!' she said.

'Not even one?' I said.

'If ye don't leave me alone, I'm warnin ye, I'll call the nurse, an ye'll be in big trouble!'

'Ye know wha yer trouble is?' I said.

'No, but you'll tell me, right? Ye cheeky little monkey!'

'Yer so mean ye'd shoot yer mammy just te go on the orphans' outin! An ye can do yer own messages in future, cos I'm not talkin te ye no more!'

An I went off, leavin her sittin wit her mouth hangin open. 'Wait till I get you,' she roared after me when I was out the door.

I was ramblin down the passage when I saw Nurse Philomena an another nurse pullin a trolley wit loads a sheets an things. They pulled the trolley inta a ward, an I followed them in. They were strippin a bed an laughin an talkin te each other. An Philomena said te me, 'How are ye, Napoleon?'

I said, 'Did ye get me socks yet, Nurse?'

'No, darling. I haven't had the time yet. I'll look later.'

'OK,' I said, an watched them makin the beds. 'Where do ye's come from?' I asked after a while.

'I'm from Tipperary,' Philomena said, 'an Teresa here is from Mayo.'

'Is tha far?' I asked.

'Oh, it's very far,' they said, laughin. Then Philomena asked Teresa, 'Did you go home Saturday?'

'I did,' Teresa said. 'I got a lift down with Mickey Doon. In his new motor car.'

'Go on!' Philomena said. 'And is anything stirring there?'

'Divil a bit!' said Teresa. 'He's waiting fer the old man to croak, and then it will be only forty acres. I'm not bothered, I'm hitting the bright lights of London when my time is up here.'

'It will be great for us, I can't wait,' Philomena said.

'So where did you head off to on Saturday?' Teresa asked.

'Oh, God, wait till I tell you!' Philomena said. 'I went to the National Ballroom. It was great crack, there was a big crowd of us. And I met this fella. He was a fine thing, I thought!' an she was laughin her head off.

Teresa held on te the sheet an said, 'Go on, tell us! I'm dying to hear.'

149

'Well,' Philomena said. 'He asked me the usual things, like, you know, do you come here often, and I said the usual, only when there's a dance on. And then he asked me what I was doin, an I told him I was a nurse here. So then I asked him wha he was doin, and he said he was in the uniform. And I nodded my head, cos I knew he meant he was a guard. And I asked him where he was stationed, and he said, Head Office. So I knew he meant the Phoenix Park, and he must be guarding President de Valera or something important like that. Then we went for a refreshment, and he bought me a lemonade, you know how hot it gets!'

'I do. Go on! Go on!' Teresa said, all eyes an mouth.

'So anyways,' Philomena went on. 'We danced some more, and I was beginning to think he was great altogether, and he told me he was from Roscommon. And when the band played the national anthem and he asked me if I wanted a lift, I said yes. And I rushed off to get my coat. I told the girls I was getting a lift home in a motor car with a fine thing who was a detective from the Aras an Uachtaran. And I would tell them everything when I saw them on Monday. Then I hurried out to meet your man outside the ballroom, and he was waiting. He had on a lovely Crombie coat, and he says to me, "Are ye right, so?"

'"I am," I says. "Where's the motor car?" And he says, "What motor car? I have me bicycle! Where did you get tha idea from?" And I looked down, and it was then I saw the bicycle clips clamped around his ankles, and I said, "I thought you were a detective?" "No! Where are ye getting yer ideas from? I'm a postman, in the GPO!"'

Teresa screamed laughin, an Philomena said, 'I told him I had to go to the toilet, and I rushed back inside to find my friends.'

'Oh, Philly! You're a scream!' Teresa said, an they both fell on the bed laughin themselves sick. I didn't understand wha they were talkin about, but I laughed anyway an jumped on te the bed. An they gave me a great spin inta the air wit the sheet.

I wandered inta the big ward, an an old woman waved over at me. 'Are ye OK?' I asked her.

Another woman shouted from her bed, 'Ida, will ye see if Granny wants somethin!'

I clattered over te see wha the granny was callin me fer, an Ida got outa her bed an dragged herself over in her slippers. 'Lyin in tha bed'd kill ye!' Ida said te the ward.

Granny took me arm an pointed te her locker, mumblin somethin. I kept sayin, 'Wha? Wha? I don't know wha ye're sayin!' an Granny shook herself in annoyance.

Then Ida came an pushed me outa the way. 'What is it, Granny? Do ye want the nurse? Here, put yer teeth in,' an she took a tumbler from the top of the locker an took out the teeth an put them in Granny's mouth. 'Now, tha's better! What ails ye, Granny?'

Granny shouted, 'I want the bloody bedpan, me bladder is burstin here fer the last hour.' An she grabbed me, 'Here, run, child, an tell the nurse te bring it quick.' I clattered off quick, makin an awful noise on the floorboards, an I woke up some of the patients who were dozin.

'Jaysus Christ Almighty, tha young one will be the death a me in them bloody shoes.'

'The heart went crossways in me, too,' another aul one agreed, but I was gone, smackin me way down the passage as hard as I could, enjoyin the lovely big noise, lookin fer the nurse.

The sister put her head outa the office an looked down her nose at me from the top of her glasses. 'Walk, child! What on earth are you makin such a racket for?'

'Sister! Sister! Granny is pissin the bed. Hurry, quick, bring the bedpan.'

'All right! Calm down, it won't be the end of the world if she does. Now, back to your ward quietly, and climb into your bed.'

I looked at her, wonderin about the bedpan. 'Go on!' she said, an she turned me aroun an tapped me arse. 'Into bed now! You'll catch cold.'

'All right, Sister!' an I dragged meself back te the ward. Ah, tha's a pity she caught me. Now I'll have te stay in me bed.

I must have dozed off, cos I shot up in the bed when I heard the tea trolley. The two women pushed the trolley over te me an gave me a big plate an whipped off the cover. Me mouth was waterin when

151

I clapped eyes on the sausages an fried egg. 'How many slices of bread do ye want, chicken?'

'Eh, gimme six,' I said, an Sadie laughed.

'There won't be any left fer anybody else! Here's three. I'll bring ye back more if there's any left. OK, me little fairy? Ah, ye're lovely. I'll bring you home wit me one of these days. Did yer mammy come up te see ye yet?'

'No, Sadie, not yet.'

'Ah, she will. She's missin ye! She has a load of other childre te keep her hands full. Don't worry, we'll mind ye! Now, I'd better get movin. I'll be drawn an quartered if this grub gets any colder.'

I was lickin the empty plate before Sadie was halfway up the ward. An stuffin the last of the lovely thick sliced bread wit good butter down me belly. An lookin over at Kathleen, te see if she had anythin left on her plate she didn't want! She was takin her time eatin it, so I said, 'Do ye want yer sausage, Kathleen?'

'Yeah!' she said.

'Are ye able te eat all tha bread?' I asked her.

'What bread? I only got two! The size of you, an she always gives ye more. She wouldn't give it te me!'

I said nothin. I had another look at me plate te see if it was really clean, an then I sat back te wait fer Sadie. I heard her comin, an she was laughin back at the people in the ward an shoutin, 'Yeah, but it would have te be a dark night!' Then she came hurryin over te me an took me plate, an gave me another one after takin off the cover. 'Here, me little lamb chop! Get tha down ye. One of the missuses didn't want theirs. Their loss is your gain.'

I took one look at the sausages an fried egg, an it was already down me neck when Sadie loaded me plate wit more bread an gave me another sup of hot tea. 'By God! I wish me childre would eat like tha. I'm always wastin food, an it's a terrible sin. I hate waste, I do. There's so much waste in the world!' Sadie took the plate back before I had a chance te lick it. 'Do ye know wha you'll do when ye're a big girl?' Sadie said te me.

'No, Sadie! Wha?' I asked.

'Well, ye should apply te tha new Queen in England an tell her ye want te be her food taster, in case anyone is tryin te poison her! Then you'll have a grand an important job an be eatin lovely food all the time. Wouldn't tha be lovely?'

'Yeah, Sadie! I'll do tha, tha's a great idea.'

I asked Kathleen if the Queen might like a child food taster, cos it wouldn't be long now till I was eight. An Kathleen threw back her head an laughed at me. 'There's no such thing. They'd arrest ye before ye even got near the Queen! Sadie was only havin ye on!'

I looked at her an said, 'Sadie knows more than you! You don't know anythin. I'm not botherin about ye any more,' an I walked off in te the next ward.

I went over te Granny te see if she wanted the bedpan or anythin else. 'Open tha locker an take out the big bag. Now, take out the other one, it has fruit an stuff in it.' I gave the bags te Granny, an she patted the side of her bed an said, 'Sit up here beside me an we'll do a bit of knittin. An here, help yerself. They're bringin me up this stuff, an I can't eat half of it.'

I stuck me nose in the bag an pulled out oranges an apples, an a bag of bull's eyes. 'Here! Gimme tha orange, an I'll peel it fer ye.'

'Ah, no, Granny! I'm not eatin tha. I don't want te look like tha Kathleen one an have me skin all yella!'

Granny looked at me an then laughed, 'Not at all, child. Ye have te eat fruit, or ye'll get scurvy.' An she peeled the orange an gave it te me in pieces. I sat on the bed an sucked me orange, an made Granny suck some, too. It was lovely an juicy.

'I enjoyed tha,' Granny said, handin me the towel te wipe me hands. Then I sucked a bull's eye an handed one te Granny. 'No, I'm all right,' she said, an took out her knittin. 'Here! Roll this inta a ball,' an she handed me the end of her knittin, which was all tangled up. I found the end of it an held on, goin in an outa the tangles.

'What are ye knittin, Granny?'

'I'm knittin a jumper fer me granddaughter. It's an Arran, an the wool is very thick, so it takes a bit longer. But it should be ready by Christmas.'

153

'How old is she, Granny?'

'Eh, let me see. I do lose track, tryin te keep up wit the lot of them. Do ye know, by God, she must be nearly eighteen now! It was no time ago when she was little like you. Ah, yes, time flies, daughter! Don't hurry it, it will come te ye soon enough. Here, have another bull's eye!' Then the sister marched inta the ward. 'Quick!' Granny said. 'Don't let her see ye up on the bed, or we'll all be sent te the salt mines!'

Sister started rushin aroun, fixin the beds an tuckin people's arms under the bedclothes. An everyone went quiet. Granny pushed the bag of bull's eyes inta me hands an whispered, 'Quick, don't let her catch ye. Get back te yer bed!'

I took me shoes in me hand an rushed past Sister, liftin me legs high in the air so she wouldn't see me. She was too busy anyway, givin out te an aul one fer bein very untidy an throwin her stuff aroun the bed. When I got back te me bed, I leapt in, takin me sweets wit me, an I asked Kathleen if she wanted a bull's eye! She looked over an thought about it. I was hopin she'd say yes, but she didn't. 'No! I won't bother,' she said, so I couldn't tell her she wasn't gettin one. Instead, I opened the bag an put one in me mouth, an sucked away, makin big sucky noises, an drove her mad!

Sunday was visitin day, an the wards was crowded wit people. Ye couldn't see in the wards wit the amount of smoke. Everyone had a cigarette. The nurses locked the tilets so tha the visitors couldn't use them. I was out on the passage wit me legs crossed, dyin te go te the tilet. I was draggin meself up an down lookin fer a nurse, but I couldn't find one. Me eyes was waterin, an I didn't know wha te do. I kept lookin up an down the passage, an I couldn't move any more. The pooley was streamin down me legs. I was cryin me eyes out, an me legs was twisted tryin te hold it. Me shoes was soppin wet, an there was a big pool aroun me feet. When the nurse finally came down the passage, swingin her big bell an tellin the visitors their time was up, she came up te me an took the big bunch of keys from her belt an opened the tilet. I swung me way in, feelin very ashamed of meself. When I did finally sit on the tilet, I thought I'd never

154

want te get up again. I gave meself a huge big sigh an emptied me shoes down the tilet. The smell of meself reminded me of me bed at home, an I got a jerk in me chest from the fright.

The sores from me head was nearly gone, an me hair was beginnin te grow back. I didn't have lice any more, an me skin was lovely an soft. But me legs was still purply lookin, an I still had the zig-zag marks across me legs from where Jackser used te hit me wit the buckle of his leather belt. I don't think about him any more, an I don't even miss me ma, cos I got used te not seein her since I came inta the hospital. I was jumpin up an down on me bed, havin a great time, bouncin on the mattress, an Kathleen said suddenly, 'Look, there's gypsies lookin in at ye, an they're laughin!'

'How can they see in here?' I asked her.

'Cos we're on the ground floor.'

'Where are they?' I said. 'I can't see them!' I didn't believe her, cos I couldn't see anyone. So I sat back down, an I was wonderin about this when a few minutes later me ma appeared in the door.

'How are ye, Martha?' she said. 'Ye look lovely.' An she was laughin.

I got a shock, an I didn't know wha te think. So I just stared at her. 'Ma, did ye see any gypsies outside lookin in the winda at me?'

'No, but we saw ye, an he was laughin at ye jumpin on the mattress. He said if the nurse catches ye, she'll kill ye!' An then she got a good look at me head an said it was nearly cured, an I'd be able te come home soon. I didn't like the sound of tha, an I just looked at her.

'When will tha be, Ma?' I asked her.

'Soon! It shouldn't be too long now. I'll have te get ye somethin te wear. I'll get ye a lovely coat an frock, an a nice pair of shoes. Where's yer old shoes?' me ma asked.

'The nurse threw them out. I have nice woolly socks instead, lookit!' I said, shovin me feet inta her face te make sure she got a good look at them.

'Right!' she said, chewin her lip. 'I'd better go. He's outside, waitin wit the pram. He told me not te be long.' Then she waved at me an stopped te look, an went off like she didn't really want te go.

When she was gone, I got all excited an said te Kathleen, 'Tha was me mammy! She came te see me! Did ya know tha, Kathleen? Did ya! Wasn't it great?' Kathleen was very quiet, an I sat back te think about me mammy. She was here! I couldn't believe it. An she was happy, cos I was nearly cured. An I'm lookin grand.

Kathleen got loads a sweets an lemonade an fruit an even a new pair of slippers from her visitors last Sunday. She was sittin on the bed sortin them out. An I couldn't believe all the stuff she had. I was hopin she'd give me somethin, but she didn't. She had a big bar a Cadbury's chocolate an a small thruppeny one. I asked her fer a bit, an she said no! But she did peel an orange, an I got a bit of tha. But I'm not mad about oranges. I wouldn't class them as sweets. I really wanted a bit of her chocolate. So when she went out te the bathroom te do herself up, I leapt outa me bed an decided te hide her sweets. But when I saw the chocolate, I couldn't help meself. I put all her sweets back where I found them an took off wit the big bar of chocolate.

I rushed in te Granny. I thought I'd be safer there. 'I'm not busy, Granny! Can I stay wit you?' I said.

'Course ye can, beauty. Come on, sit up here,' an Granny patted the side of her bed fer me te jump up. 'Wha's tha ye have?' Granny said, lookin at me chocolate.

'Do ye want a bit?' An I broke off a little bit an gave it te Granny. I sat there watchin Granny's mouth suckin on the chocolate, an I did the same. Suckin slowly, not bitin, te make it last. 'Tha's lovely! Where'd ye get tha?' Granny asked.

'Eh, Kathleen!'

'God, isn't she very good! She must really like ye!'

I had two bits left when I heard Kathleen roarin me name. I got such a shock I stuffed them in me mouth an threw meself offa the bed an hid under it. I shut me eyes tight an chewed like mad, not enjoyin the chocolate any more. I could hear Kathleen givin out, an when I opened me eyes, I was lookin at her new pink fluffy slippers. Then she ducked down an pulled me by the leg from under Granny's bed. 'Give it te me! Where is it? Where's me chocolate?

What else did ye take?'

'Hold on, what ails ye? Don't be frightenin the child!' Granny said te Kathleen.

'She robbed me chocoate! I didn't even barely get a chance te look at it, never mind eat it!' Kathleen roared.

Then the nurse came inta the ward an said, 'What's happening?'

An Granny said, 'Ah, it's only Kathleen gettin excited about nothin. Go on wit the nurse, Kathleen, ye need a bit of rest.

'Come over te me, you,' an she put out her arms an I sat meself up beside her, an she buried me head in her chest an stroked me head an said, 'Tha was a very bold thing ye did. Deprivin poor Kathleen of her chocolate. But ye're a good girl, an ye didn't mean her no harm, did ye?'

'No, Granny!' I said, lookin up inta her face. An I started te cry, cos I was sorry I had robbed poor Kathleen's chocolate.

Granny took the corner of her washcloth an made me blow me nose. An she wiped me eyes, an then she said, 'Right! Let's cheer ourselves up! Get me tha bag in the locker,' an I jumped down an gave it te her. She took out a bag of mixed luxury biscuits, an I got a pink an white fluffy one wit jam in the middle, an a lovely Kimberley one. An Granny put two aside fer her cup of tea at eleven.

This mornin, the nurse told me not te leave me bed, cos me mammy was comin te take me home. I'm waitin now, all day. An she's still not here. I'm dyin te see me new clothes. I wonder wha the coat will be like, an me new frock an shoes! I'm afraid te think of anythin else, an I'm feelin a bit sick at the thought of goin home. I keep feelin me head, an I have a few sores still. But me head feels lovely an clean, an me hair is startin te grow back. The porter said I look like a little hedgehog, but I'll have lovely hair when it grows back. I was just beginnin te think I might be able te stay when me ma suddenly appeared in the door.

'Come on! Hurry up,' she said. 'I'm late,' an she whipped me nightie off. 'Here, put this on!' an she put a summer frock over me head. It was lighter than me nightdress. Then she put a pair of sandals on me feet, an I stood up. 'Here, put yer arm out,' an she put a rubber raincoat on me. It was all cold an damp, an I was cold in it.

'I don't like this coat, Ma. Where's me new coat?'

'Tha's all I could get!' me ma said, an she was in very bad humour. 'I've no knickers or vest fer ye. An I couldn't get ye a hat or a pair of socks, but ye can wear me head scarf. It will keep yer head warm.'

I walked out the door wit me ma, an I didn't say goodbye te anyone. I knew now I didn't belong here any more, an no one would have anythin te say te me, cos I wasn't one of them. I take a size nine in a shoe, me ma says, an these sandals were a size one. So they were too big fer me. An they kept slippin off me feet. By the time we got outa the hospital grounds an walked down James's Street an onta Thomas Street, I was shiverin wit the cold. It was tea time, an everyone was rushin home from work te get outa the dark rainin night. The shops had their Christmas decorations up, an the windas were blinkin on an off wit the fairy lights. I couldn't keep up wit me ma's rushin. An she was tryin te pull me along by the hand. 'No, Ma! The sandals are cuttin me feet. I can't walk in these.' We both looked down at me feet. The sandals was miles too big fer me, an me feet was already raw an wet. 'Can we not take the bus!' I asked her.

'No! I haven't got the fare. We'll just have te walk. Right! Give me them fuckin shoes. Ye'll have te walk without them or we'll never get back, an tha bastard will be lookin fer trouble. I was out lookin fer hours, tryin te get somethin fer ye te wear. An now I'm afraid of me life, wonderin wha he'll do when we get back. Ye know wha he's like! He doesn't like te be left on his own.'

I go now fer me milk collection. Every mornin I go up te the top of Gardiner Street an onta Belvedere an collect two bottles of milk fer me ma. It's the free milk fer childre under five. I join the queue of other childre all waitin fer the door te open, then we form a line. Tha's when the pushin an shovin starts. The big young fellas throw their weight aroun an pick on the smaller childre. But I've managed te show them I'm not a softie. I'm not as big or as strong as them, but I roar like mad, an when one fella gave me a box an pushed me outa me line, I took a stick wit me the next time I went an banged him over the head. I'd searched fer hours lookin fer tha stick on the street. An now he leaves me alone. I collect a bottle of milk fer a neighbour who lives across the road, an I'm always afraid I'll drop the milk on me way home, cos it's hard te manage three bottles in me arms. She gives me one shillin an six pence a week fer gettin her the milk. An I haven't told Jackser. So I can spend the money on sweets, or what I do is keep somethin back an buy Jackser five Woodbines te stop him killin me when I know I'm in trouble. Or maybe buy me ma a bag of chips, te cheer her up. I think it's much better te spend the money on them te keep the peace than te buy sweets fer meself.

I was on me way home this mornin, it's Easter Sunday, an I'll be gettin paid me one an six. I was busy thinkin how I'll spend it, maybe buy me brother a bit of chocolate, when I dropped a bottle of milk! I couldn't stop cryin. I'll have te tell the neighbour it was her milk. I was shakin when I knocked on her door. 'I broke yer bottle of milk! It slipped outa me arms,' I said, lookin up at her.

She said nothin, just looked down at me fer a while. An then she said, 'How do ye know it was *my* bottle?'

I kept lookin at her, tryin te think. 'It was, cos they told me in the dairy it was yer milk. So tha's how I know!'

'Yeah, go on!' she said. 'More like ye'd get yerself kilt if ye went home without it. Ye know I won't pay ye fer breakin me milk! An I'll not bother ye again te collect it fer me.' She slammed the door, an I was left wonderin if I'd lost, cos I knew Jackser couldn't kill me now. I had his milk safe, an tha was more important!

Me ma's had enough of Jackser an she's decided te kill him. 'We'd never get away from tha mad bastard,' she said. 'He'd hound us. An probably end up killin us! So I'm goin te get him first!'

I looked at me ma, an me mouth was hangin open. 'Yeah, Ma!' I said, slowly thinkin. 'But how will we do it?'

'I'll poison him,' she said. 'Wit this!' an she picked up a bottle. It looked like medicine te me. 'I'm goin te put it in his tea!'

I said, 'Will he drop down dead, Ma?'

'Yeah! But I can't let him get wise te me. So I won't put too much in at first, in case he tastes it.'

Tha was decided so, an I waited fer Jackser te come back an demand his tea. I couldn't stop thinkin about Jackser droppin dead. An I was makin all sorts of plans. I'd get meself a shoppin bag, an I'd take up more milk deliveries. I'd save up an buy a go-car, one the young fellas makes fer themselves fer playin aroun in. An then I could collect the turf fer people an drag it along on the go-car. Ye get a shillin a bag, I think, fer deliverin it after collectin it from the depot. Yeah! I'd make enough money te keep me ma an me brothers. Now I'm just headin inta eight years old I've got enough sense te be able te take care of things.

When he came back, he marched inta the room, an said, 'Right, Mrs! Have ye got a sup of tea ready? I'm starvin.' Then he threw off his coat an put it behind the door, an then unlaced his boots an threw them under the bed. An then he rolled himself onta the mattress an lay down wit his hands behind his head. 'Tha fuckin labour exchange'd do yer head in. Ye'd think it was comin outa their own pockets, the way they carry on. Have ye done any work in the last week? No! Are ye lookin fer work? Yes! Well, sign this! Do tha! I'm gettin no more than I'm entitled. So fuck them!' Jackser said.

I looked at me ma as she busied herself aroun the cooker. We were readin each other's eyes. 'I have te bide me time!' she whispered.

I kept a watch on Jackser. 'Go on, Ma! He's dozin.' Her eyes were like knives as she looked over at him. An she took the bottle outa her frock pocket an poured a little inta his mug of tea. But as she was doin it, the babby had crawled under the bed after Jackser's boots an was chewin an dribblin all over the laces. He suddenly banged the shoe up an down on the floorboards an was delighted wit himself. Poor Charlie had got hold of the other one an was about te try it on himself when Jackser got a sudden shock from the babby's bangin. He shot up an reached out, grabbin Charlie an sendin him flyin, an the babby jumped an shook an squealed. He dropped the boot an took te his hands an knees, an shot under the table. Me ma screamed an threw the bottle from her hand, an it smashed inta the sink. An without thinkin, I was openin the door onta the landin, makin me getaway. Me ma turned on Jackser wit

160

the fright an disappointment at breakin the bottle, an roared, 'Don't be fuckin shoutin, ye bandy aul fucker. Ye're after frightenin the life outa everyone!'

Jackser clamped his mouth shut an rolled his eyes aroun the room, givin everyone a dirty look. 'Listen, ye whore's melt!' he said, fastenin his eyes back on me ma, who was darin him by starin back hard, an she had her jaws clamped, too! 'If I get up outa this bed, ye'll be takin a short cut straight outa this fuckin winda. Do ye read me, Mrs?'

I came creepin back inta the room against me will, but I had te shut me ma up before he kilt the lot of us. 'Do ye want yer tea, Jackser?' I croaked. 'Ma! Give Jackser his tea, he's tired.'

'Yeah!' Jackser shouted. 'Listen te tha child an give me me tea. An I want no more of yer lip!'

Me ma hesimitated, an I pleaded wit me eyes. She stared at me wit her ice-cold marble eyes, an I stared back, annoyed, an frightened, too. 'Give Jackser the tea, Ma,' I said, losin patience wit her. I knew if Jackser discovered we were tryin te poison him, he wouldn't hesimitate te kill us. An me ma was too stupid te see this. I know now I understand more than she does. I grabbed the babby from under the table an dragged him inta me bedroom, sayin, 'We'll play in here, Jackser, cos ye need te rest in peace an quiet.'

161

19

We're movin again, down te Sheriff Street. Jackser's delighted, cos tha's where he comes from. He grew up in a little laneway there. Jackser gets one of his cronies, tha's wha me ma calls them, cos she hates them – they're always leadin him up te no good, she says, drinkin an chasin dyed blondes. Anyway, Jackser turns up wit his crony an yer man's horse an cart. An they take the two beds an mattresses, an the table an one chair, cos Jackser smashed the other one. An the blankets an coats fer the bed, an Teddy's cot, an they whip up the horse an take off laughin. 'Right! We'll see ye down there,' Jackser shouts te me ma. 'An don't take all day!'

I watch them disappear, wishin we could get a ride, too. An I hurry back te me ma, who's holdin the babby an lookin at the pram piled high inta a mountain wit the babby's blankets an clothes, an our two holy pictures, an the family one of themselves. An the mug belongin te Jackser, an our jam jars fer our tea. An the two dinner plates, an the tea pot, an the spoons an knife. An her papers wit all her documents, an loads a stuff. 'Here, ye'll have te carry him while I try te manage this pram,' she says.

I grab the babby, an he slides down me legs an starts te slap me an hammer me wit his legs. 'I can't carry him, Ma!' I whined, tryin te hump him up on te me hip.

'Oh, give him here!' she shouts. An the babby happily wraps himself aroun her neck an shouts, 'Ah!' at me, in case I come near him again. 'Here! Push tha,' she says. I take the handlebars, but I can barely see over them, never mind see over the mountain of stuff.

162

I push off, an the weight of the pram immediately heads fer the road an is about te turn over off the footpath.

'Mind where ye're fuckin goin!' me ma shouts. I let go of the handlebars an race aroun the front te stop the pram. 'Ah, this is no good!' me ma says. 'What are we goin te do? We'll never get there!'

'We can put the babby on top,' I says, 'an you push, Ma, an I'll hold him.'

Me ma chews her lip an looks at the top of the mountain. 'No! He'll fall off. Ah, fuck tha bandy bastard.'

'Right! You go on wit the pram, an I'll stay here wit the babby an mind Charlie, an then ye can come back fer us,' I said.

'I'll have te go all the way down, an then walk back, an back down again. I'm not fuckin Ronnie Delaney, ye know!'

'Well, what are we goin te do then?' I roared, fed up wit me ma.

'Right! You sit there, an I'll be back as soon as I can,' an off she went, puttin her back inta the pram an then tryin te stop it runnin away as she hit the corner.

The babby went mad when I sat on the steps of the house an me ma landed him in me lap. He was stretchin an slappin an throwin his head back in an awful temper, watchin me ma disappear aroun the corner. 'OK. Come on, we go. Come on, we go.' I was pretendin, tryin te distract him. He stopped an stared at me fer a minute, an when he knew nothin was happenin, he tried te escape an crawl onta the steps. I grabbed a hold a him an roared, 'Oh, lookit the doggy!' an a mangy, skinny-lookin dog came up te us te see if there was anythin te eat. The dog stared in disgust at us roarin an shoutin. He knew we had nothin te give him an went off about his business.

I was frozen solid, an the babby was asleep in me arms, an Charlie was cuddled in beside me, wit his fists between his knees te keep his hands warm, when me ma finally rounded the corner wit the pram an hurried up te us. 'Tha bastard was givin out,' she said. 'He doesn't want the babby te catch cold. Come on, we'd better hurry,' an she took the babby from me stiff arms an put him in the pram. An she covered him up wit the blanket an put the cover on an pulled up the hood. I lifted meself up, hangin on te the railins. I was so stiff an cold, an I dreaded the walk an facin the Jackser fella. I lifted Charlie wit me an put him on his feet. The wind was blowin his coat open an smackin the legs off me.

'Ma, put Charlie in the pram! He can't walk, an he's too tired,' I said.

'No! He'll break the springs an sit on the babby's legs.'

'I'm not movin,' I said, an she was gone, flyin aroun the corner. I grabbed Charlie's hand, an he started te cry. I was cryin an roarin, too. I was in a rage wit me ma.

She kept ahead of us all the way te Amiens Street, just lookin aroun now an then te make sure we were behind her. 'Come on!' she'd shout. 'Hurry up, we're nearly there.' By the time she did stop long enough fer us te catch up wit her, she was standin under the arch next te the train station. 'Right! We're just there,' she said, an she pushed on, headin down te Sheriff Street. Me anger was now left me, an I just felt disgust fer me ma, cos all she wanted was te get down te tha Jackser. I was beginnin te think she was as bad as him. She coulda given Charlie the bit of comfort an put him in the pram.

When we finally got te St Brigid's Gardens, we went in a narra road an came onta a square wit balconies all round. We were on the ground floor, next te waste ground wit a railin aroun it, an concrete sheds in the middle of the square fer keepin yer pram an yer bike. We lifted the pram inta the hall, an Jackser came rushin te show us the flat. 'Look, Martha! We have two rooms, an you an Charlie can sleep in the bedroom. I've put yer bed up fer ye's. I'm thinkin of puttin the cot in there, too, there's plenty of room. But I won't do tha now.'

I had a winda, but it was too high up fer me te see out. An there was nothin else te look at, so I went inta the sittin room, an there was a big winda lookin onta waste ground, surrounded by other flats, an all the windas were lookin on te this patch of grass. There were dogs an childre runnin aroun, an people dumped their old mattresses an rubbish there. The sittin room had a fireplace, an Jackser had put their bed at the far wall an the table an chair in the middle of the room, an he'd got the fire lightin.

164

I've been sittin in the flat fer days now, listenin te the childre playin outside. I'd love te be out there playin wit them, but I'm afraid of me life te go near them. It's all too strange. I can't face new childre again. They won't like me, an they'll fight wit me an call me names. There sounds like an awful lot of them out there, an I'm tryin te think how I'll get aroun this. Maybe I could pretend te have an English voice. I could say I was born in England. Tha might distract them from the state I look. Runnin aroun in me bare feet tells them immediately tha I'm a pauper. Then they'll think they're better off an more important than me. The English voice won't last, then they'll call me an eejit an try te beat the hell outa me, an I'll never get any peace.

Jackser sends me up an down te the shops, an there's millions of kids aroun the place. I'm beginnin te look aroun me now an size them up. But I still don't stop te talk te anyone when I'm runnin back wit the messages.

Me ma decided te give herself an airin an put the babby in the pram, an me an Charlie went wit her down te the shops. On the way back, I saw somethin lyin on the road, just beside the entrance te our flats. There wasn't a soul te be seen down there, an I said te me ma, 'Lookit, Ma! There's an orange box lyin in the middle of the road. We could use it on the fire or maybe sit on it. Will I run down an get it?'

'No!' me ma said. 'I'm goin in here te the vegebale shop te get an onion. You stay here an mind the pram.'

I was hangin on te the pram, watchin te see wha me ma was buyin an thinkin about gettin the orange box before someone else whips it. Me ma came outa the shop, an we started walkin down the road, headin fer home. It was very quiet, this hour of the mornin. It was aroun half eleven, an all the childre were at school.

Suddenly, I saw a coupla little childre head towards me orange box, an I said te me ma, 'Ah, they're goin te take it!' Then a man got outa a big cattle truck, an he seemed te be staggerin towards it as well. I started te run, an as I got closer I saw it wasn't an orange box but a babby lyin stretched out. The man was standin a few feet away wit

165

his arms out, implorin, 'Sweet Jesus, I never had a chance! She must have come outa them flats. She was straight under me wheels before I knew wha was happenin. One minute nothin an the next a little child appears from nowhere an goes straight under me wheels!'

The man was white as a corpse an was staggerin aroun, lookin at the little babby who was mashed te the ground. She was so small she had probably only learnt te walk not long ago. I looked aroun te see if her mammy was lookin fer her, or maybe her brothers or sisters, but there was nobody aroun, only the two little childre, who were about three years old, an the man an me. Even me ma was gone. I'd heard her mutter somethin te me about, 'Oh, Jesus! Come on!'

I inched closer te look at the child, but most of her was mashed te nothin, her fair curly hair an her face was squashed. I jumped back wit the shock. 'Mister! Will I ask someone te get the police or somethin? Ye need help,' an the man looked at me.

He was in terrible shock. 'Would ye? Would ye do tha so!' An then he looked at the child again an took off his jacket an put it over the little babby.

I ran down te the priest's house an banged the door. A little aul one came out an screamed at me fer keepin me finger on the bell an bangin on the door. 'What do ye want? There's no one here.' She was about te slam the door on me, an I told her te get the police. A child had been kilt!

'Where did it happen?'

'Just aroun the corner,' I pointed, 'in front of the flats. She was kilt by a big cattle truck, an she's lyin all mashed on the ground. It's terrible! An the man who did it is in an awful state altogether!'

'Oh, God bless us an save us!' said the housekeeper. 'I'll run in an get Father.' An she rushed in, an I rushed off. When I got back te the man, there was a load of people standin aroun an lookin. A policeman was talkin te the man an tryin te keep everyone back. Suddenly, he let a roar at the lot of us an put his arms up an shouted, 'Get offa the road! Go an play in the flats. Do ye see what's after happenin now? Go on, stay off the road!'

I looked aroun me, wonderin where the little child's mammy

166

was, but there was still no sign of her yet. An I thought, she still doesn't know! The poor mammy will lose her mind. I wonder who was supposed te be mindin the child. I don't see them here either. I wandered back inta the flats an was wonderin how I coulda thought she was an orange box. When I'd looked down the road, there hadn't been a sinner about. It was so quiet, an she'd been lyin all tha time on the road an nobody te run te her.

Jackser started me at a new school, an he brought me over himself. 'This is me old school,' he kept tellin me. 'I went here before they sent me te Artane. Now I'm goin te send you. It's a great school. They'll teach ye everythin ye need te know. So be grateful te them, an if they see ye're interested, they'll be happy te learn ye all they can. Ye're lucky I'm lookin after ye, cos there's not many men who'd do what I'm doin fer ye. An if ye were waitin on yer mammy te move herself, then ye may wait till yer hair turns grey! Now, get all the edumacation ye can get outa them, it'll stand ye in good stead! Right?'

'Right, Jackser!' I agreed, an in we went te see the person in charge.

I was put inta the second class an sat there in the desk completely lost. They all had books – English books, Irish books, sums copybooks. An worst of all, they were all dippin pens inta an inkwell an joinin up letters together! These childre were all scholars! I was lookin aroun me at the lot of them, an they were very serious scholars. I hadn't even started yet te be a scholar. I never got te even finish the baby class! The teacher, Miss Flaherty is her name, is a terrible aul one altogether. She's marchin up an down wit a huge stick in her hand. An she really fancies herself. She keeps fixin her tight perm wit her free hand an smackin the nearest desk wit her stick, in case anyone is lookin up from their writin. Her hair at the roots is stone grey, but the rest of it is dyed blue.

She's walkin down the room now between the desks an pointin her stick at people's copybooks. 'Keep it above the line, you stupid creature! You, keep your head down!' an she moves on. I haven't done a thing yet. Ah, God! How do ye do this? I look at wha the young one beside me is doin, an I have a go. I'm sweatin, tryin te do them letters an sort of draw them together. But it looks like a man tryin te hang himself. An now I've just blobbed a big stain of ink. I drawed in me breath suddenly wit the fright. The young one beside me looked up an did the same when she saw what I'd done. Her mouth is hangin open, an her eyes is bulgin. She stopped starin at me copybook an moved herself down the seat, takin her copybook wit her. An she's leaned over it an put her arm aroun it, so I can't see wha she's writin an how she does it. I don't know wh. 1 te do now. An the more I stare at it, the more me head seems te be emptyin. I'm just sittin in dread, waitin fer it te be over. She's roarin an shoutin an gettin closer all the time. She's lookin at the young one beside me an tellin her, 'Good! Yes! Good girl, Agnes!' Then she looks over at mine, an me fingers are covered in ink. The copybook is a holy show.

'What on earth is that?' she roars at me. An I look up slowly an put me pen slowly down on the desk. She suddenly lunges at me an brings the heavy stick down on me knuckles. The pain shot through me, an I felt me hand was broken. I held it in me other hand, an me right arm was limp. I sort of winded out me breath an moaned, 'Ah! Ah! Me hand.' She grabbed the copybook, holdin it by the corner, an marched me te the top of the class. She was laughin at me an held me copybook up fer everyone te see. 'This is the work of a cretin!' she said. Wonder wha tha is!

The childre laughed, delighted it was not them. An happy wit her jokes, cos she didn't make many. 'Read it!' she said te me. An I didn't know what it was supposed te be, so I said nothin. I then lifted me head an looked at her. She stared inta me face, an I saw Jackser. Her eyes said, I'm master of you. An if I have te kill ye te prove it, I will. But I knew she was still a teacher. An ye can't kill people in public. So I stared back, an she roared, 'Put out your hand!'

I gave her me good one, but she grabbed the sore hand an put me arm in the air. 'Hold it there!' she roared. An when she brought the stick down, I tore me hand back an hid it behind me back. 'You'll get six on the other hand now and six more every time you draw your hand back.' I stood still an put me bad hand out. She brought the stick down as hard as she could. I never moved an inch or took me eyes offa her. I kept me mouth shut. She had a smirk on her face, an her eyes never left me face. Then she roared, 'Hold out your other hand!' an I held it high in the air fer her. She tried harder after each slap te get me te cry. Her eyes were dancin in her head, but this was Jackser, an I'm not goin te cry!

Miss Flaherty won't get the better of me, an them childre there all lookin up at me won't get much outa me either. Ye can call me names an ye can laugh at me. I have te put up wit tha. But ye're not goin te think ye're better than me. Cos one day I'll show ye's all.

The bell rang, tellin us school was over. Everybody grabbed their bags an started te put away their books. 'Quiet!' the teacher roared. 'Tomorrow, you will all bring in sixpence for knitting needles and wool. You are going to be knitting stockings, and I want no excuses. Make sure you bring in your money.'

I went home worryin where I was goin te get the sixpence. When I got in the door, I could hear Jackser roarin. 'Holy Jaysus, Mrs! Where's tha smell comin from?'

'How the fuck do I know!' me ma roared back. 'It's probably yerself! Every dog smells his own dirt!'

Jackser was goin mad, rushin aroun the room wit his head down sniffin inta corners. The babby was sittin on the floor in his vest, dribblin on a lump of cinder. He was covered in dirt from the ashes, an his little bare arse was freezin from the cold, cos the fire was out. Me ma was lyin on the bed, holdin her big belly. Her skirt wouldn't fit her, it barely covered her hips. An she left the zip opened. She was tryin te pull down her jumper te cover herself, but her belly still stuck out. An I knew another babby was goin te arrive. I looked at her, an me chest tightened, an I felt sick wit dread. I'll be left here on me own wit Jackser when she goes inta hospital.

Me ma's eyes was locked on mine. 'What are ye fuckin starin at?' she roared at me. Jackser stopped snifflin an whirled aroun. Me heart stopped. He took three long steps across the room an grabbed me by the back of me neck, liftin me off the floor. The babby roared an took te his knees, crawlin aroun lookin fer a safe place te hide.

169

He shot under the bed, an Charlie came outa his doze, sittin wit his back te the bed, an jumped in beside me ma. An she gave him a clout fer landin on her belly.

Jackser shook me, 'Do ye see tha, Mrs? Do ye?'

'Wha, Jackser, wha?' I couldn't breathe! He was stranglin me.

'Tha, ye blind eejit! Tha!' An he stuck me head inta a lump of shit the babby had done in the corner. Then he lifted me inta the air again an threw me on the floor. 'Clean it up!'

He lifted his boot te kick me, but I rolled meself inta a ball an screamed, 'I'm doin it now, Jackser! Don't hurt me, I'm sorry. I'll be quicker next time, an I won't annoy ye!'

Jackser was whirlin aroun on the balls of his feet, his fists was clenched, an he was dribblin spit. His eyes was bulgin, an I stayed very still, afraid te breathe, tryin te hold me sobs. Waitin. 'Move!' he shouted. An I shot up an sped te the scullery, lookin fer a bit of newspaper.

I came flyin back. 'Ma! I need paper. What'll I use?'

Jackser grabbed me copybook an tore out the pages an said, 'Use this, Mrs.'

'Eh, right, Jackser!' I cleaned up the shit an rushed te the tilet te flush it down, thinkin tha teacher is goin te kill me. How am I goin te get a new copybook now? Jackser was shoutin at me ma te get up from the bed. 'Get down te tha priest an see if ye can get a few bob outa him! Tell him we've no coal an the kids are dyin of the hunger. An bring me back five Woodbines. I'm dyin fer a smoke.'

Me ma was chewin her lip an lookin at me. She didn't want te go. 'Send her! I can't go out. I'm in me skin. I've nothin te wear. Anyway, tha aul bastard wouldn't give ye anythin. I'd be wastin me time.'

'Ma, you'd be better goin. The housekeeper will only slam the door in me face.'

'Right! The fuckin two of ye go,' Jackser roared. 'Or, by Jaysus, if ye continue te come the hound wit me, I'll be hanged fer ye's!'

'Come on, Ma! Get yer coat.' I could see me ma was gettin very annoyed, an Jackser would kill her if she started, an me too!

We went down te the priest's house, but the housekeeper said he wasn't in. An she wouldn't tell us when he'd be back. 'We can't go home, Ma, not without money!' I said, so we walked up te Marlborough Street an managed te get half a crown from one of the priests there. Me ma bought bread an milk, an margarine an six eggs. But we'd no money fer the Woodbines. Me ma was happy, but she said we'd better get the money fer his cigarettes, so we crossed over the river an went up te Clarendon Street Church.

I was carryin the messages, an me ma was very tired. It was gettin dark now, an she kept sayin, 'He'll kill us fer takin so long.'

'Yeah, Ma! But we can't go back without his Woodbines. If we get enough money, we can buy him ten cigarettes, an maybe tha will put him in good humour.'

The church was packed wit people gettin their devotions. An the priest was up on the altar givin out Benediction. 'We'll wait here,' me ma said, 'an catch him when he comes out.' So we stood outside the priest's house, watchin an waitin, hopin we wouldn't lose him. He might disappear out another door, an we'd be left stranded.

It was after nine o'clock when the priest finally appeared. We were cold an wet from the drizzlin rain, an it was pitch black. The priest gave us two shillins, an me ma was delighted. We rushed off an bought Jackser his cigarettes, an when we got home, he whipped the door open as soon as he heard us comin. 'Where the fuck have youse been till now? The child's been cryin wit the hunger fer hours.' He stared at me ma an then at me. I was watchin his clenched fists.

'We were hurryin as fast as we could!' me ma said.

'Youse are lucky I didn't come houndin after ye's!'

'Here's yer Woodbines. I'd an awful job tryin te get the money fer them.'

An Jackser snatched them from me ma's hand. His eyes lit up, an he started te snuffle an stretch his arm. 'Right! Get in there an get somethin on. We need grub on the table fast, Mrs!'

'Take yer fuckin time!' me ma said, knowin she wouldn't get a dig, cos he was content wit his Woodbines. 'Did ye bring in tha plank ye found? I want te light the fire fer the tea,' me ma said te me. I opened the door an rushed out te grab me plank before someone robbed it.

I'd been afraid te bring it in, cos Jackser might have smashed us over the head wit it if he was really annoyed.

Mrs Flaherty banged on her desk wit the stick an shouted fer everyone te put away their Irish books. 'Now! You, Mary, give out the knitting bags. Stand up those who have not brought in their sixpence for their knitting!'

I looked aroun me an stood up slowly. There was only one other child standin. 'I have me sixpence, Mrs Flaherty,' she said, an held it high up in the air so no one could miss it. I looked at it longinly, wishin it was mine.

'Put it on my desk!' An the young one rushed outa her seat, pulled up the leg of her knickers an went off proudly te collect her knittin.

'Now, you!' an Mrs Flaherty pointed her stick down at me. Her eyes were glitterin, an she had a smirk on her face. 'Tell us all what your excuse is today. We are all listening. Is that right, children?'

'Yes, Mrs Flaherty!' they all shouted back, shiftin in their seats wit excitement, all makin sure they were comfortable, coughin an settlin themselves in fer the show. I was shakin an tryin not te show it. I stood on one leg, leaned me hand on the desk an stood up straight, me mind racin. Tryin te find a way outa this.

'We are waiting!' Mrs Flaherty roared.

'Ah! Eh! Hm!'

'Yes?' she barked, bangin her stick on a young one's desk, makin her jump an move herself down the seat in a hurry, pushin the other one who had her leg caught in the bench an was hangin out.

'Me ma had no change,' I squeaked.

'What?' Flaherty roared, holdin her ear an pretendin she was deaf. 'Speak up! I didn't catch that!'

'Me ma had no change in her purse this mornin,' I squealed.

'You are a liar!' Mrs Flaherty said quietly, watchin me carefully, her mouth twistin an her eyes glintin.

'No, Teacher! I'm not, she really didn't have any change.'

'Liar!' Flaherty roared, an rushed at me, grabbin me arm an lashin out wit the stick at me legs, hittin the desk at the same time. She

172

dragged me te the top of the classroom an spun me aroun, diggin her fingers inta me shoulder. She bent down an levelled her eyes at mine. Her eyes are bulgin, an her face is purple, an she's spittin. 'The truth! I want the truth!'

'Yes, Miss. I didn't ask her, cos I forgot,' I said very quietly inta her eyes.

She took her head back an stared at me, thinkin, you didn't ask your mother. 'Hm! Every other decent mother in the class has paid up. But not you. Right! This will remind you. Hold up your hand,' an she grabbed me hand an started te swing the stick as hard as she could. The pain shot up me arm. She brought the stick down again an again, as fast as she could. 'Now the other hand.' She's lookin down on me, an me shoulders are breakin. I can't stop her, an I can't take me hands down. She hates me. It's cos I'm dirty. She knows me mammy hasn't got the money. I saw tha in her eyes, an she hates tha, cos it means we're dirt. I'll hold on, though, cos I can't let her beat me. She's not goin te get me. I won't cry. I won't show fear. I won't ask her te stop. She got tired an threw the stick on the desk. 'Get back to your seat.'

I was in a fog. I stayed wit me hands in the air half closed an stiff an burnin. Me eardrums was roarin, an me back was stiff an twisted. An then I turned meself aroun an staggered back te me desk. Me legs was bucklin under me.

I spent the next week runnin aroun doin messages fer people in the time I could spare when I wasn't lookin after the house an childre, when me ma an Jackser went out, or when Jackser was in a good mood an put me out on the street te play an told me not te come in unless he called me. At last, I managed te save up the sixpence, an I was sittin in me desk, waitin fer Mrs Flaherty te call out fer us te start knittin.

'OK, give out the knitting, Mary.' I was all excited, cos I had me money, an I wouldn't be gettin slapped like I did every mornin fer not havin it. I couldn't wait te learn te knit. I whipped the money outa me shoe an waited patiently.

'You, stand up!' Mrs Flaherty roared down at me. 'Have you

brought in the money?' She was wavin the stick behind her back.

'Yes, Mrs Flaherty. I have the money!' An I held it up high te show her. Her eyes bulged, an she clamped her lips together. 'I have it, Miss. Here it is,' I said quietly, afraid cos she didn't seem happy.

'Where did you get that money?' she roared at me.

'From me mammy, Miss,' I said quietly.

'You liar! Your mother didn't give you that money, you stole it!'

'No, Miss. No, I didn't! Me mammy gave it te me.'

'You couldn't have gotten it from your mother! She wouldn't give you the money. For weeks now she wouldn't give you the money. You don't have that kind of mother. You would never get the money from her because she doesn't have it. She would never be able to afford suddenly to give you that sixpence. You are a thief! Where did you steal the money from?'

'I didn't, Miss. I promise I didn't steal it.'

'Are any of you missing money?' she asked the class. I looked aroun at everyone. Some of them were shakin their heads up an down an then changin their minds an sayin no. She pointed her stick at one child, who was sayin yes an no wit her head goin aroun in circles wonderin wha te say.

'Did you have money missing, Teresa?'

'Eh, yes, Miss. One time I lost a shillin outa me bag, an I couldn't find it, Miss. It must have been took!' an she looked over at me, feastin her greedy eyes on me sixpence.

'That's enough for me! Get to the top of the class, you. Stand beside my desk!'

I couldn't understand wha was happenin. I hadn't robbed the money. I did all the messages fer the people an saved it up. But if I told her tha, I would be ashamed of meself, cos then they would all know their mammies are better than my mammy. Cos all the mammies are poor, but they still manage te give their childre the sixpence, an mine can't.

'Put the money on my desk!' I left the sixpence on her desk. Me hands were shakin. 'Come here!' I went over slowly te where she was standin. I was rubbin me hands behind me back, an now I was shakin wit fear. I lifted me head te look at the other childre, but they were as confused as me, an nobody was laughin. I think they knew I didn't rob the money, cos some of them knew I went fer messages fer people, an tha's how ye got the pennies. 'I'm going to teach you a lesson you won't forget! You dare lie to me? I will teach you not to steal! Hold up your hand, and when I'm finished, you will regret you were ever born!'

I went quiet inside as she brought the stick down on me hands. Me wrists! The pain is miles away from me. I can see her face, red an purple, an her mouth is twistin, an there is a lot of noise comin from her mouth. But I am holdin on, waitin fer it te be over. It will end. A pain wants te gush up from me, cos she hates me. An I've done nothin wrong! But I push it back down again, cos if I cry, she will be happy. An then I won't be tough any more, an everyone will beat me.

She finally stopped an rubbed her arms. 'Get out of my sight!' I couldn't move, the pain was flyin up me arms an aroun me shoulders an neck an head. I was in agony. She didn't bother where the stick landed. She grabbed me by the back of me neck an dragged me over te the corner. 'Stand with your back to the class. I don't want to see your face for the rest of the afternoon!'

At three o'clock, the bell went. I didn't move. 'Put your books away quietly and move out in a single line.' As the childre moved outa the classroom, I looked aroun an waited te get on the end of the line. 'You, Miss, and you, and you, stay behind!' Everyone else kept movin as fast as they could te get out. I tried te get on the line, but she yanked me back an threw me inta the middle of the room wit the other three. 'You will all sit here until five o'clock. You three were laughing and idling at the back of the class. So now you can wait until your mothers collect you. And I will have something to say to them about your conduct.'

'But, Miss Flaherty, I didn't do anythin! Will I have te stay?' I was shiverin from the shock. Jackser will kill me.

'Stay here, you. You are not to leave this room!' An she walked out the door.

175

I started te get a blindin headache. Wha will Jackser say? Wha will he do te me? I sat down at a desk an put me head on me arms. I was suddenly so tired an wanted te go te sleep. Oh, God, wha did I do? Don't let him kill me, ye know I didn't do anythin. But I promise te be very good if ye don't let him hurt me. I was shiverin an feelin very hot at the same time. Don't let him hurt me, God! Please.

The other childre were laughin an sayin, 'Oh, God! Me ma'll kill me.'

'So will mine.'

'Jaysus, me ma will kill her first, though. She has an awful temper, especially when I tell her she's always hittin me. Tha aul Flaherty is goin te get her just deserts.'

I was afraid te move me head, it was painin me so much, an I was tryin not te get sick, cos I would have te run te the tilet, an Mrs Flaherty would kill me altogether fer leavin the classroom.

Suddenly the door opened, an we all jumped. 'What ails ye? What are ya doin here?'

'Ma, Mammy! Tha teacher wouldn't let us out!' An a young one ran te her mother.

'Who wouldn't? Wha did youse do on her?'

'Nothin, Ma. Nothin at all.'

'Yeah!' they all shouted, an ran over te the mammy. 'We were afraid we were goin te be locked up fer the night.' An everyone was shoutin at the same time.

Then another mammy appeared. 'There ye are, Concepta! Wha happened te ye?'

'Ah, Ma, we got locked up in here! She wouldn't let us out!'

Then the door opened again an Mrs Flaherty came in. The childre started cryin an holdin on te their mammy's hands.

'Would ye mind explainin te me why ye took it on yerself te keep me child locked up here a prisoner?' Concepta's mammy asked.

'Yes! Who do ye think ye are, may I ask?' the other mammy said, gettin very annoyed.

'I beg your pardon!' Mrs Flaherty started te say, straightenin herself up.

'Don't ye beg my pardon! Ye're losin the run of yerself. Ye have no authority over me child after three o'clock.'

'Exactly!' screamed Concepta's mother. 'Ye uttered the words right outa me mouth, Mrs, so ye did.'

Then the door opened again an another mammy appeared. 'Philomena, are ye here?'

'Ma! Ma!' an Philomena galloped over te her mammy.

'Jaysus! Wha's happenin here? Was there an accident or somethin?' An she was feelin Philomena's head an lookin inta her face te see if she was hurt.

'No, Ma! It was her!' she said. 'We weren't gettin home.'

The mammy went white an looked over at Mrs Flaherty. 'Wha did ye do te me child? She's only eight years old. I was outa me mind wit worry when she didn't come home.'

'Yes indeed, Mrs. So we all were. Are ye tryin te hold on te yer job, Teacher? Is tha it?' Concepta's mother shouted.

'Ye'll be well kept,' Philomena's mother roared. 'Ye must have no home te go te an no childre or man of yer own. Tha's why ye're torturin the little innocents.'

They were all shoutin at once, an the childre were pinchin each other an laughin behind their mammies' backs. Mrs Flaherty said they should all leave now, an she ran outa the room. The mammies followed her, draggin the childre behind them. 'An another thing!' they roared after her as they slammed the door shut behind them.

I listened te the voices goin down the passage, an then they were gone. It was quiet now, an I looked over at the winda. It was gettin late. Jackser was probably on his way over, or maybe me ma would come. But I knew tha wouldn't happen. She wouldn't stir herself unless he made her. An he'd be too annoyed about me not comin back. He'd come after me himself. 'God,' I whispered. 'Are ye there? Don't let him harm me. I know he'll be annoyed I had sixpence an didn't give it te him. So maybe he'll go fer Mrs Flaherty instead, cos she got the money, an he'll put her in her place. He might just take his vengeance out on her. An then he'll forget te be annoyed wit me. OK, God. Tha's grand. I promise I'll be very good if tha happens.'

Me head was easin wit the pain, an I was content te settle down an wait.

It was beginnin te get a bit dark now an still no sign of him. Then I heard a door open an held me breath. The footsteps stopped an another door opened. I could hear voices, then a door closed an the voices stopped. I was left wonderin if tha was him, an I started te shake again. I was shiverin away wit the fear, an I couldn't stop me legs from jerkin. Please, God, help me. I promise I'll be good. I won't curse or fight wit anyone any more. I'll do wha ye say. I'll give them me other cheek when they hit me. Then I gorra picture of meself gettin milled by a crowd of childre cos I gave them me other cheek te box. An I decided tha wasn't a good idea. I'd only get kilt. Then I heard Jackser's hobnail boots on the passage, an me heart leapt. The door was swung open, an Jackser appeared wit Mrs Flaherty behind him. She had tha smirk on her face, an they nodded te each other.

'Right you! Out!' I jumped up from the desk an hurried out in front of him. Jackser tipped his cap at Mrs Flaherty an said, 'Don't worry, I'll see te her.' Mrs Flaherty smirked at me an looked very satisfied wit herself. 'Get movin, ye dirty bastard! Before I put ye under a fuckin car wit me boot.'

I started runnin ahead of him up the street, wonderin wha he was talkin about. 'She said ye were dirty. Ye had lice crawlin in yer head.' I looked back at him an stopped. I didn't know wha he was talkin about. She mustn't have mentioned about the sixpence. She made up lies, so she must have known I didn't rob it! An why did he let her get away wit the excuse of me bein dirty? Tha's her reason fer holdin me back? Lots of childre are dirty. She's not supposed te do tha. I looked at Jackser, tryin te figure him out. He has no sense! He's not like a big person at all. An tha Flaherty was afraid of him, tha's why she lied. She just hates the sight of me, tha's all. She's another Jackser! I can't understand it at all. I didn't do anythin, an I got kilt fer nothin. I'd be better off dead, it's always goin te be like this. If only I could run off somewhere an get a bit of peace.

'Move!' Jackser shouted. 'I was made a show of in there. But I set her straight. I told her ye weren't one of mine, ye were another man's leavins!'

Tha hurt me feelins, but I thought, yeah, ye're right there, Jackser! But I'm glad I don't belong te ye. An I ran faster, te get ahead of him. I didn't want him te land his boot on me.

Mrs Flaherty is ignorin me all mornin. She didn't even look at me when she called the roll te see whose missin. Tha's grand. I hope she keeps it up. I'm sittin in a desk by myself, an tha's grand, too, cos there's no one te fight wit me, an I can get a bit of peace. I lift me head an peep up at her through me fingers. An she's sittin at the top of the room wit her feet on a young one's desk. She's pattin her hair an takin crumbs off her skirt, cos I saw her earlier, sneakin a biscuit from her drawer. She'll probably start suckin her bull's eyes later when she gets everyone te put their head down wit the writin.

'Now! Can anyone tell me who were the Bold Fenian Men?'

'Me, Mrs Flaherty! Me! Me!'

'No! I don't want you to speak. Just put your hand up.'

I looked aroun. They all had their hands up except me an a few at the back. 'Concepta Sweeney, Bernie Wilson, Philomena Rafters, stop that idling!' Then she turned te the young one in front of her. 'Majella, get me my stick.' Majella dashed te get the stick an handed it te Mrs Flaherty. Then swished her lovely shiny ponytail wit the lovely long pink ribbon, an daintily fixed her lovely matchin pink frock an sat back down again. 'You will get a taste of this stick if you don't behave yourself.' Then she looked over at me. I looked down at me desk.

'Teacher! Mrs Flaherty.' I heard a squeak an looked up. It was Concepta. 'I forgot te give ye this, Teacher. It's a note from me mammy fer ye, it is.'

'Bring it up here.'

Concepta wiped her nose wit the back of her hand an pulled up the leg of her knickers, they were always hangin down. An she rushed up wit the note, bangin inta desks in her hurry. We all watched Mrs Flaherty readin the note. She looked surprised an then had another look at it, an looked at the back, where there was no writin. An then shook herself an said, 'Right! Mary, dear, would you move in here beside Majella, and you, Concepta, you sit in there beside Maria Goretti. And be a good girl. Because now I'll be keeping an eye on you.' I wish I was sittin beside Maria Goretti. They owned the fish an chip shop, an maybe I'd get free chips an fish. An we'd be best friends.

We went out te the yard te drink our free bottle of milk. Some of the childre don't bother te drink it, but I love it. Even when it's freezin cold. It was cold now, an I was hoppin up an down tryin te get warm. Me feet were painin me from all the cuts an sores from goin aroun in me bare feet. The three pals were lookin very annoyed, cos they were separated. 'Wha did yer ma say in the note, Concepta?' I asked.

'Mind yer own business, smelly!' I was wonderin if I should say somethin back, but the three of them would jump on me, an I wouldn't have a chance. 'There's an awful smell,' Concepta said, lookin at me. An then they turned their backs an walked off.

'Yeah!' I roared. 'Ye can't read, tha's why ye won't say. An ye have a snotty nose!'

Concepta roared back, 'At least I have knickers, an lookit, I wear shoes!' An she caught her foot in the leg of her knickers an went backwards, landin on her arse. I ran off laughin.

20

I was fast asleep, then suddenly I was awake in shock. Jackser was pullin me outa the bed an shoutin somethin at me. I rubbed me eyes, tryin te come te me senses. 'Get outa the bed. I told ya te go down te the fuckin road an watch fer the ambulance.' I started te look fer me frock, but the floor was lifted from under me. 'Move, ye lazy bastard! Yer mammy needs te get te the hospital!' He landed me in the middle of the floor an smacked the frock inta me face. 'Here! Get tha on ye an get goin.'

I dragged the frock over me head an looked over at me ma. She was sittin on the side of the bed wit her head down, an she was moanin. She had her fists dugged inta the mattress.

'Ma,' I whispered, 'wha's wrong? Will ye be all right?'

She looked up at me an her eyes were like daggers. 'Leave me alone! Go an get tha fuckin ambulance. Oh, Jaysus!' she started moanin, an lowered her head te the floor. I ran fer the door.

I was just whippin back down through the flats when I heard the bells of the ambulance. The cream van shot aroun the bend an up the entrance. Me heart lifted, an I started runnin back te the flat, wavin at the ambulance an pointin te show them the way. Jackser was tryin te get me ma inta her coat, an she was moanin louder. 'Hurry up, Sally! The ambulance is here. Ye don't want te keep them waitin.' The men came in wit the stretcher, an Jackser grabbed me an shouted, 'Get out there an mind the ambulance. An make sure no one's watchin. I don't want them knowin me business!'

Jackser shook me awake, I was still dozy from bein up in the middle of the night. 'Get tha babby ready. Here, give him his bottle of tea.'

181

He was standin at the bars of his cot, roarin his head off wit his tongue stickin out, an I could see he was covered in shit. Charlie was sittin beside me wit his fists stuck between his knees an his hair stuck up. He was lookin aroun him, wonderin wha was goin on an where me ma was. He didn't say a word but I could see he was really afraid. Jackser was runnin aroun lookin fer trouble.

'Here's yer trousers, Charlie. Put them on. Where's yer shoes?'

He stood up an dived under the bed, his hair gettin caught in the springs. 'Ah, me head, Martha! I'm caught.' I tried te pull him back, grabbin hold of his bare arse, an he roared even more. 'Ah! Ye're hurtin me head!'

Jackser ran over an stopped dead in front of us wit his fists clenched. There was a second of silence while Jackser took in wha was goin on, an then he lifted me by me arm an landed me at the cot. Charlie flashed out from under the bed an sat himself on the floor, puttin his two feet in one leg of the trousers an tryin te stand up.

'Get the babby ready, Mrs! I told ya,' an Jackser gave me a smack on the side of me head. It sent me flyin, then he lifted Teddy from his cot an discovered he was full of shit an whipped him back down again. 'Ah, Holy Jaysus, Mrs! I'm destroyed. Can ye not do anythin right? I'm warnin ye, clean tha child up an get him ready in his pram or I'll be done fer ya.'

'OK, Jackser. I'm doin it. I know wha ye want now, an I'll do it.'

He moved away, watchin me te see if I would make a mistake. An me head was pricklin, on alert fer the blow tha might come. I put the bars of the cot down an held the babby under me arms, tryin te make him lie down te wipe the shit off his arse an legs. He was strong an bashed me wit his fists an pulled me hair, shakin his legs an sendin shit flyin everywhere. I couldn't get him te lie down, cos he was diggin in his heels an buckin his back in the air.

'Get on wit it, Mrs! I haven't all fuckin day!'

'Yes, Jackser! I'm nearly ready.' An I grabbed the babby's feet an whipped them inta the air, an tried te clean him wit the blanket. But he twisted himself aroun an pushed himself up on his hands an started laughin. He thought we were playin a game. Jackser was in the scullery, so I said, 'Ah! Ah! Bold!' an he stopped te look at me. An I wiped him clean wit the blanket before he started te scream his lungs out. I lifted him out an put him on the floor an put his trousers on. He galloped off on his hands an knees inta the scullery. He keeps tryin te stand up, holdin on te the chair. Me ma says he'll be walkin soon, cos he's nearly ten months old.

We were ready. I strapped the babby inta his pram, an Jackser slammed the front door shut. I followed behind him, pushin the high pram, an Teddy was sittin up, lookin aroun the side of the hood. I pushed it back so he could look out. An he was content te lie there, enjoyin the sights an the rockin pram from me pushin it. Charlie held on te the handlebars, runnin te keep up. We had te rush, cos Jackser walks fast.

Suddenly Jackser stopped dead, an we nearly ran inta him. He was starin across the road at a man waitin fer a bus. 'Wha's he fuckin starin at?' Jackser said. 'Wait here, I'm goin te watch this fella, see who the fuck he's starin at!' I looked across the road te the man, who was mindin his own business, not even noticin Jackser. He was too busy watchin fer the bus. I stayed still, waitin fer Jackser te move. He does this all the time. Stops an asks people wha they're starin at. He believes everyone is out te get him, but people don't even notice him. 'People are always fuckin watchin me!' Jackser muttered. 'One of these days I'm goin te show the bastards. People'd better watch out, you mark my fuckin words! I'll get them!' He gave the man a dirty look. The man was nervous an he turned his back, pretendin te look in at the shop winda. I kept me head down, ashamed cos Jackser was makin a show of us.

People were now lookin at us as they passed by, wonderin wha was up, an Jackser was givin them all dirty looks. 'What's wrong wit him?' one aul one said as she passed me. 'Tha's a terrible carry on.'

'Move!' Jackser suddenly roared at me. An I pushed the pram up the hill as fast as I could. Charlie gorra fright an grabbed hold of the bars, afraid he'd be left behind an Jackser'd get him. We went up Seville Place, an I noticed how quiet it was. All the childre were at school. I could hear them shoutin out their lessons when we passed by the school. I was glad I was not there, but I'd be happier if we weren't wit Jackser. The women were walkin wit their shoppin bags, goin te get their messages fer the dinner. I wondered why we weren't like tha. A woman passed by me, holdin a little young fella by the hand, an he was suckin on a big orange icepop. Charlie's eyes leapt outa his head at the sight of it, an the two of them stared at each other. The little boy was about three years old, an he was wearin an overcoat wit buttons all down the front, an long trousers an boots, an a hat tha wrapped aroun his ears. His mammy was takin great care of him, wipin his mouth wit a hankie. 'Now, son, enjoy yer icepop an don't be gettin it all over yer coat.' I stared at her as I rushed past her. Gawd! I'd love her fer me mammy.

'Martha! Can we get an icepop?' Charlie looked up at me. He was about the same age as tha little boy, three years. But his face looked older, a bit like an old man's.

'Yeah! If we find money, we will. Ye never know, we could be lucky.'

We stopped at the Five Lamps on the North Strand, an I waited fer a lull in the traffic te gallop across the road, screamin at Charlie not te let go of the pram. I was tryin te catch up wit Jackser an not get us all kilt at the same time. I dodged out in front of a horse an cart turnin from Portland Row, an it was a race te see which of us got te the middle of the road first. I did!

'Whoa! Whoa!' the driver whipped the snortin horse te a standstill, the wheels of the front of the cart leavin the ground. 'Ye fuckin little bastard, ye nearly got us all put under! I'll fuckin kill ye if I get me hands on ye. Wha did ye go an do tha fer?'

I flew wit the pram, an Charlie was squealin wit fright, grippin the pram te hang on te his life. I bounced the wheels onta the footpath an had a quick look back te see if the man was runnin after me. But he was too busy tryin te steady the horse an calm him down. I slowed down, an Charlie was as white as a sheet. Me heart was goin like the clappers, but I was more afraid of Jackser than I was of the road. I didn't want te lag behind him an drive him mad. Teddy thought tha run was great gas, an he was hoppin up an down fer more, so I shook the pram, an he roared laughin.

We got te the top of Portland Row, an Jackser told me te wait. We were standin on the hill outside the Old Maids' Home. 'I'm just goin over here!' he said, pointin te the Sunset House pub. 'I won't be long,' an he rushed across the road. I stood against the railins of the Old Maids' Home an waited. I was lookin at the name, Sunset House, an thinkin, in the cowboy fillums the two cowboys say te each other, 'We'll have a showdown at sunset!' An they arrive in the middle of the street at sunset wit their spurs clankin an their boots kickin up the dust, an shoot each other. An only one walks away. The other one gets carried in a box te be buried at Boot Hill. I wondered what it must be like te think ye're goin te die at sunset. I wouldn't like te die. I want te grow up an be a fillum star.

Jackser appeared outa the pub. 'Yer mammy's gorra new babby. It's a boy! I'm just goin in fer a quick drink! I won't be long.' I was happy, not about the new babby but cos me ma would be home soon.

The babby was whingin wit the hunger, an we were sittin on the steps rockin the pram, tryin te get him te go te sleep. It was quiet again. The workers on their bicycles were long gone back te work after their dinner break. I looked up an down the road, fed up there was nothin happenin. No one had passed fer a long time. The childre should be home from school soon, so we'll be able te watch them play.

A young one about me own age came flyin down the hill wit a bicycle wheel an a stick. She was doin great, keepin the wheel straight, tappin it wit the stick an runnin fast beside it. I jumped up. 'Hey, young one! Give us a go of yer hoop, will ya?' She stopped an turned the hoop aroun, eyein me.

'Wha have ye got te give us?'

We sized each other up, makin sure we were on safe ground. She worried I might rob her hoop an me wonderin if we'd be all right together. I didn't want any trouble. She had sores all over her face, an her hair was matted. She'd no shoes on her feet, an her big toe was swollen an purple. But tha didn't stop her runnin, even if she was limpin.

'Are ye waitin fer yer ma?'

'No, she's in hospital. She gorra new babby.'

The young one sat down beside me.

'Tha aul fella is in the pub.'

'Who? Yer da?'

'No, he's not me da, only his!' an I pointed te the babby, who was starin outa his pram, takin in everythin, forgettin te cry.

'I live wit me granny aroun the corner on Summerhill.'

'Where's yer mammy?'

'Ah, I'm not bothered. Me granny says she's no good. She was out on the town, pickin up sailors. An now she's a drunkard, livin on the streets. Me granny drinks, too, though. So when she's not in the pub, she's sleepin in the bed. So I can do what I like.'

I looked at her wit me mouth open. 'Ye're so lucky, I wish I was you. An do ye have any brothers an sisters?'

'No. Me granny says me ma had a black one, it was black as the pot! An she says, "Ye're not takin tha home! Ye can get rid of it. I'm not takin care of any more of yer leavins. An don't darken me door again." An wit tha she marched outa the hospital. I was only little at the time, so I don't remember wha she looks like. But me granny tells me these things when she's drunk. I'd better go, me granny sent me fer a message. I have te go all the way up te Ballybough. An tha was ages ago. She'll kill me! See ya!' An she jumped up an hopped off down the hill, smackin her hoop.

I walked up an down pushin the pram, leavin Charlie sleepin on the steps wit his head against the railins. The babby wouldn't stop sobbin. He was exhausted an soakin wet an starved wit the hunger. The mammies had called the childre in fer their tea long ago. If only I could go home. But tha bastard would kill me. I wish he was mashed under a lorry. Why does me ma have te have more babbies? Why is she not like other mammies an make herself busy lookin after us? I hate havin te mind her. I felt like openin me mouth an runnin down the hill, cryin, I want a mammy! Get me a mammy! I'm lost, I'm on me own. Somebody mind me! Lock up Jackser, an put me fuckin ma in a home. That'll teach her. But I kept quiet. I have

186

te wait until I'm big meself, then I'll be somebody, no one will look down on me.

I heard a door slam from aroun the corner. It sounded like the pub. Then shouts. Jackser came reelin aroun the corner, hangin on te the neck of another fella. 'Come on, come on! Ye're comin wit me!' Jackser was sayin. 'Ye'll be all right!'

They lurched across the road, right in front of a bicycle. The bike swerved, an the man landed on the footpath. 'Drunken bastards!' the man roared.

'An fuck you, too,' Jackser roared back, wavin his fist.

I rushed over te Charlie an grabbed him off the steps. 'Get up quick! He's here. Let's get movin fast, before he starts.' I put his hand on the handlebar of the pram, took off the brake an started movin ahead slowly.

'Look, Moocher! This is me son.' I stopped an Moocher looked at the pram.

'Yeah! He's grand, God bless him, the spittin image of ye!'

Jackser leaned inta the pram an pinched the babby's cheek. The babby screamed wit fright, an Jackser couldn't get himself back up. I put the brake on, an he was hurtin the babby wit his elbow. I tried te get him off, an Moocher dragged him up. 'Ah! I'm sorry, I'm sorry! I wouldn't hurt me son fer the world,' he said te Moocher, wipin his long dribbles. 'I'd give me life fer him an me new son! I'm goin te straighten meself out. Nothin will be too good fer them, wait an see,' an then he started cryin. 'I'd give me life, honest te God I would. There'll be no better man. I'm goin te see te tha. Mark me words, Moocher!'

Moocher was agreein wit everythin. An smilin an lookin me up an down. I didn't like tha look in his eyes. He looked at me like I was a woman or somethin. No! I don't like him.

I started te move home, leavin Jackser an Moocher staggerin behind me. I looked back, an they were stopped. Jackser was cryin again. 'Ye're grand! Ye're grand! Ye're sound as a pound!' Moocher was sayin an pattin him on the back. Jackser was wipin his snots wit the sleeve of his coat an long spits comin outa his mouth.

'I'm not tellin ye a word of a lie,' Jackser was whingin. I moved off, hurryin on now. It was dark, an the babby'd get pneumonia from this night air. Charlie kept whinin wit the tiredness. Let us get te bed, God. Just let us get te bed. Tha's all I ask!

I put the babby inta his cot an gave him his bottle of tea an a bit of bread, an I took off Charlie's shoes an trousers an put him inta bed. 'Don't go asleep. I'm bringin ye a sup of tea. Mind tha jam jar, it's hot. Here's yer bread.'

'Mrs, would ye ever get a plate an put out me fuckin chips! They're gone cold. Fer the love of Jaysus, do I have te do it meself?'

'OK, Jackser! I'm runnin te do tha now!'

I rushed inta the scullery an opened the two bags of chips an put them on the two dinner plates we had. I put a few aside fer Charlie an the babby, an pushed two inta me mouth. Then I rushed back in an handed Moocher an Jackser their chips. Jackser grabbed the plate an shovelled a fistful of chips inta his snotty mouth. Moocher laughed an said, 'By God, I could do wit someone like you! How old are ye now?'

'Eight. I'm eight years old.'

'Ah, it won't be long till ye're out workin.'

I ignored him an went back inta the scullery an brought the few chips I'd left te the babby, who threw his empty bottle over the cot. An I managed te catch it before it broke. I took the empty jam jar from Charlie an gave him the rest of the chips. Then I went back inta the scullery an ate me bread an tea. The tea was cold, an there was no margarine left. An we'd have no bread or milk fer the mornin. Them two ate the lot. I put the babby down an covered him up. He went out like a light. Charlie covered himself up an was noddin off, too.

I hesimitated fer a minute, wonderin if I should go te bed wit them two still sittin there. 'Do ye want te go te bed, Jackser? I should put the light out! It's very late now,' I said quietly.

'Wha? Wha?' Jackser muttered. He'd been dozin in the chair. An Moocher was followin me every movement wit his sly eyes.

'Come an sit on me lap!' Moocher said, smackin his knees. I

backed away, headin towards me bed. But Moocher was outa the chair an liftin me on te his lap. I tried te wriggle free, but me frock was caught up aroun me, an I was wearin no knickers or a vest.

'No! Let me down,' I cried. 'I want te get down.' He was laughin an grabbin me arms an pinnin them down by me side. An pressin me hard down inta his lap.

'Be the holy!' Jackser snuffled an laughed. 'She's a fighter!' He kept lookin, an touchin himself, an lookin aroun, an back, snufflin, an givin a laugh. An he looked like he was enjoyin himself. Then he got up an shuffled off te the scullery, mutterin, 'I'll just get a sup of tea.'

Moocher pulled up me frock an jammed his hand between me legs, pullin an draggin at me, an rockin me very hard on his lap. He was red in the face an breathin very heavily. 'Stay quiet! Be still! It won't hurt.'

I arched me back an straightened me legs an slid off his lap. He grabbed me by me hair an yanked me back on te his lap. 'I'll fuckin burst ye!' he said inta me face, wit his eyes bulgin an his teeth gritted. 'Now stay quiet an do as ye're told!'

I couldn't understand why Jackser was lettin him get away wit this. Me heart was hammerin in me chest, an I knew this man would hurt me badly if I didn't stay quiet. He opened his trousers, an a horrible hairy long wet thing slid out. 'Here, pull this!' he said.

I looked away, it was smelly an dirty. He kept pullin at it an rubbin his fist between me legs. Jackser stayed in the scullery. An somethin came pourin outa the thing between his legs, an he pushed me belly down on top of it an nearly smothered me head in his coat. Then he lifted me off him an buttoned his trousers up. I was covered in the smelly sticky stuff an tried te clean meself wit me frock. But the frock was soakin wet, an I was wet all over. Me neck was very sore, cos he'd put his arm aroun me, nearly chokin me. It hurt between me legs, an I felt I'd been put through a mangle. I didn't know wha te do next.

I went te the bed, te climb in beside Charlie. An I heard Jackser an Moocher whisperin an laughin. When I looked towards the scullery, Moocher was givin Jackser money. 'Here's five bob. Tha should see ye straight.'

'Ah, thanks fer tha,' Jackser said. 'Do ye want a cup of tea before ye go?'

'No, ye're all right,' Moocher said.

'I'll be seein ye so,' Jackser said. An I jumped inta bed, coverin me head wit the blanket an coats. Jackser came in snufflin. 'Ah, ye know wha? I miss poor Sally. Where are ye? Get out here, I want te talk te ye.' Me heart hammered through me, an I leapt outa the bed.

'Get in there an sleep beside me! Ye can keep me company until Sally gets home.'

I stood there not takin in wha he was sayin. 'Get in, fer fuck's sake, will ye!' I crawled inta the bed an lay at the very edge an rolled meself inta a tight ball. Jackser climbed inta the bed, an I held meself very still, afraid te breathe. He grabbed me arm an spun me aroun. 'Wha's this? Get tha fuckin thing offa ye.' An he bounced me up te sit me an tore the frock over me head. Then he pushed me down an started maulin me. I went very stiff, tryin te ease the pain, cos he was hurtin me all over. 'Jaysus, there isn't a pick on ye, ye're like chicken bones. Here, pull tha!'

No! No more, I thought. 'Can I not go back te me bed? Please, Jackser, I'm tired.'

'Stay fuckin quiet. Wha's wrong wit ye? Yer mammy loves this.' An then he climbed on top of me. Me head was suffocatin under his chest, an tha hard thing was pressin inta me stomach an hurtin me between me legs an me bones. An he was rockin like mad an snortin, an the filthy smell. An I knew this was hell. I shouldn't have been bold an cursin an fightin an callin people names. If I'd been good, I would have had a bit of peace like other childre.

'Let me up! I'm smotherin!' I tried te move me head, but I was caught under him. I'm drownin. Jackser was snortin louder, rockin himself like mad, an he covered me face even tighter. I was goin te die, lights was flashin on an off in me head. An then it started te go dark. I felt somethin hot spillin over me, then Jackser rolled away. It stopped! It stopped! I'm covered in tha smelly stuff an I can't move meself. I can't straighten me legs. How can I get away from this bed?

Jackser started laughin. 'Jaysus, tha was good! Did ye enjoy tha? Whatever ye do, don't say anythin te yer mammy! She will get mad jealous an think I like ye more than her. Go on, get back te yer bed. An remember what I said. Say nothin te nobody or ye won't live very long! I don't make idle threats, ye should know tha!'

I had me frock on, an I was standin there lookin at the dirty floorboards, waitin fer him te let me go te bed. 'No, Jackser! I won't say anythin.'

Me ma came home from the hospital wit the new babby. She gorra lift home in an ambulance. All the kids came runnin from everywhere te get a look. The ambulance man helped her down the steps. I was delighted, but when I looked at her face, she was very white an tired. 'Ye're home, Ma!' I said smilin.

'Yeah!' she muttered, lookin away from me an then lookin back. Me left eye was closed an all purple. An me cheek an nose was swollen, an me mouth was swollen an cut. Jackser kept punchin me in the face when I tried te stop him climbin on top of me in the bed. 'How did ye get tha face?' me ma asked.

But before I could answer, Jackser lifted me off me feet an ran me in the door. 'Get the fuck in there! I told ye not te show yerself outside this door.'

I ran inside an waited wit me back against the wall. Please, God, don't let him hit me again. I'll be good. I won't curse any more. I was shakin.

Me ma came in slowly, carryin the new babby. She kept her eyes on me, an her mouth was movin very fast, chewin her lip. She wanted te say somethin, but I implored her wit me eyes not te say anythin. He rushed inta the scullery te make the tea. An me ma put the new babby down on the bed an gently lifted the blankets from him te get some air. He was fast asleep. She gently lifted his head an took off the white frilly bonnet he was wearin. Me an Charlie leaned over te get a look. He had long fluffy red hair an a tiny white face an lovely red lips. Then he moved his head an opened his eyes, an they were lovely navy blue. Then he started te cry like a kitten, an Charlie clapped his hands an laughed an looked at me, hoppin aroun, thinkin it was a little doll ye could play wit. Teddy stopped leapin up an down in his cot an roarin te be let out. He listened an pointed his finger at the bed, an said, 'Owo, uwu.' I went over an put the bars down an lifted him out. He flew over on his hands an knees, an grabbed the bed wit his two fists an lifted himself up te stand.

'Here!' Jackser roared. 'Bring this tea inta yer mammy an get them kids away. I don't want them tormentin her. An go down te the shop an get a pint of milk. Hurry! Hurry, Mrs! Put some coal on tha fire before ye go, an go easy on it. The coal has te last.'

I rushed in wit the tea, an me ma was changin the babby. 'Here, put this in the tilet an get me one of them napkins outa tha bag. Tell him I want the bag wit the stuff I got from the lady almoner.'

'Wha stuff? Wha bag, Ma?

'The one wit the blankets an the nightgown fer the babby.' I looked at her, not wantin te ask Jackser anythin. 'Will ye hurry!' me ma roared.

Jackser flew in from the scullery. 'Wha's goin on here? Wha the fuck are ye still doin here, are ye not gone yet?'

'I'm goin, Jackser! Ye haven't given me the money yet.'

He snorted an reached up te the mantelpiece an handed me sixpence. 'Have ye not put coal on tha fire yet, ye lazy bastard?' I grabbed the coal bucket an started te put coal on the fire. 'Rake out the ashes from the bottom first,' he shouted. 'Ye'll put the fire out.' I grabbed the poker an pushed it through the bars of the fire. 'Not too much, ye'll take the heart outa it.'

'OK, Jackser. I'll do it the right way.'

Me ma was keenin an mutterin, 'Jaysus! Why do I have te come back te this place? I wish I was fuckin dead. Ye'd be better off, at least ye'd be away from here.'

I was hurryin down te the shop fer the milk, but I couldn't go very fast. I was hurtin like mad, an I gorra stabbin pain in me head an eye when I moved. 'How're ye?' a young one from the class shouted over te me from the other side of the road. Then she came runnin over. 'Gawd! Wha happened te yer face?' She stared at me wit her mouth open.

'I fell against the wall.'

'How? How did it happen?'

'I just fell, some kids pushed me.'

'Gawd!' she said, drawin in her breath. 'An tell us, why are ye not in school? Flaherty will kill ye!'

'Ah, I don't care about her,' I said.

'But she'll send the school inspector after ye!'

'I don't care.'

'An ye'll be put away in a home!'

'So let them! I don't care.'

'Gawd! Ye're gas ye are, ye're mad.'

'Yeah! See ya! I better hurry. Me ma's waitin on the milk.'

'See ya, Madser!'

I didn't mind too much bein called tha, cos they all called me tha since Flaherty. They didn't mean I was stone mad, just tha I wasn't afraid of anythin or anybody, an I was always laughin an makin jokes so people might like me an let me play wit them. I had te try very hard te be like tha. But it was no good bein quiet or shy.

Jackser started leavin the house early in the mornin. He goes out aroun five or six o'clock when we're all still sleepin. Then he comes back aroun eight or nine o'clock wit women's knickers an slips, an skirts an jumpers. But the funny thing is, they're wet! Me ma tries them on when they're dry, an then he sends me off te the neighbours te sell them. He sent me over wit a black slip an matchin frilly knickers an a lovely white frilly nightdress te the dyed blonde woman who lives over us on the first balcony. She wears paint an powder, an lovely pencil skirts wit a slit down the back. An big high heels wit black stockins, an she's always stoppin te straighten the seams at the back an fix her hair. She's married te a docker, an every Friday night he struts out wit his chest stickin out, an walks like a cowboy, wit the Mrs on his arm. She runs beside him on her high heels, an in her tight skirt, laughin an wavin te all her friends. An

193

ye get a lovely whiff of perfume from them as they pass ye by. The aul ones, leanin on their elbows an hangin over the balconies, shout over, 'Don't do anythin I wouldn't! Or if ye do, call it after me!'

'Ah, go on!' the blonde one shouts back, laughin. 'I'm out te enjoy meself. We'll be a long time dead!'

'Tha ye will, Mrs! True fer ye! Enjoy it while ye can.' An they all nod at each other in agreement.

'Where did ye get these from?' the blonde asked.

'Me ma's sister sent them from England,' I said. 'But me ma has no use fer them.'

'How much do ye want?'

'Half a crown.'

'Ah, no!' an she looked at them inside out. 'Tell ye wha! I don't really want them, but tell yer mammy I'll take them off her hands fer one shillin an sixpence.'

'Ah, they're worth ten bob as they stand,' I said. 'Me aunt paid thirty bob fer the nightdress on its own. It was supposed te be a present fer her after she had the new babby, but me ma wouldn't wear anythin like tha. She's not as glamorous as you!'

The blonde put the nightdress up te herself again, then looked at the slip an matchin knickers. 'Yeah! Go on, then. I'll take them. Here's a half-crown, an if ye get anythin else I'd like, let me know.' She rushed in te the sittin room an said, 'Wait there!' an came back wit a slice of bread an lovely good butter on it. 'Here! Enjoy tha.'

Me heart leapt! The crust was black an crunchy, an the bread was thick an snow white an soft. An the butter was lathered on an was a lovely goldie colour. I was so happy – a half-crown in one hand, tha would put Jackser in a good mood, an a lovely lump of bread an butter in the other. I sat down on the stairs te eat it very slowly, tryin te make it last. An enjoyin the taste like I was in Heaven.

The new babby is called Harry, after Jackser's brother who went te England an never came back. I take him out everywhere in his pram, an Teddy sits at the bottom, holdin onta the handlebars. An Charlie runs beside me, holdin on, too. Harry is very good, he's very quiet. An he's content te lie wit his little head on the pilla while I bounce him along in his pram, takin in all the goins on aroun him. His eyes goes from left te right, missin nothin. The mammies stop te admire him an say he's a gorgeous-lookin babby, God bless him! An Harry jerks his little body an waves his fists an makes an O sound wit his little mouth when anyone leans in te tickle his chin. Teddy smiles, too, an points te the babby, shoutin, 'Babba! Babba!' not wantin te miss out on all the attention.

'An how's yer mammy? Is she on her feet yet?'

'Yeah! She's grand, Mrs, thanks,' I said.

An another mammy joined in te get a look at Harry. 'Ah, look at him! He's lovely, Mrs, isn't he? God bless him an keep him from all harm! Ye're a great little mother, tha's all I can say. Yer mammy would be lost without ye!' I smiled, happy wit meself. Then she looked in her purse an gave us all a penny each.

'Have ye enough there, Mrs?' the other mammy said. 'Don't leave yerself short.'

'Ah, sure it's only a few coppers. It won't break me.'

'Well, if ye're sure then,' an they moved off together, their heads bent close together, tellin each other a bit of scandal.

I rushed down te the shops te buy sweets. 'Charlie! Don't say we got money. Don't tell me ma or Jackser, or they'll kill us fer not givin it te them. We'll spend the money on sweets an say nothin, all right?'

'Yeah!' Charlie said. 'I'll buy meself loads a sweets.'

195

21

Jackser was walkin up an down the room wit the letter in his hand. He was ragin. 'Can ye beat tha, Sally? They're goin te evict us!'

Me ma was sittin in the chair, starin inta the empty grate, workin her lip up an down, chewin her lip. 'I don't know,' she was mutterin te herself. 'Ye'd be better off dead. The sooner the better I'm six foot under, it won't be quick enough fer me.'

The babby was cranky, cos he was gettin his teeth, an I was kneelin by the cot, strokin an rubbin him, an givin him his soother, tryin te get him te sleep. But I was feelin a bit exposed now. Jackser could have one of his fits any minute wit the mood he was in an turn on me, sendin me flyin wit a kick of his boot.

'Isn't tha wha the letter says, Mrs? Are ye payin any fuckin heed te what I'm sayin? We'll be all out on the street!' Jackser roared at me ma.

Me ma turned on him. 'It's not my fuckin fault ye drank the money instead of payin the rent!'

'Shush, Ma! Shush,' I whispered.

Jackser glared at me. 'You an her, an the rest of ye's, will be all back in the Regina Ceoli hostel walkin the streets again. An I'll have te go next door te the Mornin Star!'

Me heart lifted! No more Jackser! Oh, dear God, let tha come true!

'Mrs! Get up off yer arse an start thinkin. They can't put us out on the street wit the childre. I don't care what anyone says. Wha we'll do is ... go after Frank Sherwin, he looks after the poor man, an get

196

him te do somethin fer us. An if tha fails, we'll take the childre inta the Corporation an stay there. Not move until they house us. Wha do ye think of tha, Sally? Do ye think we're on the right track?'

'I don't know,' me ma said slowly, runnin her fingers through her hair, lookin fer lice. 'Ye'd be askin fer trouble. They'd take the childre away, sayin they were neglected, an put them inta a home.'

Jackser clenched his fists an rolled his eyes te the ceilin. 'Holy Jaysus, Mrs! Then have ye any better suggestions?' he roared at me ma.

'I don't know! Wha can I do?' me ma shouted back. 'We're in arrears. The fuckin rent wasn't paid in a long time, an now ye're complainin when it's too late!'

Jackser was thinkin. 'If all else fails, we can take the childre an wait until them red-neck bastardin priests are up on the altar givin out the Mass. An wit the church crowded, we march up onta the altar an expose them all – the priests, the TDs – an show the people wha holy Catholic Ireland are doin te the poor. Puttin innocent women an childre out on the streets te die! That'll make them sit up an take notice of us! Wha do ye think, Sally?'

I gorra terrible picture of the childre from school all gapin up at us. The neighbours would say we're a holy disgrace an we're stone mad! No! I'm runnin away. I'll hide somewhere. I'll find tha young one who lives in Summerhill an ask her te let me come an live wit her an the granny. Right! Tha's what I'll do!

'Do ye think tha would work, Sally?'

Me ma turned her head te the wall. 'Yeah! If ye want te get us all arrested!'

Jackser thought about this fer a minute an said, 'Pity! I'll give tha a miss. But there's nothin I'd like better than te expose them bastards fer wha they did te me an me brother Eddie fer nine long years in Artane. I was only seven years old, an me brother was eight when me poor mother put us in. She'd no way of lookin after us!'

Jackser shook his head an got lost in his own thoughts. He doesn't say much about it, but occasionally, when he's gone too far an can't stop himself from givin me an awful batterin, he'll say tha's the way he was trained in Artane. Tha it will be good fer me, a soft life never did anyone any good.

Jackser started snufflin an shook himself. 'Right! I'll have a shave. Here, you! There's tuppence. Get down te tha shop an get me a Silver Gillette blade. An don't be there till ye're back. Run! I'm goin te see tha Frank Sherwin!'

I shot outa the flats an whipped left, headin like the wind down te the shops. An suddenly, outa nowhere, an aul fella in a brown gaberdine coat an bicycle clips on his ankles te keep his trousers from catchin in the wheels slammed onta the footpath in front of me. He was in such a hurry te stop, he overbalanced the bike an was dancin his leg up an down te try an steady himself. 'Hey, you!' he shouted at me, an grabbed out his arm te hold me. He grabbed the hem of me frock, but I turned so suddenly he lost his grip an fell flat on the pavement.

I ran back, headin fer the flats, screamin in fright. 'Ah, help! Mammy! It's the school inspector, he's goin te catch me!' Me legs an arms was like propellers as I flew. Me heart was burstin in me chest from the shock. Don't let him catch me! I looked ahead te our flat an thought better of goin there. Jackser would murder me fer drawin the inspector there. I looked back, an he was turnin inta the flats, his knees pushin down hard on the pedals an his neck stuck out, tryin te pedal as fast as he could. I headed fer the stairs an tore up them, haulin meself up holdin onta the banisters.

When I reached the top, I crept along the balcony an waited, tryin te ease me poundin heart an quieten me breathin. I had te listen in case he crept up on me. Then I heard the bangin on the door an rattlin like mad on the letter box. Jackser wouldn't open the door. When someone bangs like tha on the door, Jackser knows it's trouble an won't open.

'Open up! I know you're in there. I saw you!' The inspector was bendin down an shoutin in the letter box. 'I'm warning you! This is your last warning. If you don't get that child to school, you will be brought to court, and she'll be taken away and put into an industrial school!'

I watched him, peepin over the balcony, an then he stood up an was writin down somethin in a book. What am I goin te do? I need te get the blade fer Jackser. He'll go mad I'm takin so long, especially after tha aul fella callin. I lashed down the stairs an stopped, peepin aroun te see if he was lookin. He was busy fixin his bicycle clips. I shot off an flew fer all I was worth, lookin back when I hit the corner. No sign of him. Good! I'll make it inta the shops before he comes down, then I'll have te hide an watch until he passes. There he goes! He turned right at the church, an I waited till I was sure he was gone. Then I took off, runnin as fast as I could te get back wit the blade.

Me ma went off wit Jackser, an I was mindin the childre. 'Here! Get them ready an get outside an let them get an airin!' Jackser said. I was delighted. I could get te watch all the childre playin. It was better than bein stuck in the house.

I put the babby in his pram, an he was squealin wit excitement. He knew he was goin out. Teddy was shoutin, tryin te get his shoe on the wrong foot an worried I might leave without him. 'Where's yer other shoe?' I asked him. He was lookin aroun, an I said, 'Charlie, get under the bed an see if it's there.' I got Teddy ready an told Charlie te put his shoes on the right feet or the childre will be laughin at him. We were out the door, an I banged it shut behind me.

It was still too early fer the childre te be home from school, so I headed outa the flats, wit Teddy hangin on te the handlebars. He was seventeen months now an was walkin. Charlie was hangin onta the other side. I could hear the childre playin an shoutin in the school yard. They were on their dinner break. We headed towards the bridge an stopped at the canal. But there was nobody there. Sometimes ye see the childre playin here when they're mitchin from school. The young fellas build a raft an try te paddle it along the bank. Tha's very dangerous! Cos a few of them have been drownded, but it doesn't stop them fer long, an then they're at it again, hidin their schoolbags in the bushes an fightin over who's goin te be Davy Crockett, King of the Wild Frontier!

I sat meself down, an Charlie started te look fer somethin te throw in the water. Teddy sat down on his hunkers beside me an was pokin at a long worm wrigglin in the grass. I was rockin Harry in the pram, who was sittin up contentedly suckin on his soother an watchin Teddy pokin the worm an squealin wit fright an then delight, when I heard a shufflin noise behind me in the bushes. I looked aroun an saw two young fellas crawlin in the grass. An then they jumped up an threw a stone at us. Then they laughed an ran inta the bushes. I stood up an shouted, 'Come out, ye cowards! I saw ye!' But they didn't move.

'Come over here, Charlie. Stay beside me where I can keep an eye on ye.' An I sat down again, watchin out fer them young fellas. Then one of them stood up, an I saw they were the Kelly brothers from me flats. They were big young fellas, tha one was eleven an his brother was ten.

'Keep away from me or ye'll be sorry!' I shouted. Then he threw another stone, missin Teddy's head by an inch. I stood up te grab Teddy an get goin as fast as I could. But another stone hit the babby on the forehead, an he screamed. I grabbed his head te rub it an looked te see if he was all right. A big lump was comin out, an the young fellas started laughin.

'Ye bastards!' I screamed, an tore at them, catchin the big fella by surprise. I lunged at his hair just as he turned te run, an knocked him off balance. He fell forward, an I pressed me knees inta his back, grabbin his hair an shakin his head, pressin his face inta the ground. 'Ah, ye bastard!' I screamed. 'I'm goin te fuckin kill ye!'

The other young fella came back, shoutin, 'Get up, Lasher! Don't let her mill ye. She's only a young one. They can't fight.' He kept comin closer, dancin aroun me wit his fists closed, tryin te get an openin.

'Help me, Wacker! The cow is killin me!' Lasher screamed.

'Come near me an I'll tear ye apart,' I screamed at Wacker. The childre were screamin in fright behind me.

'Let me up an I'll give ye a penny.'

'No!' I shouted. 'Ye hurt me babby brother. Ye're a fuckin coward, an I'm goin te teach ye not te pick on little kids.'

I slapped an dragged his head, feelin the rage roar up in me, an, usin what I got from Jackser, I tore inta him. The other young fella lashed out wit his foot, kickin me in the side. I let go a Lasher an whipped a hold a Wacker. 'Ah, no. I'm sorry!' he shouted, tryin te peel me hands offa his hair.

Lasher dragged himself up an shouted, 'OK, OK! You win. Let him go an we'll give ye a penny each!'

'Are ye sorry, then?' I shouted.

'Yeah! Yeah! We are.'

'Say it, then!' an I shook Wacker's head.

'We're sorry, we shouldn't a thrown stones at the babby. We didn't mean it.'

I let go an Lasher ran off wit me penny. I grabbed hold of Wacker again. 'Ah, give her the money! Let me go!'

Lasher came back slowly an threw the penny on the grass.

'Now your turn, show me yer penny,' I said te Wacker.

'Let me go, then!'

I grabbed hold of his jumper. 'Show me the penny!' I shouted.

'All right! Take it easy, I'm givin it te ye!'

I got the penny from him, an Lasher came closer. His nose was red from the bashin he got. 'Lookit, if ye don't say anythin te anybody about us, tha ye milled us, then we won't get our gang after ye! Is tha a deal?'

'I'm not afraid of yer gang,' I snorted.

'Yeah! All right, we know. But ye'd still get kilt. So will ye say nothin?'

I thought about it. 'Well, if I get inta any trouble wit anybody, will youse help me?'

'Yeah! Course we will.'

'All right, then,' I said, an they went off happy.

I rushed back te Harry, who was sittin there keenin. He had a big red lump on his forehead. I gave him a kiss an rubbed his head, an looked at Charlie, who was squattin down beside Teddy. He was white. I said, 'Come on. We'll go down an buy sweets.'

Teddy jumped up, puttin his arse in the air first an then pushin

201

his hands te get himself standin. An Charlie rubbed his hands together, laughin wit excitement. We went off slowly, headin down fer the shops, but me heart was heavy, all the enjoyment gone from me. I was frettin about wha Jackser was goin te do te me when he sees the babby's head. He'll blame me fer not lookin after the babby properly. I went te the end of Sheriff Street an parked the pram outside, puttin on the brake an makin sure I could still see the babby.

I went down the steps an inta the shop. It was dark inside, cos the sun doesn't shine down this far an the door is too narra. I lifted Teddy onta the counter an hauled meself up te get a look over at the sweets in their boxes. Teddy started shoutin an wringin his hands wit impatience. 'Yeah! Yeah! We're gettin them,' I laughed at him. 'Wha do ye want, Charlie?'

'Sweets! Gimme sweets!' He was jumpin up an down, holdin on te the counter, cos he couldn't see anythin.

'Wha do ye's want?' the aul one behind the counter asked.

'Eh, I'll have . . .' I couldn't make up me mind.

'How much have ye got?' the aul one asked me, gettin impatient.

'Tuppence, Mrs! But I mightn't be spendin it all here!'

'Oh, the Lord be! So I'd better not be thinkin of shuttin up shop fer the day, then.'

'Right! Me mind's made up! I'll have three black jacks, tha's a ha'penny. Tha's fer Charlie. I'll have three jelly babies. Tha's fer Teddy.' He screamed wit impatience when I mentioned his name.

'Hurry up!' the aul one roared. 'I haven't all day.'

'Right! I'm gettin there, Mrs. Give me time, I'm a payin customer!'

'I'll have none of yer cheek or ye can take yer custom elsewhere!'

'Right, an gimme a mouse fer the babby. It's soft an he won't choke, cos he only has six teeth!'

She slammed the sweets on the counter. 'Tha will be one penny!'

'Have ye a bag fer them, Mrs?'

'It's a pity about ye! Take the sweets an get out!'

'I only asked ye. A bit of politeness goes a long way,' I said.

'Ye's are barred,' she roared at me.

I snorted an let go of the counter. An slid down, grabbin hold of Teddy an slidin him down, catchin him wit me belly pressed against the counter an puttin him on his feet.

I walked up the steps, countin the sweets te make sure they were all there. An Charlie an Teddy roared after me, wantin their sweets. I stepped out inta the sunshine an took the brake off. 'Charlie! Help Teddy up the steps, take his hand.' But Teddy shook away Charlie's hand an came up the steps on his hands an knees in an awful hurry. I pushed the pram back up the road an sat down on the steps of an old house. The roars outa them! Even the babby was screamin an wavin his hands. He'd seen the sweets an threw his soother inta the pram, his eyes glued te the sweets.

'Here's yer jelly babies, Teddy! Sit down beside me an put yer two hands out!' I put the jelly babies inta his hands an closed his fingers. He was quiet while he had a good look at them, before puttin them in his mouth.

'Me! Me!' Charlie was shoutin.

'Here ye are! Hold yer horses, there's yer black jacks.' An then I gave the babby his marshmallow mouse. An he looked at it, wit the tail an the eyes, an then looked up at me. 'Yes! Eat it! It's lovely.' An he put it in his mouth an started suckin it. He was delighted wit the taste an took it back out te give me a big smile wit his six teeth. An me heart turned over cos of the big lump on his poor forehead. I gave him a squeeze, an he roared, cos he thought I was tryin te take his mouse.

I sat down an was enjoyin the heat from the sunshine. Teddy was happy, climbin up an down on the wide steps, an Charlie was lookin in the shop windas at the cakes. His mind was always on grub. It would be great if I didn't have te worry about Jackser goin mad cos the babby got hurt.

People were passin up an down, stoppin te talk te each other. One woman stopped wit a big fat purse in her hand an a shoppin bag in the other. 'There ye are!' she said te another woman, who had hair rollers in her head an was tryin te hide them wit a scarf tied aroun her head. 'Are ye gettin yerself ready?' she laughed, lookin at the hair rollers.

'Yeah!' Hair Rollers said. 'I'm nearly all done. This daughter's weddin will be the death a me yet! The fella she's marryin has relations comin back from England. Well, as I said, Mrs, he needn't think I'm puttin them up! I've enough of me own crowd te be worryin about.'

'Go way! Ye're right there. Ye'd only be a fool te yerself! They won't thank ye if ye're dead an buried in the mornin from all yer exertations!'

'No, indeed they won't, Mrs!' Hair Rollers was enjoyin herself no end. She was enjoyin all the glamour of it all, wit people comin all the way from England. 'I got the new wallpaper!'

The woman wit the purse checked te see if she still had it an shook herself, pulled wit the excitement of hearin it all an jealous cos it wasn't happenin te her. 'Go on! Tell us more.'

'It's only gorgeous, Mrs!' an she slapped the other woman's hand.

'Go way!' Purse said.

'Yeah, it's heavy red flock wit big white roses. I gorrit on Capel Street. Now tha it's up, I can't stop lookin at it. Even me neighbours think it's lovely. They've been in an outa the house, havin cups of tea an askin if there's anythin I want help wit. They're lendin me chairs, an old Granny Egan is lendin me her china teacups an saucers an matchin plates from her china cabinet. I'm nearly there. Me sisters are cookin the big lump a bacon an a leg a lamb I got. An the neighbours are makin a ton a sambidges. An he has a man tha works fer Guinness's, so the barrel a porter is sorted.'

'Ah, it will be lovely!' Purse said. 'I'm delighted fer ye!'

'Right then, I'd better run. I'll catch up wit ye again,' Hair Rollers said. An off they went about their business. I watched them go, takin the excitement wit them.

Fer a few minutes, I lost the run of meself. Thinkin I was part of it all. Now I felt empty. Teddy was fed up an tired. He was leanin in me lap an slappin me. He wanted te climb inta the pram an get a sleep. Harry was sleepin, so I stood up an fixed his pilla, pullin him down te stretch out an get more comfortable. I pulled up the hood te keep out the sun an said te Teddy, 'Come on, we'll see wha's in the shop winda! Charlie, you sit there an rest, an keep an eye on the babby.'

We walked slowly down te the shop an stopped te look in the winda. I looked at the lovely little dolls. They cost sixpence. If I could get the money te buy one of them, I'd be so happy. I've never had a doll. I'd get meself a shoebox an make a bed fer it. I could put holes in the arms of old rags an dress the doll. I'd never stop playin wit it. Tha would be heaven. Teddy started roarin his head off an pullin me hand. He wanted te go back an sleep in the pram. 'Come on, then, off we go,' I said te him. He wanted me te carry him, but he was too heavy fer me. I started te pretend te run wit him, te make him laugh, but he was rubbin his eyes exhausted. 'All right! Martha will put ye te sleep. Let's go.'

I started te walk home wit the pram, wonderin if maybe they might be back now. An I didn't see them passin me, so I started te hurry. I put Teddy sittin in the bottom of the pram an told him not te lie down on the babby's feet. I looked at Charlie runnin beside the pram. 'Are ye all right, Charlie? Maybe me ma's home.'

'Yeah!' Charlie said, his spirits liftin at the thoughts of gettin in fer a rest an maybe somethin te eat.

'Come on, Mrs! Hurry yerself. We want te get down te tha Corporation Office while them fuckers are still awake!'

'Ah, will ye leave me? I'm goin as fast as I can. Here, you,' me ma turned te me. 'Wheel the babby outside.'

'OK, Ma. I'll just put Teddy's coat on, then I'll do it.'

'Will ye get the pram outa me way!' me ma roared at me. 'I can't move meself in this kip!'

'Wha the fuck is goin on in there?' Jackser came rushin in an stared at me. I ran fer the pram an made te open the door, an Jackser grabbed me by me neck an lifted me offa me feet. 'Do as ye're told!' He shook me up an down. I was chokin an red in the face. Then he dropped me. I was coughin an picked meself off the floor an ran fer the pram.

'Yeah, Jackser,' I croaked, coughin an tryin te get me breath.

I stood holdin the pram, waitin. 'Don't be told te do anythin twice,' he said, pointin his finger in me face.

'No, Jackser!'

'An another thing! Ye won't be sleepin in tha bed tonight. Ye can sleep on the concrete floor in the scullery. Tha should put a stop te yer pissin the bed.'

Me heart sank, an I wheeled the pram outside. Every night now I've been dragged outa the bed from me sleep. I've been tryin te stop wettin the bed, but I dream I'm on the tilet, an then I just let go. An then Jackser yanks me outa the bed an spins me aroun the floor, an I don't know wha's happenin. He's standin over me shoutin, an I look at him not knowin wha's wrong until I get me senses, an he's screamin, 'Ye wet the bed! Look!' An I get down on me hands an knees, an he pushes me head under the bed te see the pool of piss on the floor.

I came rushin back in. 'Right, Ma! Are ye ready?' I whispered. Me ma gave me tha look, lookin inta me eyes te see if I'm all right. She was sorry she got me inta trouble.

'Don't mind him,' she muttered te me.

I looked at her without sayin anythin, but she knew I was desperate fer her te leave him. She looked away, an me heart went cold against her. I'm on me own, an I don't belong te her. She has Jackser te mind her now.

'Right, Sally. Let's go! Now, let me do all the talkin, we have te make these fuckers sit up an take notice. Ye never know, we could turn this inta our advantage an maybe even get a nice house outa them if we play our cards right. Ye have everythin?'

'Yes! Yes!' me ma said.

'Have ye the letter from the hospital? An the one from the doctor, sayin ye're under his care?'

'Yes, I told ye!'

Jackser snuffled an shook himself. 'Right, you! Stay here an mind the house. We don't want ye earwiggin an listenin te everythin tha's goin on an maybe givin the game away.'

I look at me ma an whispered when he was gone out the door, 'Ma! Ask him te let me go out an play. Will ye, Ma? Please!'

She looked at me an chewed her lip, an then gave a little cough. 'Eh, let her out on the street. She'd be better off runnin aroun.'

He looked at me, an me ma shouted, 'Go on, then, if ye're goin.' I hesimitated fer a split second, watchin Jackser, an when he said nothin, I rushed out the door. He slammed it shut behind him, an I stood there watchin them go.

When they were outa sight, I let me breath go an felt meself go lovely an light. I wandered over te the waste ground an sat at the railins. The gates were always kept locked. Nobody was aroun yet. It was too early in the mornin. The childre were gone te school, an it was very quiet. I didn't mind. I was enjoyin sittin here havin nothin te worry about an no one te bother me. I looked through the bars an spotted a roller skate someone had thrown away. It was broken, but the two halves were there. I climbed up on top of the gate. It was very high up, an the spokes on the top were treacherous. I climbed over them, takin me time, an then slid down on the inside, lettin go of the bars an jumpin on te the grass. I picked me way over the broken glass, not wantin te cut me bare feet. The roller skate was grand. If I tie the two ends together wit twine, I could skate aroun te me heart's content. I looked aroun, searchin fer a bit of twine or somethin te tie it wit, but I had no luck.

I climbed back over the gate, an a bolt of lightnin went through me from the pain of hurtin meself on the spikes. When the pain eased, I lowered meself down slowly an limped off wit me two-half roller skate, an rubbed me belly te ease the pain.

I was wanderin aroun tryin te find somethin, an then I gorra great idea! I'll try the shops. They always have plenty of twine, an I might be able te get some. The butcher gave me a big bit of twine an told me not te play on the road, te go back inta the flats. An I said, 'Thanks, Mister.' I was lookin back at him an wasn't mindin where I was goin, an I walked on a mangy dog sittin at the door waitin fer a bone. It snapped its jaws at me leg, an I leapt inta the air wit fright. But the dog missed me an didn't get a bite of me leg. I walked off

207

slowly, watchin him te see if he'd come at me again, but he threw himself back on the ground te wait. I ran off, an when I looked back, the dog gave a big screech an was sent flyin out the door wit a kick from the butcher. 'Get outa there, ye mangy bag a bones!' the butcher roared. An I ran on laughin. Serves ye right, tryin te bite me! I thought.

I tied the two halves of me roller skate together, an it held. Then I put the twine through the two holes at the back te tie it on me foot. It was grand. But then the twine cut inta me bare foot, an I had te take it off. I have te find somethin te cover me foot. I found an old woolly hat along the side of the road. It was a bit smelly an dirty. I looked at it, but I couldn't find anythin else. This'll do! It worked great, an I'm havin the time of me life runnin up an down, get goin, an lift me other foot, an I'm flyin. I had a great time all day on the roller skate. But then it kept gettin loose, an I kept tryin te fix it. But now I'd had enough.

I was sittin down wit me back against the pram sheds, watchin the other childre runnin up an down, playin chasin, an piggybeds, when a young one passed by me. I looked at her, cos she seems te be very upset. She just walks very fast an stares straight ahead. I know her te see, but I never played wit her, cos she lives in the next flats just beside mine. Her name is Nora, the same name as the song everyone is singing. I watched her walk on, not stoppin te look left or right, an wondered wha happened te her. It wasn't long after tha I heard screams an saw people runnin inta the next flats. I got up, an then I heard shouts. 'She's fallen over the balcony!' I ran in, an there was Nora lyin on the ground at the pram sheds. She was very still, not movin. I looked from her te the balcony, an I wondered how she fell so far across te the pram sheds. She was lyin on her stomach wit her left arm under her. There was no one aroun her. 'Don't touch her!' a woman screamed, an she came runnin across. She ran aroun Nora, not gettin too close, wit her arms out, wantin te keep everyone away.

We just stood starin across at Nora lyin there not movin, too shocked te take it in. 'She fell from the second balcony!' one of the childre whispered. 'I sawed her standin on the top of it.'

'She's my size,' another one said. 'She's nine, like me.'

A woman came rushin over an put a coat over Nora. Then an ambulance arrived, an a man came te put us all outa the way.

I ran up the road te the back shops. Didn't know where I was goin, but then I stopped just before I got there an ran inta the open waste ground an sat down. Why was Nora so upset? Wha happened? Me heart was bleedin fer her. Poor Nora, lyin there so still. I was afraid an I cried fer Nora, an it was as if I knew her. Could somethin like tha happen te me, too? I felt as if I was all by meself in the world an it would always be like this. But I never found out wha happened te Nora, cos we moved house.

22

The Corporation evicted us te the Corporation Buildins. Some people call it the Cage! They laugh an say the police used te have te come in crowds, cos they were afraid of their life te come on their own. It's beside Foley Street an just off Talbot Street. Ye step inta a little hallway, an there's four doors. We're on the ground floor, an there's balconies overhead. Our door is first on the left of the hallway, an we have a winda lookin onta the front. The room is very small, an we all have te sleep in one bed, cos tha's all we can fit in. The table fer eatin off sits at the end of the bed, an we have one chair beside the fireplace. An a little scullery wit a sink an a gas cooker – tha's it. We put the babby's pram under the winda, an there's very little room te move. A woman wit long grey hair, an two childre, a boy an a girl – the boy is about ten years old an the girl is about eleven – live across the hall from us. An old man lives in the other room, an the fourth room is empty. Some of the people manage te get two an three rooms as they become empty in their hallway, an pay the extra money fer each of the rooms.

Jackser's goin mad, cos the room's too cramped. We're all fallin over each other. He can't walk up an down when he's restless, an he keeps clenchin his fists an punchin his hands against each other. 'Ah, fuck this, I'm gettin outa here!' an he runs out the door. 'I'm goin te see a fella I know,' he says, an he disappears.

Me ma goes mad. 'Where are ye goin te?' she shouts, but he's gone. 'Get after him!' she shouts at me. 'See wha he's up te.'

'No, Ma! Let him go.'

'But he's up te no good!' me ma says.

210

'How do ye know, Ma? He'll be back,' I said.

'Yeah! When he gets wha he wants from some dyed blonde.'

Me heart sinks te see me ma worryin. But I'm annoyed, too. Now we have a bit of peace. 'Yeah! An there's fuck all te eat!' she says.

'Can I go out te play, Ma?'

'Ah, don't be annoyin me. Here, get the pillacase an get up te the convent an get the bread!'

I take the tuppence fer the bus fare there an back, an walk up an get the number twenty-four bus te Marino. I get off an walk up Griffith Avenue wit all the big houses an gardens an trees, an then arrive at the gates of the Cross an Passion convent an walk up the avenue an past the big front door wit the steps up te it. An go aroun the side te the back door an ring the bell only once. An then I wait fer the nun te come an open the door. If ye ring twice, they give ye nothin.

The door opens after a while, an the nun just looks at me an says nothin an closes the door again. I can be up te an hour waitin here, an it's very quiet. I sit meself down on the step an look at the green grass an admire the huge conifers – tha's what a young nun told me they were called. She came out wit a load of other young nuns. They all had black lace hankies on their heads, an they still had their lovely shiny hair, so they weren't real nuns yet. The ground was covered in snow at the time, an they came runnin out te throw snowballs at each other. I watched them havin a great time, pickin the snow up an beltin each other, an roarin an laughin, an sayin, 'Oh, blast!' Tha was supposed te be a curse! I thought they were real grand. They looked so shiny an clean wit lovely red cheeks an a Gibbs toothpaste smile full of white teeth. They thought the snow was lovely, an it did look lovely an white here. But I hated it, cos I was always freezin wit the cold, an me bare feet an hands was killin me wit the pain. I admired them no end an wanted te come an live here an be just like them, eatin an prayin, an sleepin in a bed wit white sheets. An bein shiny an clean, an have shoes an warm knickers. An rush aroun in the snow, an say 'Oh, blast!' an be very grand altogether.

I came outa me daze when I suddenly heard a noise. I looked up an saw a tramp come shufflin over. He was wearin about six coats an had a bit of twine wrapped aroun his waist. I turned away an ignored him. After a few minutes, he crept over beside me. 'Did ye ring the bell?' he whispered inta me face.

The smell of him was terrible. I moved away an didn't look at him. 'Yeah!' I muttered.

A few minutes later, I heard hissin noises. I looked over te see what it was, an the tramp nodded over te the trees. 'Come over there wit me, an I'll give ye sixpence!' He showed me the sixpence in his hand, an he was wearin black gloves wit no fingers in them. I looked at his face. It was red, an his eyes was dancin in his head. I didn't like the look of them eyes.

Me mind flew. I can't run off without me bread, an, anyway, I was here first! I jumped up an rang the doorbell. 'I'm gettin the nun fer you. An I'm tellin her wha ye said te me.'

'No! No! Don't do tha!' he said. 'Oh, Holy Mother of God!' an he rushed off, tryin te shuffle fast, hangin on te his coats.

The nun didn't come out fer a long while. 'Did you ring this bell?' She stared at me wit her lips pressed together.

I looked aroun me te see if he was still gone an satisfied meself he was not comin back. I said, 'No, Sister! A man did, but he's gone now!'

'You'll have to wait,' she said. 'I'm busy.'

'Ah, Sister, would ye have a drink of water? I'm parched, Sister.'

A while later, the door opened, an the nun handed me a tin mug wit hot water. I was disgusted! She took it from the hot tap! I drank half an handed the mug back. She had a smirk on her face an a glint in her eye. She's bad, I thought te meself. Nuns are supposed te be holy.

I took the leftover bits of bread she gave me thrown together in greasepaper. An put it in me pillacase tha was black wit the dirt an covered in blood spots from all the bites we get from the fleas. Pity I didn't get a nice nun. Once in a while, I can strike lucky an get bread an drippin, an even roast meat. The nun who gives me the bit of bacon, an maybe even a leg a lamb, doesn't seem te be there any more. Me ma will go mad an start givin out. 'Why did the nun not give ye anythin? Did ye ask her? Wha did ye say? Did ye not tell her this, why didn't ye tell her tha?' An me ma will keep at me until the next time I bring home somethin good. I always like te see me ma's face light up when she's happy, an have maybe five Woodbines fer Jackser, te put him in good form. But I've nothin te bring home, an nobody will be laughin.

I hurry over te the other convent, High Park, an pass the shops. I get an idea an rush inta the butchers. 'Eh, excuse me, Sir, but would ye ever have any bones fer the dog?'

The butcher is very respectable, an he stands back an looks at me. He picks up a chunk of lap a lamb, an wraps it an hands it te me.

'Eh, I didn't mean fer te buy.'

'Yes! Yes! That's all right,' an he waves his hand at me.

I'm delighted an put it in me pillacase. 'Thanks very much, Mister!' an I rush off.

I ring the bell at the convent, an Hairy comes out, looks at me an smirks, closes the door an I wait, hoppin up an down on the pebble stones on the ground, makin a crunchin noise under me feet. I got inta terrible trouble wit the nun once. I was dyin te go te the tilet but was afraid te go in the bushes in case she came out an I missed her. So I squatted on the ground in front of the hall door an was pissin away when the door opened an the nun's eyes met mine. We were both shocked, but I had te continue me pissin. She told me I had te send me mother, an she didn't want te see me face again. So far, I've been lucky. She hasn't opened the door fer me.

Hairy came out an handed me two stale loaves. I put them in me pillacase an put it over me shoulder, an decided te go out the back way. As I was passin the chapel, I saw a bicycle parked outside wit a black saddlebag strapped on the back. I peeked inta the chapel te see wha was goin on. The priest was sayin Mass. I shut the door quickly, tha must be his bike! I hesimitated fer a minute an put down me pillacase. I'll just have a look in the bag. I undid the straps, an the bag was filled wit ten-pack Carroll cigarettes! Me eyes lit up. Cigarettes! Jackser! Ah, no, he doesn't smoke these. He'd only smoke Woodbines. Then I had an idea. I filled me pillacase wit the cigarettes an rushed off. Aroun by the childre's home, past the farm, down the back lane, out the gate, an on te the road headin fer Drumcondra. Down the hill I flew, across Griffith Avenue wit the Whitehall police station on me right.

I stopped at the traffic lights, an gave a quick look over te see if the alarm had been raised an they were searchin fer me. Me heart was pumpin. I took out a ten pack of Carrolls an walked inta the shop an put them on the counter. 'Me da says I'm te bring these back, cos it's ten Woodbines he wants. I got the wrong ones!'

The woman looked over the counter at me. 'Did ye buy these here?'

'Yeah, I did!'

She looked at them an looked at me. 'I don't remember servin you.'

'Oh, yes, Mam! I bought them here all right!'

She looked me straight in the eye. I didn't move a muscle. 'All right, then.'

I let me breath out slowly. She handed me ten Woodbines, an change! I was out the door an inta the next shop. A few people were waitin te be served. I looked around. It was a vegebale an grocery shop. There were shoppin bags wit food lined against the walls waitin fer collection. Gawd! They're very respectable, the people livin aroun here, they get their messages done fer them.

I hesimitated fer a second – nobody lookin! I grabbed one of the shoppin bags an flew out the door. I tore up the hill an sat down on a bench outside the Bishop's Palace, an opened the bag. I pulled out a chicken wit some of its feathers still stuck te it, an it still had its head an the eyes were closed, an I was very disappointed. A chicken! But it wasn't cooked, an me ma doesn't know how te cook. I left the chicken beside me on the seat wit its two front legs stickin up in the air an looked in the bag. A packet of tea wit a picture on it of a woman holdin a basket full of tea leaves. I put tha down beside the chicken. A red jelly, an me ma can't make jelly either! I asked her once, when I came outa the hospital, te make jelly, an she said ye need an ice box.

Maybe we can eat it raw. A jar of marmalade an a packet of Jacob's Cream Crackers. Tha's the lot. I opened the side of the bag an found a purse. It had half a crown ! Ah, Gawd! Me ma'll go mad wit delight, an Jackser will be over the moon wit his Woodbines.

I put everythin back in the bag an rushed on, goin from shop te shop until I had got rid of all the Carroll cigarettes an changed them fer Woodbines. I kept the half-crown fer me ma an spent the change from the cigarettes. I bought a packet of oxtail soup fer the meat, an a half-pound of margarine, an a pound of sugar. An I bought sweets fer the childre an a banana fer the babby Harry. An a choc ice fer meself an a *Bunty* comic. I better not let Jackser see the comic or he'll rip it te shreds. He goes mad if he catches me lookin at comics. He says I'm idlin, but I just love te look at the comics, especially the *Bunty*. I can't read them, but I look at the pictures an follow the story tha way. But tha's not enough fer me any more. I want te know wha they're sayin. So I'm mad te learn te read. I know the letters, an now I'm goin aroun spellin all the signs on the buses, an the shop names, an the billboards on the walls. Anywhere I see writin, I spell it, an then break it in half an get the sound, an then put them together an say the word. I do tha now wit me comics, an I'm nearly gettin there. Soon, I'll be able te read.

Jackser's gone mad on the drink. Our nerves are gone very bad, sittin in the dark waitin fer him te come home. Me ma sits on the chair lookin out the winda. I go te bed an pray there will be no more trouble. I roll meself inta a ball, cos every night Jackser kicks the legs an back off me, cos he says I'm te get me fuckin legs away from him. I don't know I'm touchin him, cos I'm in me sleep. An he stretches his feet all the way down te me back. Me ma keeps mutterin te me from the winda. 'Oh, Jaysus! Me nerves are gone wit this bastard,' she says. 'He'll come in now, mouldy drunk, an upend the place.

'Here he is! Here he is!' she suddenly says, an me heart starts te pound.

'Don't say anythin, Ma. Please, Ma! Don't say anythin. He'll kill us. Oh, Jesus! Oh, Jesus!' I beg. Me teeth are chatterin, an I'm shakin all over. Dear God, don't let him start any more trouble. Keep us safe. I don't know whether te dive under the blankets, or get up te save me mammy. I sit up in the bed, holdin me hands, an me ma jumps up an rushes inta the scullery.

He stumbles inta the hall an slams against the door. 'Ma! Ma! Let him in,' I croak.

'Open the fuckin door, Mrs. Come on!' An he bangs on the door wit his fist. I jump outa the bed an open the door. He pushes the door an flattens me against the wall, bangin me head wit a thump. 'Where is she? Come outa there, ye fuckin aul hag, ye!' An he stumbles inta the scullery an drags me ma out. 'Ye won't keep a man locked out of his own home.' He shakes her by the neck an then starts punchin her. Me ma screams, an Harry sits up in the bed. He doesn't know wha's happenin an screams from fright. Teddy wakes up, an his face is blue from the shock, an he crawls over Charlie an puts out his arms fer me te lift him.

Jackser tears the hair from me mammy's head an throws her aroun the floor an kicks her. I jump outa the way an press meself inta the corner. 'Ah, no, Jackser! Please! Please! Don't hurt me mammy. Please, Jackser! We'll do whatever ye want,' I'm sobbin, too afraid te scream.

Jackser whirls aroun on the balls of his feet an glares at me. His eyes are mad, an the spits are leakin outa his mouth. He grabs the chair an swings it through the air, an smashes the winda. 'I'll kill ye's all!' he screams. 'I'll do time fer ye's! They'll fuckin hang me!'

The glass smashes on te the ground an inta the room, an I'm screamin. Charlie charges outa the bed an dives underneath. Jackser lunges fer the bed an just misses Charlie, an grabs Teddy instead an picks him up by the legs. An Teddy catches his breath, an he swings him out the broken winda, an me ma can't get up from the floor. She's holdin her stomach, an she gives a piercin scream an says, 'Murder! He's murderin me child! Get help, Martha! He's goin te kill the lot of us.'

I tear me face from me ma an look at Jackser flingin poor Teddy across te the bed. I charge fer the door, an he grabs me by the hair an punches me in the face. An me nose shoots out blood like a fountain. Then he opens the door an slams me across the hall, flyin through the air until I hit the woman's door opposite.

I lay like a heap of rubbish on the ground, pumpin blood everywhere, I was chokin on it. The woman came runnin out an screamed at Jackser te stop his blackguardin cos she was goin across te Store Street police station te bring back the police. She had her coat thrown on, an she ran fer the police. I was crawlin aroun, tryin te get up, but the blood was pourin outa me like a tap. An I wanted te get up te try an stop him from killin everyone, but I was winded, an the pain in me back an chest wouldn't let me breathe. I was desperately lookin out the hall, hopin someone would come, but it was dark. An the only noise was our screamin. Jesus! Jesus! Please don't let him kill us. Make him stop.

The door of the old man's flat opened, an he came out slowly, afraid of his life. 'Sweet Jesus!' he whispered, comin towards me. I pulled meself up slowly, holdin on te the wall. The blood wouldn't stop pumpin from me nose, an I had te keep me head down an let it flow, or it went down me throat an choked me if I lifted me head. He held me arm an asked where all the blood was comin from, an saw it was me nose, an said he'll get somethin te stop the bleedin. Then he let me go an put his head in the room slowly an said, 'Are ye's all right?'

Jackser roared, 'She won't leave me alone! Day an night I have te listen te her complainin! Mornin, noon an night. It never stops. Well, I'm puttin an end te it here an now. I'm goin te get rid of the lot of them. I'd be better off locked up.'

'Ah! Don't be sayin tha. It will be all right.'

'No!' Jackser roared. 'I'll fuckin finish them off.'

'Take it easy! Take it easy,' I heard the old man say.

I crept over te the door an put me head in the room, spillin pools of blood after me. I saw straight away Teddy was hurt. Blood was pourin outa him. His neck an hands an face was covered wit blood, an he was screamin. He was pressed inta the corner of the bed, his back against the wall. Harry was leanin himself against the wall, too, the side of his face pressed against the wall. An he was watchin

217

te see if someone was goin te hurt him. An he was sobbin his heart out, his chest heavin up an down, an his eyes was like huge saucers. Me ma was on the floor, holdin herself up by the side of the bed, an she was in terrible pain. She couldn't get up.

'No more! Oh, stop him! Oh, Jesus help us! Tha's enough! Don't do any more,' she was implorin.

'Shut up!' Jackser screamed at her, lungin wit his fists, bendin his head inta her face.

I screamed, an the childre were hysterical, an the young girl from next door ran in. Her mother must have told her not te come out. But she ran in, probably worried about her mammy. She took one look an grabbed me. 'Come on! Get out.'

'No! No!' I screamed, an Jackser ran inta the scullery an grabbed the knife. The young one lunged fer Teddy an dragged him off the bed an ran wit him. I got te me senses an grabbed Harry. An I was screamin, 'Help! Murder! He's goin te kill me ma. Charlie! Get outa there! Get outa there!' an I was runnin te get outa the room.

I saw Jackser jump on me ma wit the knife. He had his knee on her stomach. The woman came tearin back inta the hall an rushed past me, screamin at her daughter te lock the door. 'Lock the door!' she was screamin. The old man was shoutin, 'No! No! Let her alone!' I ran inta the room behind the daughter, carryin the babby covered in my blood. An the woman screamed, 'Jesus, Jesus! Stop! Stop! It's a slaughter house.'

Charlie came runnin in behind me, shoutin, 'Save me! Save me!' The girl was cryin an slammed the door, an opened her winda an climbed out, cos it's low on the ground, an she went runnin. 'Help! Help! He's goin te kill me ma!' she was screamin at the top of her lungs.

I heard runnin feet an people shoutin, 'It's in here!' An they came tearin in through the hall. I heard a man shout, 'Get the fuck off!' an Jackser roarin. More people came, an the girl opened the door. Two women came in wit her, an their eyes were shocked. They had coats thrown over their shoulders, an they said, 'Oh, God forgive him fer his badness.' They grabbed a towel from the scullery an started wipin the blood from Teddy's neck an face. An the other woman grabbed a cloth an was holdin the cloth te me face te stop the blood. We couldn't stop cryin. The girl put on the kettle, an the woman pulled the frock over me head. It was soppin wit blood, an I stood in me skin, shiverin an covered in blood, but I didn't care.

'Mammy! Mammy! I want me mammy,' an we were all cryin fer me mammy.

'Shush, shush! She's all right. No harm will come te her, we'll see te tha.' An they washed me down. 'This poor little fella's neck has a very bad gash.' The woman held the towel on the back of his neck, an the girl looked te see where Harry was bleedin from. But he wasn't cut, it was only my blood. When the bleedin was stopped an I was cleaned up, the woman put a frock an cardigan on me belongin te the girl. Me face was in a bad way. Me eye an cheek was swollen, an me nose was swollen, too.

The screamin from next door died down, an I could hear voices an glass bein swept up. The woman came in. 'Are ye's all right? Oh, Jesus! I never want te see the like of tha again, Mrs. I'm not the better of it!' she said te the two women.

'Ah, the man's an animal. He should be locked up fer life, no one's safe aroun him. Look wha he's done te the poor childre, he's destroyed them fer life. They'll never be the same!'

'Is me ma all right?' I asked the neighbour.

'Ah, she'll be grand. But she'll have te go te hospital fer a little while. But there's nothin fer ye te worry yerself about.' Then she whispered somethin te the two women. Me heart stopped. She must be goin te die. Wha's goin te happen te us? Charlie started cryin again. I looked at him, an his face was the colour of marble.

'Here, chicken! Drink this, it will do ye good. An eat the egg an the bit a bread an butter. It's not much, but it will bring yer strength back. Where's the babby's bottle? I want te give him a hot sup of tea.' An I looked over at Harry, sittin on one of the women's laps at the fire. He was very pale but was content te sit an let the woman rock him. Teddy was bein fed an egg by the girl an was eatin it an holdin a bit of bread in his hand. An Charlie was sittin on the floor

219

in front of the fire, eatin bread an spoonin egg inta his mouth. I gave a big sob an started te drink me tea an eat me egg. People were tired an talkin in whispers. The room was warm an peaceful, an I couldn't hear any more noise from our room, just the sound of people busy comin an goin, fixin somethin te block the winda. An there was no more shoutin.

The old man came in an smiled at us an shook his head te the women, puttin his eyes te heaven. An he looked very white an tired. 'Are ye's all right now?' he said in a very quiet voice, lookin at us. 'Ah, it's all over now. Ye's will be all right, thank God.' Then he went inta the scullery an was whisperin te the women. They made him sit down an have a drop of hot tea. An one of the women went off te her own place an said she wouldn't be long. Then an ambulance arrived an stopped outside the door. I jumped up, wantin te see wha was happenin.

'No, no! You sit there, chicken, don't move. They're only goin te take yer mammy inta hospital fer a little while. She'll be all right.'

I sat down, afraid te upset anyone, but I wanted te see me mammy, te see if she was all right. An wha was happenin te Jackser? Are they goin te take him away an lock him up? Oh, please God, get him locked up. But I was afraid te say anythin. So I didn't move an just sat quiet, an tried te stop me heart from racin. I was so afraid of everythin, not knowin wha was goin te happen te us. I was afraid te die, an I was afraid te live.

I looked at me brothers. Harry was lyin on the woman's chest, holdin on te her, his hand restin on her chest. An she was holdin the bottle of tea in his mouth an croonin te him very softly. He was lookin up at her, lettin the bottle rest in his mouth. Then he gave a big sigh an went back te suckin his bottle an nestled his head inta her chest, gettin a tighter grip of her wit his other hand. The woman smiled over at me an said, 'He's a lovely child, God bless him.' An then she said, 'I think I'll take him up wit me fer the night. He can sleep in wit me. He seems te have settled now.'

Teddy was dozin on the bed, an the girl was lyin beside him wit his head on her stomach, an she was gently strokin his hair.

The blood had clotted on the back of his neck, an the bleedin was stopped. The girl lifted the cloth an whispered, 'Mammy, the gash is very deep. It probably needs stitches.'

'Leave the poor mite where he is. Put him under the covers. An you, chicken,' she said te me, 'get in beside him, ye're all done in. Wha ye need now, the lot of ye, is a good night's sleep.'

The other woman came back from her place an brought a loaf of bread an cheese an corn beef. 'Ah, ye shouldn't have!' 'Not at all!' the women said te each other, 'There's plenty more where tha came from!' I climbed inta bed beside Teddy, an Charlie got in beside the wall, wit Teddy in the middle between the two of us.

'I'll take your little fella up wit me fer the night, an he can sleep wit my childre,' the woman who just came in wit the food said.

'Tha's very good of ye. Tha way then, I'll sleep next te Ellie, me daughter, an Maggie here is takin the babby up wit her.'

'Ah, tha's grand. We're all sorted out now. An I'll make us all a nice sup of tea. Jaysus, we could do wit it after the night we've had!' An they all laughed wit relief.

'How are things now?' an she lifted her head te our room. The man an the women whispered te each other, an I turned away, puttin me arm aroun Teddy. An he moved inta me, holdin onta me. The pain was easin in me, an the quiet whispers an the heat from the fire was soothin me. The light was off in the room, gettin light only from the scullery an the blazin fire. I started te doze, an then I felt meself sinkin inta a deep sleep.

A noise woke me up, an me eyes shot open. I tried te lift me head, but it was too heavy. An the pain shot aroun me head, an I was in pain everywhere. The woman from upstairs, Maggie, came in wit Harry an she looked down at me. Me eyes were too swollen, an I could see only through slits. 'Oh! God Almighty, ye're in an awful state, ye poor cratur!'

'Lie there, don't move yerself,' me neighbour said. 'Have ye a pram fer the babby?' she asked me quietly.

'No, it's gone,' I said. Not sayin Jackser had sold it fer ten bob down in Capel Street an drank the money.

'Never mind, I'll manage,' she said.

It was mornin, an the fire was lightin. Teddy moved beside me, an Charlie sat up an rubbed his eyes. 'I'll go off an see if I can get somethin te put the babby in. I don't mind takin him fer a few days,' Maggie said.

'Yeah, an I can keep the childre here fer a while. We'll see wha happens. Ellie, give Charlie a sup of tea an help him te put his clothes on.'

'OK, Ma.'

'Good girl!'

Charlie scrambled outa the bed, an I turned over, hurtin everywhere, an started te doze again.

I woke up again, an it was evenin. The neighbour was bendin over me wit a cup of tea. 'Come on, love, try an sit up an drink this, ye need it.' I closed me eyes, it hurt too much te keep them open. Even the movement hurt me head. 'Come on, I'll help ye.' An she put her hand under me back an lifted me. Everythin started te swim, an me head was like a ton weight. The pain was terrible. She held the cup te me mouth, an I took two sips an started te gag.

'No, no,' I said. 'I can't!'

'All right, then. Tha will do. We'll put ye lyin down again, an ye can get some rest, ye're too sick fer anythin.' I lay back down in the bed, an me head was on fire. I eased back inta sleep.

When I woke again, it was mornin. The watery sun was shinin inta the room. I slowly lifted me head an looked aroun the room, wonderin where I was fer a minute. Charlie an Teddy was sittin on the floor wit Ellie, an she was playin wit Teddy's toes an then ticklin Charlie, makin them roar laughin. 'More, more!' Charlie was shoutin, an Teddy was squealin wit excitement.

An then it all came back te me. Me head an back felt like someone had bashed me wit a concrete block, an me face was very sore. But the pain was eased an awful lot, an I felt OK when I lay down an kept still. I was content te lie there very quietly an take in the room. It was heaven on earth. The fire was banked up an glowin red, an there was a red an blue china dog sittin on the mantelpiece, an a lovely big clock tha chimed every fifteen minutes an bonged every hour. I liked the sound of it tick tockin. An over tha, on the wall, was a big picture of two soldiers in uniforms holdin guns. An they had bags on their backs. The picture looked very old. There was a small armchair wit cushions beside the fire, an a round table wit a heavy cloth an tassles hangin from the bottom, coverin it. An a lovely lace cloth lay on top of tha. An it was sittin under the winda, which had lovely white net curtains an heavy red ones, wit big yella flowers, tha ye close at night te keep out the dark, an the wind, an anyone tha wants te look in. An there was oil cloth on the floor, an ye could see yer face in it from the shine.

I could hear the mammy bangin pots an singin te herself in the scullery. There was a lovely smell of somethin cookin, an I wondered if I could stay here fer the rest of me life. I'd never complain again.

'Ah, ye're awake,' Mrs said te me, bendin down an smilin at me. I was a bit worried she might tell me te get up an go inta me own room an mind me brothers.

'Yeah,' I croaked shyly, wonderin wha's goin te happen now. I lifted me head te sit up, an it hurt like mad. But I didn't want her te think she had te put up wit us. I don't like te make a fool of meself, an maybe she hasn't enough food te stretch fer everyone, cos she's on her own.

'How're ye feelin?'

'Eh! Not too bad.'

She looked at me. 'Ah, yer poor face is very swollen, an ye must be very sore. Are ye?'

'Yeah,' I said.

'Right! Let's get ye sittin up an more comfortable, then we'll see about gettin ye a nice cup a tea. Wouldn't ye like tha?'

'Yeah,' I said, lettin out a big sigh.

She lifted me up an fixed a long sausage pilla behind me, an another one on top of tha, an I sank meself back, restin against the headboard. Then she went off te the scullery, an I heard her rattlin the cups. Oh, if only this would last for ever an me ma could be like her!

223

'Now, mind ye don't burn yerself wit tha tea. It's very hot.'

I tasted the tea, an the steam was hurtin me face, but it was lovely. Loads a milk, an it was very sweet. I supped away, an Mrs waited an then took the cup from me. 'Ye's won't have te wait long fer yer dinner. It's nearly done.'

'Oh, great, Ma! I'm starvin,' Ellie said, an she looked over at me. 'We're havin coddle. Do ye like coddle?'

'Yeah!' I said, not knowin wha coddle was. But it smelled lovely.

'Yeah, we're very lucky,' the mammy said. 'The St Vincent de Paul called last night. An when they saw me plight, wit the extra mouths te feed, they gave me an extra voucher fer ten bob an the bit of extra turf fer the fire. So now I'm well away! Ellie, run out an find Jimmy. Bring him in fer his dinner. He better not be gone far! I told him not te stray, I was doin a bit of dinner.'

'OK, Ma!' an she was out the door.

I could hear bangin plates, an then the mammy came in wit two steamin plates of stew. 'Now, babba,' she said te Teddy, who was standin himself up an sittin himself down an wavin his fists in the air wit excitement, an nearly suffocatin himself swallowin his spits. 'Sit down an I'll feed ye this.'

Charlie was sittin on the floor an hammerin his heels up an down wit impatience. 'Easy now. Easy, ye'll choke yerself,' she said te Charlie, who was coughin an splutterin, cos he shovelled too much in his mouth. Teddy screamed, cos she didn't put the spoon fast enough inta his mouth.

Ellie an Jimmy came rushin back inta the room an threw themselves at the table. Jimmy's face lit up. 'Coddle, Ma! Where did ye manage te get the money?'

'From the Vincents,' Ellie said.

'Now!' the mammy said te Teddy. 'Did ye enjoy tha?' an Teddy looked shocked at the empty plate an screamed fer more. 'No more!' the mammy said, laughin. An Charlie looked te see wha would happen next wit the empty plate sittin beside him an hoped Teddy's screams might bring more.

'All right! Take it easy. I'll bring ye somethin.' An she came back wit bread an soup poured over it. Teddy slapped his knees an roared, 'Me! Me!' until she sat down an fed him an gave the other plate te Charlie.

When they were finished, they were still lookin after the empty plates, an she said, 'Wait there, I have somethin nice fer ye's.' An she came back in an unwrapped two Sugar Barleys. 'Now, tha should keep ye busy fer a while.' An the two of them sat there suckin away on the Sugar Barleys, watchin each other take big noisy sucks, stickin out their tongues an slurpin back in again.

Jimmy was playin wit them, sayin, 'Give us a suck!' an they went mad an roared at him in case he robbed their Sugar Barleys.

'Ah, don't be tormentin them!' the mammy shouted from the scullery. 'Let them have their little bit of enjoyment.'

'I'm not, Ma!' Jimmy shouted. 'I'm only playin wit them.'

'Well, go on out an play wit someone yer own age. Cos if I catch ye touchin them babbies' sweets, ye'll get the back of me hand on ye.'

Jimmy jumped up laughin an gave a last look at the sweets an flew out the door, bangin it shut behind him. Me head leapt wit the noise, an the mammy shouted, 'Jaysus, Jimmy Dunne, one of these days I'll kill ye fer bangin tha door!

'Now, chicken. Get tha down ye!' an she handed me a plate a stew, wit sausages an rashers an black an white puddin, an carrots an onions, all floatin aroun in soup, an lovely bits of potatoes. I never tasted anythin like this before, an it was gorgeous. I ate it very slowly, cos me face hurt, but, more importantly, te make it last as long as I could. When the plate was empty, I held on te it as long as I could, te run me fingers aroun the few drops of gravy left, an only handed back the plate when it was snow-white clean.

'Now, I needn't ask, because ye certainly enjoyed tha. I was wonderin if ye was goin te eat the plate an all. Have a little sleep fer yerself. It'll do ye good,' an she pulled away the long sausage pilla, an I slid meself down under the warm blankets an felt meself dozin off inta a lovely sleep. Thanks, God, fer lookin after us. When I grow up, I'm goin te be just like Ellie's mammy an have a lovely an peaceful home an feed me childre lovely stews.

I woke up wit the sound of voices, an Maggie was in the room wit me little brother Harry. I sat up in the bed, an Maggie said, 'Ah, look, Harry! Here's yer big sister,' an she plopped him down beside me on the bed. I laughed, delighted te see him, an he looked at me an wrapped his arms aroun me neck. I held on fer a minute an then took his hands, cos it hurt me, but I didn't care. I grabbed him an gave him a squeeze, an kissed his face, an looked at him. He looked lovely an clean, an his hair was washed. Then I squeezed him again, an he had enough an tried te push me away, but I wouldn't let go, an he grabbed a hold of me hair an pulled. I roared, cos it hurt me sore head, an he wouldn't let go, an he was squealin wit delight, cos he thought it was a game. Maggie ran over an grabbed his little hands, an picked his fingers one by one outa me hair. An all the time I was roarin.

'No! No, babba!' Maggie was shoutin, an Harry gave a big squeal an a big yank before I got me head back. An I held me head, watchin as Maggie took Harry away, still squealin at me fer tormentin him wit me squeezes.

Maggie held him up in the air an shook him, laughin, 'Aren't you the little demon?' An he roared laughin. 'Ah! I'm goin te keep you,' an she shook him, an he screamed wit the excitement. Then she buried her face in his neck an blew noises at him. An he roared, an screamed wit laughin. 'An yer poor mammy will cry without ye! Isn't tha right?' an she blew inta his neck again, makin suckin noises. He loved it.

She sat down in the armchair beside the fire an put Harry on the floor. Teddy an Charlie started chasin him aroun the room on their hands an knees. 'Are ye feelin better?' Maggie asked me.

'Yeah! I'm much better, thanks.'

'Well, ye won't feel the time goin till yer mammy's outa the hospital.'

Then Mrs Dunne asked her was there any news, an Maggie whispered, lookin at me, an then turnin her back. 'She's lost it, the poor woman.'

'Ah! Lord God, isn't tha terrible.'

226

'Yeah! He kicked it out of her, the animal!'

'Well,' Mrs Dunne said, leanin back in her chair an lookin over at the picture of the Sacred Heart hangin over the bed. 'If there's any justice, he'll get wha's comin te him. An he should be locked up fer life an let them throw away the key. I hope he comes te a bad end! God forgive me,' an she blessed herself wit the sign of the cross. 'Anyway, he won't be comin back here fer a while, not where he is! Tha should put a stop te his gallop!'

Me heart leapt. Locked up! Not comin back! I was afraid te ask, cos I'm not supposed te listen, but me mind started flyin. No more Jackser! Oh, God, let it be true, but I didn't really believe it. It's hard te stop Jackser, an they might let him go free. He can talk his way aroun anythin. I felt me heart sink. No, I'll just have te wait an see wha happens.

'Ye must be delighted at seein yer mammy.'

'Yeah, Mrs Dunne, I am. I can't wait. Is she all better now?'

'Ah, she'll be fine. It'll take her a few days te get back on her feet, but she's lucky te have you te help her.'

'Yeah, I can't wait te see her.'

'What I'll do is, light the fire. Oh, yes! I must see if I can get her a bit of turf, she'll need tha te keep her goin. An I'll pick up a few scrags a neck a lamb an put on a bit of a stew. It's not nice te come outa hospital an be faced wit an empty cold room. Not after wha she's been through. Now, let's get these two little demons inta the bed, an we'll have a nice hot suppa tea. Ellie! Will ye wet the teapot fer me? I'll just throw me coat on. I want te run up te Maggie's fer a minute, I won't be long.'

Ellie put down her pencil, she was doin her sums fer school tomorrow, an went inta the scullery. The door shut behind Mrs Dunne, an she was still mutterin te herself, 'Now did I think of everythin? Did I leave aside the rent money?' I smiled te meself. Mrs Dunne was always fixin things up in her head an rushin aroun worryin about everyone. An I'm definitely goin te be like her, cos ye always feel safe an happy when ye're wit her. An she makes me roar laughin at the things she says te people when they annoy her.

227

Today she sent me fer a packet of Bisto, an I was short of a ha'penny. 'Would she not give ye the Bisto?'

'No! It was the chinny aul one, an she said te tell ye she's not standin behind the counter fer the good of her health!'

'Is tha so!' Mrs Dunne roared. 'Wait till I see her! But I'll tell ye this! Tha aul one is so mean she'd shoot her mammy just te go on the orphans' outin!' The picture of Chinny's fat ma lyin plastered on the ground, an Chinny runnin off wit the orphans, on their day out, had me in stitches.

23

Me ma got her hands on another pram. I whipped it on a gang of kids who were pushin each other aroun in it. An I bet they robbed it from the second-hand dealers who sell up on the stones on a Saturday mornin. It's just off Parnell Street. I was moseyin along when they came flyin outa the flats wit the pram, an a gang of young fellas hangin outa it. Me eyes lit up – just what the ma needs! Me head went inta action straight away. 'Quick! Quick!' I shouted. 'Did ye's not hear about the weddin?'

They came te a standstill. 'Wha weddin?'

'Down on Sean McDermott Street!' I screamed. 'There'll be a grushie.'

Yer man pushin the pram hesimitated an looked at me suspicious.

'I'm goin!' an the three sittin in the pram threw themselves out an ran like mad, headin down te the church.

'Yeah, wait fer me,' an they were gone, leavin the pram.

I looked at the wheels – grand! The springs – lovely! Just wha the doctor ordered. An off I flew in the opposite direction, turnin left an headin down past the Pro-Cathedral, an left again on te Talbot Street. But as I turned on te Corporation Street, I had te be very careful, cos they only had te look straight down an they would spot me. Te be safe, I turned right onta Foley Street an ducked left under the arch inta the buildins, an I was home an dry.

We put Harry in the pram an Teddy sittin at the bottom, an hope it doesn't rain, cos the hood is in ribbons. An we all set off fer the day. Me on one side of the handlebars, Charlie on the other, an the ma in the middle, pushin. Up the hill, onta Mountjoy Square. 'Come on! Push the fuckin pram,' me ma shouts. 'Ye's all have the heart pulled outa me!'

'I'm pushin, Ma!'

Then past Gardiner Street Church, turn right onta Dorset Street, over Binns Bridge, an up the Whitworth Road. Another hill! I look over at Charlie draggin outa the pram. Me ma's gone red in the face tryin te push. I give a little push an get annoyed at Charlie. 'Lookit, Ma! He's pullin, not pushin.'

'I'm not! Ye're pullin,' Charlie shouts back at me.

'I'll give ye's both a dig if ye's don't push this pram wit me! I'm warnin ye's.'

'Right!' I shout. 'I'm not goin!' an I stop dead.

'Stay there, then!' me ma shouts back at me.

I'm ragin as I watch me ma keep goin. 'Wait fer me!' I scream after her, cos she's gone miles up the road without me. An I run after her, cryin in temper.

Me ma laughs at me when I catch up wit her, an I jump up an down in an awful rage altogether, cos she keeps gettin the better of me. 'Ah, tha's lovely, lovely, keep it up, an if they arrest ye fer makin a show of yerself, ye needn't say ye're wit me.' An she started te hurry on without me again.

'Ye're a .. ! Ye're a .. !' I screamed after her. But I couldn't think of any names te call her. 'Fuck off!' I finally screeched, lettin all the air outa me mouth an droppin me shoulders, feelin better.

An aul one wit a black shawl wrapped aroun her head stopped te stare at me. 'Ye'll go straight te Hell fer carryin on like tha! Stop tormentin yer poor mammy. Go on. Look, she's waitin on ye.'

I took me eyes offa the aul one, an, sure enough, me ma was waitin. She laughed down at the aul one, an said, 'These childre will be the death of me yet, Mrs.'

'True fer ye, Mrs!' the aul one shouted back. 'Give her the back of yer hand, an ye won't get any more lip from her.' Then she galloped off.

I glared up at the ma, an she said, 'Come on. If we hurry, we might be in time fer somethin te eat.'

I was appeased an raced up te grab hold of the pram. We were contented again, an we raced down the hill, an then up again onta the Mobhi Road.

When we got te the Cross an Passion convent, a lovely big red-faced nun answered the door. She was wearin a dark check apron aroun her habit. 'And what have we here?' she laughed inta the pram at Harry an Teddy. 'And what age are you?' she asked me.

Me ma said I was nine an Charlie was four. 'And two lovely babies,' the nun said, bendin inta the pram an ticklin their chins. 'Wait here, I'll see what there is.' An she swung off an banged the door behind her, leavin me ma an me holdin our breaths, wonderin wha she'd bring us.

'She must be in charge of the kitchen,' me ma whispered.

'Yeah, Ma,' I whispered back.

Charlie went runnin off, chasin a black cat tha was sneakin through the trees an watchin us. Teddy roared, an me ma lifted him outa the pram, an he went after Charlie, tryin te hurry through the grass. He kept fallin down, but he picked himself up an kept his eye on Charlie an the big cat.

I could smell the lovely fresh air, an it was so quiet, so peaceful. I let out a big breath an said te me ma, 'I'm goin te run aroun the corner, an see what's in the windas.'

I was gone before me ma shouted at me te get back here, 'They'll see ye an give us nothin.' I walked along the wall, lookin up at the windas. They were too high up fer me te see anythin. I hauled meself up onta a windasill an dug me toes inta the wall, an held on wit me elbows. The winda was opened a little, but ye couldn't see in through the winda, cos the glass wasn't clear. I heard somethin – runnin water. Then the back of a nun's head appeared, an I heard a tilet flushin. I tried te look, haulin meself up higher, but me arms wouldn't hold me, an I fell back inta a thorny bush.

'Ah! Ah! Me legs, me arse, I'm caught. Ma! Mammy! Help me.'

Ma put her head aroun the corner an waved her fist up at me an clenched her teeth. 'Shurrup! Get back down here. I warned ye!' she screamed in a whisper.

I kept swingin me legs, tryin te get out, an the winda was pushed up, an a nun poked her head out. 'What on all that is holy are you doing in there?' she snorted at me.

'I'm caught, Sister! Somebody pull me out, I'm stung te death!'

She kept starin at me, doin nothin te run an help me, only shakin her head up an down, tut tuttin. Me frock was caught up aroun me neck, an I was in me bare skin, but I didn't care wha she was thinkin, I only wanted te get out!

'Unbelievable!' she barked, an slammed the winda down. I stayed quiet an steadied me breath. Easin out one leg – ah, it hurt! Then the other, stretchin meself. Then kick! An me back shot up, an I was standin again. I was full of red lumps everywhere, an me hair was standin up in all directions, wit bits of thorn leaves stickin outa me. I went back te me ma, knowin she was annoyed, but she might pity me when she saw the state I was in. I came crawlin aroun te me ma. 'Ma, lookit me! I'm destroyed!'

'Ah, don't be annoyin me. You've gone an ruined everythin. She'll come out now an put us out without anythin!' I looked at Harry starin at me an pointin te me hair. He wanted the leaves still stuck te me head. Then me ma looked aroun at me an started laughin.

'It's not funny!' I whined, an me ma laughed harder.

'Wha were ye doin?'

'I was tryin te get a look in the winda, at the nun pissin away, but I missed it when I fell.'

Me ma's nose was red an drippin, an she was wipin tears from her eyes. 'Ah, Gawd! Tha's a good one,' she said, wipin her nose.

'Yeah, Ma, but I didn't think nuns pissed! Ye never see them! Only a bit of their face an hands.'

'Yeah,' me ma said. 'They come in here te hide away from the men.'

Then the door was whipped open, an me ma jumped up off the step. 'Now!' the lovely red-faced nun roared at us. 'Have you anything to put these into?' An she leaned inta the hall an came up wit an armful of stuff. Charlie came rushin back, an Teddy was screamin at bein left behind an missin out. Me ma got excited an whipped out the pillacase an held it open. The nun swung her arms wit loaves of bread inta the pillacase. A big jam jar of beef drippin, jars wit tea, sugar an jam, white greaseproof paper filled wit cooked roast beef, another wit cold potatoes cooked in their skins, real butter in greaseproof paper, an brown soda bread, an white soda bread, an cold roast potatoes. The pillacase was nearly full.

'That's the lot,' an she reached in again an came out wit bananas. 'One for my little man here with the angelic smile,' an she peeled the banana an put it in Harry's hand. He stared at it, not knowin wha te do wit it. Teddy nearly lost his mind, screamin. 'Yes! Yes! And you, too,' an she peeled a banana an gave it te him. He looked at it first, an then took a bite, an Harry was watchin him an did the same. Charlie was wringin his hands an hummin, tryin te be patient, an she gave him a big rosy apple. He shoved it inta his mouth an nearly choked, cos he didn't chew it, just swallied. She looked at me an gave me a big yella orange, askin wha happened te me.

'I fell inta a bush, Sister!'

'Oh, now, I'd say you were up to some mischief.' An she laughed, takin the orange offa me an peelin it.

'Are ye here long, Sister? me ma asked smilin. 'It's just I haven't seen ye before!'

'Well, I've been drafted into kitchen duty while Sister recovers from a bug. I've been baking up a storm! Wonderful! I love my grub, you know. But I think the other sisters regret now letting me fly loose in the kitchen. "It's not food, it's a mountain!" the older sisters mumble into their chests.' Then she screeched laughin. 'No! I teach in our secondary school for girls. And what about you?' she asked me. 'What class are you in at school?'

Eh, I thought, forgettin. 'I'm nine! An I can read an write, an I can spell loads a things. I taught meself, so I did!' delighted te boast. 'Ask me te spell somethin!'

'Spell your name.'

'Ah, tha's easy! Ask me somethin harder.'

'Spell school.'

'Easy,' I said, an spelt it.

'Hmm, you're a bright spark. Pity to waste it,' she mumbled.

Teddy roared, cos his banana was gone, an he reached inta the pram an robbed Harry's. Harry looked at the bit he was left an looked at Teddy chewin his banana an smilin at him, an went demented. 'He robbed the banana, Sister! He robbed the babby's banana!' Charlie screamed. He was ragin, only cos he didn't get te rob it first. Charlie tried te grab it from Teddy, an Teddy bent himself in two, squashin the banana inta his stomach.

Me ma tried te separate them, an the sister roared, 'Oh, it's a calamity! Wait there, I'll see what I can get to keep you all quiet!' an she belted in again an came out wit a big bag of scones an jam buns an rock buns, an gave us all one each.

She handed the bag te me ma, who said, 'Thank you very much, Sister. I won't forget you in a hurry fer bein so good te us.'

'Listen!' Sister said. 'I have some soup left over, will I heat it up and bring you each a mug? It's gettin very cold now, and it will warm you up.'

'Oh, yes, Sister, the childre would love tha. God bless you, an I'll pray fer you.'

I lunged fer the bag of cakes, an everyone was screamin fer more. Me ma slapped me hand away an said, 'Wait! We can have them fer yer tea.'

'Just a look, Ma!'

'No, I'm puttin them away.'

She lifted up Harry an told me te hold him while she lifted the pillacase filled wit the good food, an put it at the back of the pram, an Harry's pilla on top. Then she put Harry back in, lyin on the pillas. 'Tha pram is lovely an deep. Ye can't beat the really old ones. They don't make them tha deep any more,' me ma said, all happy in herself. We all sat on the step, lookin an smilin at each other, waitin fer the soup, wonderin what it was goin te be like.

The door opened, an the nun lifted a big tray wit gorgeous steamin soup in big white mugs, an plates of thick loaf bread, lathered wit good butter, an lumps of cheese sittin on top. 'Have you a bottle for the baby?' she asked Ma.

'I have, Sister.' An me ma whipped out the babby's bottle wit the teat on, an the sister rushed in again an came out wit hot milk in it, an she'd added a drop of soup.

'Now, my beauties, that should keep you going.' An she straightened up an said te me ma, 'I'd better hurry, the bell has gone for prayers, and I don't want to be late down to Chapel.'

'God bless ye, Sister,' me ma bowed te her. An the sister waved at us an rushed through the door, an was gone.

'My God! There's not many like her,' me ma said, shakin her head. 'More's the pity. We'd all be a lot happier if only there was.' We licked the mugs an ran our hands inside them te make sure we had got every last taste outa it. An then we fixed them on the tray an pushed off down the avenue. Our bellies full, an our mouths hot wit the taste still stickin at the back of our throats.

'Ah, tha was lovely,' I said, smackin me lips an lookin at Charlie smilin at everyone.

We were all happy, an we didn't feel tired any more. We passed the butcher, an I said, 'Ma, will I go in an see if he has somethin fer us?'

'No,' me ma said. 'Leave him fer another day when we have nothin. Then we'll be glad of anythin.'

I skipped along, holdin on te the handlebars. 'Oh, Ma, this is great! Why can't it be always like this?'

'Yeah, if only,' me ma said. 'But I'd need te get me own place away from him. An as he has put the place in his name, the Corporation won't have anythin te do wit me unless he gives up the key te this place. An tha aul fella won't do tha. So I'm stuck wit him.'

'How long did he get in Mountjoy, Ma?' I asked, feelin sick, cos I never wanted te think about him ever again.

'Six months!' me ma said stone-faced, starin ahead. 'Rob a bank an ye get more! Batterin women an childre te death an ye walk away. He won't be in there fer long. They'll let him out fer good behaviour. A coward like him won't put a foot wrong, cos he's faced wit men.'

I stopped te look at gnomes in a garden. I didn't want te think of Jackser any more.

235

A dog was dozin on the doorstep an jumped up an started barkin at me. Ragin, it is, cos it can't get through the shut gate an bite the leg offa me. 'Arrah!' I barked back, pretendin I was climbin the wall. It somersaulted up the wall te get at me an crashed down again, landin on its neck, an crept off decidin it had had enough, but not takin its eyes offa me. I laughed an roared, 'Ye're too big fer yer paws, serves ye right!' an ran on te catch up wit me ma.

We went up te High Park convent an got the two stale loaves of bread from Hairy. An on the way down the avenue, I stopped at the grotto te get a look down at the holy water. Ye can't reach it, cos the water's too deep down. I said a little prayer te Our Lady, te thank her fer the lovely soup an food we got, an fer givin us all the lovely peace without Jackser. 'An will ye make sure he never comes back, Mother of God,' I whispered. I thought fer a minute . . . 'If he doesn't get himself kilt in there, then maybe if he could get an awful bang on the head an forget who he is, then he wouldn't come lookin fer us.' I blessed meself, feelin satisfied, an chased after me ma.

We went down the hill, an onta Griffith Avenue. Me ma hesimitated an then said, 'Let's do a few of these houses. We might be lucky an get a few old clothes. They do have lovely stuff here, they're very well off.'

'Right, Ma!' I was hoppin up an down delighted. Ye never know wha we'll get.

'It's after four o'clock now, so we have enough time before it gets dark,' me ma said.

We walked along the big wide footpath, wit the trees whisperin in the dark. It was an awful long road. Doors were banged in our faces, an some people looked afraid of us an screamed, 'Go away! I've nothin to give you!' an rushed in, boltin the door. Some people held their noses in the air an sniffed, an looked at us as if we were lepers. One aul one roared, 'We give charity to the blind! I'm sure there's a charity to help your kind! Now please kindly shut the gate on your way out!'

Me ma was ragin at the insult an shouted back, 'I'm sorry we're not blind te suit you! Keep yer charity, the cheek a ye!' an grabbed the pram an pushed it down the path. Then she stopped on the way outa the gate an looked back at the aul one, still standin in her porch, watchin us. 'There's no pockets in a shroud, ye know. Ye can't take it wit ye! An you've already got one foot in the grave, ye aul hag. I hope ye die roarin! Come on, Martha, let's get outa here. Them people make me sick. They wouldn't give ye the steam offa their piss!'

I rushed back an opened the gate wider. She was still standin there wit her mouth gapin open an her eyes on stalks. 'Oh! Well, really!' she said, outa breath. I made a face at her an rushed after me ma.

'Come on, I'm not ready te give up yet,' me ma said. 'They're not all like tha, just the ones who have too much an won't part wit it – tha's how they have it. Tha aul one thinks she owes herself money.'

We pushed on an then stopped at a big house in its own grounds. It had a high wall aroun it an big black gates tha were open. Me ma looked an then said, 'Come on, we'll go in here.'

I followed her through the gates an looked at all the trees an bushes on each side of the drive. There was a lamp post wit a light shinin te show ye the way, so ye wouldn't break yer neck in the dark. When we got aroun te the front of the house, it was all lit up, wit big windas nearly down te the ground an a lovely big entrance in the middle. The two big doors were open. There were two more lovely doors wit church glass, an more church glass in the frames on each side of the doors inside the big porch. An there was a big black iron stand holdin black umbrellas wit silver handles. An outside there was an iron thing fer cleanin yer shoes, me ma said. The gravel aroun the door made a crunchin noise, an it hurt me feet. Me ma looked fer the bell.

'There it is, Ma! In the wall.' I made fer it an pulled the iron knob outa the wall, an it gave a lovely chime. It sounded like the big clock in London, Big Ben! When it stopped, I wanted te pull it again. It was lovely.

'Don't touch tha again!' me ma warned. 'Ye'll only annoy them!' The door was flung open, an a fillum star looked at us. She was wearin a big fur coat an a long black frock, wit gold satin shoes an long danglin diamond earrings. An she had lovely blondie, goldie hair curlin up at the end an hangin down te her shoulders. An bright-red lips an lovely white creamy cheeks. The smell of perfume! I held me breath an gaped.

'Yes?' she asked, slowly suckin on a long silver cigarette holder an takin the smoke deep inta her lungs before she held the cigarette holder in her two fingers up in the air away from her. An closin one eye, cos she was covered in smoke.

Me ma lost her voice. 'Eh,' cough, smile, 'Eh, Lady! I wonder if ye have any old clothes ye don't want? Anythin at all!'

'What do you mean? Clothes for what?' the lady asked, lookin confused.

'Eh, well!' Me ma tried te think. 'Maybe somethin fer te fit the childre.'

'The what?' the lady asked, lookin even more confused.

'The babbies! Her!' me ma said as she pointed at me. 'Maybe ye might have an old pair a shoes tha'd fit her.'

The lady leaned out, lookin from one te the next. 'Gracious!' she muttered, an jumped back in.

'Is that the car, Henrietta?' An we stopped gapin at her te look past at where the man's voice was comin from. 'Bother! We shall be late for the opera if we don't get a move on!' There was a man in a black waistcoat an a jacket wit tails hangin from the back. An black patent shoes, an a snow-white shirt wit a collar tha stood up an looks as if it would stab ye, it was so pointy. An gold cufflinks. An he had a tumbler of whiskey in one hand an a fat cigar in the other. An a fat belly an a bald head, an he spoke like Herbert Lom in the fillums.

I took a sharp breath inta me lungs. I've never seen the like a this before. I moved closer an looked in. There was a great big hall wit doors on each side an a big wide mahogany staircase in the middle leadin up te a big landin wit more doors, an a long winda wit church glass from the ceilin te the floor. The blast of heat when I leaned in would suffocate ye. It was lovely.

The man stopped in his tracks. 'Who is it, darling?'

'Oh! It's only a beggar woman with some urchins,' she called over her shoulder, slowly lookin from us back te the man. Me ma went inta shock at this but stopped herself from lettin fly when the woman said, 'I've no idea, really, what she's about! But do give her something, Cecil. It will send her on her way!' Then she floated in, danglin her long cigarette, holdin it in the air an spillin ash on the lovely rug.

I was drinkin everythin in, me mouth hangin wide an me eyes shinin. I sobbed in a big breath, cos I was forgettin te breathe. I followed her every move aroun the corner, an she disappeared inta a room. Me eyes were foggy from not blinkin, an I had te close them shut an open them again te look at the man, who was very annoyed at us disturbin his peace. He dug his hands inta his trouser pockets an came up empty.

A boy of about ten years appeared on the landin. He was wearin a long wool dressin gown wit pyjamas an slippers, an a teddy bear in his arms. His lovely shiny brown hair was combed te the side, an it was cut above his ears, an he had a flick of hair hangin over his eye. He had lovely fat cheeks. I stared at him. 'Daddy!' he screamed. 'I want Mummy this instant!'

'Oh, bother!' Daddy said, lookin fer money te give us.

'Mummy!' the boy screamed, an Mummy floated out te the hall.

'What is it, darling? You must speak to Nelly!'

'I will not drink that horrid milk and that foul-tasting ginger stuff she puts into it.'

'Oh, darling! Be a sweetie for Nelly, and Mummy will come up and kiss you nightie night.' Then she blew kisses up te him.

'No, Mummy! No!' an he started te wring the teddy's neck.

'This is an outrage!' Daddy barked. 'The whole house is in uproar.'

Nelly appeared in a black frock wit a belt an a white lace collar, an her grey hair tied in a bun in the back of her head, an tried te wrestle the boy back te bed. The man whipped out his wallet an handed me ma a big green pound note an slammed the door shut!

Me ma kept lookin at the pound note te see if it was real! She started laughin an took hold of the pram an said, 'Come on, Martha, let's get home. We'll get in outa the cold,' an she started te run. I gave a last look back an wondered how tha boy could be so lucky te have all tha. How do ye get te be like them?

I clamped me gapin mouth shut an gave a little heave of me chest, lettin out me wind, an then shot me head aroun te run after me ma. An a big black car wit a silver ornament sittin up on the front of the bonnet whirred aroun the corner an came te a stop in front of the house. I looked in, an there was a woman in a big fur coat wit a glitterin diamond crown sittin on her head, an a man in a black dickie bow an a lovely black coat wit black velvet on the collar stared out at me. Then he opened the car door an tried te heave himself out. 'Good gracious!' he said te his wife. 'What's that?' An the two of them looked at me!

The front door opened, an the man who gave me ma the quid held his arms wide an smiled. 'Wonderful to see you, Charles!' an I closed me mouth again, rememberin me ma, an rushed off te catch up wit her, thinkin tha must be a duchess or somethin wit the crown on her head! An the way tha man did as his wife told him, even though he didn't want te give me ma anythin, tha's outa this world, it is! When I grow up, I'm goin te get meself a man just like tha. No Jacksers fer me!

We got home in the pitch black, freezin wit the cold, an me ma said, 'I won't bother lightin the fire, let's just get te bed. Everyone is worn out, an tomorrow we'll have a lovely big dinner.'

'Yeah, Ma, I'm too tired!'

I woke up te see the fire lightin, an me ma said, 'Here, have this drop a tea, an there's a chunk a lovely bread an good butter. An when ye're finished, then go aroun te the shop an get me a pint a milk an six eggs.'

'Right, Ma!' I swallied down the bread an good butter in six bites. It was too good te bother an make it last. I was starvin. 'Any more, Ma?'

'No! We're not eatin the lot now. I want te make it stretch, an ye'll be gettin a big dinner later. Here! Run te the shop,' an she gave me me two shillins.

240

'Can I buy meself a *Bunty* comic, Ma?'

'No! Bring me back the change.'

'Ah, Ma! Just two pence!'

'All right, then, but no more!'

'Ah, thanks, Ma!'

I rushed back wit the milk an eggs, an me ma gave me two pennies. 'I'm goin out, Ma, te get me comics. I'm goin te see if I can get old ones.'

'Don't be long!' me ma shouted after me as I rushed past the winda.

'No, Ma! I'll be back.'

I rambled up Talbot Street an aroun te Marlborough Street, headin fer the second-hand book shops. I bought three *Bunties* an one *Judy* second-hand fer tuppence. They wanted fourpence fer the lot, a penny each. But I managed te get the lot fer a ha'penny each. Tellin the man, cos the aul one didn't want te know, I'd bring back the comics, an he could have the lot fer a penny after I'd finished readin them.

'Go on, then!' he said, after sizin me up te see if I was genuine. I stared back at him, an he handed me the comics, an I threw down the two pennies an rushed out the door before the aul one stopped me.

I crossed me arms, holdin the comics te me chest in case someone'd try te grab them or I dropped them an didn't notice. Ye never know! Ye can lose things. I'm feelin so happy, things couldn't be better. An I had loads a things te look forward te. Then I spotted the two chairs sittin on the steps outside the Government Department Office. They must be thowin them out! I rushed up the steps an looked at them. They were like the ones in the hospital fer visitors te sit on. I looked aroun, an the shops had their bins out. Right! I put one on top of the other, an me comics sittin on them, an rushed off. I was beltin down the road an gave a look back, an there was a man lookin up an down the road scratchin his head, an he must be wonderin where his chairs got te! I ran faster. Jaysus! I'm goin te be arrested. I took another look back when I stopped te cross the road. An I saw him disappear inside. Me heart was poundin, Holy Mother of God, don't get me arrested! I thought they were thrown out!

I got in the door safely. 'Ma! Ma, lookit! We have chairs te sit on!'

'Where'd we get them?' me ma said laughin, an I told her. 'You'd better be careful!' me ma said, 'or you'll be put away an locked up till ye're sixteen.'

I didn't like the thought of tha! A lot of childre from the buildins was put away an locked up. Ye might see them rarely on a Sunday, playin pitch penny. An they'd be dressed in suits an big boots. An the suits look like the sacks the coalman used te throw over his horse on a wet day. An their heads was all shaved. An they didn't act like themselves any more. They were very quiet an kept their heads down an didn't bother te look at ye. It was like the life was gone outa them. An they were tryin te play an enjoy themselves like they used te. But it was all gone, an they were like aul men who'd seen too much a this life. An they were still only my age, some of them nine years old, an ten an eleven. Ye could see they were worried about goin back te Daingean an Artane an Letterfrack. The worry of it was killin them. I know what it's like. Tha's the same fer me when Jackser's livin wit us, so I don't know wha's worse, bein locked up or livin wit Jackser! I felt me heart sink inta me belly, cos I know he'll be back.

I looked up when I heard Charlie an Teddy fightin over the chair. 'No! It's mine! I sawed it first.' Charlie was tryin te tear Teddy's hands offa the chair. 'Get yer own!' Charlie pointed te the other chair beside the table, an Teddy looked over an rushed te get the other chair. An tried te pull it over te the fire an knocked it down. Charlie was sittin up on the chair now, wavin his legs an laughin. Teddy was screamin in frustration.

Me comics! I suddenly remembered. 'Where's me comics?' I screamed.

'I'm goin te kill the lot of ye if ye don't stop tha roarin,' me ma shouted.

I raced over te the bed an looked under an all aroun me. I was in a sweat. 'Ma! Ma! Me comics is gone!'

'They're on the floor where ye left them.'

An I looked. Harry was sittin on the floor, tearin an eatin them. I grabbed his hands an loosened his grip before he could do any more damage. An tried te put the torn bits together an took the half page still stickin outa his mouth. He sat lookin at me fer a minute. 'Ye're bold!' I said, an I went te sit on the bed. An he crawled after me, wantin them back, an screamed in frustration, tearin his hair out, when I wouldn't let him have them.

'Give him somethin te keep him quiet!' me ma roared from the scullery. I looked aroun te see if there was anythin. I knew I wouldn't get any peace te read if I didn't. I leapt off the bed an wrestled the chair offa Charlie an dragged it under the winda, puttin it on its side, an called Harry te come an play wit it. He laughed an rushed over on his hands an knees. An Teddy thought it was a great idea an dropped his own chair an came rushin over te join in. Charlie was delighted an stopped tryin te get the chair offa me an rushed back, laughin. 'Now I have me own, an no one's gettin it!' he roared.

Me ma was fryin the roast potatoes an the roast beef in the fryin pan wit the beef drippin, an I could hear the hissin from the pan. The smell was outa this world. I looked aroun me, sittin on the bed wit me back te the headboard, takin in the lovely red roarin fire an the lovely food, an the chairs we could sit on now by the fire, an took a big sigh, lettin out me breath wit all the peace an comfort we had. An I picked up me comic te read. Wha more could a body want? I asked meself. I lost meself wit 'Wee Slavey' carryin up the heavy buckets of coal te the kitchen. An I was tormented like her when all the cook an the parlour maid an the downstairs kitchen maid was screamin at her. All at the same time! She was sweatin an wipin her forehead, an tryin te hurry. 'Light the fire in the mornin room!' the parlour maid screamed. 'Ye didn't blacken me stove!' the cook shouted, an this was all in Victorian times. It was great! I was sufferin away wit Wee Slavey but feelin no pain, cos it wasn't me. An I could lift me head any time an smell the cookin, an then I was in heaven. Then I went te 'Bessie Bunter' at her lovely boardin school wit the lovely uniform an the gorgeous blazer. I'd love te be there. She was tormented tryin te get her hands on the big parcel her rich parents sent her. The head teacher had it locked up in her press, an it was full of chocolate, an sweets, an biscuits, an homemade cakes. An Bessie only cared about eatin, nothin else! An she was fat as a fool! An she got herself in an awful lot of trouble, cos she was tryin te break inta the study. She was climbin up the drainpipe, an it gave way an she landed on her fat arse an was caught when the head girl, Mary, came marchin by wit her hands in her blazer pockets an two thumbs stickin out. Tha's what a lady does! It was marvellous, an I was Mary, the head girl, cos Bessie is too stupid fer my likin. The stories take me away from meself, an I go off inta another world.

I heard the rattle of plates, an we all looked up. 'Right! It's ready,' me ma said.

'Dinner!' Charlie roared. An he threw himself offa the chair he'd been guardin an upended it.

'Take it easy!' me ma said. 'There's plenty te go aroun.' She brought in a plate filled high like a mountain wit fried roast beef an potatoes, an put it on the table. We all rushed over, an the babby screamed, cos he was caught under the chair an thought he was goin te miss out on the grub. I let him loose, an he rushed over on his hands an knees.

'Don't touch the plate!' me ma roared from the scullery. 'I'm not ready yet,' an she brought in the fryin pan wit the six eggs all mashed up an fried. I looked. Pity she can't make them yella in the middle an all white. But ye can't help tha, cos she's not able te cook. Jackser does the cookin, but then he eats it himself an we get nothin anyways, so this is better. She put fried potatoes on the clean plate, an meat an a bit of egg, an buttered six slices a bread, an put a few scones on, an we watched her, wonderin who this was fer, cos we only have the two plates.

'Here!' me ma said, handin me the plate, an I thought it was fer me! Bring this over te Mrs Dunne quickly while it's hot an tell her we had too much an I hope she enjoys it! Run before it gets cold.'

I knocked on the door, holdin the plate, an me stomach was goin mad te get me teeth inta it. The door opened, an Mrs Dunne's eyes were hangin out lookin at the plate. 'Me mammy said ye might like this, cos we've too much, an she'd be grateful if ye'd have it.'

'Ah, Jaysus, no! I couldn't, an yer poor mammy wit a roomful of childre.'

She looked at the plate as if she was starvin, an Jimmy came over an said in a loud whisper, 'Is this fer us, Ma? Take it, Mam!'

I said, 'If ye don't, it'll only go te waste!'

'Ah! All right so, seein as ye put it like tha. I don't like te see waste,' an she took the plate from me. I wanted te get back fast te eat me own dinner, an I turned me head te go, an she said, 'Tell yer mammy I said, the blessins of God on her! May she never want fer anythin. An I won't forget this.'

'Thanks, Mrs. I'll tell her tha,' an I rushed inta me own room.

'Come on, get yer dinner before it gets cold!' me ma said, eatin a mouthful of potato. 'I gave them theirs, an we'll share the plate along wit the babby.'

I looked over at Teddy an Charlie. They had their own chairs, an they were kneelin at them, eatin the meat offa the bread, an they had their potatoes lined up on the seat of the chairs an were busy stuffin the grub inta their mouths. Everyone was quiet, an me ma was standin at the table, holdin the babby an puttin food inta his mouth, an feedin herself. I helped meself te a potato an a bit of meat. It went down too fast before I had a chance te taste it, an I grabbed a bit a bread an put eggs on it. 'Oh! This is gorgeous,' I mumbled, not talkin, cos I wanted te get the grub inta me. We had a sup a tea wit the cakes, an our bellies were full.

'I enjoyed tha,' me ma said, laughin. 'Tha's wha them nuns eat all the time. No wonder they have big red necks!'

Then she took out the Oxo box wit all her papers in it, an she dipped her hand te the bottom an counted out one shillin an sixpence, an put it on the mantelpiece. 'Tha's the rent money,' she said. 'Leave it there, an I'll go over an pay it. We don't want te get put out again. After this place, there's nowhere te go, an we'll end up on the streets.'

'No, Ma! We can't let tha happen. Do ye know what'd be lovely, Ma?'

'Wha?' she said.

'If we could get our hands on a radio!'

'Yeah!' she said. 'But ye'd need money. Ye'd pay about thirty bob, or two quid, in the pawn fer one.'

'Ah, still, ye never know, we might get the money somehow! An then we could start te make a real home fer ourselves. We could get a little bit at a time. I'm goin te start te keep a lookout,' I said.

The babby started te fall asleep on the floor, an me ma picked him up an put him in the bed an covered him up. I climbed onta the bed an sat up on the other end wit me back te the headboard an took up me comics te read. Me ma stoked the fire wit the poker an put on a bit of coal. The room had gone a bit dark, an I looked at the winda, an it was startin te pour wit rain. I was glad I was lovely an cosy sittin on the bed wit me comics, an the room was lovely an warm. Teddy an Charlie had the chairs on their sides, an they were playin cowboys an injuns, an they were shootin each other wit their fingers. Me ma was washin up in the scullery. There was a knock at the door, an I jumped up an opened it. Jimmy handed me back the plate. It was shinin clean. Me ma poked her head outa the scullery. 'Are ye all right, son?' she said te Jimmy.

'Yes, Mam! Me ma said te tell ye tha was the nicest bit a grub we've had in a lifetime, an she says thanks very much. She hopes ye didn't leave yerself short, so she does.'

'Not at all!' me ma said. 'We enjoyed it, too. Tell her I'll see her later, when I get the childre down fer the night.'

'OK, Mrs! I'll tell her. See ya!' he said te me, an I shut the door an picked up me comic again.

'Ye're dead,' Charlie roared, pushin Teddy down. 'I'm still alive, so I won.'

'Bold!' Teddy roared back, an spit at Charlie, but it only dribbled down his chin.

'I'm not playin no more wit you,' Charlie screamed. 'An gimme the chair, I sawed it first!'

'Ah!' screamed Teddy, an tried te bite Charlie's head, but he ended up wit dirty mouthfuls of hair an let go, makin an awful face.

'Right! Tha's it!' me ma said. 'Come on, ye's are either playin together in peace an quiet or ye's can go te bed.'

I took no notice. I was now a champion ice skater wit 'Zelda', the girl who never gets any older, even though she's hundreds of years old an lives her life in an ice cave. I got carried away an was feelin the cold livin in a cave. I looked up te see the fire blazin. Ah! This is the life, I thought, shakin meself wit comfort.

'I won't be long,' me ma said as she went out the door. 'I'm only callin te Mrs Dunne fer a while.' Teddy an Charlie jumped up an tried te follow. 'No!' she said, pushin them back inta the room. 'You stay here. I want a bit a peace without youse,' an she shut the door. They jumped up an down screamin.

'Come on,' I said. 'Let's play school,' an I put me comics under the mattress, te keep them from harm. 'Now sit on yer chairs an say after me, one an one is two!' I held up me two fingers. 'How many is tha, Charlie?'

'Eh! I don't know.'

'It's two, ye gobshite! Ye have te know how te count when ye start school, or the teacher will kill ye.'

'I'm not playin,' Charlie roared.

'All right, then, watch this,' I said. 'If I give ye a sweet in this hand, an I give ye one in the other hand, how many sweets will ye have?'

'Two!' Charlie laughed.

'Right,' I said. 'Now! How many is this?' An I held up me two fingers again.

'I don't know,' Charlie said.

'Ah! You're pure stupid,' I roared, losin me rag.

Then there was a knock on the door, an Jimmy poked his head in. 'Me ma said te give ye these. They're broken biscuits,' an he held up a rolled newspaper, shaped like a cornet, an held it out.

While I was still lookin, Charlie grabbed the biscuits, an Teddy an himself was fightin te get at them. The paper tore, an the biscuits flew everywhere. Charlie was down on his knees, grabbin all he could an stuffin them in his mouth. I fell te the floor, tryin te pick them up, an Charlie had a handful, an Teddy was screamin, cos he got nothin. 'Ye

247

hungry bastard!' I screamed at Charlie, lungin fer his mouth te stop him eatin the lot. An he clamped his teeth down on me hand tha was caught in his mouth. The babby woke up red-faced an was cryin.

'Ah, there's no peace fer the wicked!' me ma laughed, rushin in.

'Ah, no! Don't be takin his bit a comfort!' Mrs Dunne said te me. 'Let him be an enjoy his few biscuits.'

'But we got none, an he bit the hand offa me!' I cried.

'Serves ye right fer shovin yer hand inta his mouth. I saw ye!' Mrs Dunne said, laughin. Charlie gave a bit a biscuit te Teddy, te keep him from screamin, an ran inta the scullery te hide an guzzle wha was left. I could hear him laughin an talkin te himself. I was ragin, but I couldn't run at him, cos I'd only make an eejit of meself wit Mrs Dunne watchin. Ye're not supposed te be givin yer senses te somebody who's a lot younger than ye.

Me ma put the water on te boil fer the tea, an then she fried bread fer us. It was heaven. The brown jelly from the drippin was still on the fried bread, an it tasted like the roast beef we had today. This is the best day we've ever had. It was like a feast. An I put Teddy te bed, an me ma sat on the chair by the fire, feedin a bottle a tea te Harry, an he dozed in comfort on her lap. Charlie climbed inta the inside of the bed, beside the wall, an I put Teddy in beside him.

'Ask Mrs does she want te come over fer a sup a tea!' me ma said te me, an she lifted Harry over te the bed. He had dozed off now, an the bottle was stickin outa his mouth. An me ma took it out an put it on the table, puttin him gently down at the top of the bed an coverin him up.

I knocked on Mrs Dunne's door, an she said, 'Right, childre, I'm on me way. I'll just see te the fire, an I'll be over.'

Me ma was puttin two cakes out on the big plate fer Mrs Dunne's tea, an I climbed inta bed, pullin out me comics from under the mattress. I was readin an listenin te the murmur of voices, of me ma an Mrs Dunne talkin quietly te each other, sittin on their chairs in front of the fire. An I put me comics away under me pilla an closed me eyes tha were very heavy now, an snuggled under the blankets an coats, feelin warm an snug, an enjoyin the peace an comfort.

24

I looked at the thrupenny bit in me hand, feelin the weight of it. I saved it up, doin all the messages fer the neighbours. I wanted te buy pipe cleaners te put in me hair te curl it. I couldn't wear me lovely new frock until I had me hair done in big massive curls like Shirley Temple. We got a load a lovely good clothes when we knocked on a door on Phillipsburg Avenue on the way back from collectin the bread at the convents. The woman was a lovely person altogether. She looked at us fer a minute, thinkin, an said, 'Do you know? I've just done a clear out, and I might have clothes that will fit you. Wait there!' an she went in, leavin the door open a little, an me ma an me looked at each other an laughed wit excitement.

She came out wit a big bundle of clothes. Trousers an jumpers, coats an hats, shoes, vests an knickers. 'They'd fit me brothers grand!' I was sayin, lookin at them. The woman was smilin an helpin me ma te put them in the pram. An me ma was very happy an sayin, 'God bless ye, Lady. Ye're a very kind person.'

The woman looked at me an said, 'I have a daughter about your age, and I have some clothes that will fit you. She's grown out of them now.' An she came back wit a load of clothes fer me. I got navy-blue knickers, socks an brown leather sandals, an I dropped down te the ground an whipped them on me, an they were a grand fit. The frock was dark-blue heavy cotton, wit an underskirt attached te make it stand out, an I'd be able te twirl in it. It had a lovely lace collar, an I stroked it, not believin me eyes. It was so lovely! She gave me a wool gaberdine coat wit a belt, an a black beret hat. The wool was so soft, I couldn't wait te wear them. I'm goin te be mistaken fer a spy when I wear the hat an coat. Cos tha's what all the spies wear in the fillums.

Then she came out wit a load of *Bunty* an *Judy* comics fer me. Me heart was flyin wit excitement. Me ma got a lovely green coat wit a big collar, an a load of summer frocks an winter wool pleated skirts an jumpers. Teddy had te squeeze up beside Harry, but they were happy, cos Harry was busy swingin the white rattler she gave him. An Teddy was holdin onta a big bunny rabbit, wit big ears. He kept rubbin it against his cheek. An Charlie was carryin a bucket an spade an a big red ball. 'Ma! Will ya bring us out te the seaside? I want te build a big sandcastle wit me bucket an spade. Will ya, Ma? Will ya?' Charlie kept askin me ma.

'Yeah, we will,' me ma said. 'We'll do tha when the summer comes. We'll go out te Sandymount, an we'll bring sambidges an bottles a tea. Yeah!' me ma said, thinkin te herself. 'We must do tha!'

We were happy an contented an didn't say much, cos we were savin our breath te get home in the dark, an concentrated our strength te push the heavy pram wit the mountain of lovely stuff.

I couldn't wait te hit home an fall inta me bed. It'd been a long day traipsin aroun from house te house. An it was pitch dark, an we were exhausted. I looked at the babbies, their heads wrapped aroun each other, out cold. An I wished I could climb in there an get a lift home. But I was very contented, thinkin of all me lovely stuff, an how easy our life was now wit no one te bother us.

I walked up Talbot Street, an went inta a shop. 'Have ye any pipe cleaners?' I asked the aul fella behind the counter.

'Yeah! How many do ye want?'

'One packet! How much are they, Mister?'

'Tuppence!'

'How much?' I roared.

'Are ye deaf?' he said. 'Tuppence, I said.'

'Tha's very dear, Mister. Have ye any cheaper?'

'No!'

'Gawd! Tha's robbery!' I said, an he threw them back inta the box an walked off ignorin me. 'All right, then! I'll take them.'

He threw the pipe cleaners onta the high counter, an I jumped up an took them, an put down the thrupenny bit. He threw the money inta the cardboard box he keeps fer his money an walked away. I waited. 'Here, Mister! I want me penny change. I can count, ye know! I gave ye a thrupenny bit,' I roared.

'Did ye?' he said, an walked back te his box, dippin his hand in an throwin the penny at me onta the counter. I jumped up an stretched across, an grabbed me penny.

'I'm not comin back here again!' I roared at him on me way out the door. 'Ye're a daylight robber. An I hope ye have no luck fer tha!'

'Go on! Get out before I take me hand te ye,' he growled at me.

I flew home, wantin te wash me hair an get the pipe cleaners in, then I could wear me new frock an sandals, an me lovely white socks an knickers. I wouldn't know meself. I'm dyin te look like Shirley Temple. The only thing is, she has lovely fat brown legs, an mine look like matchsticks. But I'll be lovely anyway.

When I got in the door, me ma had her good green coat on. 'Come on,' she said. 'I was waitin te go out!'

'Where are ye goin, Ma?'

'Never you mind! Watch them childre an mind the house. I'll be back,' an she was gone, flyin out the door. I boiled the water an poured it inta the basin an put it on the chair, then I poured in cold water an got the bit of red Sunlight soap we had left, an dipped me head inta the basin. I rubbed in the soap an scrubbed me head, gettin it all soapy. I kept dippin me head inta the basin, but I couldn't get the soap off. So I put me head under the tap an froze the head offa meself, but I held it there, cos it'd be worth it te get me hair lookin lovely. Then I grabbed the cloth we use fer dryin ourselves an everythin else. An I looked at it, drippin water everywhere an drownin meself. It was thick wit grease an dirt! Jaysus, I can't use tha! What'll I do? I grabbed an old woolly jumper belongin te the babby, an it wasn't much better. So I took off me frock, standin in me skin, an dried me head wit tha. Then I put it on the back of the other chair te dry it at the fire, an put the basin on the floor an sat on the chair an put me feet in the basin. I couldn't get the dirt off, it was caked inta me feet, an I had cuts an dried sores from walkin on the stones. I rubbed an rubbed, but they didn't look much better, an now they were bleedin from the rubbin an openin the sores. 'Ah, fuck it!' I shouted te meself, an washed me legs. They didn't look the way I thought they would, an I grabbed the cloth an dried me feet an legs, smellin now from the dirty cloth. I picked up me frock, an it was still wet. Ah, well! It'll do. Then I emptied the water down the sink an used the babby's jumper te mop up the wet on the floorboards.

Then I had a go at puttin in me pipe cleaners. I'd seen the way me ma used te put them in her hair when I was small. I straightened them out an wrapped bits a hair aroun them, an then wrapped the two ends together close te me scalp. When I was finished, I looked in the mirror. Grand! Me face is clean, an now I'm goin te look lovely when I take them out. I couldn't wait!

Me ma came back, an she was lookin very happy.

'Where were ye, Ma?'

'I went te see him in Mountjoy. They're lettin him out on Monday!'

'But why, Ma? Wha's happenin? He's not in long enough!'

'They're lettin him out early fer good behaviour, so he doesn't have te do the full six months,' me ma said.

'Is he comin back here?' I asked in a whisper, feelin a terrible weakness come over me.

'Don't ye know he is!' me ma said, very annoyed wit me.

'Ma, please, we're grand without him, don't let him back.'

'An where will we go?' me ma shouted. 'This place is in his name. The Corporation won't give me a place of me own unless he gives up this place, an he's not goin te do tha! Now don't be moidierin me.' An she turned her back on me an hung up her coat on the back of the door.

I sat down on the edge of the bed, the life gone outa me. I looked at me ma, an I could sense the excitement in her at havin Jackser back. She really wants him back! It's nothin te do wit her not bein able te get her own place! I couldn't believe it. She likes tha Jackser, an the hell wit everyone else! Me ma is only out fer herself. I'm only useful te her fer gettin her things an doin everythin I can fer her. There was somethin about the way she was all excited about havin Jackser back tha made me feel sick an disgusted in me stomach wit her. An I didn't care if I never saw her again. I felt me heart go cold, an it was as if I was made of stone. I didn't feel anythin, or care, or think, or look forward te anythin. I felt nothin. Just stone cold. I've another five years te wait until I'm fourteen. Then I can get a job an go te England. But I don't think I'm goin te wait tha long.

Me ma was down on her hands an knees sloshin dirty water aroun the floorboards. She dipped the greasy, smelly, dirty rag inta the bucket of dirty water. There was bits of fluff from the rag an a bit of the bottle top from the milk bottle, an lumps of brown stuff, probably shit, tha had been caked inta the floor now all floatin on top of the dirty water. She lifted the drippin rag an slapped it down on the floor again. An leaned over te a dry spot, pushin the bucket outa her way. An started spreadin the soppin rag from left te right, makin big black streaks on the boards, an spreadin the rubbish from the bucket aroun. 'Aroun the world I'll search for you,' she sang happily. I wondered why the water wasn't lovely an clean an sudsy, an the floor comin up snow white an smellin of soap an disinfectant like when Mrs Dunne an the other mammies scrubbed their floors. Me ma can't do anythin right.

I was gettin more annoyed by the minute watchin her. The floor was even mankier now than before she started. An the smell was givin me a headache. It was like rotten shit. The babby was covered from head te toe in the filthy water, dashin aroun on his hands an knees wearin only a vest an tryin te get at the bucket of water an splash it all over himself an slap the floor like me ma. An he'd blink his eyes an stop in shock when the cold water hit him, an then slap the water in the bucket again. An me ma shouted at him an pushed him away, but he kept circlin aroun her an crawlin over the wet floor, draggin the dirty water over the clean spot.

Me ma says, 'Tha's clean anyway.' An she jumped up an grabbed Harry. 'Here! Mind tha child before I lose me rag wit the lot of ye's!'

she roared at me, dumpin the babby on the bed beside me. Then she turned suddenly, slipped on the wet floor an sent the bucket flyin. An a gush of water went everywhere. Me ma's right leg shot out straight in front of her, an she landed on her back, slidin along the floor. An there was an awful quiet. We all gaped, tryin te take in the sudden shock an wonderin if me ma was kilt. 'Me leg! Ah! Me back!' Me ma crawled slowly onta her knees an tried te get up.

'Are ye all right, Ma?' I asked her, afraid te breathe.

'Lookit me floor! The curse of Jaysus on the lot of ye's, ye whore's melt! I haven't had a day's luck since I had the lot of ye's,' me ma screamed, lookin at me, eyes bulgin. I stared, an me ma suddenly lunged fer the table, pickin up the knife an throwin it at me. I whipped up me left arm, coverin me face te protect me head, an the knife caught me on the elbow, sendin a white hot pain shootin through me.

'Ah! Me arm! You've hurt me arm!' I jumped off the bed, holdin me arm, an blood dripped everywhere. The knife hit the bone in me elbow an sliced open me arm, makin a gash.

'I warned ye,' me ma screamed, 'not te torment me! Ye were lyin on yer arse, not botherin te give me a hand, an now ye got wha ye deserve. I'll be done fer ye if ye don't stop drippin tha blood everywhere!'

I looked aroun fer somethin te stop the blood, but the floor was covered in water, an I was afraid te move in case I made her even more annoyed. 'Gimme somethin te put on it, Ma!' I shouted in pain.

She picked up the bucket an squeezed out the dirty floor rag an said, 'Here! Wipe it wit tha.' I held the slimy rag, not wantin te hold it, the smell of it. But I pressed it te me arm an held it there. The pain in me bone was still stabbin through me.

'Gimme the cloth,' me ma said, an went back te cleanin the floor. I bent down an picked up me cardigan from under the bed an put it on.

'I'm goin out, Ma, te see if there's anythin happenin. I might pick up somethin.' I knew she wouldn't stop me then if she thought I might bring back anythin.

Charlie was sittin on the ground wit a stick, spittin in the mud tryin te make shapes wit the stick. He jumped up when he saw me. 'Are ye goin somewhere, Martha?'

'Yeah! Let's go fer a wander.' An he dropped the stick an followed me out the gate onta Corporation Street.

'Where are we goin, Martha?'

'I don't know yet. Let's just see.'

The shops were closed, cos it was Sunday. An people had their good clothes on. I knew I was a bit of a show wit me pipe cleaners still in me hair an tryin te cover them up wit me ma's scarf on me head, an holdin me arm wit the blood still seepin through me woolly cardigan. It was still painin me an wouldn't stop bleedin.

'What ails yer arm, Martha? Ye're all full a blood.'

'Nothin. Me ma just hit me, tha's all.'

'Let's get a look!'

'No, leave it! It's still painin me.' I pushed his hand away. 'Come on, let's go up te O'Connell Street.' I knew this was me last chance te have time te play before Jackser came back tomorrow. An I didn't want te think about him, cos it was makin me feel very sick.

We walked behind a man an a woman wit a boy of about six, holdin his hands in the middle of them. The father was holdin the hand of another child, a girl of about my age. She skipped along, suckin on an ice-cream cornet, an her long shiny ringlets bounced up an down. I admired her no end. She looked lovely wit the big white ribbon tied up in a bow on the top of her head. An she was wearin a lovely red coat wit a velvet collar an a belt at the back, an lovely red patent shoes wit straps te match, an white ankle socks. An she had lovely fat white legs, an ye could see she got a lot of good feedin an plenty of washin. I'd say she was definitely washed in hot water an soap every day. Tha's how she got te look like tha.

'Daddy, can we please go to the café and eat supper after the Phoenix Park?' she asked her daddy, lookin up at him.

'Now, now, Poppet! Mummy may have other ideas,' he laughed, lookin down at her.

'Oh, please, Daddy! You promised.'

'Now, Sarah! Do behave!' the mammy said, lookin over at Sarah.

I rushed past, wantin te get a better look at Sarah, who was shakin herself an her father's hand an her ice cream up an down in a temper, an spillin ice cream down the front of her lovely coat. An I stopped in front of them te look, an Sarah stopped actin the babby an gaped at me as if I had two heads, an moved in closer te her father. She looked up at him an then at me. An I watched her mammy take a white lace handkerchief outa her shiny black patent handbag an dab the ice cream on Sarah's coat. 'Really!' said the mammy. 'You ought to be more careful, dear. You really are a very naughty girl!'

Sarah stamped her foot an threw the ice cream on the ground, an we followed its landin wit our mouths open. Charlie looked at me an then dived on the cornet, pickin it up an shovin it up inta his mouth before Sarah changed her mind an screamed fer it back. Jaysus, I thought, rushin off. Imagine actin like tha at her age! She didn't look mental. An the mammy an daddy even let her get away wit it! How does tha happen? I suppose the toffs are all like tha. Very kind. I'd love te be Sarah. One day I'll be like tha. I'll wash every day an eat good grub an be very kind.

We stopped outside Cafolla's café an gaped in at the people all sittin at tables dressed up in their best Sunday clothes. An eatin plates of fish an chips an beans, an fried white eggs wit the lovely yella yolks in the middle. An pots of tea an bread an butter. An the childre were eatin big tumblers full of different-coloured ice cream an drinkin lemonade. An the smell comin outa the door was gorgeous. 'Why can't we go in there?' Charlie said, lookin up at me. 'Would ye need loads a money, Martha?' He was shiftin from one foot te the other an smackin his lips.

'Yeah! Ye would,' I said.

A young one stared out at me, makin a face an shakin her head at me. An puttin a big dollop of ice cream inta her ugly face an then stickin her tongue, wit the ice cream still on it, at us.

'Come on,' I said. 'Let's go in!'

I marched past the young one wit the ice cream, an her head shot aroun, watchin me go up te the counter. An she shouted at her mammy, 'Look, Mammy! Look at them dirty children comin in here. They're not supposed te be in here.'

'Shush, Mary! Eat your ice cream and take no notice,' the mammy said.

I stood up straight, tryin te make meself look important. 'Out!' the waitress screamed at us.

'Eh! I wonder if I could . . .'

'No! Out, come on!' she said, pointin te the door.

Ice-cream face roared laughin.

'What is it?' a red-faced older woman asked, turnin aroun from behind the counter.

'Could I have a glass of water fer me little brother, please? He's very thirsty!'

The woman looked down at Charlie, an the young waitress said, 'No, Nelly, don't mind them, they're only lookin fer somethin fer nothin!'

'Ah, they're only childre, fer God's sake,' an she bent down an poured out two glasses of orange squash an put them on the counter. 'Here, take them, an drink them at tha table over there. An don't be mindin Dinah, she has serious matters on her mind an wants te take it out on everyone.' Then she wiped the counter wit a wet dishcloth an roared laughin. 'Don't worry, Dinah, there's plenty more fish in the sea! Ye were right te let tha one go, he was only a tiddler. Next time ye might land yerself a big one! Maybe even a shark!' then she roared laughin again. Dinah stopped wipin the empty table an came over te the counter an whispered inta Nelly's ear. Nelly stopped suckin on her false teeth te listen an then threw her head back, an the two of them roared laughin. 'Go way!' Nelly said, wipin her eyes an nose. 'I suppose he thought it was fer stirrin his tea!' An they laughed again.

I sat at the empty table wit Charlie beside me an sipped me orange lookin over at Ice-cream face, who was gobsmacked. An I put me nose in the air an looked away from her. I wasn't goin te make a show of meself makin faces at her.

I sipped slowly, feelin I was on me way te bein grown up. This

257

is what it must be like when ye're big an ye're yer own person. I enjoyed watchin the people sittin an eatin an the two women at the counter nudgin each other an havin a great laugh. I felt like I was all a part of wha was goin on. An people were not bothered even lookin at us now, cos Nelly was good te us. They thought we were all right, too. This is so peaceful. Charlie gave a big heave outa his chest an slammed the empty glass down on the table. His mouth was red from the orange juice, an he looked at me an gasped, 'All gone!'

I poured half from my glass an whispered te him, 'Drink it slowly. If we make it last, we can stay here longer.' I didn't want this peace te end, I was thinkin te meself. I could see the crowds of people slowly passin up an down. Some stopped te look in the big plate-glass winda an then wander on, everyone enjoyin their Sunday outin.

Me elbow felt very stiff, an I stretched it te ease the soreness, then I felt the bleedin again. I pulled up the sleeve, an it was stuck te me arm. I gave it a little tug, an the blood started te flow again. Bloody hell, everyone is lookin. 'Come on, Charlie, it's time te go!' I pushed back the chair an pulled down me sleeve.

'Wha happened te yer arm?' the young waitress asked, pullin at me sleeve.

'It's bleedin,' I said, tryin te pull me arm back.

'Yeah! I can see tha, but how did ye do it?'

'I fell an cut meself.'

'Ye better go up te the hospital, tha's goin te need stitchin!'

'Will I have te?'

'Yeah! I think ye should, it won't stop bleedin otherwise.'

'All right, then, I'll go.'

We walked te the end of O'Connell Street an up onta Parnell Square. Past the strollin crowds, some of them not likin the look of us an movin apart te give us room. I didn't like the feelin of standin out. I was not wearin me good shoes yet, or me lovely frock. I'd wanted te save them till me hair was curly. So now, wit me bare dirty feet covered in black crusty sores, not te mention me ma's scarf tha didn't really cover the pipe cleaners tha was stickin outa the front of me head like horns, I look like a right eejit! But now I didn't care about wantin te look lovely any more, not wit the weight in me chest over the Jackser fella comin back tomorrow. I rushed on, wantin now te get away from all these respectable people givin me funny looks. O'Connell Street on a lovely Sunday afternoon isn't the place fer the likes of me, not lookin like this anyway. I turned right onta Belvedere, passin the school an the Jesuits, thinkin of the priest who gave Jackser the half-crown an him findin the few cigarettes in the box on the doorstep at the same time. Puttin him in great form altogether. Then we turned left an crossed the road an went inta Temple Street Hospital.

There was no other patients, so the nurse came over te us straight away. 'Right! Take off your cardigan, and we'll take a look. How did that happen?' the nurse asked, dabbin at me cut wit a big piece of cotton wool dipped in a tray of disinfectant. I said nothin. I was watchin her lookin hard at me arm, an likin the smell of disinfectant an all the other things they have fer makin ye well again. I watched her every movement as she pressed an dabbed an then dumped the dirty cotton wool in the big bin, an then dipped the steel thing wit the pointy fingers inta the disinfectant again an picked up more cotton wool. It was bleedin again, an she bent me arm an then straightened it again. It started te pour. She put a big piece of cotton wool on it an bent me arm. 'Stay here, dear. I'll just get the doctor to take a look.' An off she went, through the door.

Charlie put his nose in the disinfectant, tryin te get a better smell, an then looked up at me, sittin on the side of the high bed, danglin me feet over the side. 'Do ye think they'll cut yer arm off, Martha?'

He looked worried, an I thought about this fer a minute. 'Ah, no!' I whispered back. 'It works grand, see!' An I gave it a few stretches, droppin the cotton wool, an we both watched the blood drippin from me arm onta the floor.

The door swung open, an the nurse rushed in laughin an holdin her arse. 'Tommy O'Dowd, you're a right lecher!' she laughed inta the doctor's face.

'Ah, now! You weren't saying that the other night!' he laughed back.

Before I could wonder wha they were talkin about, the doctor marched over te me an took hold of me arm an said, 'Oh, dear! I'm afraid you will have to get stitches. Where's your mammy?'

'She's at home,' I said.

'How did this happen?'

He was rubbin me hand, an he had a worried look on his face. An he looked at Charlie, an Charlie suddenly said, 'Ye won't cut her arm off, will ye, Doctor?'

'No, of course not! What's your name?'

'Charlie!'

'And what age are you, Charlie?'

'Four! I'm four. An I'm not lettin ye take me sister's arm off. Cos I don't believe ye. Me ma says ye only go inta hospital when ye're ready te die!'

'Yeah!' I agreed, shakin me head at the doctor. 'It's true. Everyone says if ye go inta hospital, ye never come out again. They say the cure is worse than the disease.'

'Heavens above!' the nurse screamed. 'We do no such thing,' an she was roarin laughin.

'How did this happen?' the doctor asked me gently.

I looked at him fer a minute. He was very gentle, an I suddenly felt very annoyed wit me ma. Her an her aul Jackser fella. 'Me ma did it!' I said loudly. 'She threw the knife at me!' I was goin te say she probably didn't mean te hit me, but I was still annoyed an left tha bit out. The doctor looked at the nurse an then whispered somethin inta her ear. An then said, 'Will you be a very brave girl when I stitch it up?'

'Yeah, yeah. Ye mean not cry?'

'Yes, I'll be very quick!' He held up the needle an put the thread through, an then told me te look away. The nurse held me other hand, but I didn't move a muscle, cos I wanted te make the lovely doctor happy. 'Now, all over!' he said, an stood up straight, admirin his stitches. 'You were a very brave girl, very brave indeed,' an he put his hand in his pocket an handed me a shillin. 'Buy yourself some sweets.' I was so delighted wit meself, everyone thinkin I'm great, an all fer nothin! Sure, I didn't feel any pain from the stitchin at all. An they think I'm very brave! I left the hospital wit a big white bandage on me arm, wishin it coulda lasted a little while longer.

Now we're standin outside the shop on Talbot Street. I felt me heart sinkin down inta me belly. I can't let me ma see the bandage, or she'll know I was at the hospital, an Jackser might get it outa Charlie tha I told on me ma. 'Charlie! If I buy ye sweets wit the shillin will ye promise ye won't say I told on me ma? Will ye keep quiet about the hospital? Don't say we were there, will ye, Charlie? Cos Jackser will only kill the two of us, especially me, an he'd probably kill you too! Ye know wha he's like.'

Charlie shook his head. 'No, Martha! I won't say nothin.'

We went inta the sweet shop, an I gave Charlie a thrupenny bar of chocolate. He took it from me slowly, afraid it'd drop an break on him, an then said in a whisper, 'What else can I get, Martha?'

He couldn't see over the counter, an I couldn't get a good look either, cos of me sore arm. I wasn't able te hoist meself up, never mind give him a lift up. 'Do ye want a fizz bag, wit a lollipop inside?'

'Yeah! Get me one a them, an a penny toffee, Mrs, please!' I handed him the rest of his sweets. An the woman gave me sixpence change.

I looked up at all the jars on the high shelves, thinkin wha te buy meself. 'Give us sixpence worth a bull's eyes, Mrs, please.'

When we got outside the shop, I looked inside the white paper bag, an there was loads a bull's eyes. I stuck one inside me mouth, an I didn't really like the taste, it was too peppery. An suddenly I was back in the hospital sittin on the granny's bed. I could feel the softness of her chest an the lovely feelin of bein snug sittin close beside her an me back lyin on her stomach. I could even get the smell of her soap an the talcum powder she shook on herself when she washed herself in the mornin. An the two of us snug beside each other when she did her knittin an I rolled the wool inta balls. An I sucked away on her bull's eyes or munched one of her biscuits. An then fer no reason me chest filled up, an I was cryin. I missed the granny, an I wanted te climb up on the bed again an get her te smother me in her arms an rub me head an say, 'Don't mind anybody. I'll look after ye, an if tha aul Jackser fella comes near ye again, I'll put me boot under his arse an lift him outa it.'

Charlie was sayin somethin te me, an I stared at him, wonderin wha was happenin. An then I shook meself, an he said, 'Why are ye cryin, Martha? I won't say nothin, I promise! Ye don't have te cry.'

'Yeah! It's all right, Charlie, I'm stopped cryin now. Eat yer sweets. We better have them all gone before we get back, or she'll want te know where we got the money an why we didn't bring it back instead of buyin sweets.'

I took me arm outa the sleeve an looked at the bandage, thinkin, pity! I'll have te take it off or she'll know I was at the hospital an then maybe find out I told. Jackser'd start questionin me ma anyway, about wha happened te me arm, if he saw the bandage. An she'd tell him I asked fer it, an he'd only go fer me again. I threw the bandage inta a laneway an hurried on. 'Come on, Charlie. It's gettin late! Me ma will wonder where we got te, an I've nothin te bring her back. So she'll only start givin out. An we don't want her tellin tha aul fella when he comes back tomorrow tha we were causin her trouble.'

We walked down Corporation Street, an then I decided te turn right onta Foley Street. One last look te see wha's goin on an have the bit of freedom before it all ends wit the mornin comin all too soon. I stopped te look at a young one from Foley Street goin inta the shop. She was only fourteen, but she had a big belly on her like the mammies have just before they come outa the hospital carryin home a new babby. She had her mother's coat wrapped aroun her, but it wouldn't close, an her belly stuck out. An she was wearin a pair of slippers tha kept fallin off her feet. They were too big fer her. I wonder how she got the big belly, cos I knew she wasn't married an still lived wit her mammy an daddy an her brothers an sisters. But I definitely knew one thing, she's goin te be comin back from the hospital wit a new babby. Ye can tell these things, however it happened te her!

We turned inta the arch an walked inta the buildins. Young fellas were sittin on the path playin cards. Woodbine butts stuck in their mouths, an all leanin inta the middle of the ring, watchin the money thrown there, ready te snatch it back if trouble broke out an someone was cheatin. I stopped fer a minute te watch two young fellas playin pitch penny. The nearest penny thrown closest te the wall an then thrown inta a drain, standin wit yer back against the wall, or landin yer penny on top of the other fella's penny, an ye win his money. I was not bad at tha, ye need a steady arm an a good eye. Many is the penny I've won offa them young fellas. They made the mistake of thinkin young ones are an easy mark, an they let their guard down. More fool them!

I banged on the door. 'Ma! Let us in, we're back.' Me ma opened the door an looked at us.

'Where were youse?'

'Nowhere, Ma!'

I looked at the floor. It was still damp an looked black an shiny, patches here an there were dry. An the smell of damp an dirt made the room look as if it was in someone's cellar an no one lived here. The fire was not lit, an the babby was lyin on the bed whingin. His face was all white, an his nose was runnin. Teddy lifted his head, an he looked like he'd been washed. His hair was damp an standin up, an he looked very dozy, as if he was sick. I still had the bag of bull's eyes. Charlie had swallied all his sweets before we got back.

'Here, Ma! Have a bull's eye. I got them from a woman I was talkin te on Talbot Street.'

Me ma wasn't listenin, good job fer me, no questions te answer. Charlie rushed over te Teddy on the bed. 'We went fer miles, Teddy, an we went inta a big place wit loads a big people all eatin their dinners! An the woman gave us lemonade te drink, an we did loads an loads a things. Ye should a seen us, ye should! Ye should a come wit us, ye missed it all, so ye did!' Teddy slapped Charlie's head away an turned his face te the wall.

'Wha's wrong wit ye's? Here! Open yer mouth an put this in.' He looked te see what I had, an I put the bull's eye in his mouth. An he pulled it out te look at it, an sucked it an pulled it out again. He didn't really like the taste, but he decided it was better than nothin an put the sweet back in again an sucked it, lookin more contented now. I hugged Harry an put the sweet in his mouth, watchin carefully in case he choked, ready te slap his back an put me fingers in his mouth an pull the sweet out. I hadn't the heart te deprive him an wanted him te have a bit of enjoyment. It was a pity I didn't think te buy somethin fer them instead of the bull's eyes. I don't know why I did tha, wastin a whole sixpence on bull's eyes!

25

I'm runnin fer me life. If he catches me, I'm dead. The sweat is pourin off me. I can't run any faster. Me legs feel like lead. I put me hands out, racin fer the door. Me eyes are locked on the door handle, if I can just reach it. 'Mammy! Help!' Me heart is poundin. I'm nearly there. I can feel his breath on the back of me neck. He's tryin te reach te grab me. I push meself harder an grab the door handle. I turn it an race in just as he tries te reach out an grab a hold of me. I whirl aroun, tryin te shut the door an lean on it. But the man pushes on the door, an I use me might te get it closed, but I've lost. He pushes the door in, an I run again, but I've nowhere te hide. I'm trapped in the room. I look aroun desperately. Me heart is hammerin in me chest, an me ears is ringin wit the pain. I'm convulsionin wit the fear; me whole body is shakin.

'Do ye hear me, Martha? I'm callin ye! Wake up!' I shot up in the bed, lookin inta the eyes of me ma. 'I'm tellin ye te get up!' Me ma is shoutin at me an shakin me. I look aroun the room, an it's gradually dawnin on me. I was dreamin. 'Are ye awake?' me ma asks me. I look at her. She has her coat an scarf on, an it's still early in the mornin.

'Yeah, Ma, I'm awake. Where are ye goin?'

'I'm goin te walk up te Mountjoy te wait fer him outside. They're lettin him out early. By the time I get there, I won't have long te wait. You get up an give them their tea. I've poured it out. An don't take all the milk! I've only a sup left, an he'll be lookin fer a drop a tea when he gets in. An don't touch the bread! I've left ye's enough, there's one cut fer everyone. Now get up an look after everythin. I'll be back, an don't have them kids roarin! I don't want him te

265

have anythin te start trouble about. Don't give him any excuse.'

I looked at me ma, seein the worry in her eyes. An yet she seemed all excited, too. I wanted te ask her not te bring him back, but I knew it was no good. She was more excited about him than afraid. I felt a sickness in me stomach, lookin inta her eyes, an I turned away. She went out the door, an me teeth started te chatter. I was feelin shaky all over.

Teddy stirred beside me an sat up, rubbin his eyes, an Charlie shot up in the bed.

'Where's me ma?' Charlie asked, lookin aroun him.

'Ma's all gone!' Teddy said, wavin the palms of his hands. Harry was sittin at the top of the bed suckin happily on his bottle of tea.

'She's only gone up the road fer a few minutes,' I said. 'She'll be back. Come on, get yer tea.'

I got outa the bed an put me frock over me head, feelin me hair. It felt like a woolly hat. No curls. The pipe cleaners was a waste of time an money. Ah, well! I don't care any more. Fuck Shirley Temple, an her curls, an her dancin on her 'Good Ship Lollipop'. Tha doesn't happen in real life anyway.

'Tha's mine! Martha, he's eatin me bread. Tha was mine first!' Charlie screamed at me an then dived on Teddy, tryin te take the bread offa him. But Teddy had it clutched in his two hands an was tryin te hide it between his knees.

'All right, the two of youse! Let go, Charlie, there's bread here fer you.'

'No! I don't want tha, it's only a little bit.' He took the big bit I had fer meself.

'Here, take mine as well!' I roared at him.

He jumped up, grabbin the two cuts of bread. 'Do you not want any, Martha?'

'No! Eat it! I'm not hungry. An tha aul fella is comin back, an if he hears ye roarin, ye know what'll happen.'

Charlie stopped dead, wit his cheeks bulgin wit bread, an then started te chew very slowly. His eyes were worried, an I felt sorry fer him, cos he was the same as me. We were the two bastards, an me ma didn't care much fer Charlie either. She was always givin him dirty looks an callin him terrible names. I called him terrible names, too, when I was annoyed wit him, but then he was always tellin on me. But we were still the same. We didn't have anythin te do wit Jackser. An I wouldn't let anythin bad happen te Charlie.

'Come on! Get yer clothes on. Where's yer trousers, Teddy?'

I dived under the bed an brought out the clothes an shoes, an dressed Harry an put him on the floor. An took off the black hairy blankets off the bed an shook them, an then put the old heavy overcoats on top fer the extra bit of heat, an the bed was made. I rinsed the empty jam jars we drank our tea from an left them te drain on the sink. An then wiped down the table, takin the breadcrumbs in me hand an throwin them down the sink.

'Can we go out te play, Martha?' Charlie asked me, lookin very white.

'No, Charlie. Me ma said we have te stay here an wait fer them te come back.'

Charlie dragged himself over te the bed an climbed up an sat wit his back te the wall. Teddy chased Harry aroun the floor on his hands an knees. I looked out the winda. Not a soul aroun, it was still early in the mornin.

'No! I told ye te stop moidierin me, Charlie. Youse all got the last of the bread hours ago. There isn't even a drop a milk left te make a sup a tea. Now, just wait until they get back!'

'I'm starvin, Martha! When'll they come back? Ye said tha they'd be back this mornin.'

'Yeah! I know. I don't know where they're gone te. Now stop whingin.'

Harry was lyin wit his head in me lap, an I was rubbin his head te try an mollify him, cos he wanted his drink of tea an somethin te eat. But me ma must be gone off wit Jackser, an he's probably drinkin in the pub.

'Teddy, come over here an lie down beside me. I'll rub yer back.' He looked at me fer a minute an then crawled over te lie beside me an put his head in the crook of me arm. An I rubbed his back, an he closed his eyes an sucked his thumb, an I could see Harry was now dozin off.

I lay quietly wit me back against the headboard, lookin out the winda, seein the dusk comin an hearin the sounds of childre playin gettin quieter. People are now goin in fer their tea. It's gettin late. I'd better start thinkin about puttin everyone te bed fer the night. Maybe it's better if we're all asleep when Jackser finally comes back, then I won't have te face him.

I slipped off the babby's clothes an put him under the blankets. He cried fer a minute but then fell fast asleep. Then I got Teddy ready an put him te bed. 'Charlie,' I whispered. 'Get yer clothes off an get inta bed.' He said nothin but just quietly took off his clothes an climbed inta the bed. It was nearly dark now. I didn't draw the curtains or put on the light. It would only hurt me eyes, cos I had a pain in me head, an I wanted te sit on the chair by the winda an listen te the quiet an watch the odd few people goin past. I didn't feel so shut up or afraid when I could see the people an know I could run out there an be safe if somethin bad was te happen here.

I heard footsteps an laughin. I held me breath te listen. 'Will ye come on!' Tha's me ma! They're comin. I jumped up suddenly, knockin over the chair. Me head spun aroun the room. What'll I do? Will I jump inta bed an pretend I'm asleep. Too late! They're here! I rushed over te the chair beside the fireplace an whipped across the curtains an put on the light an opened the door just as Jackser staggered in. Me ma laughed, an I could see her face was red an she was all excited.

'Ah! Me topper! I'm back!' Jackser roared, lookin at me an snufflin.

'Here!' me ma shouted. 'Sit down here an eat yer fish an chips before they get cold.'

Harry an Teddy woke up cryin an rubbin their eyes. 'Yeh hoo! It's me, yer daddy!' Jackser roared at them an staggered over te the bed. Harry hid his face an turned te the wall, roarin his head off, an Teddy made a dive fer Charlie, hidin his head behind his back, an

Charlie tried te squeeze himself inta the corner of the wall but was afraid te take his eyes off Jackser.

'Ah, it's grand te be back. An by Jaysus! I won't be seein the inside of tha place again. Oh, no! I have big plans. We're gettin outa this place. I'm goin te pay off the rent arrears an get ourselves a house.' He grabbed Charlie's cheek an squeezed it. An then dived on Teddy an sank his head inta his neck an blew on it, bitin him. Teddy screamed te get away. An me ma was hoarse askin him te come an eat his grub.

'Here!' she said te me, puttin chips on a cut of bread. 'Give tha te Harry an get them up fer their tea.'

Teddy shot outa the bed when he saw the chips, an Charlie behind him. Me ma put a huge ray an a bag of chips on the plate an carried it over te Jackser. 'Here! Take this!' An he grabbed the plate, snufflin.

'Fuck me, Sally, but it's great te be outa tha kip!'

An he grabbed her arse, an she laughed an said, 'Stop, will ya! They're watchin.' But she seemed happy. I felt they were dirty, an I didn't like me ma much. I wanted te get away from her. She's dirty! Just like him.

I sat down on the chair wit me back te the room an looked at the empty grate, tryin te get rid of the picture in me head of Jackser lyin on top of me an suffocatin me.

'Here! Have yer bread an chips, Martha!'

I lifted me head an nodded te her. 'I don't want them.'

'Here! Eat them, they're gettin cold on ye. Ye have te eat somethin!'

'I'm not hungry!' I said.

An she put one of them in her mouth an said, 'Eat them, they're lovely!'

When I said nothin, she shook her head an said, 'Tha's terrible! Many's the one tha'd be glad of them!' An she gave some of them te Harry an put more in her mouth, an gave a bit of the bread te Charlie an the other bit te Teddy, until they were all gone. An then said, 'Listen, Martha! Get them all inta the bed now, it's late.'

Jackser handed me the plate an said, 'Tha was lovely. I enjoyed tha. Jaysus! I'm banjacksed! I'm hittin the sack. Don't be long, Sally! An put the light out! Turn yer head, you!'

An I went inta the scullery while he pulled off his trousers, showin his hairy bandy legs, an held the front of his shirt over his horrible privates, an rushed in towards the scullery, headin fer the tilet. 'I'm fuckin burstin!' he laughed.

'Jaysus!' me ma laughed at me. 'Tha's a terrible carry on.'

I gave me ma a dirty look an went te put the childre te bed. 'Get inta bed, quick!' I said te Teddy an Charlie, an whipped off me frock an dived inta the bed before Jackser came back. I rolled meself inta a tight ball an wondered if I should swap places wit Charlie. Too late now. I could hear him openin the tilet door.

I dived under the blankets an heard the two of them whisperin, an then me ma laughed. 'Go way outa that!' me ma said.

Jackser came rushin in te the bed, snufflin. I didn't move, holdin me breath while the mattress heaved an he settled himself. 'Hurry up, Sally! Put the light out,' he roared.

'Yes! Yes! Hold yer horses,' me ma shouted back. 'I'm hurryin.'

Then me ma shuffled inta the room an turned the light out. I waited fer her te get inta the bed so I could let me breath out an try te let me scrunched-up muscles loosen. I was so worried trouble might break out any minute.

'Come on, get in,' Jackser said as me ma climbed over him. An the mattress sank, an we all rocked from side te side wit the extra weight.

'Shush!' I heard her whisper te the babby as she lifted him closer inta the wall. Then she settled herself, an I heard them whisperin an laughin. I let out a breath then an loosened me muscles, stretchin me legs a little but not too much or Jackser would kick the back off me fer takin his room where he put his feet. Then I was out cold.

When I woke again, it was mornin. Me eyes shot open an clapped on Jackser pourin the tea. Me heart sank! It wasn't a dream after all!

'We must a spent every penny yesterday,' he was sayin te me ma.

I looked at him. His face was fatter, an his skin looked the colour of putty. An his eyes was sunk inta the back of his head, an his hair was all cropped off. Me ma opened the press beside the fire. 'There's a few nice things here. I can bring them over te the pawn.' She held up me lovely blue frock, an I held me breath. Ah, no! Not that, I thought. I never even got a chance te try it on. I was savin tha te go wit me lovely new curls! An me coat an sandals she's taken, too. I jumped outa the bed an threw on me old frock tha was so worn out ye'd think twice about wipin the floor wit it.

'Ma! Leave me frock,' I whispered. 'Ye have enough stuff there.' I looked at her coat an her skirts.

'Ah! Don't be moidierin me!' She threw the lot onta the bed an got the pillaslip an stuffed them all in.

Jackser swallied down his tea an rubbed his hands together, an shook his arm inta the air an bent himself, snufflin, an said happily, 'Tha's the way, Sally! Get them over te the pawn an try te get as much as ye can, an hurry back. I want te get goin.'

'Where are ye goin te?' me ma asked, chewin on her lip an shakin a bit wit nerves.

'I won't be long. I've just te see some fella about somethin, then I'll be back.'

'Ye needn't think ye're goin off drinkin wit the money,' me ma said, gettin annoyed.

Jackser went stiff an clenched his fists an swung his head away, an then swung back te look at me ma. 'Did I say tha? I'm only in the door five minutes, Mrs, an ye're startin again!'

'Come on, Ma! Let's go.' I grabbed the heavy pillacase an rushed te the door.

'I'm not sayin anythin,' me ma said back. 'You're the one wantin te go off an drink.'

Jackser looked up at the ceilin an held his arms tight by his side an clenched his fists. 'I'm warnin ye, Mrs!'

I went te me ma an pulled her te the door. 'Come on, Ma! There's goin te be a big queue, an we'll never get back.'

She turned then, sayin, 'Don't think ye can make a fool outa me!'

271

I carried the bundle out the gate an on te Foley Street, headin fer the North Strand.

'It didn't take the bandy aul bastard long te get back te his old ways,' me ma said.

I was annoyed meself. 'Ye're only gettin wha ye asked fer, Ma! We were happy on our own, but ye took him back. Ye can't get on without him, Ma. An he'll always be the same. He's no good, you've been told tha a thousand times by everyone who knows him. So wha's there te talk about?'

'Sure, where would we go? He'd track us down an come an kill the lot of us!'

'No, he wouldn't! He's a coward if ye stand up te him, but ye're afraid of him, Ma, an he knows it. If I was big, I'd smash everythin I could lay me hands on down on his bleedin head. He wouldn't come back a second time lookin fer more.'

Me ma chewed her lip an coughed an said, changin the subject, 'How much do ye think he'll give us, Martha?'

I thought about it an said, 'They're nearly new, Ma. Ask fer two quid, hope fer thirty bob, an take twenty-five bob rock bottom!'

'Tha'd be grand!' me ma said, laughin.

She hurried on then, an I said, 'Here, Ma, give us a hand, this is gettin too heavy fer me, the arms are fallin offa me.'

The queue was out the door, an I left me ma chattin te the other women an squeezed me way inside te see wha was happenin. The place was crowded. Women crushed up against each other, all holdin out bundles a clothes an watchin the men, three of them, behind the high counter, examinin suits, an clothes, an bed sheets, an everythin an anythin they could get their hands on te pawn.

The men rushed up an down, puttin the stuff away on high shelves an writin out dockets an arguin about money. 'Ah, Eddie! I'm tellin ye, ye gave me a pound on tha bundle last week. Tha's me best stuff in tha parcel, so it is!'

'Josie! You've been bringin tha parcel in since I was a lad, an that's not today or yesterday, need I remind ye!'

The other women laughed, an an aul one roared up from the

272

back, 'How could we forget wit yer baldy head te remind us.'

'Ah, you've gone an done it now, Mrs! He's goin te run the lot of us out the door fer passin remarks on him!'

Another woman said, 'Well, give us twelve shillins, Eddie! An I'm insultin meself at tha. Them sheets are the best linen money can buy!'

'Three shillins!' Eddie said. 'An I won't upset meself by openin the parcel an watchin them fall te bits in me hands.'

'Right, then! I'll take eight shillins!' Josie said.

'Five shillins, that's me final offer,' Eddie said. 'An I'm gettin too soft. If I keep this up, I'll have te close up shop.'

'All right, then! I'll take it,' Josie said happily.

Eddie pushed the parcel down the counter, an it slid inta the hands of another man, who picked it up an rushed off te put it on a high shelf, standin himself up on the ladder.

Josie took her docket an the two half-crowns an moved off, an another woman moved over, puttin a bundle of dirty rags on the counter. 'Eddie, love! Just give us five bob on these,' she said, fixin a little babby tha popped its head up from under her brown shawl an gave a roar. 'Shush! Shush! Here!' an she stuck her nipple inta the babby's mouth an pulled the shawl up an tightened it aroun her, an the babby was quiet, suckin happily on her diddy. Her black hair was thin, like long bits of thick thread hangin aroun her shoulders. An she put one side behind her ear te get a better look at Eddie.

'Ah, me aul flower, I'll give ye a shillin. An that's only out of the goodness of me heart!'

'Ah, Eddie! Give us three bob. I'll be back in no time te claim them out!'

'I'm not the Vincent de Paul!' Eddie roared. 'Do ye want te put me out on the street? Two bob, an that's me final offer,' he said.

'It will do,' the woman said.

An I moved me way out, gettin squashed, cos the women wouldn't give an inch of space. 'Let me out! I want te get out,' I said, tryin te lift me head up fer air.

'Here! Get out.' An an aul one gave me a dig an pushed me

through the crowd. They were all annoyed cos I was a young one an they might lose their place in the queue. 'Bloody young ones, pesterin ye!' an aul one roared after me.

Me ma was lookin very worried. 'He's goin te go mad,' she said. 'How long more have we te wait?'

'It's slow, Ma, but the queue is movin. We won't be long.'

'Jaysus, he'll go mad,' she said te herself.

Me ma was in a state by the time our turn came. She was worried cos we'd been waitin nearly two hours. 'How much do ye want?' Eddie asked me ma, examinin the clothes.

'Eh! Will ye give us . . . eh!' . . . cough . . .

'Three quid!' I said, haulin meself up onta the high counter an diggin me feet inta the panel te stop the aul ones pushin me off.

'I'll give ye a pound,' he said, lookin at me ma.

She chewed her lip an said slowly, 'Ah, no! I won't take tha.'

'Two pound ten, Mister. Them clothes are the best quality money can buy!' I shouted up.

Eddie looked at me an said, 'Are ye tryin te take me job? Thirty bob! Tha's the best I can do,' he said.

'OK, leave it at two quid. We'll be back on Friday te claim them,' I said.

'Thirty-five bob, an that's me final offer!' Eddie said, puttin the stuff back in the pillacase.

Me ma looked at me, happily chewin her lip. 'Done, Mister!' I said.

'Jaysus, ye can let her out!' an aul one said, laughin behind me.

26

I was jumpin up an down, all delighted. 'Yeah!' me ma was sayin. 'Tha aul bastard is not comin back. I got rid of him. Here, eat up tha dinner before it gets cold.'

I looked at the half-raw sausage an was about te say, 'I think it's supposed te be brown, Ma, not still snow white,' when I heard a roar in me head.

'Wake up, ye stupid bastard!'

I shot up in the bed an looked inta Jackser's face. His mouth was openin, an his eyes was starin at me. Spit was comin from his mouth, an he was roarin somethin at me. I looked aroun an the light was still on. It must still be the night, wha's happenin? I looked at him again, tryin te understand. He lunged at me, grabbin me by the neck, an hauled me onta the floor. 'Do ye hear what I'm sayin te ya? Wake yerself up an get out there an watch te see if anyone is watchin us. The St Vincents are comin te see us in a minute, an I don't want anyone knowin me business. Now move!' He bent down suddenly an picked up me frock from the floor an threw it, landin it on me head. I pulled it on fast an headed fer the door. 'An don't come back until I tell ye te!'

'No, Jackser! I won't.'

I rushed out inta the dark hall an onta the street. It was pitch black, an the freezin cold hit me full blast. I started te shiver. I stopped an looked up an down. It was very quiet, not a soul te be seen or even a sound heard. I crossed me arms an hunched me shoulders, droppin me head down tryin te get a bit of heat. An rushed fer the stone stairs te get in outa the freezin cold an the

275

wind tha would cut ye in two. I sat meself down on the cold stairs an pulled me frock over me knees. I felt me arse startin te freeze straight away an lifted meself up a little, balancin against the stone wall. Aw, Gawd, that's worse. I jumped up an started te hop, tryin te get a bit of heat. But I was too tired an sat back down again. Te hell wit it, an started te rock backwards an forwards. If only I could stay in me warm bed. He does this every week. Wakin me from me sleep an makin me sit out here te watch fer nothin. People are not watchin him at all. This is all a waste of time. Why is he not like other people? I don't see anyone else carryin on like this. He won't call me in. I'll have te sit out here fer hours an then creep up te the door an knock meself, hopin he won't kick the heart outa me cos the Vincents haven't come yet. An he'll let me in an just say, 'Right! Get inta tha bed.' But it's not long enough yet. An the cold is painin me everywhere, cos I've nothin on but a vest an me aul frock. I can't last tha long, an I opened me mouth an started te cry. An it caught in me throat, cos the fear hit me. Jackser might hear me an kick me te death fer makin a show of him. So I stopped an rocked meself harder an waited.

At last I was back. I rushed in through the gates inta the buildins. Me arms was achin, an I was tryin not te drop the messages. It was a long way from the shop in Summerhill te drag all this stuff. But ye had te go only te tha shop, cos no one else would take the ten shillin voucher me ma got from the St Vincents. An ye could only get food fer it. So tha meant Jackser couldn't spend it on drink. He was ragin. But I was delighted. I got inta the hall an banged on the door wit the heel of me foot. The bottle of milk was beginnin te slip. Me ma opened the door. 'Quick, Ma! Grab the milk before it smashes te the ground.' She caught it as it slipped from under me arm. I wriggled over te the table, an everythin was beginnin te fall. 'Ma! Take the stuff offa me. I can't hold it.' Me ma grabbed the bag of sugar an took the rest of the messages an put them on the table. I tried te stretch me arms, an they were locked solid.

'Did ye get everythin?' me ma said.

'Yeah, Ma!' I said, a bit worried in case everythin wasn't there.

'Did ye get the packet a Lyons tea? An the half-pound a margarine? An let's see, the loaf a bread!'

'Yeah! I got the lot.'

'Where's me fuckin five Woodbines?' Jackser shouted from the bed. 'Ye were long enough. I was goin te get up outa this bed an come after ye. An if I'd caught ye takin yer time, I'd a made ye sorry ye were ever born.'

'Yeah, Jackser! I got yer Woodbines! An I was hurryin very fast. But I had te wait until the shop was emptied, like ye told me te. So no one would see me handin over the voucher an know yer business. An I had te wait a long time, cos the shop was crowded.'

'Gimme the fuckin cigarettes an stop yer guff. Now get outside an play an don't go far. I may be lookin fer ye, so I want ye te be ready in case I call ye. An when I do, I'll only call once, so ye better come runnin!'

'Yeah! OK, Jackser, I won't go far!'

'An mind them kids!' me ma shouted after me as I made fer the door. 'Here! Take the babby out in his pram.'

I pushed the pram outside an went back in an picked Harry up off the floor an carried him out te the pram. His arse was bare, an Jackser jumped outa the bed an gave me a clout over the head an dragged me back inside, still holdin on te the babby.

'Here, Mrs!' he shouted at me ma. 'Would ye ever put a pair of trousers on tha child an don't be lettin tha bastard a yours make a show a this house. The whore's melt is blind as well as stupid. Couldn't she see ye can't bring no child a mine out in his skin! Lettin everyone think I'm not as good as the rest of them!'

'Ah, don't be moidierin me!' me ma was mutterin, lookin aroun half-heartedly fer somethin te put on the babby.

Harry was slippin down me legs, an I was tryin te keep a hold of him. Me nerves was goin, watchin me ma chewin her lip an takin her time. Me head was swivellin from her te Jackser, who was pacin up an down now, clenchin his fists by his sides an givin vicious side looks te the two of us.

The babby started te squeal, an I was startin te shake. What'll I do? Anytime now, he's goin te land his fists on us. I whispered te me ma, 'Give us somethin quick, Ma, te put on him.'

'I've nothin,' me ma said, annoyed an worried at the same time. 'Everythin is soppin wit piss. Ah, just leave him there!'

I put the babby down an watched Jackser, afraid te move. He whirled aroun on the balls of his feet an grabbed me. 'Go on, then, get out, an if this lazy aul hag doesn't get off her arse an do somethin aroun here, she'll find herself an her bastards out on the streets again where she belongs.' He opened the door an threw me across the hall. I managed te land on me back an roll, tight as a ball, an jump te me feet, headin fer the street, in case he decided te put the boot in me.

I ran fer the stairs an sat meself down. Me heart was poundin, an I tried te slow me breath. Then I jumped up an sneaked a look out te see if Jackser was comin after me. No sign of him. I let out a big breath an sat back down again, well hidden on the landin step. Now I'd see him before he sees me. I could look over the banisters te keep a watch. He's an awful habit of creepin up behind ye an catchin ye unawares. 'Ye won't see me comin, but I'm always watchin ye!' he roars at me.

Teddy staggered past cryin, an a young fella of about three came after him wit a stick. I leapt up an took the stairs two at a time, catchin the young fella's arm as he was wavin the stick in the air an threatenin Teddy wit it. 'Ah, no ye don't!' I said, takin the stick off him.

'Tha's mine!' he screamed.

'Why are ye hittin him? Ye can't do tha, ye're a little blackguard.'

'He spit at me!' the young fella roared. An I looked at Teddy, all black-faced an snots. An he gave a spit at the young fella, an it went nowhere, just dribbled down his chin.

I laughed. 'Ah! Don't be hittin him, he's only a babby, an you're a big fella. Look at the size of ye. If ye go aroun hittin babbies, everyone will say you're a coward. Now, ye don't want tha, do ye?'

'No! An I'm not a coward.'

'Course ye're not. I can see tha, ye just forgot he was a babby!'

'Yeah, ye're right, I forgot!'

'So will ye mind him fer me an don't let anyone else hit him?' I bent down te the young fella an looked inta his face, smilin at him.

He was thinkin about this an said, 'Yeah, I'll be his bodyguard!'

'Right! Now don't let him wander out the gates! He'll get kilt wit the cars.'

'No, I'm big, an he won't escape me!' An he grabbed Teddy's hand an said, 'Come on, we're goin te play cowboys an injuns.'

Teddy roared an shook the young fella's hand away. I grabbed Teddy an wiped the snots wit the hem of me frock. 'Go on, Teddy! Frankie's goin te play wit ye.'

Teddy looked at Frankie bendin down an smilin at him. 'Yeah! I'll be the cowboy an ye be the injun, ye can even have me stick.'

'See,' I said, givin Teddy the stick. He roared laughin, delighted, an ran off, chasin Frankie wit the stick.

I looked aroun, wonderin where Charlie was. He was supposed te be watchin Teddy, but there was no sign of him. If Jackser had caught him gone missin an leavin Teddy on his own, he would have annihilated him. Ah, fuck! I can't do anythin or go anywhere, I'll have te sit here an mind Teddy. He's too little te turn me back on him, even fer a minute. He could wander out onta the road an get kilt by a car.

'But, Ma, is it really goin te happen? Am I really goin te go te the Sunshine Home fer a holiday?'

'Yes, yes! Amn't I after tellin ye? Now will ye run down te the shop an get the milk before he starts roarin. He's waitin fer the sup a tea. Now go on,' an she pushed me outa the scullery. I rushed outa the room, throwin an eye at Jackser sleepin in the bed, an closed the door quietly, in case he woke up an started roarin. I flew te the shop, dancin in the air. The St Vincents are lettin me go on a holiday. Me heart was poundin wit excitement. I couldn't believe it!

When I came outa the shop wit the bottle a milk, I saw Emmy crossin the road, headin fer the buildins. She's my age an lives across from me, up on the balconies. 'Emmy! Wait fer me, I've got somethin te tell ye!'

'Wha? Wha's happenin?'

I rushed over an said, 'I'm goin te the Sunshine Home!'

'Ah, Gawd, tha's great! Ye go on a train, cos it's in a far-off place down in Balbriggan. An it's run by the Legion o Mary. Ye call them Sisters. They're only women, not nuns, but ye have te call them tha, so ye do, but they're all right really. They don't give out te ye like the nuns. An ye get loads a sambidges, an tea from a big pot. An when I was there last year, we had great gas. The sisters were fallin aroun the place, handin us out sambidges from a huge tray. An we kept screamin at them an puttin our hands up sayin we got nothin! An hidin the bread underneath us on the benches an sittin on them.' An then Emmy stopped te draw a breath an looked at me fer a minute an then said, 'But first ye have te go up te the head office on Mountjoy Square, te Ozanam House, it's called, fer an examination te make sure ye don't have any diseases. An they look at yer head te make sure ye haven't any nits.'

Me mouth dropped open, an me heart sank. 'Does tha mean if ye have nits, ye can't go?'

'Ah, no! It just means if ye only have a few, ye'll be grand. I mean they look at yer hair, an they don't mind ye havin the normal amount. It's only if yer head was walkin alive wit them.'

I let out me breath. 'Oh, thanks be te God. Ye don't think I'm walkin alive, do ye?'

Emmy looked at me head an said, 'Ah, no! Ye're grand. They'll pass ye!'

'Right, Emmy! I better run, me ma is waitin on the milk. I'll see ye again.'

'Yeah! See ya.'

An I took off, runnin wit the milk, wonderin an worried, happy tha I might go on a holiday. But then again, it was too good te be true. Anythin could happen. Jackser might not let me go. I didn't want te really believe it.

I was sittin on the chair by the fireside thinkin about me holiday, wonderin what it would be like, when I heard Jackser shoutin. I looked over at me ma. She was sittin wit her head down lookin at the empty fireplace an runnin her fingers through her hair, lookin fer lice. 'I asked ye, Mrs, te get them kids inta bed. Are ye fuckin deaf or wha?'

'Ah, don't be annoyin me. Ye'd put years on people wit yer carry on!'

'I'll get them inta bed, Ma!' I said, jumpin up.

Me ma ignored me an went back te starin at the empty fire. Me heart started te pound, cos it was gettin dark in the room now, an we needed te switch on the light, but I was afraid te ask Jackser, cos he was in a bad mood.

He kept walkin up an down, clenchin his fists an lookin out the winda. I looked aroun me, not wantin te get too close te Jackser in case he lashed out wit a kick or a dig. The babby was asleep on the floor, an I picked him up an carried him over te the bed. Charlie was sittin on the floor, starin inta space. 'Get inta bed, Charlie. Hurry up!' He took off his trousers an climbed inta the end of the bed. 'Come on, Teddy,' I said quietly, puttin out me arms te him an pickin him up. He was sittin beside me ma's chair, keenin wit exhaustion, an I struggled over te the bed wit him, managin te hump him onta the bed. 'Ye're gettin heavy, Teddy. I can't carry ye now. Ye're a big boy now, aren't ye?' He turned his head away from me an roared, too tired fer any more. 'Shush! All right, I'm puttin ye inta bed now.' An I pulled off his trousers an put him in beside Charlie.

'Will I get inta bed now, Ma?' I whispered te me ma, but she just ignored me. It was dark now an gettin cold, but I was afraid te move in case I did the wrong thing an Jackser went fer me, so I sat back down again on the chair, lookin at me ma sittin like a statue starin at nothin. An I wondered why she was not like the other mammies, laughin an wearin an apron, an makin tea, an shoutin an keepin everyone in order. An wipin babbies' arses, an cleanin, an shoutin she'd kill the lot of them if they didn't give her any peace! An havin a purse wit a few shillins in it, an rushin down te buy the few messages fer the dinner. An stoppin te have a talk wit the neighbours. An laughin an complainin, an rushin off again. Me ma doesn't do any of them things. She just sits there starin an doesn't bother about anythin. An Jackser won't allow us te talk te

281

Mrs Dunne any more. He hates her, cos she's not afraid of him. An when he hears her comin an goin, he shouts names an calls her terrible things at the top of his voice. But he doesn't say them te her face or even open the door. He just roars up at the ceilin, knowin she can hear him. I know it torments her, but she doesn't complain. She just acts as if we're not there an goes about her business. I feel very sorry about tha, but Jackser won't allow us te talk te anyone. He keeps frettin tha they might learn about our business.

'Hey, you!' I jumped up wit the fright.

'Yes, Jackser, I'm here!'

'A fella I knew from a long time ago said I'm te send ye up te him an he'll give me the price of a few smokes. Tell him Jackser sent ye, an he'll know what it's about. Right! Ye know the balcony te go te, an ye have the number, so get goin!'

'Right, Jackser!'

I rushed out the door an across te the other balconies, hopin I'd get the money fer Jackser's cigarettes. It would put him in good form fer a while. An he was very sure I'd get the money. I walked along the balconies until I found the right number an then knocked on the door. A man opened the door, an I looked at him. 'Jackser sent me. He said ye would give him the price of a few Woodbines!'

The man looked behind him an pulled the door close te him. He was very nervous. 'Shush!' he said. 'I'm not ready fer ye yet, she's not settled down!' he whispered te me, throwin his head behind him. 'Come back in twenty minutes, an I'll be waitin fer ye!'

'Right!' I said. 'I'll do tha!'

I wandered off te wait down the balcony, wonderin wha tha was all about. Why he couldn't give me the money now.

I decided te go an knock again, cos Jackser would come after me if I wasted any more time. 'I told ye! I'll be ready as soon as I can. She's not asleep yet!' an he kept lookin over his shoulder. 'Look! When ye come back next time, don't come here. Knock on the back room, tha one there!' an he pointed down the hall an then shut the door quietly. I was left starin at the closed door, wonderin wha he's talkin about. Jaysus! Jackser's goin te kill me fer takin so long. Will

I go back an tell him or will I wait? Oh, dear God, grant tha he gives me the money fer the cigarettes an Jackser won't kill me. An I promise te be very good from now on.

When I went back again, I stood in the hall, not sure wha door te knock on, so I knocked on one of the back rooms. The man opened the door of the first room an rushed down te me, lettin me in te the back room, an brought me over te a lovely big roarin fire. I looked aroun, there was no one else here. 'Wait here!' he said. 'I won't be long,' an he rushed out again, shuttin the door behind him. I stood in the middle of the room lookin aroun me. It was lovely an clean. The lino on the floor was shiny an smelled of polish. An there was a lovely big mahogany bed against the wall in the corner wit big black hairy blankets an lovely white sheets an white pillacases. An two little comfortable armchairs each side of the firerplace, an a big black clock on the mantelpiece goin tick tock, wit photographs of people gettin married. They were very old, ye could see tha by the way they were dressed. An there was a lovely round table wit a big heavy cloth on it, an a rug at the fireplace. Oh, God, this is lovely!

Then the door opened, an the man rushed in. He was smilin an rubbin his hands. His face was shiny an clean, like he just shaved himself. An his hair was combed an greased wit Brylcreem, an ye could smell the soap offa him. 'Are ye cold?' he said, comin over te the fire. I said nothin. I was waitin fer him te give me the money, an I'd run an get the Woodbines, cos I'd taken an awful long time, an I wanted te get back.

'Come over an lie on the bed!' he said, lookin at me an noddin te the bed.

I looked at him an looked at the bed, not understandin. 'Eh! I have te go, Mister. Jackser will be wonderin wha's keepin me!'

'Come on!' he said, whippin me off the floor an carryin me over te the bed, an put me lyin down in the middle. I sat up, confused, taken unawares. An he pulled the frock over me head an left me sittin there naked in me skin except fer me vest.

'No, let me out!' I grabbed fer me frock.

'Stay there, don't move!' he roared, pullin off his trousers.

I started te panic. Wha's he goin te do te me? An now Jackser will kill me stone dead fer all the time I wasted.

I started cryin an tried te pull the frock over me head an get me legs outa the bed.

'It's all right,' the man said, holdin me arms an takin the frock offa me. 'He won't mind. I'll give ye the money fer his cigarettes. Now lie down an be good, an I won't hurt ye. I told him not te send ye up until after dark, so don't be worryin.'

I looked at the wall an waited. He opened me legs an said, 'How old are ye?'

'Nine!' I said.

He just knelt between me legs an said nothin, just looked, an kept examinin me. I stared at the wall, afraid te shut me eyes tight in case he knifed me or somethin, or broke me bones, or tried te strangle me. Plenty of childre get murdered one way or another. An I knew I was in fer an awful lot of pain, an I needed te keep me senses about me. One thing I can't do an tha's te annoy him. Ye can certainly get yerself kilt tha way! So I lay very still an looked at the wall.

'Ye could pass fer a six year old! Ye're very small fer yer age! I'd prefer if ye had a bit a meat on ye.' Then he lay down on top of me, an he started te rock himself.

One, two, three, four, five, six, seven, I counted te meself. All good childre go te heaven. When they die, say goodbye.

'Pull this, will ye! Come on, I'm talkin te ye!'

I turned aroun lookin at him. He was kneelin up again. 'Wha?' I said.

'Pull this!' an he took me hand an put it between his legs.

'No!' I said. 'I want te go home!' I tried te sit up, an he pushed me back down.

'Do as ye're told, or I'll tell Jackser ye were no good te me an he won't get no cigarettes from me. Do ye understand tha?'

I lay back slowly, movin away from his face. He looked like he was goin te hit me. 'Jackser expects me te get me money's worth. So do as I tell ye. Now pull this, like tha!'

I looked at the thing between his legs. It was different from tha bastard. It wasn't big an hairy, it was little an white, more like me babby brother's, except fer all the hair aroun it. I looked at the wall, an I waited. I wouldn't touch it. He lay back down on me an rocked. I'm goin te the top balcony, an I'm goin te jump off. He got up an knelt, holdin his thing an pullin it like mad, an stared between me legs. I don't care any more, this life will never end unless I end it meself. So I needn't worry now. No matter wha happens te me, I can end it meself. I thought of meself flyin through the air an smashin te the ground. I saw me head explodin like a squashed tomato, an then I'd have an awful lot of pain. It would be terrible!

An then I had the picture of the other child, Nora, lyin on the ground very still. Her eyes were closed, an she didn't feel anythin. Yeah! I could put up wit the pain. It would last fer a few minutes, an then it would be gone, an I'd never have te worry again. So tha's what I'll do.

'Come on, get up!' I felt the man's weight liftin offa the bed, an I came outa me dreamin an looked aroun. 'Hurry! Get up, I'm tellin ye. I have te be outa here before the aul woman gets back from her devotions. She'll be makin her way back now from Marlborough Street Church. I only borrowed this room. I'm supposed te be keepin an eye on the fire fer her!' He was hikin himself inta his trousers an lookin fer his sock. I didn't care wha he was sayin. I slowly put me frock over me head an walked te the door, waitin fer him te give me the money fer tha Jackser's cigarettes. He put his hand in his trouser pocket an handed me two shillins. 'An here's threepence fer yerself. Now buy yerself a bar of chocolate!' I took the money an made fer the door. 'Listen! Ye know ye're not te say anythin te anybody about this, don't ya?' I said nothin, I didn't care. 'I hope ye're listenin te me, cos, number one, people won't believe ye, an number two, Jackser promised, an he means this! You'll be taken out te the country an buried alive in a big hole. An ye'll never be found!' I looked at him. 'Ye know I'm tellin ye the truth. I know Jackser a long time. He's a mad bastard! An he wouldn't think twice about it if ye crossed him!'

285

The man's eyes was bulgin, an he was afraid, too. I nodded me head, 'No, I won't say nothin te nobody.'

'Good girl!' he said happily, an he opened the door, an I walked inta the dark hall an out inta the dark cold night air.

I walked down te the shop, lookin up at the stars an thinkin, men are not nice. They want te do horrible things te me. An I wonder if any other kids get tha done te them. Somehow, I feel very old. I think I've missed me chance of ever gettin te find out what it would be like te have a real mammy an daddy te let me sit on their knee an do me hair an mind me. I'm a bit too old fer all tha now. An I started te cry. The tears rolled down me face, but I didn't make a sound. An I couldn't shout fer someone te mind me like I always did before in me own mind. Cos now I know tha won't happen. I'm on me own. I had me chance wit Mrs Dunne, but tha's over now. I'm just an aul one. Me childish days are gone fer ever.

27

I can't believe me good luck! Here I am sittin on the train goin te the Sunshine Home fer a week's holiday. I looked down, admirin me new brown leather shoes wit the straps an the shiny silver buckles, an me lovely white socks, an then brushed the dust off me lovely red an white checked frock. There wasn't a crease on it, never mind dust, but I wanted te keep it immaculate clean, cos I felt lovely in it. Jackser warned me, before he let me on the train, I was te come back wit it in the same condition I got it. An I wasn't te get a mark on me new shoes. Me heart was in me mouth, cos I thought right up te the last minute he'd change his mind an not let me go. I'd been worryin meself sick fer weeks, wonderin if I'd get te go. Ever since I passed the head examination fer lice an disease tha the St Vincent de Paul give ye up in Ozanam House in Mountjoy Square. But I did pass it. An then ye get sent te another room where they give ye a parcel wit the frock, an the shoes, an socks, an knickers an vest, an even a lovely white cardigan. The waitin an wonderin an the excitement nearly kilt me. I'd been runnin up an down fer messages wit me head splittin me, an I'd stop te vomit me guts up an then run on again. It was all the worryin tha caused it. But here I am now. An I'm so happy. I'm thinkin, all is well in the world, an God must be in his heaven.

I looked aroun me, full of contentment, an the train was crowded wit us. All young ones about me own age. They were roarin up an down the train, shoutin fer their pals. 'I'm up here. Come on! I've saved ye a seat. Move over, let her in!'

'Ma!' someone else in front of me screamed. 'Me bag of sweets is robbed!' She looked at me. I looked back but said nothin.

287

'They're here, ye gave them te me te mind!' the one wit the roarin red head an freckles sittin beside her shouted.

'Gimme them, an I hope ye didn't touch any, cos I know how many there should be in the bag!'

'I'm not a robber! An fer tha I'm not talkin te ye no more. Ye're not me pal!'

'I only said . . .'

'No!' Redhead shouted back. 'Let me out, I'm never speakin te ye again! Young one!' Redhead turned te me. 'Will ye swap places wit me? There's an awful smell in this seat!'

'Say tha again an I'll give ye such a clatter in the gob, an ye won't know wha hit ye!'

'Here! Stop fightin, ye're only goin te spoil yer enjoyment!' The young one sittin beside me leaned across te them. 'Ye didn't mean wha ye said, did ye? She's not a robber, are ye?' she looked at Redhead.

'No!' Redhead shook her head, lookin very down altogether.

'Go on, say sorry an make up.'

'Yeah! I'm sorry. I didn't really mean ye were a robber, it just came outa me mouth wrong!'

'Yeah, all right! We'll make up!' Redhead said.

An yer woman offered her the bag of sweets an said, 'Go on, Rosie, take as many as ye like! An do youse want one?' she asked, lookin at me. An the young one beside me dipped her hand in the bag an helped herself, takin a handful. An I took one, cos yer woman was lookin inta the bag an lookin very worried they might be all gone. An I didn't want her te think I was mean. We sucked the bon bons an stood up on the seat lookin out the winda.

A train roared past us, an we whipped our heads in. 'Gawd, tha was very dangerous!' yer woman beside me shouted. 'I knew a young one who was goin down te the Sunshine Home on this very train. An she leaned her head outa the winda, an her head was knocked clean offa her shoulders, an it rolled onta the ground.' She looked at us, her eyes bulgin. We all listened wit our mouths hangin open. 'Yeah!' she went on. 'An she was suckin on a sixpence at the time, an she swallied it. An when she lost her head, the sixpence fell outa her neck an dropped te the ground!'

I was shocked! Picturin the head rollin on the ground after been hit by the train. An the sixpence covered in blood an guts, an someone pickin it up. 'Did someone give the sixpence te her mammy te keep as a memory?' I asked, feelin very sad.

'Yeah! Her mammy took it an examined it an said, "Yes! Tha's the sixpence I gave me child all right. An I'll keep it for ever," an she started te cry, an blew her nose an walked off. It was awful!'

I didn't stir meself again. I was afraid te put me head near the winda in case it was knocked off by a passin train.

I was put in a room wit six other childre. An the woman who brought us up told us te pick a bed an leave our bags there. I didn't have a bag, so I picked a bed an sat down on it, waitin fer te see wha happens next. The other young ones opened their bags an took out all sorts of things. Slippers, an nightdresses, an pyjamas, an dolls, an teddies, an little bags wit soap an washcloths, an tubes a toothpaste, an bottles a scent even! One young one dabbed some behind her ears, an the smell was lovely. Then the woman came in an brought us down te the dinin hall, she called it. The room was huge, wit glass from ceilin te floor, an big glass doors goin out te a big green field wit trees an flowers. Hundreds of childre sat at long tables on wooden benches. An the noise was murder. I felt a bit afraid, cos I didn't know anyone, an I didn't know where I should sit. Everyone seemed te have their pals wit them, an I didn't want te make a fool of meself. So I stood at the door, watchin the others racin off te their pals who kept a space fer them.

'Come on!' the woman said, puttin her arm aroun me shoulders an bringin me over te a table. An she said, 'You can sit here!' I sat waitin fer the food, wonderin wha we were goin te get an lookin out at the lovely green fields an thinkin how lucky I was not te have te worry about anythin. Life can be just great.

The doors opened, an the women appeared carryin huge trays wit a mountain of sambidges, an the place erupted. 'Over here, Sister! Us, Sister!' One woman staggered over te the left side an another went down the middle of the room. Our table on the right went mad, standin up on the benches an screamin at a woman who was hesimitatin, not knowin which way te go an bucklin under the weight of the tray. She turned in our direction an landed the tray down on our table. Everyone dived on the tray, an there was screams from the ones who got nothin. The tray was emptied as it hit the table. I looked all aroun me, an some people had piles of sambidges. An there was nothin left fer the rest of us. I watched as they picked up their spoons an banged them on the table an stamped their feet on the wooden floor an roared, 'We want food! We want food!' I looked te see if the women were goin te give them a box, or even put them out, but they just put their hands te their ears an laughed an grabbed the empty trays an ran out. So I joined in the bangin an roarin. An the noise was great.

Then more sambidges appeared, an the woman held on te the tray an handed them out te people wit their hands up. 'Me, Sister!' 'No! She got some already.' An we stood on the benches an climbed on the table as the woman backed off, tryin te hold onta the tray.

'Sit down!' she screamed as people pulled each other an slapped legs, standin on their sambidges, an people fell offa the benches, an someone roared, 'Fuck off!' an I grabbed a sambidge an hid it behind me back. An got another one wit me free hand. An then I sat down an stuffed meself wit lovely egg sambidge an ham, an then she disappeared wit the tray. An I wondered if we'd get more, cos I was still hungry!

We got cups a tea from great big kettles, poured inta shiny white teacups. An when no more sambidges appeared, the ones who had more than their fair share, an who couldn't eat any more, put them on the table an asked if anyone wanted one. I grabbed two more an looked at them ... They were squashed! An I was a bit put off cos they were sat on. But the hunger got the better of me, an I stuffed them inta me mouth, cos they were too tasty, an ye can't waste good food!

I woke up suddenly, an me eyes shot open. The sun was streamin through the winda, an the bedroom was lit up all golden. I'm here! An the happiness slid from me toes all the way up te me chest, an

I stretched meself down inta the bed an laughed te meself. Oh, lovely! It's so soft an warm. An the sheets are snow white. I have two, one underneath an one on top. I had a look at me blankets, a lovely pink one an two blue ones. An on the top of them, a lovely gold heavy eiderdown. I rolled onta me belly an looked aroun the room. Everythin was quiet. The other childre were still sleepin. Then I saw the young one over in the corner under the winda lookin at me. She was lookin very worried an I thought she was goin te cry! Then she turned her face away from me an faced inta the wall. Ah, well, she's probably findin it a bit strange. Tha's a pity, cos she could be enjoyin herself. I snuggled down inta the bed, smellin the lovely sheets an blankets, enjoyin meself no end. An I wondered wha we were goin te get te eat.

Then the door opened, an the sister came in. 'Rise and shine, sleepyheads!' An she shook the blankets an tossed people's hair an laughed. The young one in the corner started roarin her head off cryin. An the sister went over te her. 'What's the matter, petal?' An then she looked at the bed an said, 'Oh, dear me! You've had an accident. Stay there, I'll be back!'

'She's after shittin the bed!' someone roared, pointin at the young one in the corner. I gaped!

'Everyone down to breakfast,' the sister shouted, clappin her hands. 'Come on, get washed and dressed, children. And leave Daisy alone!'

There was a rush te the sink. An then another young one started cryin when the sister tried te get her outa the bed. 'Me bed's wet, Sister! I wet the bed. I want te go home te me mammy!' An she roared her head off.

I sat up in me new knickers an vest, an wondered if I should get dressed. I wanted te wash meself an clean me teeth like the others all millin aroun the sink. But I didn't have anythin te wash or dry meself wit. The sister rushed past me, mutterin te herself, 'I better get clean sheets up here. Don't worry, dear,' she said, lookin at the one in the corner who was sittin in her shit an roarin her head off. Then she stopped an looked at me.

'Come along, dear. Out of bed and get washed and dressed.'

An I whispered, 'I haven't anythin te wash meself wit.'

'What?' she said, leanin down te me an lookin very distracted.

'I haven't anythin te wash meself wit, Sister!' I croaked in a louder whisper. Not wantin anyone te hear me business. She looked aroun me, an then at me vest an knickers, an saw I didn't have a bag.

'What's your name, angel?' she said, an her eyes were lovely an kind.

'Martha,' I whispered, not wantin her te go but te stay wit me all day an hold me hand.

'I'll get you a towel and some soap. Meanwhile, get dressed, darling, and I'll be back shortly.' Then she galloped outa the room.

I got a lovely white towel. An a pink washcloth an a new bar of Palmolive soap, an a yella comb. I was smellin lovely as we headed outa the bedroom an down te eat. We got cornflakes wit milk, an a boiled egg, an bread an butter, an cups a tea. Some of them had two an even three eggs lined up in front of them! An I wondered how they managed tha, cos we came in when the food was already on the table, an we had empty egg cups. We had te shout an complain, an the sisters looked at everyone suspiciously. But we got our eggs an our cornflakes, cos our sister knew we'd been robbed!

'Hey, Sally! I'll give ye two of me lemon sweets fer one of yer eggs,' a young one shouted across from me te another one sittin down from me. She had three eggs in front of her an looked at them.

'No! It's worth more than tha. Have ye still got yer Flash bar?'

'Ye must be jokin, I'm not as foolish as I look.'

'All right, then, what else have ye got? Ye can keep yer lemons, gimme somethin else!'

'Right, I can give ye two gobstoppers, take it or leave it! Do ye want te swap?'

'Yeah!' an everyone was happy except me. I was ragin. Three eggs! The bleedin robbers.

We went out te play in the playground. There was a sandpit, an I sat on the steps an watched the young ones makin pies wit buckets an spades. I was afraid te get me frock dirty, cos it had te last me the week. So I better be careful an not get a mark on it, or Jackser would annihilate me. But I wanted te get in an make pies. So I took off me shoes an socks, an tucked me frock under the elastic of the leg of me knickers, an squatted down beside a young one, an watched te see how she did it.

'Can I play wit ye?'

'Yeah, but ye have te get yerself a bucket an spade, an there's none left.'

I watched her goin aroun on her knees, diggin a trench in a circle an makin pies in the middle. She had a snotty nose, an she kept snufflin an stickin out her tongue te lick up the snots. An I wondered how I could get me hands on a bucket an spade as I watched her.

'Can I borra yours?'

'No!'

'What are ye makin?'

'A castle!'

I looked at it. 'If I help ye, usin me hands, can we take turns wit the bucket an spade?'

She looked at me. 'Yeah! All right, then, but it's my castle! An ye have te do what I say.'

'Yeah! It's your castle, but we do it together.' An I swooped up the sand wit me hands an piled it inta the bucket, an after a while she let me slap the bucket wit the spade an empty it out, but it didn't come out right an fell apart! Then she wandered off, an I was left te play wit the bucket an spade. An I spent the mornin tryin te get me pies right. But I'm not great at makin them. An I can't figure out how te build a castle.

We went in fer our dinner, an the lovely smell of cookin hit me as we went inta the house. We got handed a big white plate of cabbage an mincemeat, an mash potato. Mine was gone in a flash, an I looked aroun te see if anyone had left theirs, but everyone had clean plates, an then I picked up mine te lick off the gravy. Pity there's no more! Then we were handed red jelly an ice cream. An everyone started singin 'Jelly on the Plate'!

When tha was gone, I was still hungry. 'Do ye think they'll give us any more?' I asked a young one sittin beside me.

'No! Ye only get one dinner,' an then she gave a last lick te her plate. 'Pity though! Tha was gorgeous,' she said te me, lookin aroun te see if there was anythin left te eat.

'We're still waitin on our jelly an ice cream, Sister!' the one who managed te get the three eggs roared up at the sister collectin the plates.

'Ah! Go on out of that, you little chancer! I saw you polishing off your jelly and ice cream,' the sister laughed back at her. 'Now get your things together, because we are leaving in half an hour,' the sister said. An we all jumped up an raced outa the dinin room an headed fer our bedrooms.

I sat on me bed an watched the others change their frocks an comb their hair. An I got up an washed me face an combed me hair, an checked te see if me frock was clean an me socks still white. An then we all left an went te the playground. There was a big mob waitin fer the swings, an they were holdin places fer their pals. So I didn't bother te even try waitin fer a swing. I wandered aroun lookin fer someone te play wit, maybe chasin or somethin.

Then I saw the sister wit a mob of young ones aroun her. An she was lookin aroun fer more childre. I rushed over, an she said we were te line up an she'd call our names out. 'Mary Doyle!' An she looked at her notebook an took out a bag wit money an said. 'Two shillings for you, Mary! Patty Gibbons! One shilling an ninepence for you, Patty!'

I wondered wha was goin on. 'Why is she givin everyone money?' I asked a young one standin next te me.

'She's mindin our holiday money our mammies gave us. An now we're goin on our outin down te the shops, an we can spend it.'

Me heart sank as I watched people collectin their money an goin off one by one lookin very happy, an I knew I wouldn't be goin wit them, cos I didn't have any money te spend.

I was feelin more an more foolish standin here, knowin I'd no money te collect, an they'd all know I wasn't like them. Then the last name was called out, an the sister put her notebook in her bag. An I was left standin there, not knowin if I should follow them. The sister looked at me, an I turned away, feelin very ashamed cos I knew she'd think I was dirt. Then she came over te me an put a shillin in me hand, an I looked at it. Me heart flew inta me mouth. 'That's for you,' she whispered.

I couldn't believe it. Tha's an awful lot of money. I was worried. 'Sister! Is this all fer me te spend on meself, or do I have te give ye back some or save it or wha?'

'It's for you to spend on yourself today,' she laughed. I looked at her wit me mouth open, not believin me luck. An she grabbed me an gave me a hug, an fer a minute I was wrapped inside her coat, an then she let me go an took me hand an said, 'We're off, children, stay together.' An I skipped beside her, holdin her arm wit me free hand, an I didn't know wha was better, the hug or the shillin, but I knew I'd never been so happy in me whole life. I was light as air. I was so happy te be alive.

All the childre were runnin aroun the bedroom goin mad. They were bangin each other wit pillas an sendin the feathers flyin everywhere. The sister will go mad when she sees the state of the place!

'I can't wait! We're goin home in the mornin!' Daisy roared.

'Yeah!' the rest of them roared.

'I can't wait te see me ma an all me pals! I have all me stuff ready!' Bella wit the lovely teddy-bear pyjamas said. 'I can't wait fer the mornin.'

'Yeah! I'm goin te get ready meself,' Phillo said. Then they stamped over the eiderdowns an the pillas an the blankets thrown on the floor. An rushed te get ready.

'Here, Bella! Do ye want me talcum powder? I know ye like it!'

'Ah, no, Phillo! You keep it! Yer mammy bought it especially fer ye!'

'Ah, no, go on, take it!'

'All right, then, if ye're sure ye want te part wit it. Here look, you take me bangle, I'm fed up wit it!'

Phillo's eyes lit up. 'Gawd, Bella! Are ye sure?'

'Yeah! Me ma's goin te buy me a real silver bracelet fer me birthday, she promised me.'

I climbed inta me bed, not even botherin te wash meself. Me nerves was shakin at the thought of goin back in the mornin. I buried me head under the blankets an faced inta the wall. I was feelin too sick te talk te anyone. The holiday is over! The week went too fast. No more lovely bed or good food, an the peace was outa this world. An the lovely sister who gave me a shillin every day te spend on meself. An I would have given back the shillin fer just one hug from her. But she never hugged me again or held me hand, cos she was too busy tryin te mind all the other childre hangin outa her. An tha Daisy one always got te hold her hand. I don't know how she managed tha, cos every time I tried te get near her, I always got pushed back an ended up trailin behind them on me own.

The train pulled inta Westland Row station, screamin an snortin. An when the smoke cleared, we could see all the mammies an the daddies an the people crowded on the platform, wavin an laughin at the train. Everyone rushed te look outa the windas. 'There's me ma! I can see her!' screamed Bella. 'Ma! Mammy! In here,' she roared, hangin on the winda. Then they all scrambled fer their things an pushed an shoved te get offa the train. I looked te see if Jackser an me ma was there. But I couldn't see them. I stood up slowly an let everyone get ahead of me, in no hurry te get offa the train.

I pushed through the crowds of laughin people. 'Ma! Ma! We had the best time of our lives, but I missed ya! Where's me daddy?' one young one was shoutin, all excited. I looked aroun slowly fer me ma, but I couldn't see her. I moved down the platform, wonderin if I should go home on me own, maybe they won't be here. I know the way. I could head down te Tara Street an across the bridge, an head up Gardiner Street an then onta Talbot Street, an in back home.

As I turned outa the station, there they were, leanin against the wall. Jackser looked in bad form, an me ma was holdin onta a go-car wit Harry sittin in it, an Teddy was holdin onta the handlebars. An her face was tight an her lips clamped together. Charlie was standin on his own wit his back te the wall an his arms down by his side, lookin very worried. I got such a fright at seein them so suddenly I wanted te run in the opposite direction. But they saw me.

'Come on!' roared Jackser, wavin his fist at me. I started te run. 'Ye took yer fuckin time gettin here,' Jackser snorted. 'There's crowds a people gone on ahead of ye!' I said nothin. 'Look at the state of them clothes, Mrs!' he said te me ma, rollin his eyes te the sky an clenchin his fists. I started te move from one foot te the other, not knowin wha was goin te come next. 'Get them clothes offa her, Mrs. An let's get down te tha pawn office.'

Me ma pulled the frock over me head when I handed her me cardigan. 'Come on,' she shouted. 'Get them shoes an socks off.'

I was left standin in me knickers an vest. An everyone lookin at me as they passed. 'Ma, lookit wha she's doin!' a young one shouted, pointin at me.

The ma looked an then looked away, pretendin she saw nothin. 'Come on!' she said. 'We're goin over te see yer granny. She has somethin lovely fer ye.'

'Wha, Ma? What is it?'

'Nothin, I'm not tellin ye. Wait till ye see. If we hurry, we'll be just in time te catch the bus.' An she ran on laughin, an the young one laughed an grabbed her arm. An her little sister runnin on the other side of her mammy laughed an shouted, 'Ye won't go away again, will ye, Bettie?'

'No! I'm delighted te be home. I really missed ye, Mammy.'

An I saw the mammy strokin the back of Bettie's head, an she pulled her inta her as she rushed te catch the bus.

Me ma put on an aul rag over me head. It was damp an dirty an split under the arms, cos it was too small fer me. An I looked down at me lovely clean legs an feet tha felt soft from all the washin an wearin the new shoes. An I knew tha was the last I'd see a them! It was lovely bein clean an warm. An I wondered why good times only last a very short time an misery an worry seems te go on for ever! I don't understand tha!

297

28

The St Vincents got Jackser a job. He was te call down te see the man on Monday mornin. 'I'm very grateful te ye fer all the help ye can give me,' says Jackser, implorin the man wit his hands joined together as if he was prayin te the man.

'That's all right,' said the man. 'So long as you're there on time. Ten a.m. sharp, mind! And show you are a willing worker, you should have no problem being taken on.'

'Thank you very much, Sir! The blessins o God on ye! An I'll get the childre te pray fer ye. I'll even get the Mrs te light a candle fer ye.'

'Yes, well, that's all right, thank you!' said the Vincents man. 'And don't forget, ask for Mr O'Brien. He's a personal friend of mine. So don't let me down. He's doin this as a personal favour to me!'

'Oh, have no worries on tha end,' said Jackser. 'I'm a very hard worker when I get goin. All I need is the start.' An he gave a little salute wit his two fingers pointed at his head an then shot them at the man, lookin very serious altogether.

Jackser's gone off te see the man about the job. An he's washed an shaved wit the new tuppenny Silver Gillette blade I rushed te the shop fer this mornin. Me ma looks happy. 'It'll be grand havin the few bob if he gets tha job,' me ma said. 'I hope everythin goes all right.'

'Ah, he'll get the job, Ma. The Vincents man was certain.' Then I felt happy meself. 'Just think, Ma! He'll be out all day, an we can do wha we like! An we'll have money te spend on food! Oh, Ma, this is great!'

I looked at her, but she didn't seem sure. 'I hope so, or maybe he'll be chasin dyed blondes.'

'Ah, Ma! Stop annoyin me. Ye're always goin on about tha! Can I go outside te play an watch fer him?'

'Yeah, but don't go far. He'll be out lookin fer ye when he gets back.'

I was watchin two young fellas playin cards when I saw Jackser comin in through the gates. I rushed down an got inta the room behind him.

'Well, Sally, I got the job. I'm a night watchman on a buildin site down on the North Wall. An I'm te start tonight.' Me ma was blinkin an chewin her lip an smilin, takin it in. But I was busy tryin te work out if there was any good in tha. He'll be here durin the day an out at night when we're all sleepin. Ah, tha's too bad! But at least we'll have money. 'Right, Sally, get goin,' he suddenly said. 'I need te get me head down an get some kip. So I want this room cleared. Get them kids outa here an get me some grub te eat. Put on a stew.'

Me ma looked in her purse an handed me two shillins, tha's the last of the money! An she handed it te me an sort of took it back, not wantin te part wit it. 'Eh . . . go down an get me a quarter a sausages, an two carrots, an an onion, an a packet a Bisto. An bring me back the change.'

When Jackser woke up, me ma gave him the stew from the pot. An we all crowded aroun. 'Wha's this, Mrs?' he roared, swingin his eyes up te heaven. 'Have ye not fed these kids?'

'Don't mind them!' me ma said. 'They'll get their tea in a minute.' So we all moved away from the table, an Jackser shovelled the stew inta his big gob. I knew we'd be lucky te get tea an bread.

'Right! I'm off!' he said, standin up. 'An don't forget, send tha young one down wit me can a tea an a loaf a bread cut up. An a bit a cheese if ye can get it! An wrap it up in the greaseproof paper from the bread. An bring it down te me aroun twelve a clock tonight. Now make sure ye're on time!' he said, pointin his finger an stabbin me chest.

'Yeah, right, Jackser. I've got tha. I'll hurry down te ye!'

'See tha ye do!' An he was gone out the door. I watched through the winda te make sure he was gone, an then I let me breath out. Me ma whipped out the little packet a cheese we got on the ten bob Vincents voucher an started cuttin up the loaf a bread.

'I'll get this ready fer him tonight, an tha's the last of the bread!'

Me mouth fell open, an I roared, 'What about us, Ma?' I looked at me brothers, all waitin fer somethin te eat, our bellies rumblin wit the hunger after watchin an smellin tha lovely stew tha aul bastard wolfed down his gullet. 'We got nothin te eat all day, cos ye were savin it fer tha bandy bastard.'

'Don't you start!' me ma roared back. 'I'm tellin him wha ye're callin him when he gets back here.'

'An I'm tellin him ye're sayin he's chasin after dyed blondes!' I roared, nearly cryin wit the way she always puts him first an gives us nothin.

'Stop yer roarin! I'm givin ye bread an tea. He's not gettin the whole loaf.' An I know she was tryin te make the peace. So I let go of me rage at her an just hated Jackser even more.

I fell asleep on top of the bed, cos I knew I'd have te go out late. An there was no point in gettin inta me bed.

'Wake up! It's time te take him the tea!' I didn't know where I was, I was so tired. An I put me head down again, wantin te get under the blankets. 'Come on!' me ma shouted in a loud whisper. 'He's waitin, an I don't want any trouble.'

I got up an took the can wit the handle. It was very hot, an the tea would slop out if I didn't balance it properly. I couldn't swing it. I put the big packet a sambidges under me arm an held the can in me other hand away from me in case it scalded me. An me ma opened the door an whispered, 'Now ye know where te go? An don't dilly dally, tha tea has te be hot fer him. Down the quays, on the North Wall, past the pub facin the ships.'

'Yeah, Ma! I know where te find him.'

'Go on, then, an hurry!' me ma said before shuttin the door.

I rushed out inta the cold night air, an it was freezin. Outa the buildins an aroun te Talbot Street, headin fer Amiens Street, an then under the arch an down te Sheriff Street. Past the church on me left an up an over the bridge. Turn right, passin the shops an the flats, an go te the end, comin out where the ship docks te take ye te Liverpool. One day soon, I'll be takin tha ship an leavin here for ever. I turned left an rushed on. It was pitch black, an the wind was whippin up the river. I hadn't seen a soul. An it was so quiet, everyone was snorin in their beds.

At last I could see Jackser. He was sittin in a little box like a hut wit no door. An he was holdin his hands out, warmin them on a big metal brazier glowin red hot filled te the brim wit coke. 'It's about time ye got here!' Jackser snorted, whippin the package a sambidges an grabbin the can a tea. 'I'm fuckin starved sittin here in the freezin cold while youse are all lyin in yer beds not givin a fuck about me so long as ye have yer own comforts!' An he glared at me, shovin a huge chunk a bread an cheese down his neck an washin it down wit a big hot sup a tea.

I watched this an mumbled, 'We were hurryin, Jackser. An I got here as fast as I could.'

I moved closer te the fire while he had his fill. An when he was satisfied, he offered me a bit a bread an poured me a sup a tea. 'Here! Get tha down ya. It's a cold night. At least it took them little bastards off the streets. Young fellas! Throwin stones, they were. At me!' He couldn't believe it an shook his head. 'It's the bigger ones I have te watch. Them bastards are throwin big rocks tha'd split ye wide open if ye didn't keep wide awake. But I'll catch them! An they won't come back here in a hurry!' I finished me tea an bread, an put the mug down, wantin te collect the can an go home. But Jackser was still talkin. 'This job'd kill ya. The smoke from tha coke is gettin inta me lungs an poisonin me.' Then he gave a big cough te clear his throat, an spat inta the fire, makin it sizzle. 'Tha chinny aul bastard from the Vincents knew wha he was doin all right! Nobody else would take this job, breathin in them fumes from the coke an gettin yerself split wide open wit them fuckin young fellas!'

Then he sat thinkin, starin at the fire. 'When ye're down, it's very

301

hard te get te yer feet again,' he said, lookin very lonely. I listened. 'Nobody wants te know ye! If I had me time over again, I'd do things differently. I'd never touch the drink. Tha was the ruination of me. I put me poor mother in an early grave because of it. I gave her a terrible time, I did. I even sold the home from over me brother's head, I did. The night she was buried, I sold the key fer drink. Now they're all in England, married wit families. An they've done well fer themselves. One of them even has his own business. But they won't have anythin te do wit me! They haven't spoke te me since tha night. They all had te take the boat te England. But it's me poor mother. Ah! I broke her heart, Martha! If only I could tell her I'm sorry. I do terrible things, but I don't mean them!'

I looked at his eyes shinin wit tears, an I felt so sorry fer him. 'Ye're a good kid, Martha. I wish things were better, but you're smart, ye have it all up here,' an he pointed te his head. 'You're smarter than me an yer mammy. Poor Sally, she doesn't have your head. But I'd do anythin fer her. I idolise the ground she walks on, but there doesn't seem te be anythin I can do. She won't let me work. When I used te do the coal, she followed me te the stables an accused me of lookin fer other women. But I wouldn't do tha on yer mammy.' I knew tha was true, but I didn't know wha te say.

Every night I have te run down wit his tea an sambidges. I'll fall inta the bed aroun two o'clock an then get up again at seven an get the childre out onta the street, cos Jackser wants his peace an quiet te sleep until about four o'clock. I'm worn out walkin the streets wit the childre. An I have te spare the bread me ma gives me. An the childre are whingin wit the hunger. Me head is painin me all the time, an I get sick if I touch the bread. An we're all freezin cold an exhausted from tiredness. But nothin is goin te change. I wish he'd never got tha job.

Jackser came home on Thursday mornin wit a black eye an a big bloody swollen mouth. I listened while he told me ma wha happened. 'Sally, I got an awful beatin!' he said as he collapsed in the door. Me mouth fell open, an me ma shook an blinked, an chewed her lip, an went white as a sheet.

'Wha happened?' she asked.

'Them bastards, big young fellas they were, started their messin again, throwin stones at me. Big rocks! But I was ready – waitin fer them, I was. An when they came, I let them get close, an then I sprang. Catchin the leader, I gave him a hammerin. A young fella of about fourteen. He squealed like a pig. The bastards had been houndin me night after night. An then early this mornin, aroun six o'clock, two fellas appeared outa nowhere when I was sleepin. Out of me senses I was, an they dragged me te me feet an started punchin me in the stomach an kickin me on the ground. I never had a chance. He was the young fella's aul fella. He was a docker on his way te work, he said! The other fella said nothin. Just stood there wit his legs spread out an his arms folded, watchin. "I don't want te see you here tonight when I get outa the pub!" he said, yankin me te me feet an shovin his big bull face at me. "Or ye'll be in tha fuckin Liffey wit a big chain tied aroun yer neck. Do ya get tha?" he roared at me. Jaysus, Sally! Ye should a seen the size a them! They'd make ten a me. Built like a fuckin bus, he was! Tha's the end a me! No more. I'm not showin me face down there again. Fuck me, no!' An he collapsed on top of the bed.

Jackser's gone te collect his wages an his cards from the job, an sign back on the labour. I'm happy, cos now I might get a bit of rest at last. We took the chance, while he an the ma was out, te lie on the bed. Everyone was exhausted, even the babby was sleepin. I closed me eyes an felt meself sinkin down inta a lovely sleep. 'Oh! Thanks be te God! This is lovely,' I sighed.

We all woke up when we heard the shoutin. Jackser was comin through the door wit me ma trailin behind him. 'Can ye believe tha, Mrs? No labour until God knows when! An all cos they said I walked out on the poxy job. Sure, I was only offa the labour fer three weeks! An now ye're tellin me the Vincents are comin no more!' He roared at me ma, spittin wit annoyance, his eyes bulgin outa his head.

'It's not my fault the Vincents won't give us any more!' me ma shouted back. 'I'm only tellin ye wha they said te me. Chinny said, when I asked them te call on us, tha they can't do any more fer us. Tha they have more deservin cases te look after!'

Jackser ran at her an waved his arm in the air, pointin te the other flats. 'Ye mean they're goin te give it te them tha has plenty. While the rest of us starve!'

'Wha do ya want me te do?' me ma roared, takin off her coat an scarf.

'Right! Tha's it, I've had enough.' An he made fer the door.

'Where are ye goin?' me ma screamed in panic.

'Mind yer own fuckin business,' he said, lookin back at her.

'No! Give me tha money. Give me them wages ye got from the job.' She lunged at his pockets, tearin at his coat. He grabbed her, givin her a punch in the face, an sent her flyin. She hit the floor.

The kids screamed, an I leapt offa the bed screamin, 'No, Jackser! Please don't hurt me mammy!' I was implorin him wit me hands joined an lookin up inta his face. He hesimitated, spit comin outa his mouth an his eyes starin outa his head. I was so afraid he'd kill her an the rest of us.

We stayed like tha fer a few seconds, our eyes locked on each other, an then his face dropped an his eyes cleared. An he put his hand in his pocket an took out four green pound notes an handed me two. An he said quietly, 'Here, give tha te yer mammy. I have te get out, this place is killin me. I'll be back. Look after her.' An he was gone.

I picked me ma up off the floor, an her lip was bleedin, an her cheek was all swollen. 'Here, Ma,' I said quietly, givin her the money when she was sittin on the chair.

She wiped the blood off her mouth wit the back of her hand an looked at the money. 'Tha won't last long. He's gone off te drink the rest. What am I goin te do now?' she cried, lookin at me. I stared at her, feelin very sorry fer her. I wanted te do somethin, but I didn't know wha te do. I was still shakin, an I could feel me heart sinkin down inta me belly wit the way everythin seemed so empty. She sat there cryin quietly. An I sagged down onta the bed.

Harry was whingin an pullin at his hair wit tiredness an hunger.

His face was black an sticky, an his hair was standin up an matted wit dirt. An then he started bangin his head against the wall. I tried te pull him over te me, but he pushed me away. Teddy lay down again an just stared at the wall, not even blinkin. An Charlie just sat on the bed, not movin a muscle, an looked at me, only movin his eyes, as if te say, maybe you'll do somethin, Martha, te make things better.

I stood up. 'Ma! I'm goin out. I'll be back.'

She stirred herself. 'Where are ye goin? Stay here, I want ye. I don't know . . . ye'll have te get a few messages, I suppose.'

'OK, gimme the money! Wha do ye want me te get?'

She didn't answer me. I stood an waited. I felt I was drownin. I had te move. 'Ma! Wha do ye want me te get?' I asked louder.

'Nothin! Wait, leave me alone! I just want some peace,' she shouted back, lookin very distracted.

I turned an headed fer the door. 'Right, go yerself. Ye won't do anythin, ye just want te sit there on yer arse.' An I ran out the door, not listenin or carin when she screamed she was goin te tell tha aul fella on me.

I wandered up Talbot Street, headin fer the pillar. The old woman was sittin there under it sellin her flowers. I looked up at it. The height of it. Some people paid sixpence te climb te the top of it an look down on O'Connell Street. The people looked like ants when ye look down, someone once said. Ye can see the city fer miles aroun, I believe. An sometimes people even go up Nelson's Pillar te throw themselves down. I heard one person threw himself off an landed on the poor woman's flowers. An she's still not the better of it. Then I looked at her, but she still goes on sellin her flowers.

I wandered on up Henry Street, past Moore Street on me right. Them dealers would give ye a dig if ye tried te pick up one of the apples tha rolled on the ground. It happened te me once. I bent down te pick the apple offa the ground an put it te me mouth, an the aul one snatched it back before I had a chance te get a bite an screamed, 'Go on, get outa tha! I'm not here fer the good a me health ye know!'

305

I looked at Woolworths on me left, not botherin te go in. Lookin at all them millions of sweets sittin in their glass cases would torment me. I walked on, comin te Mary Street, an stopped, waitin te cross the road. A woman on the other side was agitated. Her head was swingin from left te right, an then she'd fix her scarf on her chin te tighten it an then clamp her hands on the handlebars of the go-car wit two babbies sittin on top of each other. The older babby of about sixteen months old was holdin on te the bars fer dear life. An the babby, about six months old, was screamin an kickin, tryin te knock him off. An then she'd look aroun her at the other three, not much older. An then make a run at the road, tryin te stop the traffic wit the go-car, only te have te make a run back fer the footpath. She almost made it te the middle of the road only te turn aroun when she heard the screams of the kids. Two were still stuck on the footpath, fixin themselves te make a run fer it, an the third was trailin behind her, screamin his head off wit fright an not knowin which way te run. She pulled the go-car back, givin it an almighty yank, nearly knockin the babby out who was sittin on the edge. An his face was purple, an he was lookin at his hands on the bars te make sure he had a tight grip. An he was sobbin, too shocked te even cry. The mammy yanked the little young fella, he was about two, off the ground by the scruff of his neck an hauled him back onta the footpath. 'I'll be done fer the lot of youse! I swear I will!' she screamed, lookin at them an then lookin te see if there was another gap in the traffic.

She steadied herself, straightenin her back an straightenin her shoulders, an whippin her chin up an down te keep her scarf on, an, grippin the handlebars, made another run fer the middle of the road. Knowin once ye got there, the traffic has te stop an let ye pass! She looked aroun screamin, 'Come on! Come on! Stay wit me, we're nearly there!' An the three little childre galloped behind their ma, their chins pushed out an their shoulders pushed back, flickin their eyes left an right, an their faces were red, an they were holdin their breath. An when they landed on the footpath, the mammy turned on them, screamin out her breath. 'One of these days youse are all goin te get me kilt! An I swear I'll be hanged fer the lot of ye's if tha happens!' Then she stopped, feelin better, an said, 'Come on! Stay wit me, an I'll buy ye's all an icepop.' An the childre's faces lit up, an they were laughin wit happiness. I was so busy watchin all this, I forgot te cross the road. I shook meself an dipped out under the traffic, makin the cars screech te a halt, an carried on up Mary Street.

I stopped outside a grocery shop an looked in. It was a bit dark, but there was loads a food stacked along the shelves, an it wasn't an ordinary shop wit everythin behind the counter. Ye could walk in an help yerself te whatever ye wanted an pay the woman sittin beside the door wit the cash register in front of her. I wandered inta the shop, an it was empty. There was only one woman mindin the cash register an another woman leanin on the counter, an their heads were pushed together tellin each other news. I stopped beside a big box of real butter. Four shillins an sixpence fer a pound! Gawd! Tha's very expensive altogether. Nobody could afford tha in a million years. I picked one up an felt the weight of it an the colour! Wouldn't I just love te lather tha on a big chunk of black-crusted fresh loaf bread an eat the lot till I had me fill. I put the packet te me nose, an smelt the butter. Gawd! What it must be like te be rich!

I looked aroun me. The women were still leanin their heads inta each other an whisperin like mad. I grabbed two pounds an put one under each arm an folded me arms across me chest, tryin te hide the butter, an slid down the shop, not makin a sound in me bare feet. An I glued me eyes on the women, ready te drop the butter an run fer me life. I slid past them, an they didn't even look up, an outa the shop an ran fer all I was worth, turnin left, past the Corporation Office on me right, where ye go when ye want te get a new house. An turned right down Capel Street, past the aul Jewish junk shops, where ye could buy a pram, or table an chairs, or whatever ye wanted, if ye had the money. I ran on, feelin the lovely weight of the good butter under me arms. I finally stopped when I hit the buildins.

I sat outside the gates on the footpath, lookin aroun te make sure no one was watchin me. Big young ones or young fellas could try

307

te rob me. I looked at the butter an thought about it. I'd have te rob the black crusty fresh loaf if I wanted te taste the butter! Tha's no good. Me ma only buys stale loaf bread, cos it lasts longer. Ye can't cut fresh loaf. It goes te pieces. If I bring this home, she'll spare it fer tha bandy aul fella. An we wouldn't get a look in. Too bad!

I thought fer a minute an then jumped up. I raced inta the buildins an knocked on a woman's door. I knew she had a husband workin an a son an daughter even bringin in money! 'Mrs, me ma sent me up te know if ye want te take this butter offa her. She bought it on the St Vincents voucher fer nine shillins, but she'll let ye have it fer seven shillins, cos she needs the money. An you'll be savin two shillins, Mam!'

She looked at me, te see if I was tellin the truth, an then looked down at the butter an said, 'All right, then, wait there until I see if I have tha much.' Me heart gladdened, an I waited, holdin in me breath in case she didn't have the money. 'Here ye are,' she said, comin out holdin her purse an openin the door wider. I could smell somethin lovely cookin. She opened her purse an smiled, lookin at the butter, an counted out two half-crowns an a two shillin piece. 'Seven shillins altogether, wasn't tha it?'

'Yes, Mrs!' I said, shakin me head up an down, handin her the butter an takin the money.

I raced down the stone stairs, takin them two at a time, feelin the weight of the money clenched in me fist, an banged on the door. 'Ma! Ma! Let me in, it's me.'

She opened the door, an I rushed past her. 'What ails ye? Wha's wrong?' she said, lookin worried.

'Look! Lookit what I got fer ye!' Her eyes opened wide as she took the money from me hand.

'Where did ye get tha?' she asked, laughin. An I told her the story. She listened an then shook her head an said, 'You'd want te mind yerself. If they catch ye, ye'll be put away an locked up in a home.'

I was quiet then, thinkin about this. It was true. Most of the young fellas in the buildins were put away te Daingean an Letterfrack, an tha was the last ye saw of them. An they were never the same again.

Then I looked at me ma's face. An she was happy, an I thought it was worth all the trouble just te see her smile. Cos when she's happy, I'm happy, an everythin is grand. 'Ma,' I said, 'don't let Jackser get his hands on the money.'

'Don't you worry,' she said, lookin very serious. 'I'll have it well hidden!'

When Jackser found out about the money fer the butter, his eyes lit up! He started snufflin an shook himself an rubbed his hands together. 'By God, Sally! This could be the answer te our prayers!'

I looked but said nothin. Me heart was sinkin. I told me ma not te tell him. But now I could sense real trouble. Ye can't trust me ma!

'You go out tomorrow an get as much butter as ye can. There's plenty a people'd take it off ye. Go early in the mornin. It's Saturday, an everyone will be gettin their messages. The shops will be so crowded they won't see ye puttin the butter in the bag. Now remember! Get all ye can! An when ye get the few bob, go back again an get yer hands on some grub. Bring back as much messages as ye can get.'

I felt sick. The room was spinnin wit the shock I'm in. I won't be able te do it! I'll get caught an be sent away. Locked up till I'm sixteen. If I don't do it, God knows wha Jackser will do te the lot of us. I looked at me ma. She was happy. She's worse than a child, I thought. I wanted te scream at her. Tell her she's me mammy. She's supposed te be mindin us. But she's so fuckin lazy. I wish I had nothin te do wit her.

I set off at half-nine, headin fer Henry Street. I was shiverin an shakin. I looked at meself in a big plate-glass winda as I passed a big shop on Talbot Street. I was white as a sheet. I'll be spotted right away, cos I'm too poor lookin wit me black bare feet te be shoppin in the supermarket. These people know tha. I rushed on, across Nelson's Pillar an up Henry Street. I went down the alleyway an in through the side door te Woolworths. I need a shoppin bag. It was still early. Not too many people. The crowds wouldn't pick up until later. I moved aroun slowly, lookin fer the bags. Keepin an eye on the shop workers fillin the shelves. Then I spotted them. I lifted down a brown leather one wit a zip across. Ye wouldn't be able te see wha's inside it. I put me arm through the two straps an headed fer the door, slowly browsin me way out an actin as if the bag was me own te get the messages. No one spotted me. I was out.

I went quickly back up the alley an headed across the road te the supermarket. I wasn't used te these places an looked aroun te see how it operates. There's cash registers all in a line, an women sit at them. Ye can walk out the way ye came in, but people line up at the cash registers an pay fer their messages an come out through tha way. I headed off te find the butter. It was in a cold fridge. I opened the bag, pullin back the zip, an looked aroun te see if anyone was watchin. A woman was comin, holdin her shoppin basket under her arm an puttin messages inta it. I can't do anythin until she goes. I better get meself a shoppin basket, or I'll look suspicious.

I had me shoppin basket in me right arm an me shoppin bag open on me left arm. I put four pounds of butter in the basket an followed behind the shoppers. When no one was behind me, I lifted two pounds a butter an dropped them inta me bag until I had the four in. Then I went back an got another four an did the same thing again. But it takes time, an then I saw a shop assistant lookin at me. She was suspicious. I saw the way she looked at me bare feet. So I picked up a packet of cornflakes an put it in the basket an decided te move on. It's time te leave! I had the zip closed on me bag, hidin the eight pounds of butter, an moved aroun the shop, slowly bidin me time, makin sure no one was followin me. An then I saw me opportunity. A crowd of people started comin in, an I moved over quickly an pushed me way through them an out the door.

I walked on, shakin inside meself, the back of me rigid, waitin te be grabbed. Nothin happened. I was safe. I turned down Moore Street an walked on, headin fer a laneway. I went down te the end of the laneway an looked aroun. Under the wheels of tha car is the best place. I can hide it there, an then go back fer more. An when I've enough, I can head off te sell it.

I went back up te Henry Street but didn't go back te the same shop. I'll give it a rest, just in case. I headed inta another supermarket, an now it was gettin crowded. Tha was more difficult. Too many people watchin. I put eight pounds a butter in the basket this time an drew attention from the women shoppin. So I moved aroun wit the crowd, everyone headin in the same direction, an did nothin until I was sure tha suspicious woman wasn't watchin me. Then when I got stuck in a crowd of people, I didn't look down but held me hand on two pounds a butter an lifted it inta me bag, holdin it open wit me left arm. No one looked down, cos we were all squashed together, tryin te shuffle in the same direction. I left the eight pounds a butter wit the other lot, under the wheels of the car, an went back again te the same shop.

By the time I was finished, it was after two o'clock, an I had forty-two pounds of butter. I headed fer the flats an knocked on doors, tellin people the same story about the St Vincents food voucher an buyin butter instead. By four o'clock, I had all the butter sold an made seven guineas. Tha's seven pounds an seven shillins. I went inta a shop on Talbot Street an changed the silver fer a huge five pound note an two single pound notes, an put them together – this was fer them. An I kept the silver – two half-crowns an the two shillin piece fer meself.

I headed back up te Henry Street an inta Woolworths, an got meself a purse te hold me money. An then I spotted a lovely red pair a sandals an put them in me bag. An then I saw a lovely pair a white socks. I put them in me bag, an just as I was about te leave, a man grabbed me an said, 'Come with me!' I knew straight away he'd seen me, an I tried te escape, but he pulled me along. An I went hysterical.

He lifted me off the ground an tried te carry me in his arms. But I was so frightened, I kicked an bucked, an I was screamin fer me mammy te help me. A crowd a people gathered aroun us, an the women started shoutin at the man te let me go. He was very nervous but wouldn't let go of me waist. I was screamin an cryin, an doin me best te fight him. An the women went mad an started hittin him te let me go. An then he dropped me, an the women grabbed me an pushed me out the door. An blocked him, shoutin,

'You've little te be doin pickin on a poor hungry child! Let her go! Whatever she has belongin te ye won't break ye!'

I flew out the door, me feet not touchin the ground, an kept runnin down alleyways an up back streets until I found meself at Jervis Street, outside the hospital. I slumped te the ground, covered in sweat. I was soakin, an me chest was heavin up an down wit the pain in it. An I was snow white. When I was a lot better, I opened me bag an tried on the sandals. They were a grand fit, only a tiny bit too big. I looked at them, red an brand new. But somehow they weren't worth it. An I felt as if things would never be the same. Everythin had changed, an I didn't like it. I stood up after puttin the shoes an socks back in me bag an moved off, headin back up te Henry Street, keepin away from Woolworths.

Jackser said I'm te bring back food, so I headed inta the first supermarket. The one I went inta early this mornin. An took a shoppin trolley on wheels. I filled it wit packets of expensive back rashers an pounds a sausages. An packets a eggs, an tea, an sugar. An boxes of cheese, an two pounds of butter. An cornflakes, an jam, an biscuits, an chocolates fer the childre, big bars! An when I had everythin, I waited me opportunity an slipped the trolley out the way ye come in an over te the counter at the back of the wall, an joined the other people all puttin their messages in their shoppin bags. I filled me bag te the brim an carried all the rest under me other arm.

The weight of the bag dragged me down sideways, nearly hittin the ground, twistin me head an back. It was too heavy. Just like the butter, all forty-two pounds of it! But I'd have te manage. I struggled out the door, tryin not te drop anythin, an headed down towards the pillar. I had te keep stoppin every few minutes fer a rest. Me arms was like lead, an me back an neck was burnin. I made it as far as Cafolla's an looked in. This is what I've always wanted te do. An in I went an sat down at a table. An fixed me shoppin on a chair beside me an ordered beans an chips an a fried egg. When it arrived, I looked at it. The egg was snow white, an ye could see the lovely yella soft yolk underneath the white. I lifted me knife an fork, an started te eat it.

'Do ye want anythin else?' the waitress asked me.

'Yeah! I'll have a plate a bread an a pot a tea.' The soft egg, mixed wit the chips an beans, slid down me neck. An a bite of white soft bread an a sip a hot tea, wit plenty a milk (me ma always spares the milk!) an two big spoons a sugar. (She saves the sugar fer Jackser!) Well . . . well, this was heaven! I cleaned the plate wit the last bit a me bread, an supped the tea, drainin the pot, an then sat back, still feelin I could eat another plate. But it was very expensive! An I sat back te watch the Saturday shoppers all millin past the café, anxious te get their final messages fer the week an somethin fer the Sunday dinner. The peace tha came over me was like I'd died an gone te heaven. I was very still in meself an felt a light buzzin in me chest of happiness. Not a care in the world. Just a quiet feelin of bein still. It was all over, an I'm safe!

I paid five shillins outa the seven shillins I kept back fer meself, an saved the two shillins, hidin it in me new socks so Jackser or me ma wouldn't get their hands on it. An then started on me struggle again, turnin down fer Talbot Street. I would try te move fast an keep goin, but it was no good. I had te keep stoppin, just like I did wit the butter.

When I finally made it te the door, it was whipped open without me bangin. They were waitin an watchin fer me. 'Holy Jaysus!' Jackser roared, delighted. 'Man alive! Did ye bring back the fuckin shop wit ye?' An he started snufflin an jerkin his arm up an down, an lookin wit his eyes out on stalks.

Me ma came rushin over te the table as I landed the bag on the floor an dropped the stuff outa me stiff arm. I felt like concrete. I handed her the purse wit the seven pounds, an Jackser roared, 'Fuck me blind! The young one's a topper!'

I helped me ma te unload the bag, an the childre all crowded aroun the table, screamin wit excitement. Charlie was hummin anxiously in case he was left out. I pulled out the bars a chocolate – an the screams, an the hands out, an pushin an shovin! 'Me! Me!' tha's all I could hear as I gave them one each. Then they rushed off te sit in corners away from each other an take off the silver paper, watchin each other like hawks in case anyone robbed them. Me ma was all excited an laughin. An Jackser was shakin his head an sayin, 'Tha's wha some workin men bring home in a week, after a hard day's graft!'

I collapsed on top of the bed, leanin meself against the wall, too drained te move a muscle. An just watched everyone. Te have everyone so happy was a great feelin. But I was very glad it was all over. I couldn't ever go through tha again.

'Listen!' Jackser said te me, snufflin an jerkin his arm. 'I've been thinkin! We're onta a good thing here.' I went rigid, lookin over at him, waitin te hear wha he was goin te say. 'People get paid on a Friday, an tha's when they go te do their shoppin. So ye could do the two days, then we'd have the double amount of money an twice as much food. An we'd be on the pig's back, an we'd never worry again!'

So now, every week, twice a week, Friday an Saturday, I have te go out an rob the butter te bring back the money an the food te Jackser an me ma. When the shops get suspicious of me, I know they're watchin an just waitin te catch me. So I can't go back there fer a while. I have te find new shops. I'm all the time lookin an readin the paper te see if any new supermarkets are openin. I travel on the bus te Rathfarnham an walk from there te Churchtown. I go out te Ballyfermot, but tha's no good. Ye're watched like a hawk. I go anywhere te find butter. I went te Blackrock, but tha's a small place wit only one supermarket, an after one day, they'd notice ye, an I'd be caught. Sometimes I'm walkin fer miles. It might be cold an pourin rain, but I have te keep goin. Jackser expects me te bring home the money. An me life wouldn't be worth livin if I didn't. An me ma would go mad, too. She'd go off inta her own world, an it would be terrible te see her like tha, not botherin te even look at us.

Things go wrong, too! I might find a quiet laneway wit cars parked down them, an hide the butter under the wheels of a car only te come back an find the butter squashed when the car drives off! Or maybe someone found it, an now it's gone! An I have te start again. Sometimes me customers might only want one pound a butter instead of two or even three. An then I have te search fer new customers, all the time, draggin the heavy bag.

I bring back fourteen pounds a week. An eight te ten pounds' worth a messages. An toys fer the childre. But it's never enough! As soon as I get in the door, me ma wants te know if I got the new jumper she wanted. 'I couldn't, Ma! They were watchin me.' An she turns away in disgust, not happy. Jackser takes the money an wants te know if I could go in on a Thursday as well, cos they need a few extra bob. 'The shops are quiet, Jackser. An I wouldn't have the customers!' I plead.

'Well, give it a fuckin try anyway!' he roars at me.

Me nerves are gone. I shake all the time. An me head never stops splittin me wit the pain. The only good day is Sunday, when it's all over. But then Monday comes, an I'm down on me knees prayin te God an his Holy Mother te grant tha I won't be caught. I feel sick all the time. An on Friday mornin on the way in te the shops, I have te stop te vomit me guts up. This hell I'm in never stops. It just goes on an on. I don't play wit the other childre now, cos I'm kept in te mind the childre an the room while Jackser an me ma goes off fer the day. He goes drinkin, an me ma just sits wit him.

He bought her a new coat, a red one wit a fur collar, an himself a Crombie coat, an a pair of jockey trousers, an a new pair of leather jockey boots te match. One way or the other, the money is gone by Wednesday. Or they might even spend it all in one day. Me ma complains she's fed up eatin rashers an eggs an sausages, an eatin mince stews. But she can't cook anythin else, an I don't know wha te bring her. She can't cook the sausages. She just gives them a look at the fryin pan an then throws them on the plate lookin snow white an completely raw. An she drops a half-dozen eggs on the fryin pan at the same time an mashes them aroun wit the knife, an then dumps them onta the plate full a black grease. An then says, 'Call him fer his dinner!' So we are no better fed, cos he gets most of it.

315

29

Me ma had a new babby. It's a girl. Jackser called her Dinah, after his sister, he says. He keeps lookin at her, sayin, 'Sally, she looks like a little saint te me! Ye know, I think she's goin te be a nun! She has tha look about her. I don't think she belongs te this world!' Then he gets tears in his eyes an crosses himself. I look at me ma in disgust, cos she keeps lookin at the babby an smilin an noddin, delighted wit herself. Happy cos her fuckin Jackser is happy! 'We have a daughter,' Jackser crows at the babby.

An me ma starts. 'Yes! She's the image of me sister Mary tha died when she was only twelve. She was very holy an a real beauty. She's goin te take after her. I can see tha,' me ma says, noddin at Jackser, who's leanin over me ma's shoulder, starin at the babby.

'Me first daughter! Can ye beat tha?' he says wit a faraway look in his eyes.

'Yeah! It's lovely havin a girl,' me ma says. 'Ye can depend on them fer yer creature comforts.' An she doesn't even look at me! I feel she doesn't want me any more. It's just her an Jackser an his childre. Cos she's always callin Charlie names. An when she does look at him, she has a sour face on her. An Jackser keeps callin me 'tha aul one', an I know I'm only ten years old, but it still pains me. Or else he's tellin me ma te get rid of the two bastards. An tha's why I think she doesn't like Charlie. She doesn't bother about me either. She thinks she only has one daughter, an tha's Dinah.

The other day we were walkin along Capel Street, pushin Dinah sittin up in her cream Walker pram. An she was lookin lovely, wit her pink coat an matchin bonnet wit the white trim lace I got fer her.

316

An her lovely big dolly sittin beside her on the pilla. An Dinah's big blue eyes, an her lovely white face an fair curly hair. She's six months old now, an she threw her rattler outa the pram, an a woman stooped down te pick it up an said, 'Oh, my God! She's an absolute beauty, God bless her!' An she started ticklin Dinah under the chin, an Dinah gave her a big smile, showin her dimples on her cheeks an her four teeth. I was delighted, an me ma was laughin. An the woman said, 'Have ye many like her?' lookin aroun at the rest a us. An me ma said, laughin, 'No, only the one. She's me first girl! The rest was all boys.'

I got such a pain in me heart it nearly choked me! But I didn't cry, cos somehow I knew fer a long time me ma didn't see me as her child. Tha I didn't really belong te her. Tha somehow I only belonged te meself, an I had te mind her. I felt very old.

Jackser sent me fer ten Woodbines, an when I got back, he was gone. Me ma was roarin an cryin. 'Wha's wrong, Ma?'

'Tha bastard's after takin all me money. As soon as he saw me takin the money outa me purse fer the cigarettes, he whipped it. Every penny I had was in tha purse. A whole five pound note an a ten shillin note an two half-crowns! Now I'm left wit nothin!'

'I don't know, Ma,' I said, feelin very weak. I sat down, sick te me stomach.

'He won't come back until he's drank all a the money. An he'll play the big man, buyin everyone in the pub a drink,' me ma cried. An then she was galvanised inta action. 'I'm goin! Gettin away from him! Here! Dress the babby,' an she handed me Dinah. 'Put tha on her,' an she gave me the babby's hat an coat. Dinah waved her arms an bounced herself up an down on me knee, delighted somethin was happenin. She always gets excited when we put her hat an coat on. I gave her a big squeeze an kept kissin her fat little cheeks, an she loved it. 'Come on, hurry up an put her in the pram,' me ma said, grabbin all the clothes outa the press an throwin them on the bed.

When everyone was ready an me ma had the pram loaded up wit a mountain of clothes, ye couldn't see Dinah. We had te keep the hood down te let her get some air. An off we went, slammin the door behind us.

317

We rushed up Talbot Street, me helpin te push the heavy pram tha had a mind of its own an kept wantin te go onta the road. 'Push!' me ma roared at me.

'I am, Ma! But you're not steerin it properly.'

'Tha bastard won't see me again,' she went back te mutterin te herself. 'He's not takin me fer a fool no more! I wasted too much a me life on him. But no more!' I looked up at her, she had a faraway look in her eyes. I said nothin, just happy te be gettin away from tha aul fella.

We turned down O'Connell Street an passed over te the GPO, headin down te the Liffey. Then we turned right onta Bachelors Walk. An I looked at all the second-hand furniture shops, wishin we could get a little place of our own. An we could buy a nice bit a furniture an have the place lookin lovely. But I was holdin me breath, afraid any minute me ma might change her mind an turn back again. Sure enough! As we crossed the Ha'penny Bridge, me ma slowed down an said, 'I think we better go back, before he finds out we're missin.'

'No, Ma!' I pushed the pram harder. 'We're not goin back! Ye don't need him! I'll take care of everythin, an we'll have a good life, livin in peace.'

I looked up at me ma, me heart in me mouth. I could see the air goin outa her, like after ye blow up a paper bag an then burst it. 'I don't know,' she was sayin, chewin her lip. 'Where will we go?'

I looked aroun me feelin desperate. 'The hostel, Ma! The Regina Ceoli!'

'No!' me ma roared. 'I'm not goin back there. Tha's an awful kip!'

'Ma, please! Let's go. Just until I get enough money together te get our own place. We can save, Ma. We won't need te spend a penny. An we'll have a lovely place of our own in no time. We can even buy lovely new shiny lino fer the floor.'

'Ah! I don't know,' me ma said, lookin far away.

Then she turned the pram aroun, an said, 'Come on! We better get back before he does.'

'No, Ma! I'm not goin back. You can go if ye want te, but I'm never goin back!'

She stopped an looked back at me. I stood me ground, me heart hammerin in me chest. But she turned away from me, sayin, 'I have te get back, Martha!' an I stood an watched her rushin away from me. An Charlie was watchin me, hopin I'd change me mind an follow me ma. He rushed on, catchin up wit the pram, an I was on me own. A few minutes ago, I thought I had me mammy an me brothers an me babby sister, an we'd live in a lovely little flat an be very happy. An then suddenly it all changes, an ye're left wit nothin! But I sort of expected tha, cos lovely things only happen in the fairy books I read or in the fillums. But they're not real!

I wandered on, lost inside meself, feelin I was all alone an wantin me mammy. But she didn't want me. I only wanted someone te like me, hold me hand an smile at me. An fuss about me hair an was I washed! An sleep in a nice clean bed. An say, 'This is my child, an I think the world of her!' But I knew I wasn't goin te find tha. I'm just not lucky, tha's all. This thought didn't lift the empty feelin inside me or take the weight inside me chest offa me.

I wandered on, turnin up the hill an comin te the house I used te live in. I sat down on the ground wit me back against the factory wall, just like I used te do a long time ago, an looked up at the windas all locked up. An the memories came rushin back. Auntie Cissy sittin on the windasill, drinkin her tea an smilin down at me, makin sure I was eatin me currant bun. Aunt Nelly wakin us, me an Barney, te give us our tea an bread, always laughin. Me ma buyin me chips on a dark cold night, an us rushin home te eat them. Just the two of us! Her happy wearin lipstick. An me heart felt it was goin te break. I want them times te come back again. I closed me eyes, rememberin. But they're gone, over fer ever. An me ma is gone, too. She went wit them times, an she'll never come back. There's nothin here any more. I stirred meself, gettin up feelin stiff. I'd been sittin on the cold ground too long.

I wandered back down the hill towards the Liffey an kept walkin till I hit O'Connell Bridge an turned down Aston Quay. I ended up under the arch at Amiens Street station. It was gettin late, nearly dark. I wandered inta a little shop an started te read the comics. I helped meself te a comic tha said 'Tales from the Crypt', an the man spotted me an roared after me, 'Bring tha comic back!'

I ran, decidin not te part wit me comic. It looked good, an I needed somethin te keep me company. A bus stopped at the stop in front of me, an I jumped on, not knowin where I was goin. It was dark now, an the conductor roared up the stairs, 'Last stop, Dollymount!' Oh, I heard of tha, it's on the seaside. I came down the stairs an asked the man wha time the next bus goes inta town. 'This is the last one,' he said. 'We're headin back te the bus station.' I got off the bus, an it was pitch black, except fer the street lights. It looked very dark in places an was very late at night.

I wandered back, headin towards some lights I could see comin outa a shop. Big young fellas an young ones wit college scarves aroun their necks were laughin an pushin each other. I looked at them wit their big white Gibbs toothpaste smiles, an clean shiny faces, an lovely long hair, an ye could see they were well looked after an not a bother in the world on them. The lights went out in the shop, an the people were sayin goodnight, an then they went their separate ways, laughin an wavin. An then everythin went dark an quiet.

I moved on, feelin very tired an cold. I passed big houses, wonderin where I was goin te sleep. I need te find a bit of shelter, somewhere in outa the cold an wind comin in from the sea. An I don't want anyone te spot me, or God knows wha might happen te me. I walked on, lookin at the houses, desperate te find somewhere. An then I stopped at a house tha was very dark an deserted lookin. I walked up the path an looked at the inside a the porch. There was a hairy brush mat on the doorstep, an I pulled it inta the corner an lay down, fallin asleep. But I kept wakin up from the cold an was disappointed te find I was only dreamin I was under the pissy blankets an coats at home. I got up an pulled the mat out onta the grass. This might be softer. But I woke up again from the cold, an I decided te look fer somewhere else. I crossed the road an found a concrete shelter on the beach. I was happy te be in outa the wind an settled meself in the corner wit me back against the wall an me feet stretched out along the bench. An I could keep an eye on the entrance, in case someone tried te creep up on me. It was very dark, but I didn't mind, just glad of the peace, an I made me plans.

Tomorrow mornin, I would take the bus inta town, an I'd have te get a few pounds a butter te get meself some money. But I didn't mind, cos it was fer meself, an I'd only need enough te feed meself wit. An now I don't have te go inta the shops every weekend an rob all tha butter an food fer them. I could give it up an only take the odd few pounds. Just enough te keep me goin. I'd better buy a candle, just in case I have te come back here tomorrow night. But I have all the time in the world te find somethin better. I was feelin very happy wit meself.

I'd got the bus inta town an managed te get six pounds a butter an sold it fer one pound an one shillin. An I'd gone up te Woolworths café an bought meself beans an chips an a fried egg. An I was just comin down the stairs when who should appear in front of me but Jackser an me ma! I got such a shock! I just stood an stared inta Jackser's face grinnin up at me. An then I turned me eyes te me ma. She turned away from me, not meetin me eyes, an chewed her lip, lookin at the wall. 'You were right,' he said te me ma. 'This was the very place te find her!'

Me ma looked at him an avoided lookin inta me eyes, an said, 'I told ye this is where she comes.'

I came back te me senses an looked past him, judgin me chances of escape. But they were blockin the stairs, an Jackser grabbed me arm an said, 'Ye needn't try te run off, cos I'll find ye, even if I have te scour these streets night an day. I'll catch ye sooner or later. Now empty yer pockets!' an he took the seventeen shillins an sixpence I had left in me pocket. He held me arm, an he marched me all the way back home.

When we got in the door, he picked me up by the back of me neck an flung me across the room. I hit the fireplace on the top of me head, an everythin went black, an I saw stars. An me dinner shot outa me neck. An Jackser grabbed me neck again an wiped me face an nose inta the sick. Me breath was cut off, an I tried te struggle, pushin up an away wit me hands on the floor. But they were slidin in the vomit, an Jackser was roarin inta me head. Then he let go an

321

gave me an unmerciful kick in me side, an I started retchin again, not able te breathe. An the pain was worse than anythin I ever had before. I was swingin meself up, tryin te get te me feet te maybe crawl under the bed te get away from him. He was hammerin on the walls an slammin the table wit his fists. 'You're not breakin up this family!' he was roarin. 'Sally told me all about ye. Gettin her te run away from me! Puttin ideas in her head! So now, the only one leavin here is you! You're gettin on tha boat tonight, an you're goin te England. Ye can stay wit her brother in Hemel Hempstead. An if I ever set eyes on ye again, you're fuckin dead! Ye're gettin this chance te walk outa here alive. But there'll be no next time.'

I crawled up on me feet, draggin meself up onta the bed. An then stood, not movin, waitin fer him te let me move. Me head was like it belonged te someone else. An me back was bent in two from the pain. An I still felt sick. Me nose was stuffed wit the vomit, an me clothes was destroyed. It was soaked inta me hair. How am I goin te clean me coat? It's destroyed! Me ma never moved a muscle, just sat starin at nothin, lookin like a marble statue. Poor Charlie was white as a sheet, an Teddy an Harry was hidin in the corner of the bed, their eyes bulgin wit fright. An Dinah was the only one screamin, an she was sobbin now, lookin from me te Jackser, waitin an watchin te see if the killins was over.

They walked me down te the boat tha night, leavin Charlie te mind the childre. He was five now. An I feel sorry fer him, cos they'll expect him te take up where I left off. We arrived at the gangplank, an crowds a people were gettin on the mailboat. 'Ma! I whispered. 'Ye have te give me the address! Where does yer brother Barney live?'

'In Hemel Hempstead,' she said, agitated.

'I know, Ma, but where?' I asked, desperate.

'When ye get off the boat, ye get on the train fer London. It takes ye te Hamel Hempstead.'

'The train takes ye te Hemel Hempstead, Ma?' I asked.

'No!' she roared. 'The train takes ye te Euston Station, then ye find yer way te Hemel Hempstead!'

322

'Come on,' Jackser roared. 'Let her get on the boat,' an he pushed me up the gangplank. I handed me ticket te the man, an he handed it back, an I put it in me pocket. I looked back, but they were walkin off, makin their way up the quays. An they didn't stop te look back at me. Other people were on the quays, wavin off their relatives an friends. But there was no one te wish me good luck. I went over te the railins te look out. But I couldn't see anythin, cos it was too high up fer me te look over. An I stood wit me back te it, watchin all the other people.

There was a crowd a fellas an girls tryin te get te know each other. 'Keep away now from tha Soho place! A lovely lassie like you will be eaten alive by them foreigners!' a culchie roared at a Dublin one. An he shook himself, roarin laughin te his friends, thinkin he was very smart.

'Here! It's you that's just arrived up on the hay lorry. I wasn't born yesterday ye know!'

'By Gawd! Lookin at them knockers, I'd agree wit ye there!' An he stuck his head between his legs an slapped himself, roarin laughin.

'Ye'll get a belt in the gob if ye give me any more of yer insults!' An she picked up her handbag an her cardboard suitcase, an shouted, 'Come on, Winnie!'

'Right! Let's go,' Winnie said. An she staggered off on her big black high heels tha would stab ye they were so pointy.

The fellas jumped after them. 'Ah, no! No! No! Don't go, tha eejit was only kiddin. Don't take no notice a him. Sure tha fella don't know his arse from his elbow. Here! Have a cigarette,' an they all pulled out their boxes of cigarettes, pullin the girls back, who didn't want te be pulled back but hoped they would be at the same time.

'We're decent people, ye know!' the girl shouted te them.

'Oh, God, that ye's are! An lovely girls at tha. Now let's all be friends, an we'll buy ye a drink, an we'll all be merry. Cos, God knows, life is short, an it's a very hard one at that. Now! Wha do ye's say?'

Yer woman took time te make her mind up. An Winnie said, 'Well, all right, then. But don't think we're easy! An we're not tha easily bought!'

The culchie slapped her on the back an laughed. An winked behind her back te his pals an shook his head te tell them te follow him. An they went down the stairs te get their drinks.

Tha left me lookin at the old man wit the red face from bein out workin in all weathers. He was lookin over the railins, leanin on his arms. An he had a faraway look in his eyes. He was wearin his best suit, but it didn't fit him. The trousers was hangin down in rolls, coverin his brown shoes. An the collar of his shirt was covered in dirt. He looked down at his cardboard suitcase tied up wit the belt of his trousers te make sure it was still there. An then he pulled out ten Sweet Afton cigarettes from his jacket pocket an counted the rest left in the packet an lit one up. An put the box in his pocket. Then he picked up his suitcase an looked aroun him. I knew he was a country man, cos he had a shifty nervous look in his eyes, an they walk wit their heads goin first an their shoulders down an their arses stuck out. An I could tell he wouldn't mix wit too many people. I don't think he has a wife an childre, an I felt sorry fer him, cos he looked very lonely. An I think he was poor. I felt very lonely an lost meself. An I wished I was like them big young ones an the fellas gone down te the bar. Only I would never take drink! Tha destroys people!

It was gettin cold out here, but I was afraid te wander off. If I sit downstairs, people will see I'm on me own an maybe ask questions. An I wouldn't know wha te say. I only have me ticket. It's one way te London, an when I get there, I don't know how te get te Hemel Hempstead. An even if I do get there, how will I find him? I can't understand why me ma didn't give me his address. I just don't know what I'm supposed te do. Maybe if I make me way there somehow, I can ask people do they know him. They didn't even leave me any money te buy meself somethin te eat. Or I might need the train fare or bus or somethin te get from London. I can't think any more. Me head is too dizzy. An I have a big lump on the top of it the size of a door knob. Ye can see it, never mind feel it. An me back an hip feels like there's hot knives goin through it. But when I stay still, it just throbs a bit. An anyway, I'm bent over from the pain, an people would be lookin at me. An I'd only draw attention te meself. So I wandered over te the stairs an found a quiet corner in a passage an settled meself there wit me legs stretched out.

I woke up suddenly an tried te lift me head. It felt like a cement block. I could see two fellas lurchin from side te side, hangin onta their bottles a porter. The ship was rockin like mad, an they couldn't get very far. 'Give us a hand, Mick!' But Mick went down, still hangin onta his bottle a porter, landin on the side of his face an rollin onta his back, upendin the porter all over himself. An then he started te vomit his guts up, turnin his head sideways.

'Ah, Paidin, I'm dyin!'

'Ah, fuck ye!' Paidin roared. 'Will ye get up outa tha!' An he spun aroun, seein nothin an spillin his porter everywhere. An then like a fountain, he spewed vomit everywhere an collapsed beside Mick, landin on his face, an went out cold. The smell was terrible, an I wanted te move. But I was like a dead weight wit the pain in me head, an me back was on fire. So I just closed me eyes an waited fer the sick feelin in me stomach te pass.

When I woke, it was mornin. An the ship gave a bang as it landed at the dock. I could hear the ship's horn blastin away te let everyone know we'd arrived in Liverpool. People started movin along the passage an up the stairs, carryin their suitcases. I pushed me hands on the floor an got meself standin up. I felt like every bone in me body was broken. I was so sore an me mouth felt like sawdust.

I climbed the stairs, followin the people, an then down the gangplank an inta the train station. The place was crowded, an everyone was hurryin te get on the trains. Men in striped uniforms wit fancy hats on their heads were busy loadin the big sacks a mail offa the ship an onta trolleys. A man's voice was comin outa a big horn stuck up on the wall, tellin everyone wha train te catch. But I couldn't understand wha he was sayin.

I stopped an looked aroun me, an got caught up in the crowds pushin forward. Men wit their heads down, suitcases in each arm, slammed inta me, knowin where they had te go an lettin nothin stand in their way. I was sent flyin an landed on the sacks of mail sittin on the trolley. 'Ye culchie bastard!' I screamed in pain, hurtin me head an back. A pair of hands lifted me up an put me standin on me feet.

'Are you all right, little hen?' I looked up inta a pair of blue eyes lookin down at me from under a striped hat.

'Yeah! Thanks, Mister,' I croaked, still feelin shaky. 'Is tha the train fer London?' I asked, pointin at a train in front of me. He said nothin but looked hard at me face.

'By gum! You've been through the wars! Where'd ye get that shiner?' An he put his hand on me face just under me eye. It was sore. I said nothin, an he stood up an looked aroun me. 'Wait here! I'll not be long,' an he was gone.

I waited an thought te meself, I must have a black eye. Now I really am a holy show. What am I goin te do? Everyone will be lookin at me. He came rushin back wit a policeman wearin a big tall hat an a strap under his chin. Me heart lurched. Ah, Gawd, I'm done fer! I looked at the train an made a shufflin run fer it. But the policeman made two big steps an had me by the arm. 'Easy now! Thanks, son! I'll take care of her.'

An he hesimitated an looked at me. 'Don't worry, me little flower, you'll be all right!' I looked up inta his face, an his eyes were very kind. An I knew he was a lovely soft kind man who liked childre. An then he turned an rushed off te collect his sacks a mail. An I wanted te stay wit him, but I was only a stranger, an now he was gone.

'Come on! Come with me!' I walked beside the policeman, wonderin what I could do te escape. 'What's your name?' he asked, lookin down an smilin at me. I said nothin fer a minute, wonderin if I should give him me real name. Wha's the point, they find out anyway. I got caught often enough in Dublin fer robbin the butter.

'Martha,' I said, feelin me heart in me belly an wonderin wha was goin te happen te me. Jackser definitely won't take me back. He only bought me a one-way ticket, an if they send me back there, I'm dead.

'How old are you, Martha?'

I hesimitated, wonderin if I could say I was fourteen. I looked up at him. 'Eh, fourteen!'

His mouth fell open, an he threw his head back an roared laughin. 'You're a canny one, no doubt! But I would say you're about seven or eight years old.'

'I'm ten!' I screamed.

He laughed again, 'Probably, but you're very small for your age.'

I felt like cryin. This was goin from bad te worse. I'll never grow up an be free. I looked at the people rushin aroun me. All goin about their business. No one te bother them. We walked inta the police station, it was beside the trains. An there were men in blue shirts sittin at typewriters clickin away an writin at a big table. They all looked up when my policeman shouted an laughed, 'Look what I found!' They said nothin but just stared at me. Then one got up from writin at the table an whispered somethin te me policeman. I stood waitin. Then he turned te me an put me sittin on a chair beside the table an sat down beside me. 'Right! Where were you going to?'

'Me ma sent me te London te stay wit her brother in Hemel Hempstead.'

'What's the address?'

'I don't know, she didn't give it te me.'

He stared at me. 'Where is your suitcase?'

'She didn't give me one.'

'So no address, no clothes. Have you any money?'

'No!'

'And so you have no money! You've run away from home, haven't you?'

'No! Me ma sent me.'

'What's your home address in Ireland?'

I said nothin.

'Look, we know you've run away from home. And you will be reported missing. So you might as well tell us the truth now and get it over with.'

I knew tha wasn't true, so I stayed quiet.

'Who gave you the beating? Was it your father? Is that why you ran away?'

'No! I didn't run away. I'm tellin the truth.'

'Well, then, give me your address in Ireland, because we have to contact your parents. Then if they tell us you didn't run away, we can find out where your uncle lives in Hemel Hempstead.'

I gave them me address in Dublin, an the policeman went off, leavin me sittin there. I was tired waitin an put me head in me arms an went te sleep on the table. I woke up when the man nudged me an gave me a glass of milk an two sambidges wit egg an tomatoes. I ate them in a flash, not realisin I was starved wit the hunger.

'It's been four hours now,' he said, sittin down beside me. 'Are you sure you gave us the right address?'

'Yes! I gave ye the right address!'

He shook his head. 'That's strange, we should have contacted them by now. And there was no report of you being missing at the police station.'

I looked at him but said nothin.

'Perhaps they have gone out to Mass?'

I said nothin.

Hours passed, an every now an then the man came in lookin more an more confused. 'Still no word! We have been in constant contact with the Dublin police, but they say they can't get a response to their knocking at the door. They know the family, and they are familiar with you. It appears you like butter, lots of it!' An he shook his head, starin at me an thinkin, but said nothin.

I kept quiet, knowin full well they were in but wouldn't open the door. They do this all the time when I get caught an I'm brought te the police station fer robbin the butter. Eventually Jackser might appear at one o'clock in the mornin te claim me, lookin like he wanted te murder me fer gettin caught, an sit there sayin nothin while I make a statement an sign me name te it. An then I'll have te appear in the Children's Court. An I always tell the same story. Tha I robbed the butter te sell fer money te buy meself sweets. They don't believe me, but they can't prove it was Jackser an me ma who sent me. Cos I never admit tha. I always stick te me story or else me ma would be sent te prison along wit Jackser. He swore he would bring her down wit him, an me ma an the rest of the childre would be locked up in a home. So I can't tell on him. I can't tell anyone wha he does te me. An this policeman is worried an confused why me ma an Jackser hasn't claimed me. But he's respectable an kind. An I would die of shame if he knew the truth of wha me ma an Jackser were really like. He just wouldn't understand.

The English police are more like you'd expect your daddy te be. They laugh an joke an don't pretend te be as important wit themselves as the Irish police. But the Irish police are not bad te me. They just leave me sittin at the table in the office an then forget about me. I could be sittin there fer ten or twelve hours, an they wouldn't say a word te me until Jackser finally decides te arrive. They don't really care. But here I'm really bein minded, an I'm beginnin te enjoy meself. So far I've got a lovely red rosy apple an a bar of chocolate.

'Here, take this and go out and buy yourself a comic.' I looked at the shiny half-crown an couldn't believe it! 'Buy whatever you want! Spend it all. And then come straight back.' I looked up happily at the policeman, an then he smiled. 'Go on, off with you!'

I staggered out the door. Me back felt like a red-hot poker, an me legs was stiff, but I felt warm in me belly, cos the policeman trusted me, an he didn't think I was a criminal any more. Now it was like I was on me holidays. An no Jackser or butter te worry about.

329

30

The day dragged on, an now I was tired. I couldn't lie down an have a sleep. Me head was throbbin an felt very hot. An I could do nothin but sit an wait an look up at the big clock on the wall tha went tick tock, hopin tha when it hit the right time, somethin might happen, whatever tha was.

I had two big black eyes. I saw tha in the mirror in the tilet. An me eyes hurt, an me face was very sore an swollen. I got a bit of a shock when I saw the state of meself. I don't want people seein me lookin like this. Earlier, the policeman said they were goin te get the doctor te look at me. But I said I was grand, an he said, just te be on the safe side, I could have somethin broken or have a head injury! But I went mad an started te make an awful fuss. So they left it. Me nerves were gone, cos Jackser never lets me near a doctor. An if they found out, me ma would go te prison, an the poor childre would suffer. No, it's not worth tha! I'm goin te have te be careful or I can find meself in a lot of trouble. The authorities are very quick te put ye in a home. I've seen too many put away.

Still no word! The policeman yawned an stretched. It was late in the day now. I lifted me head off the table an tried te look up at him. I felt so sick, the weight of me head. 'OK,' he said, lookin at me. 'We'll have to sort somethin out!' An off he went. Tick tock, the only sound. The policeman mutterin in another room lifted me a bit. Maybe he's goin te do somethin. Then I can move an maybe lie down. It was very quiet here, nothin te take me mind off meself. He came back wit two men followin behind him. They had ordinary suits on. 'All right, darling! You go with these two men, and they will take you somewhere nice to stay until we can contact your family.' An he very gently helped me off the chair an put me on me feet. I was dizzy an everythin was blurred. But I steadied meself until I got straight again an smiled at him. 'Are you OK?' he asked me, bendin down an lookin inta me face.

'Yeah! I'm grand, not a bother on me.'

He looked at the two men. 'Maybe you should have her checked out at the hospital?'

Me heart pounded, an I saw stars at the fright. 'No! No! Please! I'm grand, just a little bit tired, tha's all. Don't worry, I'm always fallin an bangin inta things. I fell down the stairs in the ship. Some drunks got sick, but there's not a bother on me.' I looked up at them, pleadin. Jesus! Jesus! Jesus! Don't let them make trouble fer me ma. Please, God! I prayed te meself.

'OK, take her over. We can keep an eye on her. She needs rest, too, anyway. A bit of a kip should see her right.'

Oh, thank God! I let me breath out an started te shuffle off, tryin te keep me back straight an get everyone movin before they change their minds again an land me in God knows wha.

We went out the door, an the policeman waved after me, tellin me not te worry. 'You don't worry, darling! These two men will take good care of you. Everything will be fine!'

I smiled an waved back. He could read me mind. I wanted te rush back an snuggle up close te him an stay there an never have a care in the world. He was a real daddy, an I felt lonely leavin him behind. But I couldn't let him find out anythin. An I wish I didn't have these worries. It's such an awful pity ye'd know I got a batterin. Cos if me face wasn't such an awful show, I could be enjoyin meself, an no one would be any the wiser.

I turned away, followin the two big men. An we got inta a big black car. I sat on the long back seat an snuggled down. The springs was lovely, an I could feel the soft leather. We flew through the city, an I could see all the big buildins an shops. But me mind wasn't on them. I was worried about wha was goin te happen te me.

We stopped outside a big house an drove in through the gates, an

331

I could see the huge mansion through the trees. I looked back, an the man from the house at the gates was closin them again. Jaysus! Where are we goin? I'm goin te be locked up. I leaned forward, wantin te say somethin, the fear risin up in me. But I didn't want te upset them. I held me breath, me heart poundin. I'll wait te see wha happens! Take it easy. I sat back, all me senses on alert. We pulled up, the car makin a noise on the stones an scatterin them.

'All right, petal, we have arrived!' The man held the door open fer me, an I got out, lookin up at the huge brown doors in the shape of a church arch. The other man pulled a big bell, an I could see a nun lookin out from one of the big windas at the side. She was smilin an then disappeared.

Then the door opened, an a nun in a long white woolly habit wit a big rope tied aroun her waist an a leather purse attached from a leather belt smiled at us an stood aside, welcomin us inta a big hall. 'How nice to see you! Do come in! Would you like to join us for tea?' she smiled at the men.

'Thank you, but we must leave,' the man wit the curly hair said, wavin his trilby hat at her.

'And this is?' she said, leanin down te me.

'This is Martha. The child we told you about.'

I looked at her, tryin te smile, but sayin nothin. 'Well, Martha, we are very pleased to have you with us.' An she took hold of me hand an waved te the men as they went out the door.

'OK, Martha, we're leaving you in good hands,' an they waved an smiled at the nun an went te the car.

When they drove off, the nun shut the door an smiled down at me an said, 'You must be ravenous, you poor child!' An we went off, her sandals squeakin on the polished black an white tiles. There was loads a big paintins hangin on the walls an big vases of flowers. The scent was lovely! An the smell of polish. An it was so quiet. We went past the big staircase – it was huge, wit big carvins on the banisters – an down a passage, passin big doors. An then she opened a big door, an we went inta the biggest room I'd ever seen. It had a long winda in the front an another one at the end lookin out te a big garden wit trees. It went fer miles. I looked at the fireplace tha went up the wall, halfway from the ceilin. It had carvins of fat babbies flyin through the air an playin. It was marble. The ceilin was the same – carvins all over it an painted in blue. An gorgeous big rugs in lovely colours. An polished floorboards – ye could see yer face in the wood. An a long mahogany table tha was polished like glass, wit big carved chairs. An lovely armchairs beside the fireplace wit carvins on them. An a long armchair tha ladies in the Victorian times used te sprawl in. I saw tha at the pictures.

'Ah! Lavinia, dear, our guest has arrived!' A girl was sittin at a round table wit a snow-white tablecloth on it. An it had plates of sambidges cut up in little bits wit the crusts gone. An plates of cakes, an lovely red an gold china cups an saucers. An silver teapots an knives an little forks. An Lavinia stood up an held out her hand te me, an she was gorgeous. She had long, sleek, shiny brown hair te her shoulders, an it flicked over one eye. An she lifted it so delicately an flicked it back over her shoulder. She had big green eyes an eyelashes like sweepin brushes, an her skin was the colour of ivory. An she was wearin a maroon an yella striped blazer, an a tunic wit a yella sash tied aroun it, an a cream skirt. An she had snow-white hands wit lovely nails. She gave me a big smile, showin her snow-white teeth, an said, 'How do you do, Martha?' An then smiled at the nun an waited fer her te sit down, an then sat herself down an crossed her ankles.

The nun pulled out a chair fer me an handed me a plate of sambidges. I didn't know whether te take the whole plate or just take the one. So I took one an waited. 'I shall pour. Do you take the milk first, dear?'

I didn't know wha te say an just muttered, 'Yeah, please!' in a hoarse whisper. Lavinia helped herself te a little sambidge, an I waited te see wha she did. She cut the sambidge inta even smaller little bits an popped one inta her mouth an chewed fer ages. I looked at me sambidge, thinkin it was only the size of one mouthful. An ye'd starve te death if ye sat here cuttin it up an spendin the rest of yer life eatin tha slow. So I picked it up an sort of nibbled at it, dyin te put the lot

333

in me mouth an finish the whole plate by meself an then start on the cakes. But it was a very slow business. Lavinia cut hers, an I nibbled mine. I was on me third, an she still hadn't finished her first.

'Lavinia, dear! Do try one of these delicious pastries!' an the nun held out a silver shovel thing.

'Oh, Madame! You are spoiling me!' Lavinia breathed, gigglin an helpin herself te a big cream puff cake.

The nun laughed an said, 'When you go up to Oxford, you shall need to keep your strength up! How is Sebastian? Doing very well at Oxford, I should think?'

'Yes, Madame! He is very well. And Mamma is happy he is settling well into his studies.'

'Yes indeed! A brilliant boy! Such a brilliant family. Your dear mamma must be so proud of you both!' An she cut her cake inta tiny little pieces an popped it inta her mouth an gave a sigh of contentment. Then she looked at me. 'How is our little charge doing?'

I was on me fifth sambidge, an they were so lovely. Egg an somethin else, cucumber, I think the nun said. But they were only makin me more hungry. 'More tea?' I hesimitated, an she took me cup an saucer, an poured more tea. An put in milk an sugar lumps from a grippin thing. 'Sandwich? Do have another!' an she put two on me plate. An I got fed up eatin so slow an stuffed it inta me mouth. They were gone in seconds. I waited fer a cake, watchin the two of them have their chat.

'Yes! Genevieve is gone to our convent in France. We shall indeed miss her.' I put me hand out te help meself te a cake, a chocolate éclair, an then put me hand back. Maybe I'd better wait. They carried on talkin. I stared at the cakes. Maybe I'll have the cream bun first, or will I have the cream horn? No! I'll have the éclair first an then the cream horn.

The nun threw down her bib, an Lavinia cleaned the corners of her mouth wit her bib an folded it, puttin it back on her plate, an they both stood up. 'What an enjoyable afternoon!' the nun said. 'I did so enjoy our little chat.'

Lavinia waved an said goodbye te me, an the two of them breezed out the door. Then the nun put her head back in the room while I was starin at the cake, thinkin I didn't even get te taste them. 'Do help yourself, Martha! I shan't be long.' Then she was gone. I was on me own wit the cakes! I snatched the éclair an swallied it in two bites, an then grabbed the cream horn, spillin flakes everywhere an smotherin me mouth an face wit cream. I was diggin inta the cream bun when she came back. An I pretended te be lookin out the winda, but I was chokin on the bun an tryin not te let her see me actin like a pig. Me head was goin up an down tryin te swalla. An she said, 'Why don't you take a little nap?' I shook me head, not meetin her eyes, sayin yeah! Then I used the bib te wipe me hands an mouth, an I was covered in flakes an white dust from the cream horn. An I knew I was after makin a show of meself.

She cleaned the table, puttin the dishes on a huge silver tray, an went outa the room an came back wit a silver brush an dustpan an swept all aroun me. An put a lovely lace tablecloth on the table an went out again. Then she came in wit a rug an pillas, an put them on the long sofa. 'Now, dear! Lie down here and take a nap. You are exhausted!' I lay down, an she covered me wit the rug an pulled the curtains shut. An she left the room.

I stretched out on me side, easin the pain in me back an head, an I felt a bit sick from the cakes. I smelt terrible. The sick was dried inta me clothes an skin. An me hair was matted an stiff. I need a wash. This convent was so grand, an the people treated me like I was a lady. I couldn't understand it. If I turned up at a convent in Dublin lookin the state I'm in now, they'd ring the police an have me arrested, never mind let me in the door. Tha girl was somethin like outa me *Bunty* comic. Like one of the four schoolgirl Marys. I'd never been up close te someone like her before. She's like someone ye'd see in a fillum. I wonder what it takes te become like her. Me own teeth are snow white. One aul one asked me once if they were false! A right eejit she was. Childre don't have false teeth! Then I was out cold.

I was sittin on the edge of the footpath, shiverin an shakin. Me teeth was bangin together, an I was watchin Jackser's back bendin up an down, mixin cement fer me feet. He was mutterin te himself, 'These will keep ye down! Ye won't come floatin te the top in a hurry. I always warned ye te mark me words well. But ye wouldn't listen te me.'

Jesus! Jesus! Jesus! Help me. Please don't let Jackser drown me! Me head was threatenin te blow off me shoulders wit the pain in me chest. Me heart was hammerin so hard, an me mind was flyin, tryin te think of a way out. 'Jackser!' I squeaked. 'I know how te get ye a load a money!' He didn't hear me. Suddenly he threw down the shovel an turned aroun, headin fer me. I tried te run, but I was a dead weight.

Somethin was whisperin an shakin me. Me eyes flew open, an I was lookin at a ghost. 'Are you OK?' it asked me, bendin over me. It was all white.

'Am I dead?' I whispered. 'Did I go up te heaven?' I waited, afraid te move.

The ghost bent down closer te me, an I could see its eyes. 'Wake up, dear! You are having a dream.' An she lifted me up. I looked aroun me, an it slowly dawned on me I was in the convent, an now I remember. Oh, thanks be te God! It was only a dream. There's no Jackser. I'm safe.

'Put your shoes on an button up your coat. You are leaving us now.' I was drippin wit sweat an still shakin from tha dream. Me legs was like jelly as I tried te hurry after her, wonderin wha was goin te happen.

The two policemen were standin in the hall when the nun rushed me in. An she whipped open the door an stood back, holdin it wide open. An the man put his hand on me shoulder an said, 'We're going to get you settled in nicely. Thank you again. Your help was much appreciated.' An he pointed his trilby hat at the nun.

She smiled an said in a loud voice, 'Indeed, it was the least we could do to help the poor wretched child!' An as soon as our feet hit the outside, she slammed the door wit a big bang.

The curly head man looked back an then looked at me an grinned te his friend, sayin, 'She'll probably have the place fumigated.'

'Aye! She was certainly in a hurry!' the other man said, an we drove off.

We arrived at a block a flats, an the car stopped. Curly took a bit a paper outa his pocket an looked at it, sayin, 'Number seventeen, Andersons. Right, I'll take her up. Won't be long!' An he got outa the car an opened the back door te let me out.

I followed him up the stairs, an we walked along the first balcony, an he knocked on a blue door wit a shiny brass knocker. The door was whipped open, an a woman in a flowery red apron wit red cheeks an a curly mop of brown hair tha looked newly permed smiled at the man an looked down at me, an laughed, 'Ye got here all right, then?'

'Yes,' the man said. 'Thanks for helping us out. She'll be no bother to you.'

'Indeed she will not! Come on, ducks! Ye're very welcome,' an she grabbed hold a me an wrapped her big massive arm aroun me an pulled me inta her body, wrappin her other arm aroun me.

The man looked down at me an grinned, 'You'll be well looked after, Martha. Tra la!' An he waved his hat at the woman an rushed off.

The woman shut the door an looked down at me, peerin inta me face. 'Tut, tut! What a sorry sight you are!' She kept clickin her tongue an shakin her head lookin at me. 'Right,' she said, makin up her mind. 'First off, you need a good feed. Yer must be starved!' An we went down the hall an inta a lovely warm sittin room. The fire was blazin, an there was a lovely big rug in front of it, coverin shiny lino. An two big armchairs. 'Sit down by the fire, ducks, an keep warm.' An she rushed off te the scullery, an I could hear her bangin pots an lightin the gas.

I looked up at the mantelpiece full of photographs. There was one of a babby lyin on his belly on a fur rug smilin at the camera. An another one of a boy about six years old ridin on a donkey at the seaside. The donkey was wearin a straw hat, wit his ears stickin out. An the boy's mammy was standin beside him, holdin him on. An she was very happy lookin.

337

This is lovely! The room is the height of luxury wit all the pictures on the walls an the ornaments all aroun the room. An the glass case in the corner, wit the lovely delft china an little statues. I'm glad te be here an out a the convent. Tha nun was very peculiar. Ye'd never keep up wit them grand people. All tha smilin. Ye'd get a pain in yer face after a while. An ye'd have te be good all the time an not lose yer temper an shout at anyone. An the good food ye'd get'd do ye no good, cos ye have te chew it fer hours. Sure there's no enjoyment in tha! I could hear sizzlin from the fryin pan an smell sausages. An I felt me heart lift an gave a big sigh of contentment. Life can be lovely. An I sat back in the armchair, listenin te the lovely music comin outa the radiogram in the alcove behind the armchair.

'Now, get this down ye!' An she put a huge white dinner plate wit beans an sausages an a fried egg, all pink on the top, an fried bread an tomatoes in front of me. An a knife an fork, an poured me a cup a tea. An went off sayin, 'I'll run yer bath fer yer, an then ye can have a good night's sleep in me son's bed. He's yer age, an he's stayin over with his auntie an granmar. They'll spoil him somethin rotten, an no good'll be had from him, bless him!'

I looked at the plate, takin in all the gorgeous food. An she roared from down the hall, 'Don't be shy! Eat up. It'll do yer a power a good.'

I looked aroun, wonderin how she knew. She must have eyes everywhere. An I started te go at it like a horse, stuffin me mouth. Oh, the fried bread is heaven. An she's lovely altogether. I was lickin the plate clean wit me tongue when I heard her comin back, an I put tha plate down quick. 'My! You was hungry,' she said, foldin her arms across her chest an laughin. 'Did ye have enough?'

I shook me head an whispered, 'Yeah, thanks very much.'

'Hang on,' an she rushed inta the scullery an came back wit a big slice a cake. 'That's a Victoria sponge. The granny sent it over fer yer tea when we knew we was expectin ye.' I looked at the two slabs a cake wit the jam an cream in the middle an took a little nibble, afraid te make meself look like a savage. 'Go on! Try it, it's delicious. I promise it won't bite yer!' An she laughed an poured me more tea.

I looked up inta her face then, te make sure it was all right. An her eyes was twinklin. An I laughed then, feelin at me ease, an took a big bite, not mindin about the pain in me face from havin the black eye. She took the plate away an left me wit the rest a the cake an said, 'Eat as much as yer like, darlin! That's wot it's there for!'

I heard her washin up, an I stared at the cake an picked up the lot an started te pile it inta me mouth. Oh! I'm havin the best time of me life. It's even better than the Sunshine Home. 'Now!' she said, comin back. 'Let's get yer washed an inta bed.'

She peeled off me clothes an checked the water, turnin off the hot tap, an said, 'In ye get.' It was hot, an I hesimitated. 'Go on, luv, ye need it te help ease all the bruisin yer got.' An she held me arm an gently lowered me inta the water. Then she picked up a washcloth an knelt down beside the bath an started te soak water all over me back an neck. She looked very worried an went quiet as she soaked me gently wit the cloth. 'Am I hurtin ye, darlin?' she asked quietly.

'No,' I whispered, ashamed she could see all the batterin I got. She'd know I'm not respectable an come from a bad home.

'What sort of a world do we live in tha could do this te an innocent child!' she muttered te herself. 'Every inch is covered in bruises!' Then she poured the cloth over me head an started te wash me hair. The pain shot through me. 'Oh! I'm sorry, I'm sorry! I can feel the terrible lumps on yer head. I'll be as gentle as I can.' An she washed me hair wit soap, without touchin me head very hard. An then she rinsed it off wit a spray.

She wrapped me in a big towel, an I followed behind her inta a bedroom. 'Now sit there on the bed while I get ye a pair a pyjamas.' An she opened a drawer an gave me a lovely pair of blue an white ones, an pulled down the covers offa the bed an switched on a night light, she called it. 'Now, I'll leave tha on fer yer! An don't worry. If ye want a drink or anythin, you just holler, an I'll be right wit ye! Goodnight now! Sweet dreams,' an she closed the door.

I snuggled down inta bed an looked over at all the toys an books on the shelves. Paddington the Bear, wit his red duffle coat, was lovely. An sittin next te him was Rupert the Bear. Another shelf was packed wit little Dinky cars an lorries an buses. Tha son has got te be the luckiest person in the whole world. Pity we can't swap places. I snuggled down more an gave a big sigh. Me eyes were lovely an heavy, an I never felt so warm an cosy in me whole life.

I sat in the armchair wit the *Beano* comic on me lap. Mrs Anderson, Flo, she told me te call her, bought it fer me this mornin. I turned the pages, but me heart wasn't in it. I looked at me coat tha was nearly new again. Flo got it cleaned fer me an washed me frock. I was spankin clean, but I didn't get any satisfaction from tha. Flo was hoppin aroun the room, givin big sighs an smackin the furniture wit the dust cloth. There was nothin te polish, cos everythin was shiny enough te see yer face in. She kept lookin out the winda. 'It'll be all right, ducks, you'll see!' I looked over at her, an she was starin back at me, her face lookin very worried. She opened her mouth te say somethin but then dropped her eyes te the duster in her hands. Then she let her arms drop an gave a big sigh. I turned away, lookin at nothin.

A whole week passed, but it only felt like a day. An now it was over. I have te leave an go back te Dublin. No more Flo pettin an huggin me, always laughin an rushin aroun doin things, bendin down te look inta me face an say, 'I gorra a nice surprise fer our dinner', or 'I'm makin yer favourite fer yer tea, chips an eggs an beans'. Or readin me *Bunty* lyin on me belly under the cosy blankets an quilt, wearin lovely warm clean pyjamas, wit the lamp on beside me bed. Me heart was very heavy sittin down in me belly. An I was feelin sick. 'I'll make us a nice cup a tea!' An she rushed off te the scullery. I watched her go, lookin at her apron tha wrapped all the way aroun her back an tied at the waist. She was wearin her pinky rosy one wit the flowers today. I like tha one. An her cosy slippers tha she always wore aroun the house. No more Flo! It feels like I'm leavin me real mammy fer ever. I took te her straight away. Now it's like we'd always been together.

'Now, darlin,' Flo said, comin in from the scullery. 'I've packed everythin you'll be needin fer yer journey. Yer sandwiches . . . I've made them with beef an yer favourite Yorkshire Relish sauce.

I spread tha over them.' An she put the white greaseproof paper package on the sideboard. 'An this one's got yer Victoria sponge Granny made special fer ye yesterday when she knew ye was . . . eh, not goin te stay, like.' I looked at her, me heart jumpin, but, no, she can't do anythin. I have te go.

Suddenly we heard footsteps, an then the knocker banged. Me heart jumped. They're here! I moved slowly, pickin up me two packages an walked down the hall. 'Oh! It breaks me heart te see her go!'

The man wit the curly hair was noddin an lookin sad, an holdin his hat an smilin when he saw me. 'All ready, then? My! Don't you look a sight fer sore eyes!' An he jumped back, grinnin down at me. I lifted me head an tried te smile. An Flo grabbed me an smothered me in her arms, an I went limp. Then she pushed me out the door an then lunged at me, givin me a kiss on the cheek, an lifted me chin an looked inta me eyes an said, 'Now, my darlin, you keep yer pecker up an always be proud of yerself. You'll be OK! Don't ye fret yerself.'

Curly shook his hat an said, 'Thanks, Mrs Anderson, thanks for everything.' An I followed him down the balcony an gave a last look back at Flo. She gave me a little wave, lookin sad, an held up her apron wit her other hand, an then I let go. She started te blur, an I turned away, feelin in meself it's all over. An I started te feel empty an cold in meself. An I stopped worryin an thinkin. An it was like I didn't care any more.

We got inta the car, an I sat in the back. I stared out the winda, lookin at nothin. We were flyin past shops, an houses wit big steps up te them, an a girl wit a straw hat on her head, tied aroun her chin wit an elastic band, an a maroon ribbon aroun the rim, an a long coat. She was in her school uniform an was laughin an holdin on tight te a lead an runnin behind a white poodle dog. An her mammy was rushin behind her, carryin her brown leather school bag. If only I was like her, God. Not havin a worry in the world. But I don't think ye're listenin! An I don't care if ye're annoyed or not! Cos ye never even listened te me ma when she lit all them penny candles askin fer yer help. I'm not talkin te ye any more. It's a waste

341

a time. So do wha ye like. I'm not afraid of ye. Strike me dead! Or better still, if ye want te make yerself useful, then give tha bandy aul bastard Jackser an awful death. An ye can make sure he dies roarin! Yeah! I gave meself a shake. I'm not goin te be afraid of anybody. An as soon as I'm big enough, I'm goin te be somebody.

'Right! We're here!' I looked up shocked. We were here so fast. An me heart started te pound. I held onta me packages, an Curly held onta me arm as we pushed our way through the crowds all headin onta the boat. 'Stop here!' Curly said, an he moved off te look over the heads of the people all movin towards the gangplank. We waited, then the man wit me shouted an pointed te a woman wearin a big felt hat an a camel coat wit a belt tied aroun it. She was holdin the hand of a boy aroun me own age, an they were followin a porter carryin her suitcases up the gangplank an onta the ship. Curly shook his head an shouted back, 'Yeah! I see her.' An he rushed up the gangplank an onta the ship. We waited, an then after a few minutes, he came rushin back down again. 'OK!' he said. 'She's agreed! She'll do fine. Come on, Martha,' an he put his hand on me back, an we climbed up the gangplank an saw the woman wit the camel coat. 'This is the child. She's travelling alone to Dublin. You will take care of her?'

'Oh, yes! I have my own child travelling with me, and she will be perfectly safe. I have managed to secure a berth, two in fact! I shall put them together.'

'Thank you very much. I know I'm leaving her in safe hands,' Curly said, bowin an wavin his hat at her. 'Bye, Martha! Safe passage and take care of yourself.'

'Bye bye, Mister! Thanks very much!' An he turned an rushed off.

'Come along, dear. We'll get you settled in. Now where is that porter with my luggage?' I followed behind her, an her son stared at me wit his mouth open until he crashed inta his mother, an she grabbed his hand an looked back at me. 'Stay close now, dear! We don't want you getting lost.'

An we went downstairs an along passages until we came te a door.

An she looked at the number an checked her ticket. 'Yes! This is our cabin.' When we got in, it had two bunks an a little sink. 'Jeremy, darling! You take the top berth, and this little girl may have the bottom one. Do pop into bed!' the lady said te me. An Jeremy was put inta his pyjamas, an he brushed his teeth in the sink an washed his hands an face. An his mammy combed his hair. An I looked, but I hadn't anythin te wash meself wit, an I had nothin te wear in the bed. So I jumped in wearin me knickers an vest. Jeremy's mammy put him te bed an then kissed him goodnight an whispered, 'Sleep well, sweet dreams!' an turned the light off an went out. Me an him didn't say a word te each other. An I went out like a light.

I woke up wit the woman shakin me. It was mornin. 'Get dressed, dear! We are disembarking. Come along, Jeremy. Put on these fresh clothes.' I rubbed me eyes, an yawned, still feelin sleepy, an watched Jeremy.

'Will Daddy meet us, Mamma?'

'Oh, indeed! He's waiting for us right this minute. Isn't it so exciting! You can give him all your news.'

Me heart gave a clatter at the mention of Daddy. Jackser! I'm back in Dublin! Oh, Mammy, help! What'll I do? He'll kill me! I jumped up, hittin me head on the top of the bunk, an rushed te get inta me clothes. I stood waitin fer them te get ready, feelin sicker by the minute. The woman snapped her case shut an tied the leather strap an fixed her hat on her head. An she looked aroun the cabin an, holdin her son's hand, passed by me in a whiff of flowery perfume. 'I'll send the porter for the luggage,' she said, lookin back at them stacked one on top of the other.

We came down the gangplank, an Jeremy flew off inta the arms of a man wearin a long navy-blue coat wit a velvet collar, an striped trousers, wit his shiny black hair combed flat on his head. An he was holdin a hat in his hand. An Jeremy screamed, 'Daddy! Daddy!' an his daddy swung him up inta his arms. The lady waved an smiled at him over the crowds, an he waved back, showin a mouth of snow-white teeth. 'You will be all right, dear?' An she looked at me fer a second.

'Yeah! Thanks very much.' An she turned an rushed off on her high heels, wearin her camel coat an her big-brim hat. An the daddy held out his arms an gave her a quick kiss on the lips, an off the three of them went, off together, him carryin Jeremy in one arm an the other aroun his wife's waist. I thought this was marvellous an was hopin fer a few minutes I might find a way te escape Jackser. I moved through the crowds an came te the entrance. No sign of them! But when I got outside onta the quays, there he was standin wit his hands in his pockets just starin at me. He turned away, givin me a dirty look when I moved towards him.

'Jackser!' I squeaked, standin a few feet away from him. 'Eh! I'm back.'

He said nothin. Just stared at me. 'Ye're not comin back te my home. Go on! Fuck off!'

Then a man appeared, he'd been standin over against the wall watchin. 'I'm a detective from Store Street. Are you responsible for this child?'

'This thing is nothin te do wit me whatsoever. She doesn't belong te me. I'm only livin wit her mammy. An she doesn't want her neither. So get it outa here. It's not wanted!'

'Listen! I can have you up for neglect an abandoning this child. Now take her home and behave yourself. And don't even think of laying a hand on her, because you are already in a lot of trouble. And we are going to be watchin you very carefully.'

'I know the law!' Jackser roared. 'Ye can't force me te take on another man's bastard! We want nothin te do wit her, an tha's tha!'

The detective sprang at Jackser an grabbed his arm. An he pulled him over inta a corner an pushed him against the wall. I stood, stuck te the ground, an watched the detective wavin his finger in Jackser's face. I couldn't hear wha they were sayin, but when Jackser started te shout at the man, the detective grabbed him by his shirt collar an shook him. An Jackser clamped his mouth shut, an his eyes stared, an then I saw the fight go outa him. The detective's head was movin up an down very quickly, an he was wavin his finger an makin punchin movements wit his fists te get his point across. An

344

proddin Jackser in the chest wit two fingers an pushin him against the wall. An now Jackser was noddin his head up an down, agreein wit everythin the detective said.

'Now be warned!' the detective said in a loud voice, steppin back from Jackser an standin wit his feet wide apart. 'No more blackguardin! Or else!'

Jackser didn't move, he stayed in the corner. 'No!' Jackser said. 'I get the point. I'll do as ye say. There'll be no more trouble.'

The man waved his finger an shook his head, an moved off, sayin, 'Ye'd be wise to heed my warning!' Then he fixed his hat on his head, cockin it te one side over his eye, an swaggered off down the quays an got inta a black car. An the other detective in the drivin seat drove off.

Me heart sank. Is tha it? Are they not goin te lag Jackser an maybe put him away or somethin? Then Jackser started te move, watchin te make sure they were gone. An he stopped te look at me. Me heart started clappin like mad. Ah, Jaysus! He's goin te kill me. I looked aroun me desperate. Oh, Holy God! The Liffey! I looked back at him, then I suddenly lifted me shoulders, stretchin me neck an straightened me arms, clenchin me fists tight by me side. 'Tha culchie's lucky,' I squeaked, stranglin meself. Jackser came closer, droppin his head inta me face. I took another heave on me chest te get a breath. 'I'm only sayin, tha red-neck culchie copper is one lucky man! Cos if you hadn't held yerself back, they'd be shovellin wha's left of him now offa the road!'

Jackser's eyes narrowed, an he bared his teeth, watchin me eyes, ready te clock me. Then he cocked his left eyebrow an gave his shoulders a good shake an thought about it fer a minute. I held me breath. 'Yeah! Yeah, ye're right there! He didn't know wha he was up against. But I spotted the other bollocks sittin in the car. They'd be down on me like a ton a bricks. Mind ye! I could take on the two a them. Let them come! One at a time, I'd show them! The bastards. No better man!' Then he snuffled an rubbed his hands. 'Ah, fuck them! Come on! Enough time's been wasted.'

Me heart lifted. Thanks be te God. An I ran down the quays te keep up wit him. He was rushin. 'Ye better get home fast an collect the shoppin bag. There's fuck all in the house te eat. So when ye get the money, make sure ye get as much food as ye can. Now go on! You get runnin, there's no time te waste.'

I took off at a sprint, leavin Jackser te take his time. An me head was spinnin again. When I hit the end of the quays, I turned right an headed over the bridge an inta Gardiner Street. Me heart was sick, an I couldn't find a way out. I opened me mouth. 'Ah! I can't take any more. I wish I was dead,' I roared me head cryin, an people looked at me. I kept runnin, me mouth wide open, tears an snots pourin outa me. I don't care. An old woman holdin her shoppin bag tight on her arm stopped te stare at me. As I came closer, she said, 'What ails ye?' I hesimitated, lookin inta her face. But then I moved meself even faster. She can't do anythin.

I looked aroun me, runnin an lookin inta the faces of people. Some looked away quickly. They don't care. Nobody can do anythin. I don't want te get caught by the police an be locked away. I hate me ma. She's no good, she's always wantin me te bring her things! Ah! I wish she was dead. I hate the whole world. I'll kill meself. I'll throw meself under a fuckin car. She's a whore's melt! Me heart is pumpin, an I'm soakin wet. I tore onta the road, headin fer a lorry comin straight at me up Talbot Street. The driver sees me, an he's tryin te brake. I dare him, lockin me eyes on him. An he's turnin the wheel an brakin an slidin, an he's still headin fer me! I'm not afraid. It's goin te be all over. The truck skins me, headin up onta the footpath. I stand rooted, smellin the burnin rubber an seein smoke pourin up from the back. People are stoppin an starin, their mouths open. An now they're runnin. A woman grabs me arm. 'What's wrong, are ye all right?' she's shoutin inta me face. I look at her.

'Why did ye do tha?' another woman roars at me. I look at the truck driver. His head is lyin on his arms on the steerin wheel, an he's white as a sheet.

'Come off the road!' The woman holdin me arm walks me onta the footpath. I can't think. Everythin's a bit strange, an me head is swimmin.

'Ye ran inta tha truck,' a man roars at me, pointin his finger in me face. 'Tha was deliberate!' he says, lookin at the two women beside me.

'I think she's in shock,' a woman says, lookin at me. 'Get her a cup of sweet tea. Is the poor lorry man all right?'

I look up, an he's talkin te a crowd a people standin aroun the lorry. He's shakin. I gave him a fright. I pity him now I see the bad state he's in. I go up close te the winda an look up at him. 'Mister!' His eyes are still shocked, an I'm now feelin ashamed of meself. 'I'm sorry. I'm very very sorry!'

He stared at me. 'I could have killed ye! I didn't see ye until the last minute!' An he shook his head slowly. 'Ye ran outa nowhere.'

I shook me head slowly, agreein wit him. 'Yeah! I should've minded where I was goin.'

'Here's the policeman!' a woman says. Me heart leapt. I looked aroun, an sure enough a copper was headin straight fer me. I took off wit the fright an lashed down Talbot Street.

'There she is!' a woman roared after me. 'Gone runnin, ye little blackguard! Ye nearly gave tha poor man a heart attack!'

I ran, lookin left an right, waitin fer a break in the traffic before tearin across the road between the cars an hoppin onta the footpath, takin a quick look back. Nobody runnin after me. An I shot down Corporation Street an inta the buildins.

347

31

Me ma was kilt lookin out the winda. 'Jaysus Christ, where is he, Martha? He should a been here an hour ago! Wha's keepin him?' She looked over at me sittin on the bed readin me *Bunty*. I looked up, seein her chewin the inside of her lip, an blinkin her eyes, an snortin an breathin big sighs out the winda again.

'Ah! He'll be here, Ma. Stop yer worryin.'

'Oh, Jaysus! Quick. Here he is! He's comin,' she said, whisperin, rushin te put the kettle on. I leapt offa the bed an made meself look busy.

He came in the door an looked at me. 'Where's yer mammy?'

'I'm puttin on the water fer a cup a tea,' she roared from the scullery.

He rubbed his hands together an snuffled, shakin his left arm up in the air an swingin it aroun like he was goin te throw a ball. 'Fer fuck's sake, will ye get out here! I want te talk te ye.'

'All right! I'm comin. Wha's happened?' she asked, smilin up at him, an chewin her lip, an blinkin, waitin.

'We're elected!' he roared, laughin an spittin wit excitement, throwin down a bunch a keys on the table. 'Fuck me! By Jaysus! I knew we'd beat them. Keep after them, I said. Hound the bastards! Day an night. An now we have a house! A real house wit a garden an rooms on the upstairs wit a washroom.' Me ma was chewin like mad, standin an smilin, lookin at the keys.

'Where's tha tea?' Jackser roared. An me ma headed off te the scullery, givin a big laugh tha sounded like a horse neighin.

Jackser went in behind her, roarin his head off wit excitement, an

348

grabbed me ma's arse. She laughed an said, 'Don't be doin tha, tha's a terrible carry on.'

He rushed back out an picked up Dinah off the floor, givin her a fright cos he grabbed her so fast. An her breath caught an she went, 'Ah!' He kissed an sucked an smacked his spits all over her cheek an neck. An she didn't like it an squealed an gave him a box in the mouth wit the back of her little fist. Teddy an Harry started laughin an rushed over te join in, an he dumped Dinah back on the floor. An she screamed up at him an waved her arm at him. Then he lunged fer Harry an dug his face in his belly, growlin like a dog, an Harry screamed laughin. Teddy reefed an tore at Jackser's trousers, screamin, 'Me! Me! Do it te me!' Then Jackser's trousers slid from under his belt an fell down aroun his ankles, exposin his hairy arse. He dropped Harry on the floor, an Harry rolled, givin a terrible scream from the sudden shock.

'Ah! Fuck me!' an Jackser grabbed his trousers. An Teddy stood in fright, chewin his fingers, not movin, just lookin up te see wha would happen.

'Jaysus! Tha's the end of tha!' an he turned away, laughin.

Me ma looked out from the scullery at me laughin me head off, pretendin I was lookin out the winda. 'Tell tha eejit te stop his carry on.'

'Right!' Jackser shouted. 'Let's get movin. The sooner the better we're outa this kip the happier I'll be. Away from all these wasters! They wouldn't work te warm themselves! No! We're goin te be respectable from now on! No more anybody lookin down their noses at us. We'll be as good as the best of them. I'll rush up an get Thompson te come down wit the horse an cart. He owes me a few favours, so he can shift himself! No . . . better still, I'll give the bastard a few bob. Tha way he can't say I owe him anythin. How much have ye in tha purse?'

'Eh! How much are ye givin him?' me ma asked half-heartedly. She was blinkin an chewin an tryin te look in her purse without openin it too wide. She took out a pound note an a red ten shillin note, turnin her back tryin te hide the pound.

'Gimme tha,' Jackser said, leanin over her shoulder an grabbin the pound note.

'No!' me ma roared, tryin te snatch it back. 'I need tha. Then I'll only have ten bob left te keep us goin.'

'What are ye complainin about? Sure ye can always send the young one out, an she'll bring back a few bob.'

Me ma looked at me. I gave her a dirty look, sayin nothin. 'Eh! Could ye see if ye could go an maybe bring back a few bob, Martha?' She stood lookin at me, smilin an chewin.

I stared at her. 'Today is only Tuesday, Ma. The shops will be empty, an I'll get nothin. If I go now, I'll only get caught, an I'll be up in court again. If I end up in court now, they'll put me away. Ye know I've been caught too many times. I'm on me last chance! I can't, Ma,' I whispered, lookin down at the floor, feelin all the life goin outa me.

'Ah! Fuck her, Mrs! If she doesn't appreciate what I've done fer her, gettin us this house, then I can fuck the keys back at the Corporation. I don't give a fuck. All the same te me. Stay here! The lot of ye's. I'm takin meself off fer a drink.'

'No, wait!' me ma panicked. 'She's goin. Get the bag, Martha,' she shouted at me.

He swung himself aroun, roarin an spittin at me face. 'Ye can all fuckin rot here. Why should I bother when the rest of ye's wouldn't even shift yer arses? I'm goin.'

'Jackser!' I ran te get the bag from the press, shakin an feelin sick. An pushed past him, starin me out the door, an ran outa the buildins.

'Don't be too long! We have te move all this stuff by tonight!' he roared after me as I disappeared past the gate.

Where will I go? Me face is too well known in them shops. An they'll be all empty. Nobody does their shoppin until Friday an Saturday. Maybe I'll try Henry Street. I haven't shown me nose in town fer a while. I always go outa the city, takin the bus te them new supermarkets openin up. Yeah, OK, an I'll just aim fer makin two quid. Then I'll only have te rob twelve pound a butter. An when

I get tha, I'll have te look fer new customers. Cos me regular ones won't want their butter until Friday or Saturday. Where'll I go? I'll go te the flats. Tha means I'll have te knock on every door. Jaysus! It will take me for ever.

I hurried on, up Talbot Street, feelin me heart bangin, an me legs was like jelly. I'm feelin cold, like ice, an shiverin. It's me nerves. I'm always like this when I have te go fer the butter.

'It's the best butter, Mrs, an me ma'll let ye have it fer three shillins an sixpence. It cost her four shillins an sixpence on the St Vincent de Paul voucher. Ye can only get food on tha voucher. An the butter is no good te us, cos me ma needs the money te pay the rent, or we'll be put out!' I stopped, lookin up at her, tryin te keep me face earnest.

She stared at me, not sure, then looked down at the butter. 'I don't know, love. I'm not sure if I have the money.' Me heart was sinkin. She was a lovely old woman wit snow-white hair all wavy an tied back on her head wit clips. She looked at me closely then, wit her lovely baby-blue eyes, an said, 'Will ye take a half a crown?'

I hesimitated, not wantin te push her. But no, I need te make up tha two quid. An this was me last pound a butter. 'I can't, Mam! It has te be the three an sixpence. Look, ye're gettin a bargain. Savin a whole shillin. An feel it! Look at the make an the colour. It's gorgeous on fresh crusty bread!'

She lifted it outa me hand an laughed, weighin it up an down. 'That'd be grand if I had me teeth.'

I said nothin, just waited, holdin me breath while she thought about it. 'Ah! Go on, then. Come on in till I get ye the money.' Me heart leapt. I followed her down the hall, slappin along in her fur brown slippers. Ye could see yer face in the shiny oil cloth coverin the floorboards.

The sittin room was spotless, every bit a furniture shinin like the coloured glass ye see in the church. She reached up te the mantelpiece, takin her purse from behind the big black clock an opened it. 'Now, put out yer hand, an I'll count it out te ye.' I held me hand out wide. 'Right! Here's a half-crown, an wait, I should have a shillin piece here.' An she lifted it up te check it in the light from the fire. I could see straight away it was, but I waited fer her te let her be sure of herself. 'Yes! Now we have yer three shillins an sixpence.'

'Thanks very much, Mam. An I hope ye enjoy yer butter.' Then I backed away, headin fer the door.

'Will ye have a sup a tea before ye go?' Me heart went sad, cos I knew she wanted me te stay fer a while. An I'd a loved nothin better than te sit in the armchair by the roarin fire an talk an ask her te tell me stories about when she was young. But it was pitch black out, an God knows wha tha Jackser fella is goin te do te me.

'Mam, I wish I could stay an have a cup a tea wit ye, but me ma will be wonderin where I am. She told me not te be long.'

'Ah, yeah! Ye're right there, child! Always do wha yer mammy tells ye. It's not easy rearin childre. I should know! An ye can tell yer mammy fer me ye're a credit te her, so ye are. Very mannerly! There's a lot more about who could follow yer example.'

Me heart rushed up te me neck, an the gladness flushed all aroun me body wit delight. 'Thanks very much, Mrs,' an I kept grinnin an noddin at her. 'Goodbye now!' An I waved an shut the door behind me an rushed outa the flats. Jaysus! It's pitch black. Wha time is it? I ran like mad. Dear Holy God, don't let me get inta trouble. I'm prayin tha Jackser will be in good humour when he sees the two pound I have fer him. God, don't let him go mad. I'll be very good from now on, I promise.

I belted in through the open gates an slowed down when I got te our winda. There's no light on. Wha's happenin? I could hear the childre cryin. The door was wide open. 'Ma!' I squeaked, creepin inta the room, waitin fer Jackser te jump out from behind the door an land me wit a kick.

'Where in the name of Jaysus have you been? I'm waitin here fer hours fer ye.'

I looked aroun. No Jackser! Charlie was sittin on the floor, dozin against the wall, an Teddy was lyin on the dirty smelly floorboards on his side wit his arms under his head, tryin te sleep. An Harry was pullin at me ma's skirt, wantin her te lift him up, cos he was exhausted wit the tiredness. Me ma pushed him away. 'Will ye leave me alone!' An she gritted her teeth. He fell back on the floor an screamed in rage. 'Jaysus Christ!' me ma moaned, pushin Dinah up an down in the pram tryin te get her te stop cryin an go te sleep. 'Will I ever get any peace away from the lot of ye's!'

'Where's everythin gone te, Ma?' There wasn't a stick a furniture left in the room.

'Where do ye fuckin think it's gone te! He went off hours ago, takin everythin on the horse an cart wit tha Thompson fella. He'll go off drinkin now. An when we finally get there, we probably won't be able te get in te the place, cos he has the keys.'

'How far is it, Ma?'

'It's out in the country. A place called Finglas. An by the time we walk there, it'll be Christmas. Come on! Lift tha young fella an put him on top of the pram. We better get goin.' I lifted Harry onta the end of the pram, an Dinah screamed, not wantin him there. Me ma dashed at Dinah an grabbed her under the arms an yanked her sittin her up te make room fer Harry. She looked shocked an stared at me ma fer a few seconds not movin, wonderin if she could give a big scream. Me ma stared back an said, 'Ah! Ah!' an waved her finger. Then me ma laughed an said, 'She's very darin.'

Then Dinah grabbed a hold of Harry's hair when he tried te lean back beside her. 'Eek! Eek!' she screamed, takin her annoyance out on him.

'Ah, Holy Jaysus!' me ma moaned. 'Will they ever stop?'

'No, Dinah, bold!' An I undid her fingers one by one, an she latched onta me hair, pullin like mad. 'Ye're bold! Let go, bold girl.' She let go, an I moved away.

'Gimme the money! How much did ye make?'

I handed her the purse, 'Two pounds, two shillins, Ma.'

'Is tha all?' she asked, lookin at me an chewin her lip.

'I can only get the butter at the end of the week, Ma! I had an awful time tryin te make tha money.'

'Yeah! It will do. We better get movin.' She tried te pull her skirt up an tie it aroun her belly, but her skirt was miles too small fer

353

her, an she just pulled down her jumper te cover her skin. An even her coat wouldn't button all the way down. I turned away hatin her. Another babby on the way. She's every bit as bad as the bandy aul bastard. 'Go on! Push tha pram out, or we'll never get there.'

Teddy jumped up off the floor. 'Ah! I'm tired, Mammy. I want te lie down,' an he grabbed hold of me ma's skirt. I pushed the heavy pram out the door, nearly topplin Harry out tryin te get it down the steps.

I waited until me ma banged the door shut. An she said, 'Have I left anythin behind, Martha? Cos we've no keys te get back in. He gave them in te the Corporation.'

'Yeah, Ma! We have everythin.' She hesimitated, chewin her lip an blinkin, tryin te think. 'It's all right, Ma. Ye have everythin. Have ye got the purse wit the money I gave ye?'

She felt her pockets. 'Yeah! It's there,' an she laughed, an Teddy held onta her coat, an Charlie trailed behind. An I pushed off, me ma hurryin te catch up.

'It must be very late now,' me ma puffed her heavy breathin, tryin te hurry behind me.

'Yeah, it's definitely very late.' I leaned out, tryin te save me breath te push the heavy pram.

'Ma! Can we stop fer a rest?'

'No, keep movin!' an she came up alongside me, holdin Teddy's hand an restin her other hand on her belly.

We looked in at the dark cemetery. 'There's an awful lot of dead people lyin in there, isn't there, Ma?'

'Oh, indeed there is!' me ma whispered back, lookin through the railins inta the pitch black. 'Ah! Sure they're more better off than we are!' me ma said wit a sour face. 'Their troubles are over. I wish te God I was gone meself!'

I felt sick at the thought of me ma dead. 'Ye know, Ma, Jackser brought me in there one time te see his mother's grave.'

'Yeah? Pity he didn't fuckin stay there,' me ma said.

'Yeah,' I agreed. 'I'd love te see him fall inta a hole, an when he tries te get out, ye can hit him over the head wit the shovel the grave digger left behind, Ma! I could do it fer ye.'

Charlie roared up at me ma, all excited, 'No, Ma! I could do it.'

Me ma laughed at me. 'Will ye go away outa tha, ye'd never get near him, he'd kill ye first!' I was feelin very let down fer a minute. I thought we could do away wit Jackser, but me bleedin ma wouldn't hear of it. She likes tha aul fella too much. I pushed the pram harder te get away from her. She makes me sick.

Now we were past Glasnevin, an nothin aroun us but fields. It was pitch black, an the road was narra, an there was no footpath on the other side of the road, but ditches. Then we saw lights up ahead in a big buildin wit gates inta it. The big sign said 'Merville Dairies'.

'Wha's tha place, Ma?'

'Tha's where they do all the milk,' me ma whispered, lookin aroun her. It was in the middle of nowhere, an we couldn't see any sign of life. 'Come on, hurry,' me ma whispered. 'It must be the middle of the night, an I'm afraid of me life someone is goin te jump outa them bushes any minute an knife us all te death. There's nowhere te run fer help.' An me ma blessed herself.

I looked all aroun me at the dark after leavin the Merville Dairies behind us, wonderin what I'd do if someone jumps out at us. I could feel meself shiverin wit the fear. 'Come on, Ma, hurry!'

'I am! Go on, you, go on!' me ma croaked an puffed. 'No, wait!'

I rushed on, wantin te get outa this dark. Then I heard a noise. I stopped dead, an me ma crashed inta me. 'Wha's tha, Ma?' I screamed, losin me mind wit fright.

'Fuck ye!' me ma roared. 'Will ye mind where ye're stoppin. Wha noise?' An she stopped te listen. 'It's nothin,' she said, slowly lookin aroun her. I followed her eyes, feelin me heart poundin. Then she suddenly lost her rag an gave me a dig, 'Go on! Move, move!' Her eyes was bulgin. 'Stoppin here is doin us no good. I don't hear anythin.'

Then it hit me. 'Maybe it's the dead from the cemetery, Ma!'

She turned white. 'I'll fuckin kill ye stone dead if ye don't shut up an push tha pram.'

'But, Ma!' I whispered, tryin te explain.

'I'm warnin ye, Martha!' she said, grittin her teeth.

'Then come up beside me, Ma. I'm afraid of me life.'

'How can I? There's no room on the footpath. We're goin te break our fuckin necks in this dark if we're not careful! Go on, I'm behind ye.'

I pushed on, holdin onta the handlebars tight. Then a big black thing shot out in front of us. 'Did ye see tha, Ma? Did ye see it?' I roared in a loud whisper.

'Wha? See wha?' me ma asked, stoppin suddenly.

'A rat, Ma! The size of a cat it was!'

'Jaysus, tha's all we need. Well, make sure they don't jump inta the pram. They'll go fer the babby's throat. Keep a watch out,' an me ma was lookin aroun her in the ditches an down aroun her feet.

I pushed an stared at the pram. 'Oh! I don't think we're goin te make it, Ma. We're sure te get kilt by somethin. Ma, I don't like the country, let's go back.' I was shakin.

'If ye don't push tha pram, I'll be hanged fer ye, Martha! Me nerves are gone listenin te ye.'

'So are ye not afraid then, Ma?'

'Yes! No! Oh, sweet divine Jaysus, if ye don't get goin,' an she lunged out at me.

I pushed the pram harder, not wantin te get her too annoyed, cos we were on our own in the middle of nowhere in the pitch black.

Then we saw lights up ahead. 'We're gettin there,' me ma muttered from behind. I rushed on, wantin te get up te the lights in the distance. 'Take it easy,' me ma croaked, tryin te get her breath. I stopped te wait an have a rest. Charlie leaned his head inta the pram, exhausted, an me ma was half draggin an half carryin Teddy under her arm. Then we moved on. We came te a row of houses well back from the road wit a field in front of them. An we turned left, leavin the hill in front wit all the shops. 'Not too far now,' me ma said. Lookin over at the convent on the left, I could see loads a houses ahead a us. I pushed harder, tryin te get the pram up the hill.

'Ma! I'm so tired. How long more will we be?'

'Not long now,' an she looked up at the street lamps. 'We're grand

356

now, we have the light. Jaysus! He'll go mad. It must be two or three o'clock in the mornin.'

I didn't bother answerin. Fuck him! He got a lift out on the horse an cart. An I'd roar tha at him if only me ma would not be so afraid of him. He's only a coward. If she'd only hit him wit somethin, he wouldn't come back fer more.

We passed the houses wit gardens in a row. Everyone was asleep, no lights on. I kept pushin, first me right hand an leg, droppin me head, then fall back an push me left side. Ah! I'm so tired, I'll never walk again. 'Lift yer feet, Charlie!' His head was stuck in the pram, an I was havin te drag him along. I hate the country! It must be hundreds a miles away out in the arsehole of nowhere! We passed a big buildin wit loads a windas, an the gates were locked. I barely lifted me head te look. The houses were on the left.

'Ma!' I stopped. 'Where's the house?' I could hardly get me breath.

'We're there,' she said, an kept movin, not liftin her head te look up. I turned, leanin on the pram an pushin wit me chest. We turned a corner, more fields! An crossed the road. I looked up. Tha looks like a bit of a hill. Ah! I can't do it, I'm goin te die. I'm dead already. 'Go on, we're there,' me ma muttered, comin up behind me. 'Turn here!' I turned inta a road wit houses. 'It's across the road.'

I stopped in shock, watchin me ma cross the road. I galvanised meself inta action, droppin the pram down the steep footpath onta the road, an jumped on the handlebars te stop it topplin over. An then I pushed like mad wit me head down, an yanked the pram down te get it up the footpath on the other side, an did me weightliftin te get it back up again. Me ma was turnin in a gate. I pushed like mad, draggin Charlie offa the pram. 'Quick! Gerrup, we're here, Charlie.' I left him te stagger himself awake, an, stretchin me back an legs wit me head down, went flyin in the gate. Me ma was bangin on the letter box, an I looked at the garden. It was full a green grass so high ye could hide in it. An the smell of the fresh air was lovely.

I looked aroun me. Everythin was so quiet, an all the houses had the different-coloured doors an curtains on the windas, an all the gardens was done up wit flowers. An, Jaysus! The house next door even has a motor car sittin outside!

Jackser opened the door an looked out, squintin wit the sleep in his eyes. 'Mother a Jaysus! Did it take ye's a week te get here?'

'Come on, come on! Let us in!' me ma barked.

'Holy Jaysus!' Jackser laughed, snufflin an rushin out te grab the pram. 'The state of ye's,' he laughed. 'Go on, gerrin there. Wait till ye's see the place.'

Charlie was missin. I rushed out the gate, an he was stretched out against the wall, sleepin wit his head in his lap. I lifted him by the shoulders. 'Come on! Gerrup. We're here.' An dragged him in the gate. 'Look, Charlie! Grass!' He didn't hear me. I went in the door inta a hall. Lovely clean floorboards, nearly white, an white walls. An stairs wit banisters. I shut the brown door an walked down the hall an inta a room. There was a huge winda, an ye could see the grass, an a fireplace. Our table was in the middle of it, wit one chair. The other two was over beside the fireplace, one each side. An the pram was in the corner, beside the press. It looked a bit bare.

'Where's the bed?' me ma asked.

'Upstairs,' Jackser snuffled. 'Fuck me, we're sleepin in the stars. Come on! Come on!' he shouted, wavin at us te follow him.

Me ma eyed me, chewin her lip, an snorted a laugh. 'Fuckin eejit! Here! Take him outa the pram,' an I grabbed Harry under his arm an lifted him up. He was fast asleep.

'Come on, Harry! Ye're goin te bed.' I humped his arse over the side of the pram an grabbed him aroun the waist, clatterin his legs onta the floor, an held onta him, draggin him out the door, still holdin him by the waist. Me ma lifted Dinah. 'Come on, Charlie. Let's go! He was standin by the fireplace, tearin an scratchin at his head, not knowin where he was.

'Are ye's comin or wha?' Jackser roared down through the ceilin.

'Gimme a hand wit this child!' me ma roared back.

Jackser came runnin down, 'Holy Jaysus! Do I have te do everythin meself?' He pushed past me, an Charlie came rushin himself behind me. Dinah was screamin.

358

'Come on, Charlie! Grab Harry's legs. He won't wake up!' I went up the stairs backwards, holdin Harry under his arms. Charlie held his feet, an we slapped his arse on the stairs goin up. An he woke up twistin himself an kicked out, knockin Charlie off his balance. An he tried te stand up an fell backwards, takin me wit him. An we all rolled down the stairs, screamin in fright just as Jackser came rushin aroun the corner wit Dinah screamin in his arms. An he toppled over us, sendin Dinah flyin te land on me lap as I was tryin te get up. He hit his face straight inta the stairs an was stretched out on top of the lot a us.

'Wha happened?' Jackser asked, lookin aroun in shock.

Me ma came rushin wit Teddy rubbin his eyes. 'Wha happened?' me ma asked, lookin shocked.

'I think me chin is broken, Sally!' Jackser said, slowly rubbin it.

'I don't know,' I said, lookin at Dinah sittin in me lap, lookin aroun wonderin wha happened.

'It's them bleedin stairs!' Jackser said, haulin himself up by the banisters. 'I knew they were bad news as soon as I clapped eyes on them.'

'They're very treacherous, all right!' me ma said, grinnin an rollin her eyes up te heaven, lookin down at me an pretendin te cough inta her hands.

'I'll put a sup a tea on,' Jackser said. 'They left us the gas cooker. You go on up te bed, an I'll bring it up.'

I carried Dinah up the stairs, restin her on me knee an holdin onta the banisters. She held me tight aroun me neck an wrapped her legs aroun me belly, an looked back at me ma comin up behind us. We came onta a landin wit three doors. I went left inta a huge room wit a big winda an a fireplace, an a big press just inside the door. The bed was under the winda, an I put Dinah down in the middle, an then I went over te the press in the wall an opened it. It was huge, enough room te keep all the clothes.

Me ma struggled in, tryin te get her breath. 'Jaysus! I'm not the better of them stairs.'

'Look, Ma. A big press! Ye can put yer coat in here.'

'Come on! Put these te bed,' she said, whippin Dinah's hat an coat off. Charlie landed Harry up onta the bed, an they were laughin, makin straight fer the winda te look out. Teddy was tryin te climb inta the press, but he couldn't get his leg up. I grabbed Harry, pullin his shoes an trousers off. An Teddy gave up an came rushin over te climb up on the bed an look out the winda.

'Lookit! Lookit! We're in the air,' he shouted.

'Ye'll be flyin through it if ye don't get them clothes off!' me ma warned him. 'Where's the cot?' me ma asked, lookin aroun.

I looked. 'There it is, Ma! Down in the corner behind the press.'

'Put her in fer me.' I carried Dinah over te the cot an put her lyin down. She was delighted an closed her eyes straight away as I covered her up. The rest a them dived under the blankets, coughin an stretchin an titterin, delighted te be in bed at last. Me ma slipped outa her skirt an hauled herself inta the top of the bed. 'Put the coat in the press fer me an get inta bed.'

I threw me ma's clothes inta the press an dived in beside Teddy, pushin him te make more room fer meself. An I went out like a light.

'Come on, will ye ever get a move on, Mrs. The day will be gone before ye get goin!'

'I'm comin! Jaysus Christ!' me ma shook her head at me. 'Will tha man ever take his time?'

'Yeah, Ma! OK, go on.'

'Now remember! Make sure ye look out fer them Vincents deliverin the bed. Stay by the winda where ye'll see them comin!'

'I'm fuckin leavin without ye!' Jackser roared in the hall.

'Go on, go on, Ma!'

'Jaysus, me heart is broken wit tha man,' me ma moaned, rushin herself after him an down the road, tryin te catch up.

I shut the front door, not wantin the gang a kids all leanin against the wall outside, gapin in wit their mouths open, seein any more of our business. Charlie was lookin out the winda at the childre playin outside. 'Do ye want te go out an play, Charlie?'

'No!' he shook his head slowly. 'No! They don't want te play wit us. Me an Teddy went up an tried te play chasin, or cowboys an injuns, an they just threw stones at us an wouldn't let us play. An a big young un said we were gypsies an we were smelly.'

'Don't be mindin them. Go on out an play in the big back garden. Or do ye want te play school? I'll be the teacher.'

'No! Cos ye always hit me. I'm goin te play on me own!'

'Go on, then, see if I care.' I was annoyed, cos I had te watch the winda an wouldn't be able te play while Jackser was gone out.

I leaned me head on the glass, watchin the young ones playin piggybeds on the footpath outside. 'My turn! Ye skipped on the line, ye're out!' An a young one ducked down te pick up the polish tin. Ye fill it wit stones or sand te make it heavy when the polish is all gone.

'Gimme tha back! I'm not out!'

'Ye must be blind then! Cos I saw ye.'

'Right! Tha's it, gimme back me tin box. I'm goin home, an I'm never playin wit ye again fer callin me tha!'

'Take it!' the big young one wit the mop of roarin red hair screamed, throwin the tin down. 'I'm goin te get me own, an it's a lovely new one tha had the good lavender polish in it.' An I watched her swing herself aroun an march off wit her head held high in the air. Me eyes peeled on the other one, standin there wit her mouth open. She was ragin.

'Ye're a liar!' she screamed. 'Yer ma never polished anythin in her life! Youse don't have anythin te polish. An another thing, ye's don't even wash yerselves!'

'Wha did ye say?' screamed the red-haired one an came flyin back. God! They're goin te kill each other. I leaned over te get a better look.

The other young one stood her ground fer a minute then flew off screamin, 'Ma! Ma!' Aw Jaysus! I'm missin it, I can't see a thing.

The door behind me was pushed open, sendin Dinah flyin outa the way. She'd been crawlin aroun the floor, happily mindin her own business, lookin fer somethin te put in her mouth an chew on. Sometimes ye have te watch her, she can choke herself. Everyone

361

was screamin. 'Teddy fell on Harry's head!' Charlie screamed.

'I didn't. He threw stones at the cat sittin on the wall next door!' screamed Teddy. Harry screamed an rubbed his head, an spat at Teddy.

I ran te pick up Dinah, lyin on the floor roarin her head off. Then there was a bang on the door. We all caught our breath, then I remembered. The bed! I rushed te open the door. 'We have yer bed from the St Vincents!'

'Yeah! It's this house, Mister.'

The door opened in the next house, an a man an his son, he was about twelve, an a young one about ten, my age, came out an gave us a queer look an marched on. An the childre gave us a quick look an hurried after the da an got inta the black shiny Ford Anglia. I admired them no end. God! They're very respectable altogether. The motor car started, an a yella arrow shot outa the side of the car te show he was movin off. An the childre gave us looks from the back of the car, lookin like they were afraid of us or somethin!

'Open the door wide fer us, will ya!' I sprang inta action, closin me mouth an shook meself te wake up. I grabbed the door. 'Right, Harry! Up the stairs,' an the two men twisted an turned the big bed spring te get it over the banisters. The man roared, 'Get them kids outa the way!'

Jaysus! Dinah will be kilt, she was crawlin under the men's feet tryin te make it out the door. 'Charlie! Harry! Get inta the sittin room!' I lunged under the bedspring te grab Dinah, gettin meself a kick in the head.

'Where's yer mammy?' shouted the older man, tryin te get the spring inta the air an up the narra stairs.

'Wha's goin on?' roared Jackser from the gate. Me head nearly swung offa me shoulders wit the fright at seein Jackser appear from nowhere.

I shook Dinah on me hip. 'The bed's here, Jackser!'

He looked at the bed an forgot about me. 'Martha!' me ma roared, hangin onta the gate. 'Tell him te hurry himself. I think the babby's startin.'

'Wha? Wha babby, Ma?' I looked at Dinah gettin heavier on me knee.

'This babby!' Her eyes looked like daggers.

'Oh, yeah!' I said, lookin at her stomach hangin te the ground. I rushed up te Jackser, me ma draggin herself in behind me. 'Jackser! Me ma wants ye,' I roared up the stairs.

'Put her in the pram an get me a loaf a bread an milk,' me ma said.

I rushed te put Dinah in the pram. 'Charlie, get them outside te the back garden!' I whirled aroun the pram an pushed Dinah out te the back garden. 'Come on, youse!' I screamed at Teddy an Harry.

'Are we gettin anythin te eat?' Teddy was whingin at me ma.

'Yeah, eat!' Harry was moanin.

'In a minute,' me ma roared. 'Get them outside!'

'Come on, Charlie. Grab them.'

I shut the back door, leavin them roarin an bangin on the door, an rushed in, takin the half-crown from me ma. 'Don't be long!' she roared after me.

I was back in minutes, an Jackser was waitin at the door fer me. 'Gimme the messages. Run te the phone box an call fer an ambulance.'

I raced up the road an aroun the corner. A woman was talkin on the phone. I waited, an she kept talkin. I watched, hopin she'd see me, but she kept her back te me an kept on talkin. I waited a long time, but she wouldn't stop talkin. Then I knocked on the phone box. 'Yes?' she looked at me.

'It's me ma! I'm te ring fer an ambulance fer her, she says the babby is comin!'

'Why didn't ye say tha! I didn't know!' An she put the phone down an rang fer an ambulance. 'Come on,' she said, rushin outa the phone box an gallopin down the road on her high heels.

We hurried in the gate an the door was wide open. Jackser heard us an came rushin down the stairs. We could hear voices from upstairs an me ma roarin an gruntin. 'It's too late! We can't move her now,' Jackser shouted.

The woman rushed up the stairs, an Jackser flew inta the bedroom. I rushed up behind the woman. 'No! No! You can't come up here, ye have te stay outside.'

I moved back down the stairs, slowly lookin back, feelin very disappointed. Lovin te see wha was goin on upstairs.

32

I was on me knees on the floor wit me arms out wide ready te catch Dinah. 'Come on. Come te me, Dinah.' She grabbed the bars of the cot an pulled herself up again, watchin me an half smilin, ready te let go. 'Yes! Tha's it,' I said slowly an quietly. She let go an staggered a foot, then the other one, an flew, takin three steps, an I shot forward, catchin her before she hit the floor. 'Hurray!' I screamed, kissin an squeezin her. She screamed, delighted, an dropped on her knees, headin fer the cot again. This time she was too fast, turned aroun, took a half-breath an lifted her chin an tried te run. Smack! Down she went. 'Ah! Dinah fell! Bold floor,' an I smacked the floorboards. She lifted her face te me in shock, not knowin whether te cry or laugh. 'Whee!' I lifted her up, laughin. 'Let's have another go,' an she giggled wit excitement. I put her down at the cot, an she looked up at me. 'Yeah!' I shook me head up an down. 'Ye're walkin. Come on, over te me!' An I knelt down, waitin wit me arms held high. She stood up an hesimitated. 'Come on!' I saw her eyes measurin the distance te me, an she lifted her leg slowly, then the other one, then got movin an kept goin. I crept back slowly, not takin our eyes offa each other, an she was halfway across the room before she went down. I grabbed her, screamin wit delight. 'Dinah's walkin! Wait till me ma sees ye, Dinah!'

Then I heard the others screamin an shoutin down the stairs. 'Martha!' screamed Teddy, slammin in the door. 'Tell him he's dead!'

'I'm not!' screamed Charlie.

'I'm the injun, an I got ye wit me bow an arra. An then I even took Harry's scalp.' Harry was cryin an rubbin his scalp.

'Youse are all dead. I'm the cowboy!' screamed Charlie. 'I shot ye's wit me gun.'

'Ye haven't got a gun,' screamed Teddy. 'Ye only have yer hand. I have me arra. Lookit!' Teddy screamed, an held up a piece of stick. Charlie grabbed the stick, an Teddy nearly lost his mind. 'Martha! Me stick, me arra.'

'Gimme me tha stick!' I roared at Charlie.

'No!' an he laughed an whipped out the door. Then I heard the gate openin, an me heart lurched. 'Quick! Everyone stay quiet. They're back.' I grabbed hold a Harry an rubbed his head te stop him cryin. 'Shush! Shush! Ye're all right now, me ma's back.'

I heard the key in the lock, an Jackser came in wit a long face on him. 'Give yer mammy a lift in wit the pram.' I waited till he was past me, an he lashed out at me head wit the back of his hand. 'Move, ye lazy aul hag!' An I shot forward te lift the high pram over the step an inta the hall.

Me ma's eyes locked on mine. 'Jaysus! All tha fuckin waitin fer nothin. A few nappies an the cans a Cow an Gate milk fer the babby.' I backed up the hall, pullin the pram wit me.

'Are ye all right, Ma?' I whispered, not likin the look a her. She was very white an tired lookin after the new babby.

'A course I'm not! I'll never be fuckin right wit him in there tormentin me day an night.'

Me heart sank. Wit me ma sick an up in the bed most of the time now, tha aul fella can get his hands on me whenever he wants. I felt meself gettin desperate. 'Ma!' I said suddenly, lockin onta her eyes an leanin inta her an puttin me hand on her arm. 'I don't like bein left on me own wit Jackser,' I whispered, holdin me breath, feelin me heart poundin.

She stared at me, an we stayed like this, readin each other's eyes. Then the light went outa her face, an she gave me a dirty look an turned her head away slowly, lookin at nothin. An she closed her eyes an clamped her mouth shut. An took a big breath, an said, 'Oh, leave me alone. I've more than enough trouble! Don't be botherin me!' Then she reached inta the pram an lifted out the new babby. I felt me shoulders heave, an a terrible pain went through me, like someone put me in the bin, thinkin I was only dirt. Fit only fer the dump. I was born a child, but I'm not a child. I couldn't get a breath. I'm suffocatin.

I raced fer the door an whipped it open, hesimitatin fer a split second. Jackser was in the scullery makin the tea, can't go tha way! I lashed up the stairs an inta the big back room, an raced over te the winda. I opened it an let in the air, an leaned me head out. I hate me ma! I never want te be like her. I looked at the young one flyin up an down on the swing next door, gettin pushed higher an higher by her friend. I'd love te be in the garden wit them now, playin an laughin, but they won't even look at me. They're too well dressed an respectable. Their daddies have jobs, an they're very quiet, an they even give the young ones pocket money.

I looked aroun me at the new bed from the Vincents. It was black iron, but Jackser kept the black hairy blankets tha came wit it an gave me the aul overcoats te put over me, an a smelly aul blanket te sleep on tha's full a holes an smells a piss. The bed is full a hoppers an tears me alive at night, eatin the skin offa me. I have te keep runnin down at night te the scullery te get the box a DDT te shake all over me an the bed. But it doesn't kill them! There's too many! I looked aroun the room. Nothin te look at, only the bed an the bare pink plaster on the wall. No wallpaper an bare floorboards. But I don't care, cos I can sleep here by meself. No, I can't! I feel sick again, cos tha Jackser bastard sneaks in an jumps inta the bed beside me when he gets an opportunity. Now he's doin it more an more. I felt a rage comin up inside me. The bastard! I'll hang him, I'll get him lagged. No! They'll only put us all away. Jackser promises te bring me ma down wit him if I ever say anythin. An everyone will be locked up, he says. No! I can't do tha. I'll run away te England an make sure I don't get caught.

'What are ye fuckin doin up there?' Jackser roared up the stairs.

I jumped an ran te the landin. 'I'm comin down, Jackser.'

As I reached the bottom step, he lifted me off me feet by the neck. 'Get the fuck in there an help yer mammy wit them childre. I'll give ye idlin!' An he gave me a kick in me back an sent me flyin inta the room, smackin the side of me head against the pram.

'Mind wha ye're doin!' me ma screamed at him. 'Ye nearly knocked me over wit the babby in me arms.'

'Then stop complainin nobody's helpin ye!' Jackser roared, an went back inta the scullery te eat the grub he'd cooked fer himself.

I staggered te me feet, rubbin the pain outa me back an rubbin the shootin pain in me head. Me ma stood up an carried the new babby girl over te the cot, leavin the half-empty bottle on the table. 'She won't take any more fer me. The nurse in the clinic said she should be takin the full eight ounces by now!'

I sat down on the chair, watchin out fer Jackser, suddenly too tired te move or care. The life was outa me. 'Get me one of them nappies an the borax powder!' me ma asked.

'Ask him!' an I pointed te Charlie.

Me ma swung aroun an gritted her teeth. 'I'm fuckin warnin you. He'll tear ye apart if ye give me any more of yer guff!'

I looked at the door an stared at me ma, darin her. 'Yeah, Ma! An I'm runnin away from here. An ye can look out fer yerself!'

'Get him in here!' me ma said te Charlie.

I jumped up. 'I'm gettin it, Charlie!'

Me ma turned back te the babby an started te take off the dirty nappy. The shit was yella, an she rolled it up an handed it te me. 'Here! Put tha in the tilet an rinse it out, an then leave it in the bath fer washin.' I emptied the nappy down the tilet an rinsed it in the sink under the cold water. An then looked at the bath full a dirty clothes tha had been lyin in the dirty water fer months, waitin te be washed. I put it on top an pressed it down inta the water tha smelt te high heaven. We never got te have a bath in tha, cos it's always full a dirty washin!

Jackser roared outa the scullery at me. 'Tell tha woman te come in fer her dinner. It's gone fuckin stone cold!'

'Here!' me ma roared at me. 'Give the babby the rest a the bottle, an make sure ye wind her or she'll get sick.' I sat on the chair, an me ma handed me the new babby, fixin her back an head on me arm, an I lifted me knees an held her in tight te me, afraid a droppin her. Me ma put the bottle in the babby's mouth an lifted me arm. 'Keep the bottle up, an don't let any air in.'

The babby started te suck an then stopped te look up at me. 'Yeah! It's me,' I said, shakin me head an laughin at her very quietly. She started te suck again, an I looked at her huge blue eyes starin up at me. 'Ye're gorgeous,' I whispered, starin back at her. She gripped me little finger wit her tiny hand, then stopped an went red in the face an gave a huge fart, shittin inta her new nappy me ma'd just put on her. I took the bottle outa her mouth an looked at it. Only one ounce left. She had enough an started te doze off. So I leaned her forward, restin her chin on me arm, an held her belly an started te rub her back very gently, cos her little bones are like matchsticks. An her wind came up wit a drop a milk dribblin down her chin. An I wiped it wit the clean torn aul nappie me ma keeps fer her. An I carried her over te the cot an put her lyin down te sleep. She didn't stir, an I looked at her. She was like a livin doll. She never cries an only wakes fer her bottle. An she's nearly seven weeks old. Her name is Sally, after me ma. Pity tha, cos she would've been better wit a name like Sofia, like the fillum star.

'Did ye not tell her yet?' I heard Jackser shoutin back te me ma as he came inta the room.

'Ah, don't be botherin me,' me ma shouted back.

'Holy Jaysus!' Jackser said, lookin up at the ceilin. 'They're after us again te get ye te school, or they're puttin you away, so get yer arse up te tha church at half-eight, first thing in the mornin. An there's a bus waitin te drop ye outside the school.'

'Yeah, OK, Jackser.' I tried te make sense a this. It's well over a year since I was in tha school, an even then I hardly showed me nose in the door. Maybe only fer a few weeks they sent me there in all tha time. I won't know where te go or wha te do, an I have no pencil or copybooks. Jaysus! Them nuns'll kill me. They're very strict altogether.

Me ma came in moanin. 'What am I supposed te do wit all them childre on me own? An who's goin te go fer the messages, may I ask?'

'Don't I do everythin fer ye, Mrs? Do ye want them te take tha young one away? Then we'll be truly fucked!' Jackser roared, an pointed his finger at me ma's chest.

'Ah! I don't know. She should be able te finish school by now, she's eleven years old, fer God's sake.'

I am? When did I get te be eleven? This is the first time she mentioned tha.

I was out the door an flyin fer the bus, up the hill an across the road. Wonder where the bus is? Through the church an out the gate again. Where's the bus? Ah! Mammy, I'm goin te miss it. There it is! Over by the shops. I flew across the road, not mindin the Morris Minor car tha came aroun the corner. I made it stop, an the man waved his fist at me. I looked again. Ah! Tha's me ma's doctor, hope he doesn't know me.

I made it up behind a gang a kids all squeezin onta the platform, squashin the conductor inta the corner as he tried te hold onta his bell te stop the childre from bangin it. 'Go easy! Go easy!' he roared, as everyone tried te make it up the stairs before it filled up an the rest of us got kicked downstairs. 'There's plenty a room inside!'

I squeezed inside an made fer the end of the bus, wantin te sit at the back on the long seat where ye could see everythin happenin. 'Inside now! No more seats upstairs!' roared the conductor, jumpin on the stairs te block the childre goin up. Everyone banged the bell, hopin te make the driver take off an leave the rest of them still rushin from all directions te catch it.

The bus was full now, an childre were still rushin on. 'Push up there! Let us on!' The conductor pushed all the childre havin te stand now down the bottom, an I couldn't see a thing. The bus was burstin.

'Geroff the platform!' screamed the conductor. An pushed even more down.

Jaysus! I'm suffocatin. Then the bell gave three loud quick bongs an another three bongs. An the driver pushed back the little winda behind me back an looked fer the conductor but couldn't see or hear a thing wit the noise. 'OK, Tommy!' screamed the conductor, swingin outa the bar an leanin offa the platform. 'We're off!'

The bus farted an gave a big bang, an puffs of blue smoke blew up outa the back. It took off, an we're hardly movin. Kids banged on the winda an roared inta the driver, 'Hey, Mister, we'd be faster runnin! Do ye want us te ger out an push? My aunt Lizzie she lives in number eight, she has two diddies, like a ball a . . .'

'Cut tha disgustin singin out,' screamed the conductor up the stairs. The windas were all open, an everyone was pushin an shovin te lean out.

'Hey, Jenny! Are ye not goin te school?' A young one standin on the seat in front of me screamed out at another one on the other side of the road.

'No! I'm not well!' she roared.

'It's well fer ye!' screamed the one on the seat.

'Tell the teacher fer me, will ya?' shouted the other one back.

'No! I'm tellin her ye were mitchin!'

The bus lurched an got a second wind, an took off flyin, rockin from side te side. An everyone standin was now collapsed on top of the childre sittin. 'Geroffa me! Ah, me leg! This is my seat! Mister, she hit me!' Everyone was roarin.

The conductor took no notice. 'Fly me to the moon!' he sang, puffin on his Woodbine. Then we got te Dorset Street, an the conductor suddenly gave two bongs te the bell, an the bus came te a skiddin stop, sendin everyone flyin again, landin on seats an the floor.

'We're stopped!' shouted the childre, an the conductor waved at the driver, who shot back his little winda te see wha's goin on.

The bus conductor flew inta a sweet shop. An everyone shouted, 'Come on! He's gone inta the shop! Buy me a penny toffee, will ye? Here's me money.'

'Get's a fizzy bag!' screamed another young one. An gangs of childre roared in after the conductor.

They all came flyin back out again. 'Get back on tha bus!' roared the conductor, grabbin childre by the arms an carryin them onta the bus. An he lashed out wit his foot, tryin te stop others escapin back inta the shop. 'I'm tellin the head nun on the lot of ye's if ye're not back on tha bus right now,' he screamed, tryin te grab them scatterin in every direction.

'Ye're not tellin on us, Mister! Lookit us, we didn't geroffa the bus,' roared childre from the top winda.

The driver was watchin an waitin. 'Have we got everyone?'

'Yeah, Tommy! I think so,' the conductor said, outa breath, lookin outa the bus te make sure. 'No, wait!' An a young one came outa the shop suckin an icepop.

'Tha's not fair, Mister! We want te get somethin. We're entitled!' screamed childre from the platform.

'I'm reportin you!' screamed the conductor. 'Get on the bus before I put the lot of youse off.'

The young one galloped onta the bus, an the conductor jumped on an bonged the bell three times. An the driver shut the winda an then opened it again an roared, 'If any one of youse bang on this winda again, I'll leave the whole pack of ye's stranded where ye's won't be found fer a week!'

'Ye can't do tha, cos we'll report ye te CIE. We know our entitlements! Yeah! An we won't think twice about it neither.'

The driver slammed the winda shut, an the bus roared an gave a big bang. An blew a big cloud of black smoke, an tore off, sendin everyone flyin. An then rocked back, an everyone went flyin in the opposite direction. An the conductor opened a new pack a Woodbines, peelin off the wrapper an throwin it offa the platform. An he stuck a cigarette in his mouth an lit it wit a match, an took a big drag inta his lungs, an shook himself, mutterin under his breath, 'Jaysus! This job will be the death a me yet!'

We drove inta Mountjoy Square an turned right. 'We're there!' childre shouted.

'Come on, where's me schoolbag?', 'Oh, Mammy! I forgot me copybook', Lend's a pencil!', 'Oh, Gawd! I didn't do me exercise, the teacher's goin te kill me.'

'Hurry! Geroffa the bus.'

Everyone was goin mad. All shoutin, an frettin, an pushin, an standin on each other when some were crawlin under the seats tryin te find their things. I took me time, in no hurry te get in them gates. Me heart was beatin like a drum. These young ones have been goin te school fer years. An they know wha te do an where they are. I know nothin. An I hate te look like an eejit. Pity I didn't know sooner. I could've fixed meself up wit a copybook an pencil.

I was bein pulled along by the crowd. 'Come on, youse! The bell is gone, we'll be late!'

We went through the doors, an everyone flew in different directions. I stopped an looked aroun me, wonderin what I should do. 'What do you think you are doing, standing about here?' a voice barked at me. I got such a shock when I saw a big black figure flyin at me. Me eyes blurred, an I was seein three of it. 'I asked you a question! Are you deaf?' she screamed. I looked up inta the white face – the cheeks were hangin down, an it was squashed inta a white cap covered in a big black veil, an a long black habit, ye couldn't see her shoes. An she was pointin a big bell at me an starin down at me wit her watery faded blue eyes waitin fer an answer. I forgot wha she asked me, so I stared back, waitin fer the question again. 'You stupid girl! What is your name?'

'Martha, Sister. I was here before.'

'Are you a new child? Who sent you here?' she looked aroun te see if anyone brought me.

'Eh! Not really new, only a little, cos I was here before!'

She looked down at me, tryin te figure out what I was talkin about. 'When? When did you last attend here?'

'Eh! Maybe a year ago, or it could be more. I don't really remember. Ye see, me mammy told me te come back te school or I'm goin te be sent away,' I tried te explain as she stared at me.

'Are you on our roll?'

I stared at her, thinkin. 'Eh! Wha roll is tha, Sister?'

'Follow me, you stupid creature! Stand against that wall!'

I stood up against the wall outside her door, an she marched in an slammed the door behind her.

373

I could hear childre chantin their lessons inside all the classrooms down along the passages. 'No! No! Sit up and pay attention!' I could hear a teacher roar, as she banged her stick on a desk. I shivered at the thought of havin te go inta one a them.

The door swung open, an I stood up straight. 'Come with me quickly!' an she marched off down a corridor, past classrooms wit foggy glass at the top of the door so ye couldn't see in. But ye could hear the noise comin out, no problem. Teachers shoutin an childre repeatin all together wha the teacher was tellin them.

We stopped outside a classroom, an the childre inside were chantin numbers. 'Nine ones are nine!' An the nun listened until they were finished an then knocked on the door an opened it. All eyes swung on the nun, marchin over te the desk te talk te a fat little nun wit a red face. 'Ah, Sister Vianney!' An they turned their backs on the childre an whispered, puttin their heads close together.

I stayed half in an half outa the door, watchin the nuns. Then I looked at the childre as they swung their eyes aroun catchin sight a me. They nudged each other an whispered wit their hands over their mouths. 'Who's tha? Gawd! Lookit the state a her!'

'Quiet!' the fat nun suddenly barked. An then the other nun turned an walked out the door. I crept inta the room, listenin te the quiet while the little fat nun pulled out a big book from a drawer in the desk an wrote somethin in it. Then she slammed the book shut an put it back in the drawer, an stood up from her desk an looked at me, then looked at the back of the classroom an pointed te an empty desk an said, 'Sit down there.'

I followed her finger an spotted the place she wanted me te go. An walked down the middle of the room, wit dozens a pairs of eyes all pinned on me. Me legs was shakin, an I felt very foolish, cos some of them were titterin behind their books.

'She's real scrawny!' one young one was whisperin behind her hand.

'Back to work!' roared the nun.

I sat down an looked at the empty seat beside me. Glad of tha.

No one te bother me. I had a big winda on me right, an I could look out the winda an see up tha Mountjoy Square.

'Marie Byrne!' the nun shouted down from her desk, pointin her stick at a young one. 'Come up here an give me the nine times table.'

The young one crawled up te the top of the class an stood lookin down, twistin her fingers an lookin up at the ceilin. 'Start!' roared the nun, bangin her stick on the desk.

'Nine ones are nine,' she squeaked, then coughed an started again. 'Nine ones are nine, nine twos are ...' an she looked up at the ceilin, 'are eighteen, nine threes are ...' an she tried te count on her fingers without bein seein. 'Nine twos are eighteen, nine threes are, are ...'

'Stand against the wall with your back to the room!' screamed the nun. 'I will deal with your idleness later. Now! The rest of you, open your table books at nine times division.' An everyone started chantin out the nine times division. It was just a dronin noise te me. I didn't know wha they were sayin, so me mind wandered off te look out the winda, an I longed te be grown up like tha aul woman rushin past te get her messages. On her own an no one te bother her. She disappeared outa sight aroun the corner an up the hill. Tha left me watchin the aul mangy dog sniffin aroun the waste ground hopin te find somethin te eat. Even the dog can go about his business. No one te mind wha he's doin. But no! I wouldn't want te be a dog. I'm better as I am. There's always a chance fer me, but a dog has no chance. A dog can be put down anytime. At least as a child they can't be too quick te put me down. No! I'll just have te watch meself here. An it will all pass eventually.

'Go on, get goin!'

'Right, Jackser. I'm goin.' I rushed outa the door an started te run, feelin Jackser's eyes watchin me from behind the curtain. Ye always have te run everywhere. Jackser doesn't like me te walk. He thinks I'm idlin if I walk. I kept up a slow run until I turned the corner. Then I slowed down, feelin very tired an not in the mood te face another walk in an back te tha school. I couldn't understand why he was sendin me inta school when there's a bus strike on. An yet the week before last he kept me out fer the whole week, even though I was only four days started in the school. At least it's Monday. I'm glad Friday an Saturday is over. I didn't get caught robbin the butter. An I needn't worry fer another few days. Not until Wednesday or Thursday, anyway. Tha's when I start te get very sick, worryin meself half te death about it.

I arrived up at the church, ready te head down the hill when I saw a crowd a people over at the bus stop beside the shops. An they were climbin up onta the back of army trucks. I rushed over. 'Wha's happenin, Mrs?'

'They've brought in the army te get us te work.'

'Where's this truck goin te? Hey, Mister!' I shouted te the soldier helpin the women up.

'Inta town, me little darling!' he laughed as he lifted me up an whooshed me through the air, landin me sittin on a bench beside a woman chinnin her head scarf up an down. I was delighted, lovin tha spin. An feelin very contented at gettin a lift inta town.

Another woman leaned herself down beside me, an the two of them leaned inta each other an started talkin. 'Isn't this grand, Mrs!' said Chinny, restin herself on top a me.

'Oh, it's lovely!' said the fat woman. 'The blessins a God on the army! What would we do without them, I'll never know.'

'Ah! They're grand all right!' coughed an old man sittin on the bench opposite, chokin on his Woodbine.

'Hey, sonny! Where's this one takin us to?' another man roared down the lorry te the soldier. Everyone waited fer his answer.

'O'Connell Street, outside the Metropole!'

'Lovely! Tha suits me fine,' an everyone shook their heads in agreement, noddin te each other.

The lorry filled up, an the soldier slammed the back shut an jumped up beside the driver, an we took off, flyin inta town faster than the bus. I was lookin out through the back, an people were watchin us flyin past an wavin at us. The truck stopped, an the soldier helped everyone down. An I waited me turn an lifted me hands, an sure enough I got another spin, flyin through the air. An he landed me on me feet an patted the top of me head. An I laughed, feelin giddy from the excitement of it. Then I headed up Parnell Street an left up the hill, an slowed down before I hit the gates. I'm on time, an the lorries are pickin us up at five o'clock te take us out te Finglas. I can hang aroun till then, an Jackser will never know the difference. He'll think I've walked!

There was very few childre at the school when I came in the school yard. The nun was ringin the bell, an only the childre from the city centre was here. I'm the only one from Finglas who's come. They probably don't know about the army trucks yet. The nun twisted her mouth up inta a smile when she saw me. 'You must have left home at dawn to get in to school on time?' she said, holdin her bell te stop it ringin.

'Eh! Yes, Sister,' an she shook her head, thinkin about this. An started ringin her bell again, shakin it in the face of young ones stragglin behind me.

'Come along! Hurry, you lazy idlers.'

I went down the corridor, headin fer me classroom, smilin te meself. She thinks I walked in this mornin. Grand, let them think I'm great. It feels lovely when people like me.

33

I was just headin in the gate from school when Jackser whipped the front door open. 'Here, you! There's half a crown. Run up te tha van an get me five Woodbines. Hurry!' he barked.

I took the money an flew. When I came rushin back, I saw me ma standin outside the gate. An Jackser was standin outside the front door, screamin at her. 'Go on, ye whore! Get movin. Ye're not comin back te my house!'

I came up te the gate, an Jackser roared at me, 'Come on, you, get in here!'

Charlie an Teddy was standin behind him, screamin, 'Mammy, Mammy! Don't leave us.'

Me ma roared at me, 'Don't go in there, Martha! He'll kill ye!'

'Get in here, ye bastard!' Jackser roared at me.

Harry came runnin out, screamin, an Jackser jerked him back by the neck of his jumper an landed him in the hallway. I hesimitated, not knowin wha te do. 'Come on! Come wit me,' me ma screamed at me, runnin down the road.

I threw the packet a five Woodbines in the gate an took off, runnin after me ma. When we got aroun the corner, we saw Charlie runnin behind us. I stopped, an me ma stopped. 'Ye're te come back,' he said te me ma.

'No!' me ma said. 'I'm not goin back there. Tell him tha.'

'No, Ma!' Charlie said. 'Take me wit ye!'

I looked at him, his little face was white an he was shakin. 'We'll take him, Ma.'

'No! He has te stay an watch the childre,' an she turned her back an ran.

I hesimitated, lookin at Charlie an watchin me ma rushin off up the road, not knowin wha te do. 'Go back, Charlie!' I said, an turned te run after me ma. I looked back, hearin Charlie scream, wringin his hands. Then he turned an ran back te Jackser. He's only six, he'll have te do everythin! Jackser will kill him, cos he doesn't want another man's bastard. He hates poor Charlie as much as he hates me.

'Hurry!' me ma puffed. 'He'll come after us.' We rounded the corner at the church an hid in the shop, waitin fer the bus an keepin a look out fer Jackser.

'Here it is, Ma!' I said, finally seein the bus headin down towards us. We galloped across the road an jumped on.

'Gimme tha change,' me ma said. I handed me ma the one shillin an tenpence change from the Woodbines, an she paid the fare. 'Tha bastard took all the money from me an headed off inta town wit it this mornin. He was only back just before you arrived. Well! He's not livin off me any more. Tha's the last of me he's goin te see!'

I said nothin. I was tryin te make sense of wha's happenin. 'But what about the childre, Ma?'

'Let him take care of them! I've wasted enough of me life,' me ma said, tightenin her lips an lookin away from me.

We arrived at Parnell Street an got off the bus an walked down Moore Street, just wanderin. 'It's an awful pity he got his hands on the money,' me ma muttered te herself. 'I'm goin te have te hang on te the shillin I've left.' I saw her look longinly at the café we passed. An the smell a chips turned me mouth te water. I'd love te go in there an sit down an have a cup a tea. But we just moved on, wanderin aimlessly. 'I wonder where we can stay fer the night,' she said, lookin at me, thinkin an chewin on her lip. 'It's beginnin te get dark, an we can't stay on the streets.'

'Let's go down te the buildins. There's a very nice woman I know. She's one of me customers. Maybe she'll let us stay the night.'

When we got te the buildins, it was dark an I knocked on the door. 'Mrs!' I said when she squinted out at me, wonderin who was knockin on her door this hour of the night. 'I wonder if ye wouldn't mind lettin me an me ma sleep on yer floor fer the night? We've nowhere te go, an me ma had te run fer her life when Jackser threw us out.'

'I'm sorry, love. I'd love te help ye's, but I've no room! Isn't there anyone else ye can ask? I've a houseful of childre.' An she opened the door wider, an we looked inta the dark room an saw childre sleepin on a pull-down bed in the corner.

'Ah! I'm sorry te bother ye,' I said in a whisper. 'We'll be all right. We'll find somewhere,' an I went te move off.

'Wait!' she said. 'Is tha all ye're wearin?'

I looked at me thin frock an cardigan. 'Yeah,' I said.

'You'll freeze in tha,' she said, rushin inta the room an comin out wit an old overcoat. 'Put tha aroun ye. It's not much, but it'll help te keep the cold out.'

I took the coat, sayin, 'Thanks very much, Mrs, an I'm sorry again fer givin ye any bother.'

'No! No! Not at all. I'm sorry I have te turn ye away,' an she put her arms out, showin me the room full a people. She closed the door, an I put the heavy old coat, miles too big fer me, aroun me shoulders, an followed me ma up the cold stone steps. We sat down on a step on the landin, an me ma pressed in against the wall. An I pushed in beside her, sittin on the hem of her coat, wrappin the big coat over the two of us. We sat without movin, listenin te the quiet. I stared at the dark, wonderin wha was goin te happen. I looked at me ma, lost in herself, the wind gone outa her now when it hit her we had nowhere te go. I could feel a coldness creepin over me chest. Maybe she's thinkin of goin back te Jackser! Tha can't happen now. He'll kill her an blame me fer puttin ideas inta her head. An he won't show me any mercy. An wha will happen te the childre? Ah, Jesus help us! This is an awful mess. An we don't even have any money. If I go an rob any butter tomorrow, I could get caught. Then me ma would be left stranded, an she'd have te tell Jackser. No! Forget tha. But wha then? I'm afraid te ask me ma, in case she's changed her mind an thinkin of runnin back te him. 'Ma,' I croaked. 'Eh, wha's goin te happen now?'

'I don't know, there's no one te take us in. Where can we go?'

I said nothin, thinkin.

We'd fallen asleep. An I woke wit me ma shakin me. 'It's beginnin te get bright, Martha. It must be nearly mornin.'

I sat up, rubbin me neck an feelin stiff as a poker. 'Jaysus, Ma. I'm freezin!'

'Yeah! This is a terrible carry on. I hope tha bandy aul bastard dies roarin!' me ma snorted.

'Yeah! But, Ma, we're away from him! An I know wha te do. Don't worry yerself. I'll come up wit somethin.'

Me ma looked at me, chewin her lip. 'Yeah! But, Martha, we've no money. We need te get our hands on a few pound. Then we could go te England! He'd never find us there.'

I felt me heart leapin. 'Right, Ma. I've made up me mind. Follow me!'

Me ma laughed. 'Where are we goin?'

'Let's just see, Ma. But first we need te spot a milkman.'

'A milkman!' me ma laughed.

'Yeah! Wait an see, hurry!'

I left the coat on the stairs, an we made our way down, watchin our step, cos it was still a bit dark. The early mornin damp hit us, an I thought about runnin back fer the coat, but I'd only look like Mutt an Jeff wit tha thing trailin along the ground after me.

We left the buildins an headed up Talbot Street. I looked from one side of the road te the other, lookin in all the shop doorways. 'No milk yet, Ma!' We turned right up Gardiner Street, not meetin a soul. 'It's too early te be out yet, Ma,' I whispered. 'So we're goin te be spotted an look suspicious. So keep yer head down if ye see anyone, an walk fast.'

Me ma looked aroun. 'Come on, then, we don't want te be arrested fer nothin. They pick ye up fer idlin,' me ma said, hurryin.

We crossed over an down Parnell Street. 'Look, Ma! He's made deliveries.'

We looked over at a crate of milk bottles sittin outside a shop. 'Great! Let's move.'

I had a quick look. No! Only milk. We rushed on. 'Ma! Ma! Look!' I pointed over te a box. 'Watch there's no one comin!' An I dived on the box. Butter! Twenty pounds. Jaysus! I grabbed the box, tryin te lift it, an then dropped on me arse an hoisted it up te me chest. 'Anyone comin, Ma?' I croaked.

'Eh! No! No!' Me ma's eyes were swivellin in all directions.

I staggered off, tryin te hurry. 'We have te get outa here, Ma, quick!' I was gaspin fer breath. I heaved the box out in front of me chest, propellin meself across the road an turned right down Gardiner Street, not stoppin. I kept movin, me arms breakin, an me heart threatenin te burst in me chest. I kept goin. Left down by the Diamond an right onta Corporation Street. I stopped an dropped the box gently. 'Ma! Can ye grab a hold of one end, an we'll be faster.'

'Jaysus! The weight of it,' me ma puffed, liftin it awkwardly.

'Lift it, Ma!'

'I am! Wait!' she laughed. 'Come on,' an we took off, walkin sideways. 'Hold on, it's slippin!' me ma roared.

'Grab it, Ma! If we're seen wit this, they'll know we've robbed it, an we'll be arrested straight away.'

Me ma got a hold, an we rushed on, crossin the road an inta the buildins. 'Head fer the stairs where the coat is, Ma.' We hoisted the box up the stairs, me goin up backwards, an plonked it down on the step. 'Cover it wit the coat. We don't want it te be seen,' I said, collapsin onta the step, tryin te get me breath back.

'Oh, Jaysus! I'm glad tha's over,' me ma said, landin down beside me.

'Yeah, Ma! We're steeped in luck gettin tha butter. An not just tha, but it's Friday, an me customers are expectin me.'

'Jaysus! Tha's grand altogether,' me ma said, smilin. Then she said, 'Eh! How much will we get, Martha?'

'Eh, let me think. Three pounds an ten shillins.'

'Oh, God! Tha's great, tha's enough te keep us goin, but we'll have te go easy on it.'

'Yeah! We can't go mad,' I agreed. 'I'm wonderin, Ma, if I should leave the box wit ye an just carry aroun a few pounds or wha? It's very awkward carryin the box without the shoppin bag.'

'I don't know, wha de you think? It wouldn't look good if anyone sees me sittin here.'

'Yeah,' I said, thinkin.

'An what if he finds us? He could be headin in here right now lookin fer us,' me ma said, her eyes bulgin.

Me heart leapt wit the fright. 'Yeah, ye're right, Ma! He knows where te find me. Look,' I said. 'We're goin te have te be very quick. We'll wait here until everyone starts gettin on the move. An then I'll start goin aroun te me customers. You stand up there, keepin an eye out over the balcony. An keep the box beside ye, covered wit the coat. Tha way, if anyone sees ye, they won't pass any remarks. They'll think ye're waitin fer someone. An ye'll be able te keep a watch out fer tha aul fella. I'll be as fast as I can.'

'Yeah!' me ma said, worryin. 'I only hope te God everythin works out an he doesn't come lookin in here fer us.'

'No, Ma. He won't, not yet. He'll think I'm aroun the shops. It's still too early fer me te be here. Tha's wha he'll be thinkin. So he'll be scourin Henry Street an hangin aroun O'Connell Street, tryin te spot us. Tha's if he isn't off drinkin the money. So we still have a head start on him. Don't worry, tha bastard is not goin te catch us,' I said, feelin hot in me chest. Then we stayed quiet, feelin satisfied. Just waitin fer the time te pass.

'We won't have enough fer the boat, though, tha takes us te England,' me ma said slowly, lookin at me.

I felt me heart sinkin. 'No, I suppose not, but ye never know, Ma. We'll find a way,' I said, feelin meself liftin again.

I was gettin impatient an stood up an walked up the stairs te look over the balcony. I saw people movin down Corporation Street. 'We won't have te wait much longer, Ma. It's much brighter now, an people are on the move.' I sat down again te wait.

'This waitin'd kill ye,' me ma said. 'Me nerves are gone, sittin here waitin fer him te jump out at us from nowhere.'

I was gettin very worried meself. 'Right, Ma! Let's get this box up onta the landin, an we can watch from the balcony. We lifted the box up an put it between us, coverin it wit the coat, an leaned our elbows on the balcony te keep a watch out. I had te stand on the box or keep jumpin up te see over. 'OK, Ma,' I said at last, rippin open the box an takin out six pound a butter. 'I'll go.'

'Don't be long!' me ma said after me, soundin very worried.

'No! I'll be back as quick as I can.' An I shot off, hurryin te me first customer, hopin they'd got paid their money an not be tellin me te come back later.

I was knockin on doors. 'Eh! Ye're here early today. Oh! The butter is lovely an hard, not mashed like the usual!'

'No! I was able te collect it yesterday.'

'I'll take an extra one today, so give me the three.'

'Thanks very much!' an I shot off, rushin back te me ma. 'Here, Ma! Take the money.'

I was doin great, only five pound a butter left. I grabbed it an took off, leavin me ma countin the money, laughin an lookin very happy. Only two pound left. I knocked on the door. 'Ma! It's the butter young one,' a little young fella of about seven shouted.

'Tell her two!' the mammy shouted out, comin wit her purse, countin the money. 'Oh, tha's lovely an fresh lookin,' she said, takin the two pounds a butter an smilin. 'It's usually all battered.'

'No, it's lovely, isn't it?' I said. 'I didn't have te carry too much today in me shoppin bag, so it's not gone all soft.' I took the seven shillins an sixpence, an said, 'Thanks very much, Mrs,' an I was gone back te me ma waitin at the bottom of the stairs. I was sweatin an all red in the face. An me ma was delighted when I handed over the money.

'Let's go,' she said, an we rushed out onta Foley Street an headed down the North Strand. An turned right at the Five Lamps, headin down towards Sheriff Street.

We got te the quays an walked down the North Wall slowly, me ma lookin at the boats. 'If only we could get on tha boat tonight an get te England. Then we'd be grand!' me ma said, lookin longinly at the ships. 'We need never worry again about lookin over our shoulders te see if tha mad bastard is after us.'

'Yeah!' I said, feelin desperate, tryin te think of a way aroun tha. 'We can't hang aroun, Ma, tryin te get more money, cos sooner or later tha aul fella is goin te catch us. An we'll be up against the police as well if we get caught robbin the butter.'

'Jaysus Christ! What are we goin te do then?' me ma said, lookin aroun her.

'Let's just keep walkin, Ma, an don't be worryin. Ye never know wha will happen.'

I was feelin down meself now, cos I'm afraid, when I see me ma get desperate, she might change her mind an run back te tha aul fella.

We walked on past the pub wit aul fellas standin outside, their backs against the wall an hoppin from one foot te the other wit their hands in their pockets an their eyes hoppin from one end of the quays te the other, lookin fer someone te buy them a drink. I saw their eyes flickin over me ma as they swivelled their heads lookin down the quays an then turned back te spit, so they could get a better look at her. Tryin te play the hard men an cockin their eyebrows te try an make themselves good lookin. Thinkin they were John Wayne or Roy Rogers! Me ma looked away.

'More Jacksers, Ma! A gang a fuckin wasters,' I said.

'Oh, indeed!' me ma said. 'Well, I've had enough a men. Never again!'

'Yeah, Ma! An I'm never havin anythin te do wit them neither.'

We walked on, an there was a woman singin outside a café in a loud voice. 'I'm a rambler, I'm a gambler, I'm a long way from home.' We stopped te watch her. She sounded grand, an the workin men sittin an eatin at the tables inside were clappin an roarin. Then she went inside an made a collection, passin her hat aroun. An the men threw money in. When she was finished, she turned te us an said, 'Ye have te do somethin te eat!' An she laughed. I liked her. She had a big red happy face, an her eyes was dancin in her head.

'Sit down an have a cup a tea,' she said te me ma. We sat down at an empty table, an she asked fer a pot a tea, callin the waitress over, an asked me did I want any bread an butter.

'No, thanks very much!' I said, not wantin te spend her hard-earned money.

'How did ye come te be singin on the streets?' me ma asked her, smilin.

'Ah, it's a long story!' she said, rollin up the sleeves of her cardigan, showin her massive arms an wipin the sweat offa her forehead. 'But I'd prefer te have meself out singin an makin me own way in the world than te be dependin on any man te keep me!'

'Oh, indeed! Ye're right there,' me ma said. 'Have nothin te do wit them, they're only bad news. An they'd put ye in an early grave!' Me ma was lookin very serious altogether.

'Are ye not married then?' I asked her.

'No! I'm not,' she said, shakin her head, half smilin an half serious. 'An I never will be!'

'So does tha mean ye have no childre, then?' I asked.

She looked at me, hesimitatin. 'I had one,' she said, 'a long time ago. An they took her away from me.' I could see hurt comin inta her eyes, then she shook herself an smiled at me ma. 'She's a grand child! How old is she?' noddin at me.

'Yeah!' me ma said. 'She's eleven. An she's grand company fer me. I'd be lost without her.'

'Well, ye're a very lucky woman. There's many a one would love te have a child, so ye must be happy an count yer blessins. I'd better get movin,' an she stood up an laughed. 'Mind yerselves now,' an she waved at us an disappeared out the door.

I sat watchin the space where she'd been. Empty now! An I suddenly felt very lonely. A minute ago, it was like someone turned on a light, an everythin was warm an goin te be all right. Now it was dark an cold again. An I didn't want te bother lookin at me ma, mutterin te herself, 'I don't know. I don't know wha we're goin te do!'

'Ah, shut up, Ma!' I said, feelin very annoyed.

We've been sittin here fer hours now, dozily watchin people comin an goin. Not sayin much, just sittin an starin. Then me ma muttered,

'I think they're gettin fed up wit us sittin here. Maybe we should get a pot a tea!'

'Yeah, Ma, good idea!'

I sat up, feelin meself beginnin te stir. The woman brought over two cups an saucers an the pot a tea, an me ma poured it out. I took a big mouthful, an the warm tea hittin me belly began te make me think again. 'Ye know, Ma, maybe we should go down an take a look at the boat when it comes in tonight.'

'Yeah!' me ma said. 'I was just thinkin the same. Ye never know, maybe we might get the chance of findin someone te let us slip on.'

'Yeah,' I said happily. 'We have te try everythin.'

We sipped the tea slowly, makin it last. Then me ma said, 'I think it must be nearly time te go.'

'Yeah, Ma,' I said, feelin me heart flutterin.

We walked slowly down te the ship, watchin it. People were slowly makin their way up the gangplank, stoppin an handin their tickets te the man at the entrance. Then suddenly more people began te arrive, an I felt me heart begin te race. 'Ma!' I suddenly said. 'Quick! Let's get on the ship.'

Me ma looked at me, starin. 'Here's wha we'll do. I'll run on, an you keep right behind me back. If I'm stopped, I'll say I'm lookin fer you. He'll be so busy mindin me, he won't notice you, so just keep goin, an if he calls ye back, don't look, lose yerself in the crowd, an I'll come an find ye. Now if he stops you, say you're lookin fer me, an I'll be watchin, an leave the talkin te me. An go along wit everythin I say. But we'll have te be fast, Ma. Right?'

'Right!' me ma said, lookin very nervous an beginnin te shake. We watched, holdin our breath.

A big crowd was swarmin aroun the ticket collector now, an he was on his own. 'Come on, Ma!' I grabbed her coat, pullin her wit me. I rushed up the gangplank, rushin past people quietly, an when I got te the ticket collector, wit the crowd aroun him, I squeezed past them, mutterin, 'Ma! Mammy, wait fer me!'

I was on! I looked back te see me ma comin up te the ticket man, an she was lookin in his direction an then saw me on the ship wavin down at her. 'Come on. Come on,' I was whisperin. She laughed at me nervously an then slid past the man while he was checkin someone's ticket, an she was up an on the ship. I grabbed her coat, an we disappeared inta the crowd, only stoppin when we were well away from the ticket man.

'Oh, Jaysus! We made it,' me ma said, laughin.

'Yeah, Ma! Yeah! We're on the ship. We're goin te England!' Me heart was flyin wit excitement, an I stood up an watched the seagulls flyin aroun the ship. An they sounded as excited as meself. 'Oh, Ma, we got away from Jackser. I can't believe it. We're on our own again after all tha time.' I ran up an down on the seat, feelin I could do what I liked. 'How are ye's, Mister?' I shouted te a gang of fellas standin by the rails lookin at the water, feelin miserable in themselves. They took no notice a me.

'Let's get downstairs an get ourselves a seat before they're all taken.'

'Yeah, Ma!' an I jumped down an followed her down inta a room wit cushy seats. We sat down an rested ourselves, content te take it easy now an just watch the other people comin an feelin we were the same as them. All startin a new life. An the lovely quiet an peace tha came over me was like I'd died an gone te heaven. I never felt so happy before. I wasn't worried or afraid any more. Oh, God must be lookin after me. Maybe he likes me after all.

I sat back watchin the people, lookin at their faces. One aul fella was sittin next te his wife, an she had a babby of about nine or ten months sittin on her lap, an another one of about two lyin on the seat beside her wit his head slumped against her. The aul fella kept fixin their two huge suitcases beside him te make sure no one robbed them. None of them looked happy. 'When are we goin te get movin?' he kept mutterin te the wife. She said nothin. Just looked at the little fella lyin beside her.

I watched his eyes, hard as nails, slidin aroun the room, landin on the women an lookin up under his eyebrows te check the men weren't watchin him. Then slidin back te the wife, givin her a dirty look. An seein her move nervously, lowerin her eyes down te the child on her lap. Not lookin anywhere, in case he might accuse her of lookin at other men. An then, satisfied she's not enjoyin herself, he looks away te take in the room again an say, 'See! Lookit me, I'm a big man. I keep me wife an kids under control, an they know wha's good fer them. I'm yer man fer handlin women an childre. But I'm not interested in gettin inta a fight wit men, cos I couldn't handle tha, tha's why I don't look them in the eye.'

Another fuckin Jackser! I thought. But the woman annoyed me more. Why is she so afraid of him? Just like me ma! Why can't they wait their opportunity an then pick up somethin when he's sleepin an split his head wide open. An when he wakes up shocked, scream, 'Ye can hit me, but ye'll fuckin have te kill me, cos every time ye touch me, I'm goin te cripple ye until ye stop! Do ye understand?' I think them cowardly bastards would back off quick enough. Cos they don't like ye playin them at their own game. Me heart was flyin wit annoyance.

I shook meself, te get rid of the feelin, an looked at me ma. Her eyes were closed, an she was dozin. Me poor Ma, she's too soft an doesn't know how te work her way aroun anythin. A lot of women are like tha, waitin fer the men te tell them wha te do. I'm not goin te let any man tell me wha te do. Nobody's ever goin te get the better a me.

Me ma stood up an whispered, 'Martha, I'm just goin out te the tilet. I'll be back in a minute.'

'OK, Ma. I'll go wit ye.'

'No! You stay an mind the seats. I won't be long.' An she headed off out the door. I took me shoes off an wrapped me feet under me, gettin more comfortable. Then a man poked his head in the door, wearin a cap pulled down over his eyes an a big overcoat wit a belt tied aroun it. An grabbin a tight hold of an aul suitcase under his arms tied shut wit string, he crept inta the room on his toes, wit his arse still out the door, an looked slowly aroun. An then his shifty eyes lit on me ma's seat. An before I could open me mouth, he was over an dropped his arse down on the seat an put the suitcase down beside him, an stretched his legs out, an slid his head an neck down inta his overcoat, an pulled the cap down restin it on his nose, makin himself very comfortable.

I shot up in the seat an roared, 'Hey, Mister! Tha's me ma's seat!' An he didn't move an inch! 'Hey! I'm talkin te ye, Mister!' An I shook his arm. He lifted his head an looked at me under his hat fer a second an went back te his comfort as if I hadn't said a word. I looked aroun me at the other people, an they acted as if nothin was wrong. I sat gapin at him, ragin. Then I used me two hands an tried te push him offa the seat. 'Are ye bothered or wha?' I roared.

He shook me off wit his elbow, liftin his head, an muttered outa the side of his mouth, 'Whist! Go away outa tha!' an settled himself back inta more comfort. Then me ma appeared in the door, an I saw her face begin te shake an her eyes blink at the cheek of someone takin her seat. She walked over slowly an looked at me, blinkin an coughin. 'Wha happened?' Cough! Blink! 'Wha's this man doin in my seat?'

'He won't get up, Ma! An he's pretendin not te hear me.'

Me ma coughed an blinked. 'Eh! Excuse me, Mister! But tha's my seat ye're sittin in,' an she poked his shoulder wit her finger. 'Do ye hear me? Jaysus! He's not takin a blind bit a notice a me! Come on! Get up!' me ma said, shakin him.

An he looked up at her fer a second an said, 'Find somewhere else! I'm here now,' an he nodded his head te the door an then dropped it back inside his overcoat.

Me ma looked aroun in desperation, an a woman nodded her head at me ma, mouthin, 'Keep away from him, he's not all there.'

I stood up. 'Ma! Leave it, you sit here, don't mind him,' an I headed fer the door.

'Where are ye goin?' me ma asked nervously.

'I'm not sittin beside him, but there's nowhere decent left te sit.'

'Jaysus! Tha's an awful pity we lost the seat. We'll never get a bit a sleep now!' me ma kept sayin.

'Look, Ma, go on, sit down. I'm just goin te take a wander. Ye'll be all right.'

An she looked at the seat an said, 'Well, don't be gone too long, then.'

I wandered aroun, feelin the boat rockin, an heard singin an laughin. An I followed the noise up the stairs an saw a crowd a men drinkin an laughin. The room was blue wit the smoke. I looked aroun an saw a gang a fellas hangin onta the counter an throwin back glasses a porter, an shoutin at each other an laughin. 'Go on there, me boy! Give us another belt.' An a big roarin red-neck culchie threw back his head an roared in a hoarse voice, 'When Irish eyes are smiling'.

'Tha's it! Tha's it!' roared a mallet-headed fella wit a flat nose, an threw back his head an lowered the glass a porter down his neck, an slammed the glass back on the counter, wipin his mouth wit the sleeve of his donkey jacket, an slammin his hobnailed boot hard down on the floor, an givin a scream like a red injun. 'Tha's the stuff!' he roared, lowerin his head an shakin his fist in the air.

I pushed me way through the crowd an stopped beside him. 'Hey, Mister!' I said, tappin yer man on his arm.

He looked down at me. 'Wha?' he barked.

'Isn't he a lovely singer?' I said, pointin at yer man croakin his lungs out, nearly stranglin himself throwin his head back, an the veins on his neck blue an stickin out.

'Ah, by Gawd, he's tha all right,' he agreed, noddin his head up an down, nearly tears in his eyes, an lowerin another pint a porter down his neck. 'Where did you come out of? Are ye lookin fer someone? Is it yer father ye're after?'

'No, Mister! I've got no father! He's dead.'

There was a silence while he tried te figure this out. I wasn't goin te tell him I had none, cos he wouldn't have any time fer me knowin I was a bastard. 'Tha's terrible!' he said. 'When did he die?'

'Eh! Before I was born!' He looked at me. 'Yeah! Me ma said he was drownded at sea, on the way back te Ireland.'

'Oh, tha's shockin! Shockin altogether!' he said, shakin his head an thinkin about it.

I looked closely at his face, an he was studyin mine. He's a boxer,

I thought, makin me face look very mournful. 'An what are ye doin in here?' he asked me. 'This is no place for you,' he said, lookin aroun at all the men drinkin.

'I lost me seat, Mister! I was sittin down beside me ma, ready te go te sleep, an a man came in an pulled me offa me own seat an took it fer himself, an me ma is nearly cryin. An the man won't take any notice of us when we tell him te give it back. An everyone is afraid te say anythin te him.'

'Is tha right now?' he said, his eyes narrowin.

'Yeah!' I said, shakin me head up an down sniffin. Me eyes was very sad altogether, lookin inta his face.

He tightened his jaw an took hold of me arm an said, 'Show me where this bowzie is!'

I rushed out, makin sure he was followin me. 'Go on, I'm right behind ye!' he said, in a hurry te meet the robber.

'There he is!' I pointed, pointin me finger at yer man stretched out in me ma's seat.

The boxer took a short run at yer man an lifted him by the coat an dragged him te his feet. Yer man's eyes swung aroun in his head, not knowin wha was happenin te him. His hat flew off, an he shook his head, 'Me hat! Where's me hat? Who are you?'

The boxer grabbed him by the arse of his trousers, an had another hand grabbin his coat tight aroun his neck, an rushed him out the door. 'Go on, ye blackguard! Pick on someone yer own size!'

'Me case! Gimme me case!' An the boxer dropped the man, who staggered, still tryin te figure out wha was happenin te him.

Then the boxer lunged in an grabbed the suitcase an smacked him wit it, sendin him flyin back up the passage. 'An don't be back here botherin people!' he shouted.

I stood stock still, an me ma's eyes was blinkin like mad. People were starin wit their mouths gapin open at the suddenness of it all. 'Are ye all right now?' he came steamin back inta the room an looked at me ma.

She nodded her head up an down, smilin, an said quietly, 'Yes! Thanks very much, I was afraid a me life a tha fella.'

The boxer looked aroun the room, an people who caught his eye nodded at him, sayin, 'I'm glad he's gone.' The hard man wit the nervous wife puffed out his cheeks an rolled his eyes. He said nothin but was lookin te say, 'I'm glad tha's over.'

'Ah, ye're all right now,' the boxer said te me, pattin me on the top of me head. 'He won't be back in a hurry.' Then he put his hand in his pocket an took out a roll a money, an peeled off a ten bob note an handed it te me. 'Here! Take tha fer yerself,' an he was gone.

I stood lookin at the red ten shillin note in me hand. An me ma said, 'Jaysus Christ! Who was tha, Martha?'

'Oh, just someone I met, Ma.' An I handed her the ten shillins an sat down in me ma's seat.

She laughed as she put the money wit the rest of it. Then me ma started te roar laughin. 'Yer man didn't know wha happened te him!' an she bent over, tryin te get the big laugh outa her.

Other people started laughin, an the woman who nodded at me ma said, 'Is he a relation of yours, love?'

'No!' I said. 'I never met him before in me life!'

There was silence fer a minute, an then everyone started te roar laughin. 'Ah, Jaysus! Tha's a good one! An tell us then, how did ye meet him?'

I told her wha happened, an everyone was listenin an laughin in between me story. An when I finished, they were rubbin their eyes an sniffin from all the enjoyment. 'Ah, but I think he was a poor unfortunate,' another woman said. 'He wasn't weighted down too heavily up there,' an she pointed te her head. People nodded their heads in agreement, lookin sad.

'I don't know about tha!' me ma said. 'He was mad in the right way te pick on her,' an me ma pointed te me.

'Oh! I don't know about tha,' the woman said. 'He certainly picked on the wrong one when he picked on tha child.' An everyone started roarin laughin again. An people started talkin te each other an tellin their stories, about why they were leavin Ireland, an who they were goin te stay wit until they got settled. Me ma listened, an I felt very tired an started te nod off, very content in meself.

34

I woke up, an me ma was shakin me. 'We're here, Martha!' she said quietly. I looked aroun, an everyone was gettin their things together an movin off. 'Come on!' me ma said. 'We have te try an get on the train.'

We followed the crowd off the ship an inta the station. 'Now boarding, the London for Euston,' the voice said comin outa the loudspeakers.

'Hurry,' me ma said. An I rushed after her through the crowd, listenin te the whistles blowin an the roar an the steam puffin outa the steam engines. An the noise of people's feet runnin on the platform, tryin te make it onta trains. An the different voices of the culchies, an the Dubliners, an the English, all mixed together. An the air smelt different. An the excitement ran through me. Nothin bad could happen te us now. We were on our own. An we didn't have te worry any more. Me ma jumped on the train, an I hesimitated, lookin down at the tracks, afraid I'd fall down. Then I gave a jump, an I was up. An the whistle blew, an the train shook, an the noise was deafenin, from the roar of the steam. An I followed me ma down the train, lookin fer a seat. 'Sit down here!' an we sat down next te the tilet. 'We'll stay here,' me ma whispered. 'An when we see the ticket collector comin, we'll hide in the tilet.'

'OK, Ma,' I said slowly, not sure. 'Ma! Won't he knock on the door te check if anyone's there wit a ticket?'

'We'll just have te take tha chance,' me ma said, lookin worried.

After a while, me ma got up an looked at me te follow. We went inta the tilet an locked the door. 'We'll stay here,' she said. 'It's safer.'

I held onta the sink, an she stretched her back against the wall. The train was rockin like mad an flyin. Nothin happened fer ages. An we just stayed quiet, waitin an listenin. Then there was a knock on the door, an we stared at each other, tryin te judge if it was the ticket collector. We heard the feet movin off after knockin again. Me ma raised her eyes te heaven an puffed out her cheeks. 'This waitin would kill ya,' she mouthed. I nodded me head, wishin it would end. Then the train stopped, after hours an hours of bein locked up. An we opened the door very slowly, puttin our heads out te see wha's happenin.

'Changin at Crewe for the London train!' an English voice was announcin.

'Come on, quick!' me ma said. 'We're gettin off. When's the next train fer London?' me ma asked the man in a uniform.

'Not for another forty minutes, Madam!'

'Grand!' me ma said, smilin te me. 'Come on, let's get a cup a tea.' We went inta the station café. 'You sit down over there, an I'll get us a sup a tea,' me ma said, headin over te join the queue at the counter. I watched me ma movin up the queue, an when it was her turn, an the woman handed her two cups a tea an saucers, I rushed over, takin the tea, an she carried over a plate a bread an butter. The bread was gone in no time. We were starvin. 'That'll have te do us,' me ma said. 'We have te go easy on the money.'

'Yeah!' I said, feelin very hungry after the lovely tea an bread.

We headed out onta the platform an climbed up onta the train fer London. 'Come on,' me ma said. 'We have te go easy on the money. We won't bother sittin down.' An we went straight inta the tilet.

It didn't take long fer people te start bangin on the door. 'Who's in there?' a woman's voice roared in, but we stayed quiet an listened te people complainin te each other outside.

'It's been locked for a long time. I'm sure there's someone in there! Open the door!' Someone banged wit their fists, but we didn't move an inch, just stared at each other, wonderin wha was goin te happen. Then the noise stopped, an we let out our breath.

'Jaysus!' me ma whispered. 'I can't take much more a this!'

We waited, wit the guts gettin shaken outa us from the rockin of the train, afraid te breathe too loudly. Then there was a big bang on the door, an a man's voice shouted, 'Tickets!' We held our breaths, afraid te move a muscle. Then another bang. 'Tickets, please! I'm waitin to check your tickets.' We opened our mouths, lettin air in an out without makin a sound. Then it went quiet, an we waited again, droppin our heads from one shoulder te another, afraid te make a sound.

A long time passed. But then sure enough there was another bang on the door. 'Tickets! Will you come out, please!' Me ma put her face in her hands, an I stared at the door. 'Open this door, please. I'm not leavin until you open the door!' Me ma dropped her hands, an she was white as a sheet. She put out the palms of her hands te show we were caught.

'I can't come out, Mister! I've an awful pain in me belly!' I moaned. 'Ah! Me stomach is killin me!' an I gave a big fartin noise outa me mouth, stickin me tongue out.

'How long are you in there?' he asked after a minute.

'Ah! Oh, me stomach. Just before you knocked. An I'm not comin out fer a long while,' I moaned, 'cos someone else got here before me. An they made me wait an hour.'

'All right, love, sorry to bother you.'

'Ah! Mammy! This is terrible,' I moaned. Then I opened me eyes after I heard his footsteps goin. An me ma was suffocatin herself, stuffin her coat in her nose an mouth, tryin te stop herself from laughin.

'God Almighty! I thought there fer a minute we were had.'

'He's gone, Ma!'

'Yeah! But he might come back.'

I slid against the sink, tryin te ease the stiffness in me. An we waited. At last! The train slowed down an then came te a stop. We waited until we heard the crowds movin an the doors openin, then we pulled the door open quickly an moved inta the crowds an got carried down the station, keepin our eye on the ticket collectors at the gate.

We moved past them quickly, without lookin at them. An we

were free! Out an onta the street, an we stood lookin at London. Red buses flyin up an down. Taxis, cars an crowds a people headin in all different directions. 'Where will we go, Ma?' I said, feelin I owned the world.

'Paddington!' me ma said. 'We'll go te Paddington.'

'Oh, Ma! This is the life. We made it!'

'Yeah!' me ma said, laughin. 'Come on this way. We'll go fer the bus.'

I knelt on the seat beside me ma, an we were on the bus headin fer Paddington. I stared inta the face of two black men wit woolly hair, talkin te each other in a foreign language. They stopped talkin when they saw me starin at them. An they stared back. I didn't blink, an just stared harder. I'd never seen a black person before. Only half-castes, but these men were black as the ace of spades. An their teeth was so white. An I wanted te study them.

'How did ye get so black?' I asked them.

Their mouths dropped, an they looked at each other, an one fella said, 'You are a very rude little girl!'

'Ye're very touchy!' I said, gettin annoyed. 'I only asked ye a civil question. An I wouldn't mind, but ye's weren't sayin tha when the nuns at school roared at us te bring in a penny te help the little black babbies an then bring in more money fer the missionary priests te go out an convert ye's all in Africa.'

I said it all in one big breath an then waited te hear wha they had te say. They just stared at me, sayin nothin. I was very annoyed. 'Yeah! But there's somethin else ye should know.' I paused; they waited. 'None of ye's got my penny, cos I wasn't bothered about any black babbies needin te know about God. Ye's could find tha out fer yerselves, cos I was spendin the penny on meself. So wha do ye's think about tha then?'

'Well!' yer man said, smilin at me. 'I think you were a very wise little girl.'

'Yes,' I said, feelin happier wit them. 'An I think them nuns kept back half the money fer themselves. Did ye's get much money from them?'

397

'No, we didn't!' they said, laughin.

An I was just beginnin te enjoy meself when me ma stood up an said, 'Come on! This is our stop.'

'I have te go now, we're gettin off,' an I waved at them. An they waved back, smilin.

We got off the bus, passin shops, an I wanted te wander in an have a look. 'No!' me ma said. 'We can't dilly-dally. We have te find somewhere te stay.'

'OK, Ma,' I said, rushin after her.

We passed the train station an then came te rows of big houses. Some were big houses wit steps up te them. An some had railins aroun them. Me ma was lookin from one side of the road te the other. 'To Let,' one sign said in the winda. 'No Irish! No dogs! No coloureds! No children!'

'They don't like the Irish, Ma,' I said.

'No! Too much trouble,' me ma said.

'Why, Ma?' I asked.

'Ah! They're always drinkin an fightin.'

'Yeah! Ye're right there, Ma. But no childre? They won't take me?'

'No!' me ma said. 'It's hard te get a room wit childre.' We walked on, lookin fer rooms te let.

'Ma!' I said. 'Tell them I'm yer sister. Ye'd pass fer tha, an maybe I'd get away wit tellin them I'm thirteen! Tha's not a child! Will we do tha, Ma?' I said, lookin at her. 'If ye tell them I'm eleven, they'll only keep shuttin the door on our faces. Them last three houses we knocked on just took one look at us an slammed the door. "No children," they roared when they saw me. So if you go in on yer own, an I'll wait up the road, we'll have a better chance.' Me ma looked at me, chewin her lip an thinkin. 'Try tha, Ma,' I said, feelin desperate. 'I'm gettin very tired. We've been walkin all day.'

'OK, I'll try in here, you wait aroun the corner,' me ma said.

I sat down on the steps of a big house te wait, hopin me ma would get somethin. It'd be lovely if she got somewhere fer us te stay. But how are we goin te pay fer it? Me ma's not great at findin her way aroun things. I'll have te start thinkin. But wha? I'm too tired te bother about anythin this minute. I just want te lie down an get a good sleep.

I pulled me frock aroun me knees, feelin the cold go up me now. It must be near the evenin. I watched people goin past, all in a hurry, goin in different directions. People looked at me an turned away, like I'm not supposed te be sittin here. A lot of them were better dressed than ye see in Dublin, but they didn't stop te talk te ye. Some of them give ye such a bad look ye'd think they were afraid of catchin a disease from me. Pity about them!

I heard knockin an looked aroun te see where it's comin from. An aul one wit a blue rinse in her hair an glasses on the end of her nose was starin at me like she wanted te commit murder. 'Go away, shoo!' she roared through the glass. I kept lookin, wonderin who she was tellin te shoo. I looked aroun me, but there was no dog shittin on her steps.

'Me!' I mouthed, puttin me hand te me chest.

'Yes!' she shook her head up an down.

I was ragin. 'I'm not a dog! Ye can't tell me te shoo!'

'I'm callin the police,' she roared.

'Fuck you an yer police!' I roared back. 'Ye aul hag.'

She dropped the curtain an rushed off. I stood fer a second, me chest still heavin up an down wit the rage! I'm not dirt, I thought. The cheek a her! Treatin me like an animal. Still, I'd better clear off. An I rushed aroun the corner, headin fer the house me ma went te. I was runnin up the steps, ready te ring the bell, when the door opened, an me ma came out wit a woman. Me ma was smilin. 'There ye are, I was just comin te get ye.'

I looked back te see if aul blue rinse was after me, an I puffed out, 'Ma! Wha's happenin?' An the two of them stopped te look at me. Me ma's face went red, an she started blinkin. I knew somethin was wrong, but wha?

'I thought you said she was your sister, and she certainly looks a lot younger than thirteen!' The woman was lookin at me, very annoyed, an then te me ma, waitin fer an answer. Ah, Jaysus! I gave the game away.

'Eh! Mrs, she is me sister, aren't ye, Kathleen?' Me ma blinked an coughed, lookin very confused altogether. 'But ye see, Mrs, she's been lookin after me since me granny died as a babby.'

'Your granny?'

'Eh! No, I only say tha cos I think more of her. Kathleen is like me mammy, ye see! An I am thirteen. I'm just very small fer me age. Ye're not alone at all, Mrs, fer thinkin me a child. I just look young, but I'm not! Everyone's always mistakin me fer a child!'

I looked at her, hopin she'd let us stay. She let go of me eyes an turned away, headin down the hall. 'I'm not really sure,' she was mutterin. 'My policy is no children. We only take workin people here.'

Me ma dug me in the ribs wit her elbow. 'I'll kill you! I told ye te stay outa sight,' she muttered through gritted teeth.

Ah, fuck! Nothin's goin right, I thought te meself as yer woman showed us inta the vacant room. 'This is the room, then.' I looked aroun. It was a single bed under the winda, wit one chair an a little wardrobe. The room was tiny, an there was room only fer one person at a time. The woman stood in the room an I peeped in the door, an me Ma leaned over me.

'Yeah!' me ma said happily. 'As I said, I'll take it! It will do us grand, won't it, Martha?'

'Oh, yeah! Ma! Kathleen.'

'Fine,' the woman said. 'Well, the rent, as I said, is three pounds a week, and you pay the first week in advance. So if you give me three pounds now, you can take the room.'

We all watched as me ma counted out the three pounds an handed it te the woman. She gave us a key fer the room but no hall door key. 'I'm always awake,' she said, 'providing you don't come back too late. I will answer the door and, please remember,' she said, lookin at me, 'you have to be quiet. We have people getting up very early and leaving for work.'

'Yes, Mrs!' I said.

'Thanks very much, Mam!' me ma said. An she was out the door an gone.

400

I looked at the bed an out the winda. Me ma looked aroun the room. 'Jaysus! I'll bet they used te keep the sweepin brushes in here,' me ma said, lookin very downhearted.

'Yeah,' I agreed. 'And the bed is very narra.'

Me ma looked at wha was left of our money, foldin up the ten bob I got from the boxer an countin the silver. 'Fifteen shillins an threepence! Tha's all we have left te last us.'

'Tha's not much, Ma. We're goin te have te find a way te live. An we're not stoppin here long.'

'No! We're gettin outa here as quick as we can,' me ma said, takin off her coat an shoes. 'Let's get inta tha bed, I'm worn out.'

'Good idea, Ma,' an I whipped off me shoes, sittin on the bed. 'Jaysus! Lookit, Ma. Holes in me shoes, they're gone. An me socks are in ribbons as well.'

'Ah!' me ma said. 'Mine are not much better, an I haven't even got a comb te tidy me hair.'

'Ah, never mind, Ma, we'll be grand,' I said, pullin the frock over me head an divin under the white sheets an blankets. Me ma climbed in beside me, an I was squeezed inta the wall. 'Give us a bit a room, Ma! I'm suffocatin.'

She laughed an pushed out a bit. 'You an yer sister. An then tellin her I'm Kathleen.'

'Yeah, Ma! Ye never give them yer right name.'

'I know tha. But then the poor aul one was blind, bothered an bewildered when ye started on about the granny! She knows bloody well we're tellin her a pack of lies!' We laughed our heads off, an then I snuggled inta me ma's back an started te doze off.

I woke up, shootin me eyes open, an me ma was sittin on the side of the bed. Me heart lifted. We're in London! I sat up an looked out the winda. Traffic was flyin, an people were on the move. 'God, Ma, we slept. It's late!'

'Yeah! It must be aroun the eleven mark. We better get movin before tha aul one comes in an starts askin questions.'

'Right, Ma! Let's go,' I said, jumpin outa the bed an inta me frock, an puttin on me dirty socks wit no feet in them, the hole went right up the back, an the shoes wit the soles gone outa them. I wet me fingers an pressed me hair down, waitin fer me ma te button up her coat.

'Right! Have we got everythin?' she said, lookin aroun the room.

'Yeah! Have ye got the money?' I asked.

'Yeah, I have it here,' an she pressed her hand on her pocket, an we headed out the door. We walked down the long hall wit the strip of carpet in the middle an doors on the left an stairs leadin down te the basement.

The door down the stairs opened, an the landlady poked her head out. 'Are you off out, then?'

'Yes,' me ma said. 'We're just goin out. We won't be back until later.' An she slammed the door an went back in, takin the lovely smell a rashers an sausages wit her. 'Miserable aul cow!' me ma muttered under her breath. 'Hope she chokes on her rashers. God forgive me!'

'Yeah, Ma! No fear of her offerin us any,' I said, bangin the door behind me.

We went down the steps, an the excitement hit me on seein all the strange people an cars an red buses. A policeman wit a huge helmet on his head an a string under his chin was rockin backwards an forwards on his heels. He was standin on the edge of the footpath watchin the traffic. 'Lookit him, Ma, a policeman.' I stood te stare. Then a woman in a brown fur coat, holdin a little white poodle on a lead, walked past. 'Look, Ma, a poodle.'

'Yeah! Come on!' me ma said, walkin on.

I stooped down te pet the poodle, an it yelped an bit me. I whipped me hand back, suckin it, an the woman whipped the dog up inta her arms, sayin, 'Oh! Mamma's little Tiddles got a fright from that naughty child,' an she glared at me.

'The cheek a you, Mrs!' I roared. 'Tha thing nearly took the hand offa me.'

'How dare you touch my dog!' she screamed, an marched off.

I watched her go, an then I saw the policeman lookin at me, an I whirled aroun lookin fer me ma, an she was gone! 'Ma! Ma!' I roared, runnin up the street, wonderin where she'd got te without me. I couldn't see any sign of her, an it hit me, I'm lost! 'Where are ye, Mammy?' I screamed in rage an fright. I ducked in an outa the crowds a people, an when I got te the traffic light, I didn't know which way te go. Cross here or turn right, which way? Me face was gettin hot, an I was startin te cry. She's gone off an left me! I ran halfway across the road an then turned back, runnin inta cars an buses, an makin them stop, an headed up the right turn instead, an kept runnin.

Then I heard me name called, an stopped, lookin aroun at the crowds te see where the voice was comin from. 'Martha! Here! Here I am!' I couldn't see her. I was whirlin all aroun, runnin up an down lookin fer her. 'Over here, Martha!' An I looked on the other side a the road, an there she was, standin an wavin at me outside a café.

'Ma!' I roared, delighted te clap eyes on her again. I raced across the road, not waitin fer the traffic te stop. An they all honked their horns at me. An I leapt onta the footpath, roarin at me ma. 'Ye left me! Ye went off an left me,' I said, cryin.

'I was here,' me ma said, laughin. 'Waitin fer ye, but ye didn't see me. Ye ran off in the opposite direction.'

I looked at her an thought, there's nothin te laugh at. I didn't want te talk te her.

'Come on in here, an we'll get a pot a tea,' she said, tryin te make peace wit me. I followed her in an we sat down at a table.

'What are you hollerin about?' a workman sittin at the next table wit another fella asked me, laughin an shovellin a big plate a rashers, an sausages, an beans, an fried bread inta his mouth.

Me ma laughed. 'Oh! She's a devil,' me ma said. 'She won't stay wit me. Every time I look aroun, she's gone.'

The waitress came over an me ma asked fer a pot a tea. 'An bread an butter, Ma!' I said.

'No!' me ma said. 'The prices in here are too dear. We'll get a loaf a bread later an a bit a cheese in the shops. I have te watch the money,' she said, leanin inta me. But I could see the men were listenin. They never took their eyes offa us.

'Are you over from Ireland?' they asked me ma.

'Yes! An we're still tryin te find our way aroun.' The waitress put the pot a tea on the table, an me ma poured it out, puttin plenty a milk in.

'I've got a place across the street. I'm doin it up now if you want to come and take a look. The rooms are big, and the rent is cheap. It shouldn't take me too long te finish it. Do you want to come?'

Me ma looked at me. 'Tha would be lovely if we got somewhere of our own. Wouldn't it, Martha?'

'Yeah, Ma! Let's go an take a look,' I said, delighted. We drank our tea, emptyin the pot, an the men waited fer us an brought us across the street an inta a hall an closed the front door behind us. I looked up at the high ceilins, an the plaster was gone off the walls. An there was no staircase, only a ladder leanin against the landin.

'Come on!' the man said te me, pushin me up the ladder.

'Oh! I'm not gettin on tha,' me ma said, lookin at the ladder. 'I'm afraid of me life a heights.'

'It's no bother,' he said, pushin me up the ladder. Then I was on the landin, an the man was takin me arm. I was lookin down at the ladder, an me ma wasn't comin up. 'In here,' he said te me, pullin me inta a room wit only a bed an shuttin the door. I stood lookin aroun, wonderin wha was happenin. An he pulled down his trousers, exposin his horrible hairy arse an the long thing stickin out between his legs. Me heart started te pound, an he grabbed me an threw me down on the bed. An he pulled up me frock an tore me knickers, rippin them offa me body wit one hand, an holdin me chest down wit his other hand. I started te panic an kicked me legs tryin te turn meself. An he was on top of me an tryin te push tha horrible thing inta me. The pain was like a red-hot knife, an I gave a piercin scream. He stopped an grabbed a pilla te put under me arse. 'Now, now! This won't hurt you,' he kept sayin.

'Let me go! Please, Mister!' I was whimperin. I could hear me ma askin fer me downstairs, but she wasn't comin up. The man tried te push himself inta me again. An I started te get sick. But I couldn't breathe then, cos he was on top a me. An he kept pushin, an the

404

pain, an tryin te get sick. I could feel everythin goin dark.

Then it was light again, an the pressure was gone, an the pain like a knife goin through me was stopped. An the man was kneelin over me an wipin himself wit the blanket. An me belly an between me legs was sticky wit somethin, an it was just like Jackser all over again. I jumped up, feelin a terrible pain between me legs. An I was standin on the floor, lookin fer me knickers an me shoes. I saw me pink knickers on the bed, an I couldn't put them on, cos they were torn, an I bent down te put on me shoes. I was shakin an afraid fer me life. Cos I didn't know wha he might do te me next.

Then he went te the door an opened it, an I was grateful te be gettin outa here. An I followed behind him. But he pushed me back, an the other man was outside, an he smiled an came in. I started te make whimperin noises, an I could hear me ma sayin, 'What are ye doin te her up there?' An I screamed, 'Mammy!' An the man came in, an the other fella said, 'Don't worry! I'll see yer woman downstairs won't bother you. I'll keep her occupied.'

I wanted te scream, but I was afraid they would hurt me mammy. Somethin was tellin me not te panic, or it would make things worse an they might harm us. But I had te find a way out. 'Please, Mister! Don't touch me! I want me mammy! Just let me go!' I was tryin te back away from him an make him change his mind about wantin te hurt me. An not get on the wrong side of him in case he turned vicious an murdered us.

'Get on the bed!' he said. He was younger than the first man an jumped on top of me an was pressin even harder. The pain was nothin like anythin I ever had before. I gave a piercin scream, an he pushed even harder.

'Police!' I screamed, not carin, wantin the pain te stop. He put his hand over me mouth, an I was suffocatin. I'm dyin! It won't last, I can't breathe, an the pain is wha hell is. I was flyin through a tunnel. It was gettin darker now, an the noise in me ears, an the terrible pain, an the man's heavy breathin, an the panic, is goin further away. I'm leavin it behind, an I know I'm dyin. An I don't really mind, cos then it will be all over.

'Are you all right?' The man was starin inta me face, lookin worried an annoyed. I didn't know wha was goin on. 'Ye blacked out!' he shouted inta me face. He was slappin me cheeks an shakin me aroun by me shoulders, an I was sittin up by the side of the bed. He was tryin te get me on me feet, but I couldn't stand. I was made of air, an me legs wouldn't work.

The older man came inta the room, lookin down at me. 'Is she all right?' He looked worried.

'Yeah! She'll be all right. Just a blackout!' the younger fella said, brushin his hair back wit his hand, sayin, 'I want te get out of here. I thought she was a goner!'

'No, we'll get her out.'

It was comin back te me, an I wanted te stand an go as fast as I could. I stood up, feelin me legs like jelly, an held onta the bed. An I started te make me way te the door. 'There you go,' said the older man. 'She's right as rain.' Then he put his hand inta his pocket an handed me six shillins. I looked at it, not wantin the money. He's no right te give me money after wha they did te me. It's like he's sayin we're quits. Givin me six shillins means he did me no wrong, but I didn't give it back. Instead, I made me way te the ladder an went down backwards, holdin on tight, afraid I would fall, cos I was so weak. An I felt me legs like jelly. I got te the last step, an the men came down after me.

Me ma was standin at the end of the ladder, an her face was shakin, an her mouth was twitchin. 'Wha happened?' she looked at me an then at them. Nobody said anythin. An I headed fer the door, desperate te get out. 'Wha did youse do te her?' me ma asked, lookin at them an followin me.

They laughed, an the older man said, 'Ah! She's all right,' an he opened the door, an I rushed out wit me head down, feelin at the mercy of everythin an everyone. He slammed the door shut behind us, an me ma said nothin. When I handed her the six shillins, sayin, 'The man gave me that, Ma! You take it,' she gave me a queer look, like I'd done somethin terrible wrong. An somehow I felt very old an like I wasn't like ordinary childre. An men weren't like the daddy

I wanted them te be. Ye have te be a child te have a daddy. An I wasn't a child, even though I still felt like one. But I'd have te give tha up an watch meself. Ye can't take chances wit people. Most men will hurt ya, an there's nothin at all me ma can do fer me. So women are not much good either.

I hurried away, walkin close te the wall, wantin te touch it. Afraid of everythin – people, noise. I stopped te retch, tryin te get sick, but only the tea came up quickly, then I couldn't bring anythin else up. But I was still heavin me stomach. Then I stopped an leaned against the wall, lookin at the ground. 'Wha's wrong wit ye?' me ma asked, leanin down te look in me face.

I lifted me eyes, sayin nothin, an tried te wipe away the dribbles hangin outa me mouth. 'I gorra shock, Ma,' I mumbled.

'Jaysus! Ye're the colour of a corpse!' me ma said, shakin. 'Them bastards!' an she looked back te where we'd come from.

I walked on, wantin te be somewhere else. I didn't want te talk te me ma. There was nothin she could do. Maybe if she'd lost her head, they might have murdered the two of us – I sensed tha. Maybe we're lucky te be alive! God! Why did I not see it comin! I didn't even think they were interested in me ma. I usually keep wide awake te men. Ye can usually see it comin a mile away. Men are always interested in goin after me ma. I see them lookin at her. An even the ones who go after childre, they're easy te spot, the way they mooch up te ya. An ye can get away from them. But not this time! Lord God, I fell inta their trap. There's nothin but Jacksers everywhere. God, why can't I just die? But I don't want tha, an I don't want te live either. I just feel afraid of me life.

'Come on!' me ma said, clampin her mouth tight an lookin away from me. 'Let's get movin.'

We walked slowly together, not sayin anythin. 'Where are we goin, Ma?' I asked after a while.

'I don't know,' she muttered, not lookin at me.

She doesn't want te be wit me either, I thought. She's actin as if I've done somethin wrong on her. I looked at her, an she turned her face away. I don't care about you either, Ma, I thought. Ye can be as fed up as ye want, I'm not bothered about anythin. Wha's the point in tryin te be happy? It doesn't last. One minute I'm feelin very happy, an the next it's gone. The only thing tha lasts is misery. People are no good. Ye never know when they're goin te strike an do ye real harm if ye let them get the chance. The heart was gone outa me. An I just wanted te go te bed an sleep. I was still feelin sick an shivery.

'Ma, let's go back te the room!'

'Wha?' me ma said, lookin at me sideways.

I didn't like tha look she was givin me. 'I'm tired. I want te go an rest meself.'

She said nothin, just tightened her mouth more an looked away, not wantin te see me.

'I'm goin back,' I said. 'I'll find me own way.' Not carin wha she said. An I turned aroun ready te find the way we came.

'Wait!' she said. 'Ye can't go back now or tha aul one will be askin awkward questions. Come on, we'll go te the pictures.' She was lookin at me now, but when I tried te look inta her face, she looked away. Not able te look at me. 'Come on, we'll go in here.' An she went up the street an inta a picture house. I followed her in, an we walked inta a very plush place wit all red soft seats. The usherette took the tickets an showed us up the back, shinin her torch te find the way. An the advertisements was on, showin a woman wit long hair ridin a horse on a beach. The music was lovely. An we sat down. Somehow the music made me feel very lonely, an tears rolled down me cheeks. Where's God? He's supposed te care fer me, but I know he's not bothered. Why can't I be happy fer long? Why doesn't it last? If only I'd never been born, then I wouldn't have te worry about livin or dyin. But now I'm stuck. Me mind had wandered, an the fillum was started, *The Three Faces of Eve*, an the actress was Joanne Woodward. I sat starin, not takin it in.

35

I woke up sensin there was somethin different. Me eyes looked aroun the room. It was quiet! Me ma! Where's me ma? I shot up in the bed. She's gone! Me heart started poundin, an I jumped outa the bed. I wanted te scream, 'Help! Me ma's gone! She's left me!' But I held it back, an I was makin keenin noises outa me chest. No! No! Maybe she's just gone out te the tilet. I opened the door an listened. Nothin, not a sound, it was too quiet. I wanted te go out an look, but I'm afraid someone will see me. I don't want te talk te anyone. I shut the door, easy, an crept back over te the bed. Why would she leave me? An where's she gone? If she was comin back, she'd a woke me an told me te wait. Maybe she got fed up wit me not wantin te say much. An I wasn't bothered about gettin us anythin or even comin up wit ways te get us some money. I didn't listen when she kept complainin te herself about what are we goin te do, an the money is nearly runnin out.

In another two days, the landlady will be after us fer the rent. An I don't know wha we're goin te do then! Maybe tha's why she's gone an left me. Cos I'm only draggin outa her now. I'm no help any more. Yeah! Tha's wha's happened. She's decided she's better off on her own. I heard noises out the winda, an I looked out, hopin it was me ma. No! Only two women stoppin te talk te each other an laughin. One was holdin a shoppin basket wit vegebales an fruit stickin out. Me heart dropped, an I leaned me head against the winda, feelin like a babby, keenin an moanin, 'Ma! Mammy! Where are ye, Ma? I want ye. Don't leave me, Ma!' I was moanin quietly, knowin nobody could hear me, cos I didn't want anyone te see

409

me actin foolish. But it helped me, an rockin meself backward an forward stopped me from losin me head an goin mad wit the fear. I kept rockin meself fer an awful long time. An me moanin an keenin has stopped. An I'm just rockin gently an listenin te me breathin an watchin the daylight goin. An the street lamps are comin on, an it's beginnin te drizzle. People are hurryin an puttin up umbrellas an tryin te hold them te stop them blowin away. An it's gettin very windy, an suddenly it's gettin darker. An I look aroun at the door, an no one is goin te come in, an I'm safe in here. The landlady won't knock, cos she won't bother until Saturday, when she's due the rent again. So I'm OK.

I sat meself in the middle of the bed, restin me chin on me knees, an held onta me legs tight. Rockin meself an hummin, 'I see the moon! The moon sees me!' I keep hummin an hummin. I liked tha song. I used te sing it when I was very young an I was happy, just me an me ma, an me aunt Nelly an me cousin Barney. Me heart is jerkin at the thought of them times. I want them back, I want te be happy again. But noooo . . . they're gone. I'm singin te meself, an now the tears are pourin down me cheeks. An I want someone te hear me. Maybe God is listenin! Or someone who won't laugh at me an think I'm foolish. Maybe there's a ghost in the room. I look aroun seein the walls an the little brown wardrobe. An lookin at the chair wit me frock an me cardigan sittin on it, an me shoes wit the big holes in them. One is sittin on its side, an I stare at the big hole, then I look at the dark corners of the room. I'm not afraid if there's a ghost. Cos it might even be like Casper, the friendly ghost in the comic books. He won't laugh at me or call me names or try an hurt me. He'll like me, an we can play together. He'd talk te me an tell me all sorts a things. An he'd treat me like I'm not any different from other people. An when I'd cry, he'd know it's cos I'm very sad cos nobody's really bothered about me. Yeah! That'd be nice.

It's very dark now, an I listen. No, there's nobody here. No Casper, no ghost, an God's not listenin, or he wouldn't leave me on me own. I rubbed me arms, an they're like ice. It's only just hittin me now, I'm freezin wit the cold. I move up an cover meself wit the sheet an blankets. An curl meself inta a ball. Ah! Tha's better. I'll have a good sleep fer meself, an I know what I'll do. Tomorrow I'll go out an look fer me mammy. I'll keep on walkin the streets until I find her. An I won't talk te anybody, cos tha's too dangerous. Yeah! Tha's what I'll do. An I felt meself liftin. I know wha te do.

I was fast asleep when the light suddenly went on an me ma appeared outa nowhere. I lifted me head tryin te see, but the light was blindin me. 'Is tha you, Ma?' I was shieldin me eyes, an they were stingin me.

'Yeah! I'm back!' she said, smilin. Me heart leapt wit excitement. An then I had the fear I might be just dreamin.

'Am I awake, Ma?' I asked her, lookin inta her face te make sure she was real.

'Wha's wrong wit ya?' she asked, laughin. 'Were ye fast asleep?'

I looked at her puttin down a loaf a bread an a little box a cheese. An a bottle a milk an a bar a chocolate. An a big packet a newspapers filled wit fish an chips. She put them all on the bed. 'Tha bread an cheese will do us in the mornin,' she said, takin off her coat. I watched her in wonder. She looked very happy, an I couldn't believe all this was happenin te me. 'Come on!' she said. 'Eat these while they're still hot.' An she opened the newspaper an handed me a big piece a fish.

The smell nearly kilt me. I took a big bite, an it was gone down me neck in only a few chews. An I polished the rest off an dipped me hand in the newspaper again an took out a handful of chips. 'Here!' me ma said, handin me the bottle a milk. 'Take a sip a this. Oh! I'm enjoyin this, them chips is lovely,' she said, puttin a handful in her mouth.

'Where were ye, Ma? I was worried!'

'Wha?' she said.

'Why did ye go off on yer own without tellin me?'

'Ah! I had te hurry, an you were sleepin. An I knew I'd be quicker on me own!'

'But where did ya go te?'

'Ah! Don't be talkin,' me ma said, laughin. 'Where didn't I get

411

te, would be more the question. Look!' she said. 'We've plenty a money.' An she counted out eleven pounds!

'Where did ye get all a tha money?' I whispered, not believin me eyes.

'Well! First, I went down te the Welfare Office an got money offa them fer the rent. Tha aul one gave me a letter statin we're livin here. An money fer our keep. Then I went te see someone I used te know, an I got a few pounds from them. An I went inta a café in one a them big shops. An they were offerin work in the kitchen. So I started tha straight away.' Then she started laughin an nearly choked on a chip. 'Jaysus!' she said, wipin her nose an eyes wit the sleeve of her cardigan. 'They put me in the scullery wit a mile long a pots an pans, an gave me a big rubber apron, down te me ankles, an a huge pair a rubber boots, an told me te get crackin. I thought the money was grand until I saw what I was lettin meself in fer! I was swimmin in water. "Ah, no!" I said, after I dragged meself up on me feet after then scrubbin huge floors. "This won't suit me at all. Ye can give me the wages I've earned, I'm not comin back."'

I couldn't believe me ma took a job! I didn't think she had tha in her. I looked at her in wonder. She seemed different somehow, younger! 'How old are ye, Ma?'

'Who, me?' me ma asked. 'Eh! I'm twenty-seven.'

'Tha's young, Ma! Not very old at all,' I said, thinkin me ma could look lovely if she did herself up. 'Ma! We'll be able te pay the rent!'

'Wha? No! We're not stayin here. Tomorrow, we'll go te Shepherd's Bush te the markets. An we'll go te Petticoat Lane. We need te get ourselves a few clothes. I'll be glad te see the back a these rags we're wearin. Then on Saturday, we'll head off te Birmingham. Come on. I'm gettin inta bed before the legs drop offa me.' An she tidied away the food an put the papers under the bed. An put out the light an pulled off her frock an climbed in beside me. I snuggled up te her back, feelin I was on top of the world an God is lookin after us, an I was happy knowin He's still there.

We got off the bus at Shepherd's Bush markets. An me ma was in a hurry. 'Come on, Martha!' she said, laughin, an her head was flyin

412

from one side te the other tryin te decide wha te look at first. 'Ah! We need te get ourselves a bag,' she said, rushin off.

'Wait, Ma, I don't want te get lost!'

'Come on,' she said, hurryin. 'We've nothin te carry the stuff in.' She flew past stalls, an then her eyes lit on a pile a suitcases an shoppin bags an handbags. Me ma picked up a big suitcase an winked at me. The market was crowded, but there was only another woman beside us browsin at the handbags. An the owner was sittin on a big high stool drinkin a mug a tea an suckin on a cigarette. He was watchin his stuff like a hawk.

'Come on, Ma,' I said, pullin her sleeve.

'Ah, wait,' she said, smilin. 'Gimme time.' Then she picked up a big leather shoppin bag. 'How much is this? Eh, Mister?' An she gave a little cough an a laugh.

Yer man held the cigarette in the corner of his mouth, closin one eye against the smoke pourin in an sized me ma up wit the other. 'Ten bob! An that's cheap. You'll pay fifteen bob in the High Street.' He saw me ma's face drop. 'But I'll tell yer wot I'll do! I'll let yer have it fer eight bob. An I'm robbin meself. But I likes the look a you!'

'Come on, Ma!' I roared, an I moved off.

'Ah, tha's very dear!' me ma said te me back as I walked off.

I walked up a bit an waited fer her te catch up. 'Did ye not like tha, Martha? Tha bag would suit us grand,' she said, chewin her lip.

'No, Ma! We can't afford te pay tha kind a money on just a bag. An tha fella is a robber.'

'Yeah! Pity, though,' me ma said, lookin woebegone. 'But we need te see if we can get somethin te carry stuff in first.'

'Yeah! Wait until there's a crowd aroun him, then we'll whip it,' I said.

We moved on, stoppin at a stall wit mounds a clothes. 'Look at this!' me ma said, liftin up a brown coat tha was doin the rounds when Queen Victoria was livin. 'Go on! Try it on,' me ma said. 'It'll keep ye nice an warm. There's nothin wrong wit it.'

I put the coat on, an it had a mangy fur collar. It felt damp, an the linin was torn, an there was a hole in one of the pockets. It was faded an old lookin, like it had definitely seen better days. 'Tha's grand on ye,' me ma said, standin back te look.

'Yeah, OK, Ma, it will do,' I said, lookin up te see if there was anyone watchin. I kept the coat on an moved away. I had no intention of even givin the time a day fer the coat never mind partin wit money.

I looked back te see how things were at the bag stall, an there was a few people moochin aroun. The owner was arguin the price wit a man holdin a suitcase. He was puttin it down an walkin off, an yer man was chasin him wit the case. 'All right! All right! I'll tell yer wot I'll do.' An the man turned back.

'Quick, Ma! Grab the bag!' I flew down lookin fer it, an me ma rushed over, pickin it up from the back.

'Here it is!' she whispered, liftin her eyebrows an lookin aroun te see if anyone was watchin.

'Give it te me!' an I grabbed the bag, puttin it down by me side an throwin a glance at yer man who was still arguin an pushin the suitcase inta the other man's hand. His back was turned te me. An I turned aroun an slowly headed off in the opposite direction. We kept walkin until we were outa sight an then stopped at a stall wit a huge mountain a clothes. I couldn't reach up. 'Tha's beautiful,' me ma said, pickin up a jumper fer herself an rollin it inta a ball, an winkin down at me, an flickin it over the edge te land in the new bag. I was holdin it open! Nobody could see me over the clothes. So all I had te do was wait fer them te drop an catch them in the bag an squash them down in the blink of an eye an wait fer more.

'How much is them lovely sheets over there, Mrs?' me ma said, pointin te the back of the woman. Skirts, slips, knickers an shoes landed in me bag. An shoes banged me in the face, cos me ma was busy concentratin on the woman. I leaned forward te catch the stuff fallin te the ground an got the buckle of a belt in the eye. 'Ah, no, not them, the other ones!' me ma roared te the woman.

I had te slap the leg of a fat woman tha was standin on me hand. 'Ah, my Gawd!' she screamed, jumpin back an lookin at me.

'Sorry, Mrs! I'm tryin te fix me shoe, an ye stood on me.' I jumped up, liftin the heavy bag twice the size of meself, an took off lookin like I was goin on me holidays wit all the clothes. Me ma hurried after me, an I was strugglin wit two hands tryin te carry it. 'Grab the bag, Ma!' I puffed. An she looked back te make sure no one was after us an grabbed the bag, hurryin off laughin.

We kept movin. Then I spotted a stall wit boxes a soap an lovely smellin things, an I stopped te get a look, sayin, 'Wait, Ma, look!'

'There's towels,' me ma said, eyein the pile a new towels. I picked up a box of smellin stuff wit soap an slid it under me arm. Then I examined a towel, an when no one was lookin, I folded it up an moved off. 'Come on,' me ma said. 'We have enough.'

We got off the bus in Paddington an hurried back te the room. Me ma emptied the bag out onta the bed. I grabbed a frock an held it up te get a look. Me ma was examinin a black skirt. 'How does this look, Ma?' I said, standin back an straightenin meself up.

'It's a bit big fer ye.'

I looked. Yeah, it's fer a big young one twice the size a me. It was swimmin on me an halfway down me legs. 'Here!' me ma said. 'Put them on ya.' I tried on a big blue pair a knickers, an the legs dropped down past me knees.

I kept lookin at them. 'These are fer women, Ma. They don't fit me!' I said, disappointed.

Me ma was tryin te squeeze herself inta the black skirt. 'They'll keep ye warm,' me ma said, puttin her hand on her mouth an laughin.

'Ye're makin a laugh a me!' I roared.

'No!' she said, searchin fer the other stockin an lookin at me holdin up me frock an starin at the size of me knickers. 'Where's the other nylon te go wit this?' An she held up the stockin. 'Ah! There it is!' I watched her puttin on the nylons. I'd never seen her put anythin on her legs before. 'Ah, fuck!' she said when she stood up te admire herself an the nylons fell down. 'I've nothin te hold them up wit!'

I picked up a big red, white an blue jumper wit Ba, Ba, Black Sheep on it. I pulled it over me head, an it went down te me knees.

I stood back, wonderin if I was lovely in it or not. 'Wha do ye think, Ma?'

'Eh! It's lovely! Keep ye nice an warm.' I examined her face te see if she was tellin the truth. She put her hand te her mouth an turned away.

'Where's the jumper I got fer meself?' she said, buryin her head in the clothes. 'Ah! Here it is!' An she held up a tight-fittin baby-blue jumper an held it up te the skirt.

'Ye're laughin at me, Ma!' I roared. 'Cos ye know I look like someone let outa Grangegorman fer the day!'

Me ma roared laughin. 'Come on,' she said. 'Keep lookin! There must be somethin decent here te wear. Oh, look! There's a lovely pair a navy-blue gaiters tha should fit ye.'

I whipped the trousers on, an the strap under me feet was a bit long, an they hung down in rolls. I'm not wearin them. They're too big. I whipped them off. 'Do ye like tha?' me ma asked, standin back te admire her jumper an skirt.

'Yeah! But ye're all hangin down in the front, Ma.'

'Hold on,' she said. 'There must be a brassiere here somewhere. I know I saw one. I had it in me hand a minute ago. Oh, look, Martha! Here's the boots I got ya. They should fit ya.'

I looked at them. All fur on the inside an a zip up the side. I shot me feet inta them an zipped them up, lookin down at meself. They were grand, just a little bit big. But they didn't look right wit me bare legs an frock. Somethin was missin. I whipped them off an put the trousers back on an took off the frock. An now I was standin in me boots wit the trousers pushed inside them an the jumper on top. An I stood back happily. 'Wha do ye think, Ma?'

'Yeah! Them's lovely!'

I walked up an down, feelin inches bigger in me furry boots. An I was lovely an warm in me knickers an trousers. An the jumper looked lovely now, over me trousers.

'Wha do ye think of this?' me ma said, smilin an lookin down at herself, movin from side te side.

'God, Ma! Ye look lovely! Did ye get the jacket te match?'

'Yeah!' she said. 'It's a suit.'

I stood back lookin at the lovely black suit. The jacket fitted her grand, an she looked lovely in the jumper. An her diddies were standin up an pointin wit the brassiere on, an I'd never seen her look like tha before. 'Wait till ye see these,' an she put on a pair of black patent high-heel shoes an tried te balance herself walkin up an down. She kept wobblin, an I roared laughin. 'Come on,' she said, takin them off, 'before I break me neck. Let's put these away, an we'll go up te tha Woolworths. There's a few things I need. I want te get a bit of elastic te keep me nylons up. An we'll buy a comb. An I might even get a tube a lipstick. Then we'll get somethin te eat. We'll get ourselves fish an chips.'

'Right, Ma. Hurry!' I said, all excited.

The landlady slammed the front door after us as we left the house. 'She's ragin, Ma, cos ye didn't give her the rent.'

'Let her rage! We only stayed a few extra days.'

We made our way fer the bus. Me ma tryin te balance on her high heels. 'Take it easy! Stop pullin at me an hold the bag up. I'm goin te break me neck in these high heels,' me ma roared.

'I am, Ma! But we'll never get te Euston station if ye don't walk faster.'

'Ah! Holy Jaysus, wait! Me nylons is slippin down.'

I dropped the handle of the bag te watch me ma. She took a quick look aroun te see if anyone was watchin an then pulled the stockins up under her skirt an put a tighter knot in the elastic. A big whistle came from somewhere, an me ma's head spun aroun, an she tore her skirt down. 'Cor! What a gorgeous bit a stuff!' An aul fella pedallin his bicycle winked an nodded his head at me ma as he puffed past.

'Ye dirty aul sod, ye!' me ma roared after starin at him wit her mouth open. He turned his head back, blowin kisses at me ma. An she laughed an picked up the handle of the bag, sayin, 'Go easy. We'll get there if ye take yer time.'

The bus arrived, an we tried te get on. 'Hold this! Take the bag!' me ma said, tryin te grab a hold of the bar an haul herself up. I took the

417

bag an watched her hoppin her leg up an down, tryin te get onta the platform. But her skirt was too tight. 'Jaysus!' she panted. 'Give us a hand, Martha!' but the conductor flew past me an grabbed me ma aroun the waist an hoisted her up wit his arms wrapped aroun her, an her exposin the tops of her stockins an the legs of her knickers. 'Ah, Jaysus! Put me down,' she laughed, tryin te fix her skirt an pull up the stockins tha rolled down. Everyone was leanin forward te get a good look. An the men clapped, an some of the older women muttered te each other tha she was disgraceful!

I walked down the bus lookin fer an empty seat, an everyone was laughin. 'Wait, Martha,' me ma roared, makin a show of me. An she was laughin, makin herself even more foolish. I sat down, pushin meself inta the winda an stared out, not mindin me ma talkin te herself an laughin about not bein used te the high heels.

The conductor came rushin up an wrapped his arm aroun the back of me ma. An rested himself against the seat an sang. 'You are my heart's desire,' an then whispered somethin in her ear. Me ma roared laughin, delighted wit herself.

'Oh! Tha's shockin,' she said. I ignored them, an the rest of the people, all gapin. I wish she wasn't actin so foolish. Ye'd think she was a young one, the way she's carryin on. Not like a mammy should.

'Is this your little daughter?' he asked me ma.

'Eh?' said me ma.

'Yes, I am!' I roared. An I was just about te tell him she had five more when I saw the look on me ma's face. An I knew I'd hurt her. I'd said enough. An I turned back te the winda. They went quiet then an started talkin about the weather.

'This is our stop,' me ma said, gettin up. I took hold a the bag an dragged it down the bus, leavin the conductor te help me ma off.

'Be seein you!' he winked at me ma, holdin out his hands, still feelin the weight of me ma in them.

She was laughin. 'Wait, take yer time!' she said, clatterin after me. I was holdin the bag wit me two hands an tryin te get ahead so people wouldn't know I was wit her. 'Hold on, me nylons!' An she stopped again te pull up her skirt.

'Ah, fuck off!' I screamed, makin a show of meself an not carin who heard me.

I puffed me way inta the station. This bleedin bag is too big an awkward te carry! I stopped an looked aroun, most of the seats was taken up. A lot a them by down an outs. I pushed past an aul woman takin up a whole bench te herself wit all her old newspapers an rags tied up wit bits a twine.

An aul fella in a dirty raincoat wit a shoppin bag under his arm an a greasy aul cap pulled down over his eyes, an a cigarette stickin outa his mouth, leanin against the pillar an watchin everythin goin on, spotted me, an his face lit up. I saw him look aroun te see if anyone was wit me. An he slowly made his way in my direction. I stopped an stared right back at him, givin him a dirty look. An he stopped an looked away, surprised I was onta him, but he didn't move off. He would wait fer a chance te try an get me if he thought I was on me own. I watched the door, waitin fer me ma. 'There ye are!' she shouted, wavin an laughin at me. When she appeared, I watched yer man move off in a hurry an disappear out the other door when he saw I wasn't on me own.

'Come on, Ma. Let's go inta the tilet, an you can change outa them things.'

'Yeah! An it's not soon enough fer me,' she muttered.

'Ah, tha's more comfortable,' she said, sittin down in her frock an coat an flat shoes. 'We'll sit down here an watch fer the train comin in. We can see wha's happenin from here.

'Right! The queue is beginnin te move, Martha. We'll walk over slowly an wait our chance. You take one side of the bag, an as soon as he's busy, we'll make a move.'

'Quick, Ma!' We pushed forward as he was pointin out directions fer a train te some woman.

'Platform four, Madam!' he was sayin as he turned in our direction.

'Keep movin, Ma. I think he's seen us.'

'Jaysus! Is he lookin?'

'I don't know. Let's move faster.'

We were nearly gallopin, wit the bag bangin against me legs. I kept me eyes on the open door an held on until me ma jumped up, then I let go of the bag. Me ma nearly tumbled out wit the weight of it overbalancin her. She screamed an grabbed a hold of the bar, half in an half out. I rushed forward, givin her a push back, an she landed on her arse, takin the bag wit her. 'Fuck ye, anyway!' she roared at me, tryin te get up off her arse. 'Ye nearly kilt me!'

'Come on, Ma! Get up! Are ye hurt?'

'No thanks te you I'm not!' An she stood up, rubbin her back an arse, an brushed her coat down. 'Come on, we'll get an empty seat an have the bit a comfort while we can. He won't be along fer a while.'

We were flyin outa London, an I sat back in me seat, enjoyin watchin all the houses an buildins flashin past, an smoke blowin outa the chimneys, when me ma stood up, gettin nervous. 'Come on, Martha, we'd better go. We can't take the chance of the ticket man catchin us here.'

'No! Ye're right,' I said, lookin back at the people sittin in their comfortable seats, enjoyin themselves at their ease, lookin out the winda.

We made our way te the tilet an locked the door. 'Say a prayer he doesn't catch us,' me ma said, leanin against the wall. I sat down on the bag, cos it was takin up most of the room, an we stayed quiet, waitin te hear the ticket collector. Charlie's face came inta me mind, an me heart fell down inta me belly. An all the other childre. Oh, dear God, please look after them. If only we had them wit us. But we'd have nowhere te bring them. We have te try an find somewhere te live. Then me ma can take them as fast as possible. I feel terrible in meself, leavin them behind te the mercy of Jackser. But I couldn't bear te stay wit him. I had te run an take me chances wit me ma. It's hell on earth fer the poor little things not knowin wha's happened te them. They must be sick an cryin day an night fer me ma. We have te do somethin. But wha? I'm afraid te ask me ma in case she takes it inta her head te run back te Jackser. So I'd better keep quiet. We have te find somewhere first an then start plannin. Yeah! We have te do tha. We sat lookin at each other an listenin. People moved up an down the passage, an then we'd hold our breath when we heard a knock. Time was passin, hours an hours. We didn't talk, just sat, me ma dozin on her feet, restin her back against the wall.

At last the train pulled in. 'We're here, Ma!'

'Right, get ready,' me ma whispered.

She opened the door an went out first. 'Come on!' she whispered. 'They're gettin off.'

We walked wit the crowds an got through the ticket collectors, me goin first, an me ma pushin behind me. 'We made it, Ma!'

'Yeah! Let's get a bus over te the Social Welfare.'

'This is it!' me ma said, lookin up at the buildin. We went in, an me ma said, 'You sit down here an mind the bag.' She pointed te a bench. I sat down an watched me ma go over te a hatch an sit down talkin te a man. I tried te listen, but I can't hear wha they're sayin. The man was talkin te me ma an then lookin at me. I wonder should I go over an see if I can help her. The man keeps shakin his head like he's sayin there's nothin he can do. An me ma looks worried. She keeps lookin from side te side like she's not able te get through te him. Then he gets up an walks aroun te me. An me ma gets up an comes over an takes the bag off me.

'Will you come with me, please?' an he takes me arm.

'Eh, Martha!' me ma is standin lookin like she's in shock.

'Wha, Ma? Wha's happenin?'

'Come with me, please,' the man says, pullin me arm. I hesimitate, me heart in me mouth.

'They're sayin ye have te go inta a home until I find accommodation.'

'A home, Ma!' The room starts te blur, an me ma doesn't know wha te say or do. I let meself get taken by the man inta an office. An he's talkin on the telephone an says I'm te sit down on a chair at a table an wait. Me ears are roarin, an me heart is pumpin, an I can't take in wha's happenin. Time is passin, an I sit here while the man fiddles wit papers an writes an talks on the telephone. How did this

421

happen? Why did we come here? Me ma said we'd get help, but this is worse than the police.

The door opened, an a woman wit grey hair an a thin baldin man wit glasses came in. They spoke te the man, tellin him I was goin te some place. But nothin they're sayin is makin any sense te me. I can't hear the words, only a buzzin noise in me head. I'm tryin te get me senses back, but everythin is just a confused jumble. 'Come along!' the woman says, wit a half-smile on her face. An she opens the door, waitin fer me te follow her. I move after her, keepin me eyes down. An we go out a different way. An I can't see me mammy. 'In you get!' an the woman pushes me inta a car an gets in the back beside me.

The car moves off, an I don't see anythin. I stare at me boots. Wha's goin te happen te me? How long will they keep me? The car stops outside a big house, an a woman opens the door. She smiles, lookin down at me, an then te the grey-haired woman. I don't look at her but past her inta an empty space. 'Come in,' she says, rushin me through a hall an down a flight of stairs an inta a brightly lit room. An a young one wit fluffy slippers an a dressin gown shouts, 'Hello' at me. 'Come and meet Nettie,' the woman says te me. 'She's been waiting up for you. And she's the oldest girl at sixteen.'

The girl's face drops when she sees me. 'Oh! You're very small for thirteen, isn't she, Mum?'

'Yes! We were expecting to see a much bigger girl.'

I dropped me head, lookin at the floor an thinkin, I'm even small fer eleven. They're goin te know me ma is tellin a pack a lies. An they'll find out who we really are, an then we'll be in serious trouble. Me head started te pound, an I felt like gettin sick.

'Would you like a cup of tea an some bread an jam, Mary?' the woman asked me.

I looked at her, an she was waitin fer an answer. Oh! Is tha supposed te be me name? 'No, thanks,' I muttered, keepin me head down.

'What pop groups do you like?' the young one asked me.

I shook me shoulders, not knowin anythin about pop groups.

'Do you like films?'

'Yes,' I said, feelin shy.

'What film stars do you like? I like Tony Curtis!'

I said nothin. I wanted te say Shirley Temple, but she would have said I was foolish. The young one looked at the woman, an they kept givin each other looks, wonderin wha te make a me. 'Up to bed with you, Nettie. You've stayed long past your bedtime,' said the woman.

'Yes, Mam! G'night, Mary.'

'Night!' I muttered, an she rushed outa the room.

'She's disappointed you're not a big girl. She was hoping for someone her own age,' said the woman.

I said nothin, feelin foolish.

'Follow me, and I'll show you where you're sleeping.'

I followed her up the stairs an along a passage. She opened a door an switched on a dim light. 'Over here,' she whispered, bringin me over te a corner bed under a winda. 'Here's a nightdress. Get changed and be quiet! Everyone is sleeping.' Then she left.

I woke up te shoutin. I shot up in the bed, an two young ones were fightin. 'Oh, give it back! That's mine,' said a young one of about eight, tryin te pull a teddy bear off another one of about ten. 'That's my Paddington Bear!'

'No, it ain't! You give it to me, or I'll bite you!' screamed the younger one.

A woman came inta the room. 'Come on, down to breakfast, now!'

'Auntie! She's got my Paddington Bear!'

'Katie! Give Renee back her bear,' an the woman snatched it off Katie an pushed her out the door. Katie looked back, stickin her tongue out at Renee. I got outa bed an started te get dressed. 'Come on, Renee,' shouted the woman up the stairs.

'What's your name?' asked Renee, lookin at me.

'Mary,' I said, thinkin first.

'How old are you?'

'Thirteen.'

'You don't look that!'

423

I said nothin.

'Where are you from?'

'Ireland!' I said. 'Dublin!'

Then the auntie put her head in the door an said, 'Come on, slow coach! Mary, come for your breakfast.'

I followed them down the stairs an inta a big kitchen wit two long tables full a childre.

'You sit here,' a baldy man sittin at the top of the table said te me, pointin at an empty chair. I sat down, an he closed his eyes an joined his hands. An everyone started te sing, 'Thank you, God, for the food we eat, for the flowers that grow, for the birds that sing'. Then everyone started te eat. I put the knife in me mouth, eatin me sausage. An he let a roar at me. 'Take that knife out of your mouth!' I jumped, an he looked at me sayin, 'Never put a knife in your mouth! You will slice your tongue off! Sarah!' he roared at the other table. 'Elbows off the table and sit up straight. And stop giggling, Rebecca.'

Everyone was quiet, an the man an woman talked, eatin their breakfast. Then it was over, an everyone rushed off te get ready fer school. The man got up an left, then everyone disappeared. An I was left at the table listenin te the noise comin from somewhere in the house, an the bangin an thumpin of feet on the ceilin, an then the slammin of doors. An then the house was quiet.

The two women came inta the kitchen an started talkin. I didn't look at them, an they ignored me as if I wasn't there. I wondered what I should do. So I waited, but nothin was said te me. Then they started te clean the tables, an the auntie told me te go outside an play, an she opened the back door inta a yard. 'Sit on that bench,' she said, 'and don't move.'

I went outside an looked aroun. There was only a high wall wit a bench against it facin the kitchen winda, an a concrete ground. I sat on the bench, not movin. An I saw her at the winda washin the dishes an preparin the dinner, peelin the vegebales an keepin her eye on me. I had nothin te look at, an she was watchin me. I had the feelin they didn't like me. An I couldn't understand their ways, either. Me stomach keeps churnin at the thought of me an me ma in trouble. Where is she? An wha's happened te her? An wha's goin te happen te me? Will I ever see me ma again?

All mornin I've been sittin here now, an me legs are stiff, but I'm afraid te move. The wall is high, but I'm sure if I stood up on the bench an had a leap at the top of the wall, I could get up there an take me chances jumpin down on the other side. I could try it when the auntie turns her back. But even if I got away, how would I find me mammy? I wouldn't know where te start lookin. No! It's best I stay here an wait. She'll know where te find me. But then tha's only if they tell her. Maybe they won't tell her where I am! An if they do catch me tryin te escape, they won't give me a second chance. They'll probably lock me up somewhere else or watch me even more closely. No! I'll wait te see wha happens. More time passes, an the watery sun is movin away. It's gettin very chilly here now, an I can't stop meself worryin.

Then I heard noise in the house. The sound of the childre comin back from school. The back door opened, an the mum put her head out. 'Come in, Mary!'

I got up from the bench, an me arse was creakin from the stiffness. 'Oi! Here's the Irish girl,' an three girls, about eight an nine an ten, were starin at me.

'You're not big! I'm bigger than you!' The ten year old said, comin over te stand next te me an measure herself. 'Look, Mum, I'm bigger than the new girl.'

'Yeah! Look, and I'm nearly as big as her,' roared the eight year old.

I stood there not knowin wha te say or do. 'Yes! Mary is small for a thirteen year old,' the woman said, lookin at me like there was somethin very suspicious about me. Then she went back te settin the knives an forks.

'Mary is a midget! Mary is a midget!'

'How old are you?' I asked the one tormentin me. I felt like givin her a box.

'I'm eleven,' she smirked. 'And I'm bigger than you.'

I looked at her. She's my age, an, yeah, she's definitely bigger. An fatter. An she has lovely long curly hair past her shoulders. But if she keeps on tormentin me, she'll be sorry. An fuck tha aul one! I looked at her te see if she was goin te tell them te stop, but she went on about her business, gettin the dinner ready, an wasn't even listenin.

'Oi! You're a Paddy!' the nine year old said te me.

'Yeah! An you've no mammy!' I said, wantin te hurt them back.

'Stop that at once!' A roar came from the baldy aul fella comin in the door. He marched over te me an barked, 'You will call me Dad, and you will call my wife Mam, and you will call the other lady Auntie! Is that understood?' He stared down at me.

'Yes!' I mumbled, lookin down at the floor.

The other three witches sniggered behind their hands. Then he roared at us, 'Upstairs and wash your hands for dinner. Hurry! The lot of you.'

They rushed out the door, an I followed behind them. Like hell I will, call them Mum an Dad! I thought te meself. Then it was back down te the tables, an when everyone was sittin down, it was the 'Thank you, God' prayer again.

I looked aroun, an they were all sniggerin at me, the bastards. There must be about sixteen childre here. An they're all ages. From about six te sixteen. I looked at me dinner – green peas, potatoes an a chop. I started te eat, watchin te see how ye use the knife an fork. Ye hold the meat down wit the fork, an ye saw wit the knife. OK, I've got tha. I made sure te keep the knife away from me mouth an watch the aul fella, who was keepin an eye on everyone an lets out a roar if ye do somethin wrong.

'Oh, you rotter! That hurt. I'm telling!'

'Quiet over there!' roared Baldy at the other table, an he stopped eatin te glare at Renee an Sarah.

'Dad! Sarah was in very big trouble today for throwing water at everyone and flooding the bathroom floor.'

'Liar!' screamed Sarah.

'Yes, Dad!' puffed Renee. 'Miss Pennyfeather grabbed her ear and marched her off to Mr Jones, the janitor, to get the mop and bucket. And she was made to clean it up.'

'No, Dad! It was Renee. I was trying to stop her,' screamed Sarah.

'Shut up!' roared the dad.

'And Renee bit me on my arm,' shouted Rebecca, sidin wit Sarah.

'Quiet the lot of you!'

'No, she did not, Dad! Rebecca was pulling my hair, and Sarah ...'

'Shut up!' screamed the dad at a little fat young one sittin next te me. I dropped me eyes, cos he was lookin at me te see if I was joinin in the fight.

'You're a beast,' whispered Sarah, givin Renee a slap.

'That's enough,' roared Auntie, sittin opposite them. Renee started cryin.

'That's it!' roared the dad. 'One more word from anyone, and you will go to bed early without supper!' An he glared at everyone, snortin an flickin the bit of hair tha flew inta his eye. An he took a stab wit his fork at the chop, an it shot off the plate. There was a silence as he watched it land on the floor an muttered as he bent down te pick it up. 'My sainted grandmother!' an everyone started sniggerin, then he flung it on the plate. An the laughin got louder. I buried me head in me plate, not wantin him te see me laughin.

'Dad's got a flyin chop,' roared the fat one sittin next te me.

'Dad's got an empty tummy,' muttered Baldy.

'Would you like some cheese, dear?' asked his wife, smilin.

'No, I won't bother. I've lost me appetite.' An he stood up an lifted his newspaper from the little table by the fire an sat himself down in an armchair an started te read.

Everyone started te move, bringin their plates over te the sink, an the mother shouted, 'Get your schoolbooks out! It's time for homework!'

'Mum! Mum! Someone pinched my pencil case. My treasured one,' whined a young one, openin the belt of the mum's bib tied behind her back while she was tryin te wash the dishes.

'It was Tracy who pinched your pencil case!' said Ida.

'Out, now!' screamed the mum, pushin Ida away an grabbin anyone she could get her hands on te push them out the door. 'Homework! Bring your schoolbag now,' she roared.

Baldy lifted his head over the newspaper an barked, 'Brush your teeth!' an looked at everyone, droppin his readin glasses down on his nose, an then shook his newspaper an buried his head in it again.

I headed te the bathroom, but it was crowded, wit everyone pushin an shovin te get at the sink.

'Oi, Paddy!' a young one said te me wit a toothbrush stickin outa her mouth.

'Shut up! Don't call me tha or I'll stick tha brush down yer neck.'

'Ooh!' screamed bloody Renee. 'I'm goin straight to Dad to tell him what you said to our Sammy.'

'Go on, I'm not afraid!' I shouted, an she rushed out the door, an Sarah roared after her.

'Yeah! Tell Dad wot she said.'

'Shut up, you!' I roared.

'I'm telling!' she screamed, an she rushed out the door after Renee.

The little fat one slid out past me an roared, 'You're an Oirish Paddy!' an ran down the stairs so fast she slipped an grabbed onta the banisters.

I headed fer me bed, bumpin inta some young ones robbin Renee's Paddington Bear. The two of them glared at me an then pushed past, laughin an sayin, 'We'll hide it in Sammy's bed.'

'Yeah!' said the other one. 'And she'll get the blame.'

I dived outa me clothes an jumped inta me nightdress, shuttin the door, an hopped inta bed, pullin the blankets over me head, hopin the dad wouldn't come after me an I'd be in trouble. An hopin the others wouldn't bother me, an I'd get a bit a peace.

36

I've been here fer weeks now, seven weeks, an I've had no word from me mammy. It's gettin worse, the same routine every day. I sit in the yard on the bench every mornin after breakfast. I get a cup a tea an a sambidge at lunchtime. Then I have te sit on the bench again an wait fer the childre te come in from school. The heart is goin outa me. I'm not bothered about eatin. I don't feel hungry. An the childre don't talk te me, only te fight wit me all the time. An the people don't bother wit me, except te side wit the childre when I fight back wit them fer pickin on me an callin me names. The English people don't like the Irish. An I definitely don't like the English.

'Mary! Go and take your bath. I've run the water for you.'

'OK!' I said, followin the auntie te the bathroom.

'Now don't be long.'

'No, OK,' I said as she closed the door.

I stepped inta the bath, dippin me toe in first an then lowered meself in. Lovely! I took up a huge bar of Sunlight soap an started te wash meself. Then I washed me hair. The door opened, sendin in a draft. An the auntie poked her head in. 'Hurry up, Mary! Come out of the bath now and get dressed. Quickly!'

'OK,' I said, disappointed, enjoyin meself in the bath, cos this was the only place no one could get me an start tormentin me.

I got dressed an was dryin me hair when the auntie rushed in an said, 'Come quickly! There's someone waiting to see you.'

Me mouth dropped open, an me heart gave a jump. Me! I rushed out, followin the auntie up inta the parlour, an there was me ma! I gaped at her, an the auntie went out, closin the door behind her.

'Quick!' me ma said, openin the door quietly. 'Come on!' an she opened the front door an grabbed me. 'Run, Martha!' an she ran down the street an jumped inta a waitin taxi. 'Go, Mister!' An she poked the driver in the back, an he hesimitated te ask where to now, an she said, 'The city. Hurry!' An we took off just as the front door opened, an the auntie an the mum an dad an young ones all came rushin out te gape after us. Me ma looked back an muttered, 'They won't fuckin get us again!'

I looked back, an the man was rushin back inta the house while the women stared. The auntie had her hand on her head, an the mum had her hand on her mouth. The young ones were runnin up an down the path laughin, an some were gapin.

'Wha's happenin, Ma?' I turned te look inta her face, an she winked at me not te say anythin in front of the driver.

She leaned forward an said, 'Can ye go a bit faster, Mister? I'm in a hurry!'

He shot forward, an we fell back in the seat. Then we hit the city centre, an me ma looked aroun. 'Pull over there, Mister!' an she pointed te a big shop. The man pulled in, an me ma said, 'We're gettin out here.'

I jumped out, an me ma paid the driver, an then we rushed inta the big shop an out through another door, an walked through crowds a people. An then she said, 'Come on in here!' an we went inta a café, an she ordered a pot a tea. 'Them bastards wouldn't tell me where ye were. I couldn't find out where they'd put ye. They said I could visit ye when I had a place of me own an I could be classed as fit te take care of ye.'

'So how did ye find me, Ma?'

'I met a very respectable man who took pity on me. I was sittin on a bench in a park cryin. An when he heard I'd lost you, cos I had no home of me own, he said I could stay in his home. An he's willin te take you. He's a real respectable gentleman. So then I was able te tell them I had a home fer you. An they gave me the address after checkin wit the home ye were in. An they said I could come an visit ye. I told the taxi man te wait fer me, an I left him a few houses down so they wouldn't see him. Tha way we were able te get away quickly before they knew wha was happenin.'

I looked at me ma. Her eyes was shinin, an she was very happy. But she looked very tired, too. It's only hittin me now. I'm out! Back wit me ma, we're together again! Me heart lifted, an me belly gave a jump wit gladness. Me ma stares inta me face. 'Wha happened te you? You're lookin very white, an ye're still very thin.'

'Yeah, Ma! I'm white from all the washin I got. An I didn't like the food any more.'

'Yeah!' me ma said, starin inta me face. 'Were ye frettin?'

'Yeah, Ma! I was. I missed ye somethin terrible.' An I felt me chest fillin up. I wanted te start cryin.

'Well,' me ma said, lookin away from me. 'Them bastards won't get a second chance te do tha te us again. We'll keep away from the authorities!' Me heart jumped in fear at even the mention of tha word.

'Come on,' me ma said. 'We'd better get movin.' Then she headed inta the tilet, an I followed her in. Another woman was there wit a young one about my age, an I watched the mammy comb the young one's hair. It was lovely an shiny an straight, parted down one side an a big clip in it. I stared while she buttoned her coat up wit the navy-blue velvet collar an a half-belt at the back. An the young one stood still while her mammy fussed aroun her. She looked lovely, an I wished I could look like tha. Me ma came outa the tilet an said, 'There's no paper in there,' an laughed at the woman, but the woman ignored her.

An I said, 'Never mind, Ma! The English don't shit, tha's why they look as if they're in pain all the time.' I stared at the woman, feelin fire in me belly. An she turned the young one te the door an flew out.

Me ma laughed an looked at me. 'Wha happened? Why did ye say tha? Did she do somethin on ye?'

'No, Ma! But people seem te think we're dirt.'

'Ah, fuck them!' me ma said. 'Let's go.'

431

We walked through a big shop, an I stopped te look at the childre's coats. I tried on a pink coat wit brass shiny buttons an a half-belt, an wandered down te show me ma, who was lookin at jumpers.

'Look at this, Martha! Isn't it lovely?'

'Yeah, Ma,' I said, lookin aroun te see if anyone was watchin me.

'Come on, I'm goin,' me ma said, an headed fer the door. I followed her out slowly, ready te roar, 'Wait, Ma! I want ye te buy this coat,' if I was followed. Tha way no one could say me ma was robbin, an I could play the innocent. But no one followed. An I rushed off, catchin up wit me ma an havin another look aroun before I started te walk wit her.

We got off the bus an walked te the man's house. The house was huge, an I stood on the step while me ma rang the doorbell. An I was delighted wit me new coat. I looked very respectable. The door opened, an an elderly man, he could have been in his forties, or even in his fifties, smiled at us an said, 'Come in!' An he stood back, holdin the door open, an we stepped inta the long hall wit a shiny mahogany table an a big statue sittin on it of a woman wit an arra in her hand. I could smell furniture polish an food cookin. An there was a lovely rug hangin on the wall wit old pictures, an a carpet runnin down the centre of the polished floorboards.

'Come in, my dears! Let me take your coats.' I took me new pink coat off an handed it te him. He bent down an smiled at me, 'And you are?' he said, takin me coat.

'Martha!' I said.

'What a lovely name,' he said as he hung me coat on a coat stand beside a big pot holdin walkin sticks wit silver tips an black umbrellas. Then he hung me ma's up an rushed us inta a big room wit a huge fireplace an a roarin fire. 'Make yourselves comfortable. Come close to the fire,' an he smacked a big cushion, fixin another on the back, an waved me ma inta a big leather armchair beside the fire, wit a table an a lamp lightin on it. Me ma hesimitated, smilin at me, an sat herself down on the edge. Then he looked at me, standin not knowin wha te do. 'Come! Sit over here by the fire, dear,' an he pulled a big leather stool over beside me ma, right in front of the fire.

432

'Thanks, Mister,' I said shyly.

'Call me James,' he said, givin a big smile showin a mouth of gorgeous white teeth. Then I stared at his face. He only had one eye, the other one was marble. An he had a terrible scar under it. It was all white an pulled together in lumps. He saw me lookin an watched me wit his one eye, lettin me take it in. He was still smilin, so I looked at his good eye, wantin him te know I didn't think he was ugly.

'Thanks, Mister!' I whispered.

He nodded an whispered back, 'Thank you, Martha.' Then he rubbed his hands together an said, 'You must be famished. The food's in the oven. Dinner won't be long,' an he walked out, closin the door behind him.

'Ma! He's a terribly nice gentleman,' I whispered, leanin close te her.

'Ah, indeed he is,' me ma said, smilin an lookin aroun her. 'It's true wha they say, strangers will help ye when ye're down, quicker than yer own family.' I remembered me ma's family, an them throwin us out onta the street when I was young. There's no point in botherin them.

We heard dishes rattlin outside the door, then it opened an the man rolled in two trays on wheels, an left it, rushin over te bring a small table in front of the fire. 'Supper by the fire! More cosy!' he said, an set the table wit knives an forks, an a plate wit a silver cover on it. An he whipped off the cover, an there was lovely meat, an gravy, an carrots, an white lumps tha looked like potatoes. 'Casserole and dumplings! My favourite,' he sang. 'Tuck in!' he said te me. I looked at him an laughed. 'Go on! Put some meat on those bones!'

I started te eat, an it was meltin in me mouth. 'Did you cook this all by yerself, Mister?'

'James!' he said, swallowin a big mouthful. 'Yes! Indeed I did, little lady.'

'Do ye not have a wife te cook fer ye?'

'No!' he said, concentratin on gettin a piece of meat onta his fork. 'I'm a widower,' he said, munchin on his food an lookin at me wit his good eye.

433

'Do ye have any childre?' I asked, lookin aroun te see if any appeared.

He went quiet an looked at the fire. I said nothin, feelin he was a bit hurt. 'Yes, I did once,' he said slowly, thinkin. 'Two . . . a boy and a girl, but they died with my wife. A terrible car accident took them away from me,' an he sat starin at the fire.

'I'm very sorry, Mister,' I whispered. 'Ye're still missin them, aren't ye?'

Then he looked at me an said slowly, very quietly, 'Yes, I do. Very much!' An he put his knife an fork down, not finishin his dinner, an looked at me ma, eatin her dinner. 'Is that hot enough for you, my dear?'

'Ah! It's grand,' me ma said, smilin an puttin down her knife an fork, feelin shy.

'Did everything go well for you today?'

'Ah, yeah! I have her back,' an she nodded te me.

'Yes! That's all that matters,' he said, jumpin up. 'Pudding!' he said te me. I looked at him wonderin did he mean black an white puddin. 'Chocolate pudding! Always a favourite with children. Hm! Yes?'

'Eh, yeah!' I said happily.

'Sir will be back with Madam's order in a jiffy,' he bowed, rushin off wit the trolley.

I laughed. 'Ye're a funny man!' I said.

'Oh! You ain't seen nothing yet!' he said, soundin like Humphrey Bogart. An he swung the cart out the door, closin it behind him. I wanted te run after him. But he was gone, an I didn't want him te think I was runnin loose aroun his house. So I watched the door, waitin fer him te come back.

The room was a bit dead without him. I looked at some of the photographs sittin on the piano. There was one of him in an army uniform wit wings on the shoulders, an he was holdin his hat under his arm an standin very straight. He looked a lot younger, an his face hadn't a mark, an his two eyes were perfect. An he was lovely lookin altogether, wit black curly hair an gorgeous eyes. Then there was another of him half sittin on a table wit his arms wrapped aroun a blonde woman wit wavy hair, an wearin a skirt an jumper wit a matchin cardigan an a pearl necklace. An another one of an old woman wit a blouse buttoned up te her neck. It was all frilly. An she had a brooch at her throat, an her hair was gathered up in a bun, wit soft waves at the front, an she was holdin a little girl of about three wit blond curls. An a little boy of about five or six was standin beside the granny's chair. 'Look, Ma! Tha must be the man's family, there's his wife! An I bet ye tha's his childre. An tha's their granny,' I said, gettin a closer look.

'Yeah!' me ma said, not movin from her chair. 'He's a lovely man altogether.' An I could see me ma was tired an noddin off from the good food an the heat off the fire. I heard him comin, an I rushed back te me stool.

The door pushed in, an the man rushed in wit the cart again an stopped. 'Bad news, little lady, no choc pud!' Me face dropped! 'But no fear!' An he waved his finger in the air. 'I managed to save us some smelly cheese from our resident mouse.'

'Oh!' I said, gettin worried, cos I don't think I like the sound of smelly cheese. An I watched his face an kept me eye on the bowls wit the cover on them.

'But some would think me a magician! So . . .' an he waved his hands over the bowls, sayin foreign words, an then whipped the cover off te get a look an shouted, 'It worked!' wavin the lid in the air. I looked, an it was hot apple tart an ice cream wit melted chocolate on top. 'You must be very special,' he said, shakin his head at me, lookin very serious. 'My magic only works for special people.'

I wonder if tha's true! He's lookin at me so seriously, an I know he wouldn't tell lies. But I don't believe in Santa, or anythin like tha, I never did. Only once fer a little while a few years ago. But tha came te nothin, an I learnt very quickly not te be kiddin meself. No! James is only messin. I dipped me spoon in an it slid down me neck, makin me face shiver, it was so sweet, an landed in me belly before I could stop it. 'Yum! Delicious!' James said, smackin his lips an laughin at me makin faces. It was so gorgeous.

'Were you fightin in the war, James?'

'Yes,' he said, lookin at me. 'Royal Air Force.'

'An wha did ye have te do?' I asked him.

'Oh!' he said, lettin out his breath an thinkin. 'I flew ahead, marking out the spots for the other chaps coming behind me to show them the way and where to drop their bombs. They called us "The Pathfinders"!'

'So you were a fighter pilot?' I asked him, shocked with surprise. 'Yes!'

I kept lookin at him, not knowin wha te say. He's so nice, ye'd never think him a very important man tha'd make funny jokes an talk te us an treat us like we were important, too. 'I read about youse in the *Hotspur* an the *Victor*. I read boys' comics when I've run outa the *Bunty* an the *Judy*. An youse fighter pilots were very brave altogether!' I could hardly get me breath, thinkin about him flyin all them planes.

He looked at me, shakin his head an smilin. Then he leaned over te me an waved his finger, sayin quietly, 'You know, you too are not without courage, little girl! There's plenty of fire,' an he leaned closer, lookin inta me eyes wit his one eye, 'in those blue velvet eyes. You have courage! And one day you will become a wonderful woman!' Then he jumped back an clasped his hands. 'Right!' he said, gatherin up the dishes. 'Time to dispose of these.'

I felt me chest risin, an I got a tingle in me belly, an I lifted me shoulders an raised me head, straightenin meself up. I felt very proud in meself altogether. He says I have great courage! A bit like them fighter pilots. Me! I really admire James no end. If I was a boy, I'd want te be exactly like him. He's the nicest person I've ever met in me whole life. An ye'd never think te look at him he was a great man. But he certainly is. 'Ma, do ye want te know somethin?'

'Wha?' me ma said, her eyes half closin an her face red from the heat of the fire.

'James is better than an aul fillum star, isn't he?'

'Oh, yeah!' me ma said, shakin her head in agreement.

I sat meself in James's chair, makin meself comfortable. God, we're so lucky. Then the doorbell rang. Me ma opened her eyes, lookin at me an listenin. The front door opened, an we heard a man's voice. 'G'night, Sir. We are looking for a woman and child, Sir, believed to be living at this address. A Miss Kathleen Smith and her daughter Mary.'

'Step in, Officer,' we heard James say. An another door opened. The front door was shut, an we heard footsteps goin inta another room an the door closin.

'It's them, Martha!' me ma said, grabbin me. The room started spinnin, an I felt the blood drainin outa me. Me ma's eyes were starin in fright, an she was the colour of a ghost. 'Come on, quick! Let's get out before they come in,' she said, lookin aroun.

'No, Ma! No!' I whispered. 'Wait, they'll catch us if we go out there. Do nothin. Wait, let's see wha happens.'

'Jesus! Jesus! Jesus!' me ma joined her hands lookin up te heaven. I was shakin an watchin the door.

The other door opened, an the men's voices said, 'Thank you, sorry to bother you.'

'No bother,' James said, shuttin the door.

He came in, an we stood starin, holdin our breaths. 'The police, I'm afraid,' he said, runnin his hand through his hair. 'They want to interview you. They believe . . . it was reported to them, you absconded with the child without authority.'

Me ma was rubbin her mouth wit her hand an lookin at me. 'We have te go. They'll put her away again. An this time they won't let me near her. I'll never get her back.'

'No, no, my dear!' James said, puttin up his hands. 'Don't panic. We can sort this out.'

'No! Thanks fer all yer help. But I'm not takin tha chance.' An she said, 'Come on, Martha. We'd better move before they come back.'

James stood away from the door an said, 'No, please, there is no need for this! I have contacts. We can have this sorted out.'

'Ah, no!' me ma said. 'When the police get involved, then tha's trouble.'

'No, no!' James said, puttin his hand out te me ma. 'These chaps are only doing their job. They must follow through with their enquiries, we'll . . .'

'No!' me ma said. 'We're goin now. Where's me coat?' An she grabbed her coat off the stand an then grabbed mine. 'Come on, Martha,' an she made fer the door. I was standin beside James an didn't know wha te do. 'Come on, I'm tellin ye,' me ma roared.

'Please, at least stay the night. You are putting yourself and this child in great danger by walking through the streets at this hour. Tomorrow morning, after a good night's rest, perhaps you will see things more clearly!'

Me ma hesimitated. I looked at her, wringin me hands. 'No!' she said. 'Once they get their hands on ye, they don't let go. They might even lock me up.'

'Good gracious! What in heaven's name would they do that for! You are not a criminal!'

'No!' me ma said. 'But tha's not how they see it! I'm goin. Come on, Martha.'

I looked at James, an he was very downhearted. My heart was breakin, too. 'I am sorry, dear, very sorry!' he said te me in a whisper.

I turned after me ma, flyin out the gate an stoppin te look up an down the road, then she headed off in the direction of the bus. I hurried after her, lookin back at James. He lifted his hand slowly an gave me a wave, then turned away an went in, closin the door. I felt like me whole world had emptied, an there was no one left but me . . . an me ma.

It was drizzlin an dark, an I pulled me collar of me coat up, thinkin me new coat will be destroyed wit the rain. Only a short while ago I was in heaven. Now we're worse off than ever before. I had a feelin it was too good te last. Nothin good ever lasts fer long. An now it's gone. Me ma looked aroun at me trailin behind her an started te run. 'Hurry up, Martha. The bus is comin.'

I rushed after her an jumped on the bus. We sat beside each other, not sayin a word. Then I remembered, 'Ma! Where's the bag wit our clothes?'

'Ah, them!' she said, turnin her head away in disgust. 'They're gone long ago. Someone robbed me bag when I put it down beside me in a café.'

'So everythin's gone,' I muttered, lookin out at the dark streets, drizzlin, not a soul in sight an everythin closed up fer the night. I could see houses flashin past wit big gardens an trees an lights on. The people cosy inside, probably sittin beside warm fires, thinkin of stirrin themselves outa their armchairs an headin off te warm beds wit soft mattresses an big eiderdowns te snuggle under. I looked aroun the bus. The conductor was sittin restin himself wit his eyes closed an his legs stretched out. A coloured man wit a big turban on his head, wearin blue overalls an a big heavy overcoat, sat starin ahead, goin wit the rockin of the bus an holdin his sambidges, wrapped in bread paper, loosely between his hands on his lap. The whites of his eyes was bloodshot, an he looked like he was very tired, but this is somethin he just has te do, an there's nothin tha can change it. I wanted te ask him was he fed up an tell him I was feelin the same. An maybe he's feelin lonely, an we could cheer each other up an laugh. An maybe put our heads together an come up wit a plan te make life easier, tha we could be family or somethin. I stared at him, thinkin, no, he wouldn't know what I was talkin about, an I'm still a child. People just laugh at the likes of me. Things are not workin out the way I thought they would. I'm not able te bring in any money, so we're lost without tha. I don't know wha te think or do any more. It's just beyond me.

'Come on, move,' me ma said. 'We're gettin off,' an we stepped onta the shiny wet footpath. All the shops were closed, an the rain was gettin heavier now. It was blowin inta our faces, pushin us back, an we had te fight te keep movin. 'Jaysus Christ! What a fuckin night.' Me ma was startin te cry. I looked at her face collapsin, an she moaned, 'No one gives a fuck about ye when ye're homeless. We might as well be dead fer all anyone cares.' An she looked aroun her at the empty streets, her face red, an her nose runnin. An she wiped her nose wit the edge of her headscarf.

'Don't cry, Ma. It's all right! Look, Ma, we're together again, nothin's changed. We need te be careful, tha's all. An we'll come up wit somethin. So stop worryin, Ma!' I held her eyes, an she quietened herself down.

'Yeah! There's no point in lookin fer anyone te help us. Fuck them!' she said, lookin aroun her te curse the world. We walked on, rushin through the rain, in a hurry te nowhere.

We passed a church an stopped. 'It's all locked up,' me ma said, lookin at the dark church. 'We can't go in there.' We moved on, lookin at the dark streets ahead of us. There's nowhere we can go in an sit down. 'Jaysus! I curse the day I was ever born,' me ma started te cry again.

'I'm really fed up, too, Ma! I'm freezin from this rain, an I'm exhausted.'

I was talkin te meself. Me ma was mutterin away, lost in her own world. 'We'll go back,' she said.

'Go back where, Ma? To the man?'

'No! Tha's no good. Te the childre. I'll get me own place in Dublin. An tha bandy aul bastard won't stop me.'

Me heart was sinkin. Even the mention of tha aul fella was makin me want te get sick. 'No, Ma! Tha's not a good idea at all. Keep far away from him, Ma. He's no good.'

'Yes, I know tha!' me ma shouted. 'But what else can we do?' An she waved her arms aroun her. 'Anyway, I'm not goin back te him. Not on yer life I'm not. No! I want te get the childre, an I'm not goin anywhere near him.'

'But how are ye goin te do tha, Ma?'

'We can watch an wait. An go in when he's not there. He won't be expectin us te turn up.'

'OK, Ma,' I said slowly, thinkin it would be lovely te see the childre again. I left it at tha, too tired te ask any more questions, like how are we goin te get our own place?

'We go tomorrow. I have the ten pounds tha man gave me when I was goin out te get ye today. We'll buy our tickets, an this time tomorrow night, we should be on the mail boat headin back.'

We walked on, stoppin at traffic lights, wonderin which way we'd go. Only a dark road up ahead wit houses an trees, nothin up there. Down te the left, a high wall wit fencin over it an a big factory behind it. We turned right, headin down past shops shut up fer the night an a picture house showin a cowboy fillum startin next week. I had a look. Mexican outlaws swaggerin on their big boots wit spurs hangin outa them, holdin a gun in each hand an wearin big hats. '*Desperados on the Run*', it said! It would be nice te see tha, wonder how much it costs te get in. I looked, an me ma was halfway down the road. I hate tha, now I'd have te run te catch up. She never waits fer me. 'Wait, Ma!'

'Come on,' she said, turnin aroun, then moved off again. We crossed the road an turned onta a narra street wit cobblestones an old houses tha looked like they were ready te fall down. People came outa a pub, slammin the door open, an it swung back wit the force. An two aul fellas were shoutin an singin, 'I Belong te Glasgow', an then one of them started te tap dance on his bandy legs. When he got te 'So what's the matter with Glasgow, cause it's going roun and roun', he sang it very fast, an I sidestepped him, keepin me eyes on him at a distance. 'Come ere, chicken. Do a dance wiv me!' he said, roarin an wavin his arms out at me. The younger fella eyed me ma, who was standin waitin fer me.

'Come on, Martha,' she shouted, an I moved off.

'Ah, no! Don't go. Come back in an ave a drink wiv us!' the older fella wit the flat nose roared, makin a run fer me ma wit his arms wide open.

He wrapped himself aroun me ma, who was laughin an tryin te get free, sayin, 'Ah, no! I don't drink, an we're in a hurry.'

I went up an stood beside her, watchin yer man an sayin, 'Come on, Ma. We have te go.'

'Go on, Martha. Tell er te stay, sure ya only live once.' I was eyein him, an the young fella was watchin an laughin.

A woman about me ma's age came down the street wit a newspaper filled wit chips. 'Jimmy MacVeigh! Yer missus is lookin fer ye! Ye're te go home.'

Jimmy pulled away from me ma an looked at her. An puffed his chest up, dribblin all over his chin, an clenched his fists, shoutin, 'Tell tha woman te go an mind her own business. I'm about me man's business.'

The woman laughed, an opened her parcel a chips, an took a handful, an said, 'Tell her yerself. She's on her way down te get ye.'

Then she filled her mouth, an Jimmy was watchin her an said, 'Give's a few a them chips, Angie, me darlin.' An he staggered over te Angie te help himself te her chips.

The younger fella said te me ma, 'Ye don't live around here, then. Where are ye goin this hour?'

'Ah, we're movin on,' me ma said. 'There's nothin here fer us.'

'Look, do ye want te come wiv me an have a cup a tea an a few chips?'

Me ma looked at me. 'I don't know,' she said. I hesimitated, thinkin of the chips an hot tea.

'Come on,' he said, grabbin me ma's elbow. 'It's just aroun the corner.'

We went inta a café an sat down at an empty table. An yer man went up te the counter an ordered three plates a chips an three cups a tea, an came back an sat down beside me ma. I sat opposite them an waited fer me chips, an yer man was talkin away te her. The chips an tea arrived, an I made short work a them. When the plate was empty an the last of the tea drained outa the cup, I put it down, feelin very sleepy now. It was nice an warm in here, an lovely te sit down. They were still eatin, an yer man was talkin away, usin his hands all the time te make his point. Me ma was listenin an half closin her eyes an lookin away. She does tha when she's wit strangers. 'I know, yes, tut, tut, tha's terrible!' she kept sayin an smilin.

I looked aroun me, an two people were sittin at another table. An aul one wearin a head scarf, wit her ears stickin out an the scarf tied on her chin, was talkin away te an aul fella. 'I sez te him, I sez, there wos ten fags,' then she stopped te think, lookin up te heaven. 'No! I'm tellin yer lies. There wos nine fags in tha packet!'

'Yesh! Go on,' the aul fella was noddin, leanin his belly against

442

the table an puttin his elbows down wit his greasy fingers in the air, nearly sittin on top of her across the table.

'Wot wos I sayin?' she asked the ceilin, as yer man dipped his hand onta the plate an shoved a handful inta his gummy mouth, not botherin te use the fork, an started te chew, his bottom lip stuck out an kept goin up an down, coverin his nose as he tried te eat the chips wit his gums. 'An nows they're gone,' she said, wavin her arms an starin at him wit bulgin eyes, an her lipstick was plastered all over her face, not just on her mouth.

'Yesh! I wos perceptible te him.'

'Yes, you wos!'

The woman waved her finger at him in agreement. 'I sez tha to myself. You wos perceptible to im. You wos onta him right aways, you wos.'

'Yesh, I wos, washn't I?' the aul fella said happily.

'Right! We'll be off,' the fella said, gettin up.

An me ma said, 'Come on, Martha! He's givin us somewhere te stay fer the night,' she said, smilin.

'No, Ma! Don't go wit him!' I watched him go te the door an wait fer us. He was smilin, but I didn't like the look of flint in his eyes. He's a vicious bastard, I thought. 'Ma! Let's keep goin!' I said, followin me ma.

'No, we can't,' she said. 'If we stay on the streets, we'll be picked up.'

'Listen te yer mam,' he said te me, grabbin her arm an rushin her out the door, leavin me te trail after them.

'He's no good,' I muttered after me ma, an he looked aroun givin me a sneer tha was supposed te be a smile, an shook his head at me ma, sayin, 'She's a lippy one, an no doubt about tha!' Then he grabbed her arm again, sayin, 'Cor, it ain't half chilly! Let's be movin,' an he started te trot, pullin me ma behind him. I had te run te keep up. An I was cursin me ma fer bein so soft.

He turned inta a hall an up stone steps wit an iron banister, an along a cement passage, an put the key inta a door. An he went inta a dark passage an opened another door, an switched on a light.

443

There was a big bed in the corner against a winda, wit a gas cooker in the other corner, an a table an a dresser holdin cups an plates. 'Roight, let's hit the bed,' an he switched off the light an pulled off his shoes an trousers. I sat on a chair, pullin off me boots, an didn't look in tha direction. I heard the bed springs creakin. An I got in at the bottom, leavin me ma te climb in beside him. I pulled the hairy blankets over me an shut me eyes, bringin me feet up under me an rollin meself tight inta a ball.

Then the noises started, an me ma was complainin. I didn't want te hear. I put the pilla over me head, blockin out the noise, an waited fer the rockin an creakin of the bed te stop. I was holdin meself very tight, not takin a breath, an I felt I wanted te scream. I can't stand it. Me ma is a fuckin cow! Why is she wit him? She's always walkin inta trouble. The noise just won't stop. I can't believe she's lettin him do horrible things te her. Why is she such a fuckin eejit?

'Ma!' I roared, pullin the pilla off me head. 'I want te go now or get some sleep.' Yer man stopped an pulled away from me ma. An then it was quiet. I was just dozin off when I felt his foot tryin te get between me legs. I leapt up. 'Get yer bastardin foot away from me!' I roared at him.

'Wha's happenin?' me ma asked, raisin her head offa the pilla.

'Sorry! I wos stretchin meself.'

I looked at him, an he turned over, buryin his head under the blankets, an me ma said, 'Shush, go te sleep.' I lay down again, movin meself well outa his reach, an lay at the edge of the bed, finally dozin off.

'Come on,' yer man was sayin, bucklin up his trousers an searchin the floor fer his socks. Me ma was fixin her skirt, an I jumped outa the bed an looked fer me boots. I didn't take me trousers off goin te bed. 'I've got te be movin.' An he tied up his shoelaces an grabbed his overcoat.

I put on me pink coat an waited fer me ma te button up hers. 'Are we right, then?' she said te me. An I rushed past him holdin the door open fer us, ready te slam it shut behind us. An we're on the street again. He gave a half-wave te me ma an hurried off in the other direction.

'Come on, Ma. Let's go,' I said, anxious te be away from him an this place.

Me ma was lookin after him an turned te me. 'I suppose we'd better get the bus down te the train station?'

'Yeah, let's find out where we get it.'

She stopped te ask a woman fer directions, an I moved on ahead, not wantin te be beside her. 'Wait!' she laughed, rushin up te me. 'It's down here, the woman said. Come on!' I let her go ahead an trailed after her. When we got on the bus, she asked the conductor te let us off at the train station. I looked out the winda, leavin her talkin te herself. 'Pity we couldn't get a place here. We coulda brought the childre over, an we'd be well away from him.'

'Ah, fuck off! Ye're only good fer findin Jacksers,' I wanted te say. But I just kept lookin out the winda.

'Next stop train station!' the conductor roared up.

'Come on, this is our stop,' me ma said, gettin up. I followed her offa the bus an inta the station. She went up te the ticket hatch, an I watched a big black hairy dog stop an cock his leg against the pillar an give a big piss, sprayin the leg of a woman in a big hat wit a feather stickin out, an she jumped an shook her leg, an I roared laughin. She was complainin te the railway man about the dog, an it came back an sniffed her cloth travellin bag she left beside the pillar, an then it lifted its leg again an gave another piss all over the bag. 'Mrs!' I roared. 'Look what it's doin now.' Enjoyin meself no end.

'This is outrageous!' she screamed, pickin up her bag an droppin it again. 'It's ruined!'

Me ma came back, holdin the tickets. 'We've an hour's wait. An we won't get te Euston station fer hours. Then we've te catch another train te take us all the way te the boat. An we'll have te get off tha one an change again. Jaysus! It's goin te be a long aul journey.'

We sat down te wait. 'Ma! Can we get somethin te eat? I'm starvin.'

'I haven't much money left. We'd better go easy on it. Come on, then, an we'd better be quick. We don't want te miss the train.'

We went inta a shop across the road, an me ma bought a packet a biscuits an a bottle a milk. An we went back te the station an sat down an had two each, savin the rest fer later. An I took a few sups of the milk.

'Train for London now sitting on platform two!' the man's voice roared outa the loudspeakers.

'Come on, tha's us!' me ma shouted, jumpin up.

The man checked our tickets, an I ran ahead. 'I'm here, Ma!' an we rushed inta an empty carriage an shut the door behind us. 'We have it all te ourselves,' I said, stretchin me legs out on the seat. Oh, lovely! No smelly tilet. The door whipped open, an the woman wit the feather hat an the smelly bag put her head in. She looked at us fer a minute, then shut the door an moved on. I looked at me ma, 'She doesn't think much of us,' I said, laughin.

'Ah, fuck her!' me ma said, laughin. Then we heard the whistle blowin, an the train shook, an I looked out. The man waved his flag, an the train took off.

I dozed, lookin at the fields an cows an houses flashin past. An then I was out cold.

'Get up, Martha! We're here.' I lifted me head, an the train was pullin inta Euston Station. Me ma opened the door, an I followed her out, holdin onta her coat, cos I was still dopey. 'Wait here,' me ma said, leavin me standin beside a pillar. Then she appeared back, wavin an shoutin. 'Come on, quick. It's over here.' An she took off, vanishin in the crowd. I woke meself up an raced in the direction I saw her headin. An she was givin her tickets te the man. 'Hurry!' she said te me.

'You have to be quick, Madam! The train is leavin in three minutes.'

We ran down the platform, an the man was standin wit his flag an his whistle in his hand, an he saw us comin. All the doors were bein banged shut, an we leapt up onta the train, an the door was slammed shut behind us. We hurried down the passage, lookin fer an empty seat, an the whistle blew, an the train got ready te move. 'In here!' me ma said, openin a door. An we sat down in an empty carriage. 'Jaysus! Tha was lucky!' me ma said, tryin te get her breath back. Then the train moved, an we took off outa the station slowly.

I looked out at the rain pourin down, an it was very dark. Thunder was roarin an flashes of lightnin. 'God, Ma, the weather is very bad here.'

'Yeah! Just as well we're not out in it,' me ma said, openin the biscuits an givin me one. 'Here, have a sup a milk.' We ate another biscuit, an me ma said, 'We'll save these fer later.'

'Yeah,' I said, still feelin hungry. Then I lay down, havin the whole seat te meself, an dozed off again.

'Wake up! We're at the boat,' me ma said, shakin me. I stood up, ready te move. 'No! Sit down, wait till the train stops,' me ma said, lookin out the winda. It was pitch black outside, an I hated havin te move. 'Right! Let's go. We have te hurry if we want te get a seat.'

But we needn't have worried. There was plenty a room on the boat, cos there was very few people travellin. I followed me ma over te the long seats in the corner of the room, an we shut the door behind us. It was empty. I put me back te the wall an stretched out. Then the door opened an two more people came in an sat down at the other end an put their bags on the seat an stretched themselves out, the aul fella restin his head on his suitcase. An his wife got up an shut the door. 'Here, have a biscuit,' me ma said. 'We might as well finish them. An ye can drink the rest a the milk.' I put the empty bottle on the floor an lay down, puttin me hands under me head.

'I wonder if we've done the right thing,' me ma asked, lookin at me.

'Goin back te Dublin? If it was up te me, Ma, I wouldn't be goin back.'

'Jaysus!' me ma said, lookin worried. 'I wonder how the poor childre are.'

I started te feel sick at the mention of Dublin. Jackser came rushin back te me, an I could feel his grip tightenin aroun me. It was as if we'd never left him. 'No, Ma! We're still in Liverpool. Let's get off.' I tried te pull her up offa the seat.

'We can't! It's too late,' she said, chewin her lip. 'We'll only be locked up if we stay here wit no money an nowhere te stay.'

Me heart was poundin, an I was lookin aroun. The other people were starin at us. 'Come on, sit down. We'll be all right. We'll have a better chance of gettin somewhere te live once we have the childre back.'

I looked at her. 'How, Ma? How?'

'We'll go te the Corporation, an we'll stay at the Regina Ceoli if we have te, but there's no good te be had from stayin over here.'

I looked inta her face, not knowin wha te think. Then I lay down on the seat just wantin te sleep an wake up. Wantin everythin te be OK.

37

We made our way off the boat an headed up the quays. 'So tha's it,' me ma said. 'We're back here again!'

I didn't answer. The seagulls were screamin in the air an flyin down low aroun the ship. People were laughin an shoutin at each other, their relatives an friends delighted te see them again an pickin up their suitcases an walkin on. Some were on their own an hurried away, anxious te be where they were goin. I smelt the Irish air, an a bit a me knew I belonged here. I walked on wit me ma, feelin the damp mist get inside me. Aul fellas standin against the wall watchin the world pass by spat an choked on their Woodbines. I didn't know their faces, yet I felt I'd known them all me life. Lazy bastards, they make me sick. We crossed over the bridge, an an aul woman coverin her head wit a black shawl caught me eye an nodded te us. 'Cold aul weather, isn't it, Mrs?' she said, passin us by an hurryin on about her business.

'Ah! Indeed it is!' me ma answered.

How is it ye don't see such poor people in London? Even the tramps is better dressed, even if they are wearin forty coats tied up wit string. But people here seem te have such worn-down faces. Even the young ones look old. I wonder why? I lifted me head, comin away from me thoughts, an noticed we were walkin down Parnell Street. 'Where are we goin, Ma?'

'I'm thinkin,' she said, lost in her own thoughts.

An aul one wit a red-raw face, her scarf slippin offa her head showin grey hair, was walkin up an down in front of her stall, stampin her ankle boots inta the ground te keep out the damp. 'Do ye want a few potatoes, Mrs? Look! They're lovely.'

'No!' me ma said, shakin her head an walkin on. Then me ma screamed. 'Run, Martha!' an took off runnin. 'He's seen us!' she screamed as she flew off headin towards O'Connell Street.

I stopped dead fer a split second, me head swingin on me shoulders tryin te see wha's wrong. Then I saw him. Jackser! His legs pumpin towards me, holdin his overcoat gripped in one hand across his legs when he means business an he's runnin fer his life. I turned, already too late. His hand was reachin out te grab me. I stuck me body out an leaned me head back, me legs goin like propellers, an he missed me by inches. I headed down onta the hill, an I could feel his hot breath on me neck.

'Stop, ye bastard!' he roared in me ear, reachin his arm out fer me. I ducked, divin across the road an roun the corner. I hesimitated fer a split second, duckin sideways te avoid a woman comin towards me, an Jackser's hand plunged out, grabbin me by the collar of me coat, yankin me offa me feet an chokin me. 'Get back here, ye bastard!' he panted, swingin me aroun te look at me. 'Where's yer mammy?' he roared, his eyes bulgin an big spits hangin outa his mouth. I stared at him, not able te get me senses back. He shook me, roarin inta me face, 'Where is she?'

Jaysus! Wha's happenin? Me teeth is rattlin in me head, an I can't stop shiverin. 'Come on, ye whore's melt. I'm takin ye te the police!' An he dragged me off in the direction where he first spotted me.

Police! Wha for? Fuck him, he's bluffin, they can't do anythin. He hasn't got me ma, there's nothin he can do. 'Let me go!' I roared.

'Shut the fuck up!' he said, givin me a box on the side of me head.

'No!' I screamed in a rage. 'You're nothin te me.'

He stopped an looked at me. 'Wha did you say?' His eyes narrowed, but I didn't care.

'I don't belong te you! Ye're not me father! I'll tell the police all about ye if ye don't let me go.' I was stiffenin meself an starin at him, tryin te get me breath.

He blinked, then ground his teeth in a snarl, an I went tighter, waitin fer his fist te fly at me. Then he caught his breath, an his face

450

sagged. 'Look, ye're a good kid, just tell me where Sally is. I'm lost without her,' an he started te cry.

I stared at him, keepin me face straight. Yer soft soap won't work wit me, I thought, waitin fer him te relax his grip, an I was off. I looked aroun te see if anyone would help me. Then I saw me ma puttin her head aroun the corner. Ah, fuck! Why is she there? Jackser looked in the same direction, lettin go of me, an I took off as he chased her, screamin, 'I've got ye now, ye whore!'

I tore up Parnell Street, lookin back te see Jackser grab a hold a me ma an pin her against the wall. I slowed down an stopped. He has her! Jaysus! What am I goin te do? I rushed back, stoppin a few feet away. Now he was roarin inta her face an pointin te the sky. 'They're gone, ye whore, gone!'

'Where are they?' me ma was askin, white as a sheet an shakin.

'I fucked them inta a home. Wha did ye think I'd do? They're split up in all directions. Did ye really think I was goin te take care of them? Did ya?' he screamed.

'But where are the childre now?' me ma asked, shakin like mad.

'I told ye, ye're not listenin te me. They've all been put inta different homes,' he roared, stabbin the air wit his pointed finger an lookin at her wit his eyes starin an his jaw droppin open, soundin very satisfied wit himself. Me ma started te cry. 'It's too late fer tha now, Mrs,' he said, standin back from her. 'An I'm on me way over te the Corporation now te hand them back the keys of the house.'

'I want te see the childre,' me ma said, lookin at him. 'Where are they?'

Jackser stepped inta me ma's face again. He had an evil sneer on his face, an he said quietly, 'Ye won't be seein them again. They're gone fer good. I signed them away, as you're not fit te take care a them. Remember, whore! You were the one tha abandoned them! An ye've no home te take them to. So you can fuck off now. Cos I've already got another woman lined up fer meself,' an he laughed, throwin his head back.

Me ma stared at him, tryin te work out wha was happenin. 'Yeah!' he said, shakin his head slowly at her an laughin again. 'They're gone, every last one of them, an you'll never find them. Ye can start searchin, Mrs, but they won't tell ye fuck all.'

Me ma looked at me in desperation. 'Jaysus Christ! The childre are gone, ye poxy bastard,' she roared at him. He sneered at her, enjoyin himself. 'An ye're goin te give up the keys of the house? Ye can't do tha! Tha's my home, too.'

'No, Mrs! Ye're wrong there,' he said happily. 'Tha house is in my name. An I can do what I fuckin well like.'

Me ma was blinkin like mad, tryin te think. 'Ma, tell him, tell him, Ma, you were comin back te him. Tell him ye missed him an the childre!' I looked at him. 'Jackser, she missed ya! She never stopped talkin about ya!'

The bastard's face lit up, an he looked at me ma. She looked at me, 'Yeah,' she said, blinkin at him an chewin on her lip.

'Well, tha's different. Tha's a different story altogether! If I thought ye were back fer good, an I knew ye'd never try anythin like tha again, maybe I'd see me way te lettin ye back. But there would be changes, mind! Ye're not gettin off tha easily!'

'Yeah!' me ma said, noddin agreement. 'So let's go, then. I want te get the childre back. We'll go now.'

Jackser snuffled happily an looked at me, noddin away, agreein wit everythin tha was bein said. 'Right! The first place is Cheeverstown. Tha's where Dinah an the babby is. An you! Go on home. Charlie will let ye in. I kept him back te look after the house.'

'Ye didn't put Charlie away?' me ma said, lookin confused.

'No, he's your bastard, an I needed him te get me messages. Go on! Are ye still here?'

'I've no money fer the bus fare.'

He put his hand in his pocket an took out two pennies an threw them at me. 'Here, get runnin fer tha bus.'

I sat on the bus lookin out the winda seein nothin. Caught! Just like tha. An everythin's gone. We couldn't let him give up the house, cos he's right, the bastard. We'd never get the childre back. At least this way we have a chance. We can try te find a place of our own once we have the childre. An poor Charlie! He kept him wit him.

Tha child is only six. He wouldn't be able te do much, an Jackser was sure te beat the hell outa him. I looked up, an the bus was comin te my stop. I jumped up, an the conductor banged the bell wit his fist. I didn't wait fer the bus te stop. I held onta the bar an jumped off backwards when it started te slow down. An then I ran forwards te keep me balance. The conductor thumped the bell again, an the bus picked up speed without stoppin. I like doin tha, cos it tests me te see how fast I am on me feet. I'm always testin meself. Jumpin off high walls, climbin things. If I'm afraid of somethin, then I have te have a go, to test meself an beat it.

I started runnin, wantin te see Charlie. In the gate, better close it or tha aul fella will go mad. I banged on the letter box, the knocker's gone. An Charlie opened the door. He stood starin at me, an I couldn't take me eyes offa him. I came in slowly. Jaysus! Wha happened te him? He looks like an aul man. His eyes were sunk in the back of his head, an he had big purple marks under his eyes. An his hair was matted, an he was in his bare feet an wearin a pair of short trousers tha looked like they'd belonged te a twelve year old. An the rest of his face was grey. A dirty grey. 'Where's me ma?' he stood starin at me.

'We're back, Charlie!' I said slowly, smilin, tryin te take him in.

'Yeah!' he said quietly, turnin his back on me. 'An ye's went off leavin me behind.' An he walked off slowly inta the sittin room. I followed him in. Jaysus, the place is a mess. Porter bottles everywhere. An jam jars wit tea, an plates, an spoons, an filth on the floor walked inta the filthy dirty black floorboards. The smell was terrible. I opened the curtains an the windas te let in the air, an the fuckin chairs was broken an smashed against the walls an thrown in the corner. Christ! Me heart was sinkin down inta me belly.

'There's nothin te sit on,' I said, lookin aroun the empty room wit only the table still standin an dirt everywhere. I looked at Charlie, an he said nothin. 'Wha happened, Charlie?' I asked him quietly. He looked away, sayin nothin. 'Did he go mad?' No answer. 'Did he kill ye, Charlie?'

He shook his head up an down. 'Youse left me wit him, ye's

453

wouldn't take me,' was all he said. He looked like a very old man standin there in the trousers too big fer him, an his legs, ye could only see a bit of them, was like two matchsticks hangin under curtains. An his feet were black. His eyes was dead, though. An his face was all grey an purple.

'Yeah! It was a terrible thing we did te ye. Leavin ye behind. I should've made me ma bring ye wit us. Later, when it hit me, I knew he'd kill you, cos ye don't belong te him, an he'd take it out on you! I'm sorry, Charlie!'

Charlie stared at me listenin, then he turned his head away, takin in a breath, an said, 'Yeah! He hates us, Martha. He wishes me ma didn't have us.'

I shook me head, 'Yeah, Charlie! Ye're right. He thinks we're only the bastards, but who cares wha tha mad bandy aul bastard thinks. Come on, let's pick up this rubbish before tha animal gets back.'

I started te pick up all the porter bottles, an I headed fer the back door, puttin them in the corner, cos the dustbin was overflowin. 'Jaysus, he went mad on the drink.'

'Yeah,' Charlie said. 'He brought aul ones back, an they were laughin an drinkin all night.'

'Wha?' I said. 'Here, in the house?'

'Yeah. One aul one came in already drunk, an she was plastered wit lipstick all over her teeth an her mouth. Jackser wanted me te cook black an white puddin an eggs fer them. But I couldn't light the gas. An he gave me a smack a the fryin pan, an I woke up lyin at the back door. I was vomitin me guts up wit the pain in me head. Here, look on the top! Ye can still see the sore.'

I bent down, an his head was matted. It was hard, the blood must of caked in an dried it stiff. 'It bled fer weeks, Martha. An I had a headache all the time, cos I must a touched it in me sleep, tha's why the sore kept openin.'

'Go in, Charlie,' I said, feelin terrible. 'This is hell. We have te get the fuck outa here.'

'Ye're takin me wit ye's. I'm not stayin no more,' Charlie said, lookin up at me ashen-faced.

454

'Yeah, Charlie. Don't you worry. Me ma's takin everyone. We're goin te get a place of our own an get away from tha mad aul fella.'

'When?' Charlie asked.

'Me ma's goin te get everyone outa the homes, then we'll start lookin,' I said happily, thinkin about it.

Charlie lifted his shoulders te give a big sigh an sorta smiled, then he dropped them again. I was happy te see him liftin up a bit. But he didn't look well, an it broke me heart.

'Let's make a sup a tea, Charlie,' I said, headin fer the kitchen.

'There's no milk, Martha.'

'Ah, Jaysus, tha's too bad.' I was disappointed. An there's no bread, so tha's tha then. We'll just have te wait.

I was lookin at him when I heard the front gate openin. I leapt te me feet, an Charlie was screamin in fright. He was tryin te get up in a hurry. I was already halfway te the door, an I rushed back, helpin him te his feet. 'Take yer time, Charlie! Sneak through when they're in the sittin room,' I croaked, me heart poundin.

The door whipped open, an Jackser glared at me, puttin Dinah down on her feet. She started te whinge. 'Where the fuck are you hidin, Mrs? Why the fuck didn't ye have the door open fer us?'

'Sorry, Jackser. I was rushin te get it open.' He pushed past me, headin fer the scullery.

Me ma came in carryin Sally. She raised her eyes te heaven, lookin at me. 'Jaysus, he's startin again,' she said. I shut the door, an Dinah stood rooted, starin at the floor an keenin.

'Come on, Dinah,' I said, takin her hand, an she pulled away from me.

Jackser came runnin inta the hall an punched me on the side of me head, sendin me flyin. 'Get the young one in,' he roared, stoopin over me wit his fist raised in the air.

'Right, Jackser,' I said, seein stars an tryin te watch his fist. 'Get her in,' he roared, draggin me by the back of me neck an liftin me te me feet. Dinah screamed, buryin her face in her arm. I lifted her under her arms an carried her inta the sittin room. Sally was cryin an frettin, too.

'Jaysus, Sally. Will ye ever shut them kids up?' he roared, goin inta the scullery.

'Jaysus Christ!' me ma moaned, lookin at me. 'Wha did I come back te this for?'

'Hey, Mrs!' Jackser roared, comin in. 'Get up te tha van an get a pint a milk an a loaf a bread.' An he threw two shillins at me. 'Hurry!' he roared.

I was out the door when he roared after me, 'An another thing! First light in the mornin, I want you outa tha bed an inta them shops. An ye'd better bring back the money an get them messages. There's fuck all money or food in this house. So ye better get back te work, you've a lot a catchin up te do. An I heard all about yer gallavantin.' An he looked at me ma. She got annoyed an didn't know where te look. Jackser laughed, an me ma made a face sayin, don't be mindin him! An Jackser said, 'It's true, isn't it?' an pinched me ma's arse an looked at me wit a glint in his eye. 'She was . . . ye know,' he was lookin at me ma an mumblin. 'Wasn't she? Tha's wha ye said,' an he was shakin his head an pointin down at me ma's arse. 'Fuck me,' he said, laughin an takin sideways looks at me an snufflin.

I felt sick an looked at me ma. She was laughin, an liftin her head, an givin quick looks at me, an didn't know wha te do wit herself. She told him! She knows wha happened te me in England wit them two men. But she thinks I'm a woman! Tha I would want tha te happen te me! An now Jackser thinks tha's great. He's lookin at me like I'm a grown woman an I would want wha they do te each other. I wanted te scream, 'Ye fuckin bastardin whore! I'm a child. I'm only eleven years old. Ye're not supposed te be treatin me like a woman, ye dirty filthy animals. Ye're a whore, Ma, an I hope ye die roarin!'

I took outa the house an ran as fast as I could up te the van. An when I had the bread an milk in me hands, I walked back slowly. Me heart was breakin. Me ma knows wha Jackser likes. He likes te get his hands on me. She must have known tha. An she went an told him wha happened te me. She must have thought I wanted te be wit them two men. So she tells Jackser te make him happy. So the fuckin whore is happy te be back wit him. She must have missed him, tha's why she came back, not just fer the childre. An te think I fell fer her lies. No! She's no good.

Me anger slowly left me. I can't depend on her. I'm on me own, an so is Charlie, an we've nowhere te go. If I complain, wha would I say? An they would deny it. An, anyway, no one would do anythin about it. The police made him take me home tha time I was sent te England on me own, even though they knew I didn't belong te him an he didn't want te take me back. But they forced him. So there's nothin I can do about it other than kill meself. But I'm not goin te do tha. I want te be big. Then I can do what I like. But tha's too far away. God, are ye there? Will ye look after me an me brother Charlie? Cos he's got longer te go than me. But on the other hand, I can always take him wit me. Will ye make sure no harm comes te us, God? An ye know wha me ma an Jackser are like. I don't want te ever be like them, God! So will ye look after us, God? An I'll be very good. Thanks! I felt better. God is lookin after us, an he'll make sure we're OK.

I started te run wit the bread an milk. An when I got in the door, Jackser came runnin an snatched the bread an milk offa me. 'About fuckin time! Were ye milkin the cow?'

'Eh! There was a big queue at the van,' I said, talkin te his back.

'Go an give yer mammy a hand,' he shouted, makin the tea.

I wandered inta the sittin room, not really wantin te be near me ma. 'Look at this poor child's head, Martha,' she said, holdin Sally on her lap an sittin on the floorboards. 'The child's head is covered in sores.' I looked at Sally, an she looked sickly, her eyes dead in her head an not lookin at anythin. Her head was covered in sores an a few aroun her forehead. 'She picked tha up from tha place out in Cheeverstown! They're full a diseases them places! As soon as I saw her I said I was takin her home. They were tryin te stop me, but I told them they had no rights. An tha aul fella said he was responsible fer signin them in, an now, says he, I'm takin them out. An don't try te stop me.' Then me ma laughed. 'They were afraid of their life, cos they knew they were in the wrong. There's nothin they can do when ye have yer own home. So fuck them!'

Me ma was ramblin on, but I wasn't listenin. I was lookin at Dinah sittin beside me ma an lookin away when she saw anyone lookin at her. Her eyes were dead, too, an her face was very white. I tried te lift her. 'Come on, Dinah,' I said, smilin at her, an she let her head fall back an keened, not really cryin, an actin like she didn't know me. I put her back down on the floor beside me ma, an she just lay there. Not lookin at anythin, no life in her.

38

Jackser was pacin himself up an down the sittin room watchin fer the gate. 'Now ye know wha te say te him! Don't ya?'

'Yeah, Jackser!' I said, wishin te get it over wit.

'Tell him nothin! Keep yer mouth shut. An keep yer eyes on me. I'll let ye know when te answer somethin. If he asks any awkward questions, leave it te me. Just pretend te be stupid. But the main thing is te say nothin, ye can't be hanged fer wha ye don't say! Have ye got tha now?'

'Yeah! Right, Jackser. I'm te say nothin.'

'Right! Fuck this waitin, he should be here by now,' he said, lookin outa the winda. 'Wha's tha smell?' an he sniffed his way aroun the room. 'Did ye make sure te clean up tha shit the babby did over there?'

I looked over beside the corner near the fire. 'Yeah, Jackser! It's all cleaned up.'

'Well, check aroun again,' he roared, clenchin his fists. 'I can still smell somethin. I told tha lazy aul hag te get this room cleaned up.'

I rushed aroun lookin in corners. The floorboards was caked black wit dirt. 'Yeah, it's OK, Jackser,' I said, keepin close te the door, well away from him over at the winda.

Then he pointed at the ceilin. 'Get up there an tell tha aul one te keep them fuckin kids quiet. I can hear them movin aroun.'

I rushed out the door. An then I could hear the gate squeakin open. 'He's here, Jackser!' I said, rushin back in.

'I know tha!' he said, grabbin me an pushin me outa the way. He

459

opened the door himself, an a man came in carryin a leather bag. He stopped just inside the door, takin in the room. An his mouth dropped open, an his eyes flew aroun the room, then lit on me. Then he looked at his shoes, not sure if he should come in or go back out. Jackser came up behind him, sayin, wit a big smile on his face an droppin his head te show respect, 'Eh! Martha's in here, Sir!' an he rushed over te the table tha was bare now. Me ma had te clear all the dirty jam jars an milk bottles away fer the man's visit. 'Eh! Sit here, Sir!' an pulled out the only chair tha wasn't goin te collapse when ye sat on it.

The man sat at the top of the table, an I sat on his right. An Jackser sat on his left, starin straight at me. 'Now!' the man said, openin his bag an takin out a big bunch a forms. 'You know why I've come here? I have been sent by the court, because the judge wants a report on Martha. My name is Dr Carroll. And I want you, Martha, to answer my questions.'

I looked at Jackser, an he shook his head an winked at me. I shook me head an said, 'OK, Dr Carroll.'

'Right, let's begin,' said the doctor, lookin at me an then pullin out a piece a paper. 'Now! I want you to look at this picture and tell me why you think this man is running.'

I looked at Jackser, an he winked, so it was OK to answer the question. Then I looked at the picture. It was a big field. An a man was runnin fer his life, an he looked so afraid he'd even let his hat blow off an didn't wait te pick it up. I stared at the picture fer a few minutes, then I said, 'Tha poor man is after gettin an awful shock. He was goin home, makin his way across tha field. It was probably a short cut. An he saw a man hangin from a tree. An he's not the better of it. An he's rushin te tell someone an get help.' I then let out a big breath after workin tha one out. The man was starin at me wit his jaw hangin down. An I looked at Jackser te see if I'd done all right, an his eyes was rollin te heaven.

Ah, Jaysus, did I say somethin wrong? I was thinkin, when the doctor said, 'Yes! Fine, now, can you tell me where Mars is?'

'Mars? Do ye mean a Mars bar?' I looked at Jackser, an he was rollin his eyes an pointin his finger te heaven. 'Oh! Ye mean space?' I asked the doctor.

'Yes, that's right,' the doctor said happily.

'Oh, yeah! I know all about tha,' I said. 'I remember years ago, when the spaceship went up. I was listenin on the radio, an I waited fer it te come back. But it never did. So I gave up wonderin about it.'

'Good!' said the doctor. 'Now, can you tell me what is charity?'

'Oh, tha's when ye get somethin fer nothin. Or when ye help yer neighbours out or they help you. It's lookin out fer each other!'

'Very good,' said the doctor. Then he was delighted when I read a page outa a school reader fer him.

'I can read the lot if ye want me to,' I said, delighted he was listenin te me read.

'No, no! That's very good,' he said, takin back the book.

I waited fer more, enjoyin meself. He'd asked me sums ye do in yer head, an I had the answer out before he finished the question. Ye have te be quick, or I'd be robbed blind when I'm sellin me butter. 'Now, spell forbidden,' he asked, lookin at me. The first spellins were fer babbies, but now he thinks these are harder, but they're not.

'F-o-r-b-i-d-d-e-n!' I spelt, waitin fer more.

'Good!' he said, puttin away the last of his papers an slammin his bag shut. 'That's the lot!' An he stood up, headin fer the door.

Jackser jumped up, bowin an smilin, an said, 'Thank you very much, Sir!' An tipped his forehead wit two pointed fingers an rushed te open the door fer the man an let him out.

I waited te see if I'd done anythin wrong. 'You an yer fuckin Mars bar!' he said, lookin at me. 'Wha put tha idea in yer head? Lucky I warned ye.'

'Yeah, Jackser, ye were very smart there, all right!' I said, butterin him up. Then he snuffled an laughed.

I let me breath out. An me ma came in sayin, 'Jaysus! Is he gone? Me heart was broke tryin te keep them kids quiet!' An she ground her teeth an gave Charlie a box in the head, cos Sally was annoyin her cryin.

461

'Wha did I do?' Charlie muttered, duckin an rubbin his head.

'So wha's goin te happen now, Martha?' me ma asked, chewin her lip an blinkin. Sally was now screamin in her arms, an me ma was gettin very agitated. 'Here! Sit down there,' me ma roared, dumpin Sally on the floor te crawl aroun.

'Well,' I said, thinkin about it. 'Now I have te go back te court. An tha doctor is goin te give him the report about me.'

'I don't know,' Jackser said, rubbin his head. 'I don't like the look of this. Tha judge never asked fer anythin like tha before. Usually he just gives ye the probation act an lets ye off wit a warnin! But this time it's different! Wha did they catch ye fer this time?'

'Six pounds a butter, Jackser,' I said, waitin te hear wha he was goin te say. I was gettin worried again. The thought of havin te face tha court again in another few weeks was makin me feel sick.

'Tha's not too bad in itself. But ye've been up before him at least seven or eight times in the last two te three years.'

'Yeah,' me ma said, 'an she'll be twelve in another few months. Then we could get ye te leave school fer good. They don't bother about ye when ye're older like tha.'

'But I don't go te school anyway, Ma!' I said, gettin annoyed wit her.

'Yeah, but I'm sayin, once ye're over age, ye don't have te worry!'

'Will ye never mind about tha, Mrs!' Jackser roared. 'We have te get this court case outa the way first, or the young one will be put away!' He glared at me ma. 'An where will we be then, Mrs? Eh? No fuckin money comin inta the house. An ye can kiss goodbye te yer lumps a steak, an yer fried rashers, an yer good butter on yer bread!'

'Ah, shut the fuck up!' me ma roared back. 'An you won't be fillin yer gut wit any more drink!'

Jackser slammed his fist on the table, an I ran fer the door. 'Right, Mrs! If ye don't want te listen te what I have te say, then fuck ye,' he roared, snortin, an glarin, an spittin big dribbles at me ma.

'Go on, then!' me ma said, shakin. 'Say wha ye have te say. I'm listenin!'

Jackser stepped back, takin a big breath inta his lungs, an said, 'We may have te get her a solicitor. It will be money well spent. An you get a letter from the doctor, sayin ye're expectin another child. An get him te say ye're in bad health. An ye suffer wit yer nerves. An the young one is a great help te ye at home. An without her, ye won't be able te manage. Tha it will cause great hardship. Have ye got tha?'

'Yeah!' me ma said, not lookin too sure she understood everythin he said.

Jackser watched her, 'Did ye understand tha, Mrs?'

'Yes! I told ye,' me ma said, gettin annoyed.

'Look, Martha, you go wit yer mammy te the doctor, an ye can explain the situation te him better. He won't make head nor tail outa what tha woman is tryin te say, an this is too important te mess aroun wit. Cos if you get sent down, then tha's it, we're all fucked! We need the money comin inta the house.'

'Yeah,' I said.

'Will ye ever light tha fire,' me ma roared at Jackser. 'It's fuckin freezin in here.' She was blinkin an chewin her lip, still agitated at the thought of all she had te do. She hates havin things facin her, like the doctor, or the courts, or havin te do anythin.

'There's no coal left,' Jackser said, lookin in the empty tin bucket standin next te the fire. 'Here! Give tha young one the money an send her up te Cappagh te get a stone a coal. Go on,' he said, lookin at me. 'The sack is in the shed outside.'

I rushed out te the back an grabbed the sack. Me head was startin te pain me, an I felt a bit sick. Jaysus, I'm not in the mood te walk all the way up there an drag tha coal back. 'Give us the money, Ma,' I said, holdin out me hand, wantin te get movin.

'Eh! Get me a stale loaf an a bottle of milk,' me ma said, thinkin an takin her time.

'I can't carry all this, Ma! How am I goin te carry the coal, then?' I said, snarlin at her in a loud whisper.

'Well, we need the milk an the bread!' she said, glarin at me.

'Get a fuckin move on,' Jackser roared over at us while he raked out the ashes.

'Here, ye can go up te the van then when ye get back.'

I snatched the half-crown an rushed out the door, headin fer the farm shop up in Cappagh where ye can buy the coal. I was thinkin of the time a few weeks ago when I walked inta the farm yard, headin fer the shop, an I saw the nanny goat chewin on a ten bob note. It stopped chewin fer a minute when it saw me lookin. An I was afraid of me life of tha goat, cos it chases ye. But I only hesimitated fer a few minutes, takin in the picture of the red ten shillins, an me fear was gone. I dived at the goat, grabbin her mouth an forcin it open an snatchin the ten shillins. Wha was left of it. The goat got such a shock she just stood there lookin after me flyin out the gate. Then when it dawned on her tha she'd been robbed, she lowered her head an ran after me. Too late! I was down the road an headin fer the bank in the village before she even hit the gate. I told the man in the bank the babby got a hold of me ma's purse an chewed the money. An he laughed an took the three-quarters of the note tha was left an gave me a shiny new one. I had a great time spendin it an even brought home fish an chips fer everyone. Jackser didn't think te ask me where I got the money from! Tha was a great day.

I looked up, realisin I was here. Me day dreamin passed the time, an I headed inta the shop waitin me turn. Then I suddenly felt somethin hot comin down me legs, an I looked down, seein blood pourin outa me. I had no knickers. I was just wearin a thin aul frock an a pair a shoes, an the blood was pourin outa me an onta the floor. I froze, afraid te move, an looked at the other women an childre te see if they noticed wha happened te me. I don't know why I'm pumpin wit blood, but it's comin from between me legs, an I've no knickers te wear. Oh, Jesus, wha's happenin? I feel sick wit the shame of it. I looked aroun me, wantin te run, but they'll see me. I looked down at the pool a blood pourin onta the floor an moved up a bit. I was destroyed. Me legs was soaked in blood. I bent down suddenly an wiped me legs wit the sack, coverin them in coal dust. But I kept rubbin, lookin at people's backs te make sure no one was lookin. Then I turned, headin out the door, an flew up the country road, headin towards Cappagh Convent.

There's not a soul aroun, thank God! I went inta a field an sat down, liftin up me frock so as not te destroy it. The blood was caked inta me. I felt a cramp in the bottom of me stomach an a huge clot a blood came rushin out from between me legs. Jesus! Wha's this all about? Is it somethin te do wit women? I have a feelin it is. I stood up again, movin away, leavin the clot of blood behind. An sat down again, grabbin handfuls of grass te clean meself. I need water, an a washcloth, an a pair of knickers, an a rag te soak it up. Where am I goin te get tha? I kept rubbin wit the grass, an it was damp, so tha's good. I looked at meself. Me legs was clean now, an I wiped between me legs, but the blood kept comin out. Jesus! What am I goin te do? I can't ask anyone fer somethin te wear. Wha would I say? I'm ashamed of me life. Me heart was slowin down now. Fer a while I nearly lost me mind in tha shop. I thought I was goin te get hysterical an start screamin. But I'm OK now. It definitely must be somethin tha happens te women. If only I had somethin te wear! I kept on rubbin the grass all over the top of me legs an in between, an then I stood up, lookin down at meself. Me legs were fine, nice an clean. Even the coal dust was gone. But as I started te move off, I felt it pourin outa me again, an I moved me legs apart, holdin me frock, an it trickled down onta the grass.

Me head was poundin me now wit pain. An then I started te get sick from the sudden sharp pain in me head when I moved it. I heaved up the sick, an the pain got worse. An then I started te panic from the thought tha Jackser's waitin fer the coal an I can't get movin. I started te cry, lookin aroun me wonderin what I could do. I bent down an picked up the sack, an started walkin outa the field, still roarin me head off cryin, an then stepped onta the footpath, headin off inta the country. I can't go back there, everyone will see me. An I looked down at me legs, the blood still streamin outa me. What am I goin te do, God? I asked, lookin aroun at the empty fields, all shinin wit wet, an the bare trees, an no one te help me. I walked on slowly, keenin te meself. Jackser's goin te kill me fer bein so long, but there's nothin I can do. I can't walk through the streets like this or go inta tha shop. So I wandered on, comin te the gates of the convent. They had a hospital here, too, fer people wit broken bones an people tha couldn't walk.

I wandered up the avenue, hopin te find a rag or somethin, or maybe by some miracle a pair a knickers. Then I stopped at the front door, lookin at the brass plaque tha said Mother Mary Aikenhead, an I looked aroun me. Not a soul or a sound te be heard. The fields was white wit all the frost, an it was covered wit the January mist. I was standin so long lookin at the door an wonderin what I could do tha the frost was inside me bones now, an me teeth started te chatter. Tha was makin me headache even worse. Then I heard a sound, an I looked aroun. A little nun was headin towards me wearin a long black coat buttoned from the neck te her toes over her long black habit. 'What do you want?' she asked me, comin closer.

'Eh! Sister, nothin,' I said, freezin up. I put me knees pressed together an looked down at me frock wit the big red stain of blood in front, an turned away from her, not able te bear the shame.

'Stop! Come here,' she barked at me. I turned, lookin down at the ground. 'What? Why?' she asked me in a rush, lost fer words an lookin at me from head te toe. I lowered me head te the ground, feelin meself gettin very light, the shame smotherin me, an just hangin on, waitin fer her te feast her eyes on the terrible state I was in. An then say wha she had te say, an then I'd walk off, an she could leave me alone. It won't kill me, I can disappear an never have te face her again. 'Come with me,' I heard her say. I lifted me head a little an she was walkin off. 'Come on,' she said, hurryin. 'Follow me!'

I moved after her, an we came te a side door, an she opened the door an said, 'Hurry.' Then she headed off down a passage an went through another door an down a long passage wit doors on each side. 'Go in there,' she said, 'and wait. I won't be long.' It was a bathroom wit a huge bath an a tilet an a sink. She shut the door behind me, an I waited, lookin at the bath. Me heart lifted. The nun is a saint, I thought te meself. Thanks, God, fer lookin after me. I heard footsteps, an then the door opened. The nun rushed in wit a towel an soap an a washcloth, an put them on the stool, sayin, 'Have a quick wash here,' an she put in the plug an turned on the tap an

466

hot water gushed out. 'Now, take off your things and step in quickly. I don't have much time. I need to catch the bus.' Then she looked at me. 'What size are you? I'll take a look and see if I can find you somethin to wear.' I said nothin, just tried te smile at her, an I kept me eyes on the floor. Then she was gone out the door.

I whipped off me frock, an the blood streaked me chest an neck. It was a terrible sickly-sweet smell. An I wrapped it inta a ball an put it on the floor an kicked off me shoes an stepped inta the huge bath, shiverin. The steam was risin, an I left the water runnin. It was a bit hot te sit in, an I kept sittin an standin until I got used te the heat. Then I sat down, an it was lovely. The water turned red. An I pulled the plug, lettin out some of the water. Then I picked up the bar a soap. Palmolive, it said. The smell was lovely. I lifted me foot an soaked meself wit the soap, an the hot water poured down. Oh, thank you, God! This is lovely. But me belly was nervous at the thought of wha they were goin te say te me when I eventually got back. I'll have te think up somethin. I put the plug back in an then ducked me head under the water. Might as well wash me hair while I'm at it. I was lovely an warm an covered meself in soap again, an dipped me feet under the hot tap, enjoyin meself no end. Ah! This is lovely. I'll definitely have te think up some good excuse fer Jackser. But wha?

Then the door opened, an the nun rushed in wit clothes under her arm. She kept her face turned away from me. 'What did you say your name was, dear?'

'Martha, Sister.'

'Right, Martha. Like a good girl, will you step out now and get dressed, and these, dear, are pads. You put one inside your underwear, and it will soak up the blood.' She opened up a package an took out a white long pad, she called it, an it looked like a thick bandage. An put it on top of the clothes she left on the stool. 'I'll be back shortly,' she said, not lookin at me an headin fer the door. 'So be quick, Martha!' As soon as she closed the door, I stood up, pullin the plug, an lifted the big soft towel an dried meself. Then I stepped out an looked at the clothes. A big pair a navy-blue cotton knickers

467

wit elastic in the legs. I pulled them on then looked at the white pad an put it on the knickers an pulled them up. Lovely! Warm an dry. Then I picked up a cotton vest wit a frill at the top, it was soft an light as a feather an long. It covered me arse. Then a long dark-green frock, it's really heavy wit a white frilly collar. It's a bit long an wide fer me. But it's grand an warm an clean. An even a coat wit a wide collar an buttons. I put it on an looked down at meself. It was miles too long, but I didn't care. It'll keep me lovely an warm. I'm always freezin wit the cold.

I picked up the brown paper bag, an there's two packages of pads. Southalls it says. Now I have loads a pads. I looked aroun, an me frock was gone. She must have thrown it out. No socks! Ah, well! Ye can't have everythin. Then she knocked at the door an put her head in. 'Are you ready?'

'Yes, Sister, I'm grand now.'

'Come along so. I must be on my way,' an she headed off down the passage, an I followed behind her.

When we got outside, I said, 'Thank you very much, Sister! I'm very grateful te you!' Then I lowered me head, an I mumbled, 'I didn't know wha te do.'

She put her hand on me shoulder an said, leanin inta me, 'It's a natural happening, child. It means you are becoming a woman. This is nothin to worry yourself about. It happens to all women of child-bearing years. Pray to our Blessed Lady, she will watch over you and protect you. She's doing that all the time. Even when you don't know it. Who do you think led you to me, child?'

I looked up at her then, an she had the most gentle eyes. I looked at her white face, soft an covered in wrinkles. But I knew she was a saint, even if other people tha looked at her only saw an old woman. I won't ever forget her an wha she's done fer me. 'Thanks, Sister. I'm goin te say a prayer fer you, an I'll light a candle, too.'

She squeezed me shoulder an smiled, sayin, 'That would be lovely. You do that, child.'

'I'd better hurry, Sister,' an I turned an waved back at her an rushed off te get the coal, the pain in me head easin off.

468

39

We walked down Lord Edward Street an turned right, headin in under the arch tha led inta the Dublin Castle where the Children's Court was. I looked up at the sign on the wall tha said 'The Sick and Indigent Roomkeepers Society'. I always look up at tha sign when I pass it goin te the court an wonder wha the Indigent means. It must mean they're annoyed cos they're sick an have no money. I don't blame them! It's terrible te be at the mercy of the world when ye have nothin an nowhere te go. I was shiverin wit fear. The thought of havin te face the courts an not knowin wha was goin te happen was killin me. I followed me ma an Jackser in the door te the court an turned left inta the waitin room, an we sat down on a bench. Jackser was very quiet, an me ma was like ice, just starin an sayin nothin. I didn't want te even look at them, never mind talk. Women an childre were millin aroun, walkin up an down, white as sheets, not talkin either. They were mostly young fellas, not young ones like me.

Everyone was listenin anxiously, waitin fer their name te be called. A name was roared down, an everyone jumped. We cocked our ears an looked at each other, the other mammies askin, 'Who was tha? Listen!' An the name was called again.

'Brown! Emmet Brown.' The man came inta the room, an a mammy jumped up, grabbin her son by the arm.

'Here! That's us!' she said, rushin Emmet outa the room. He tried te pull back, goin white as a sheet, an the mammy pulled him, sayin, 'Come on! Come on! We're here, Sir!' an she followed the man up the stairs. We all sat back, waitin our turn an feelin sick. No one looked at anyone. Me thoughts were on the waitin. I could hear me heart flyin in me ears, an me stomach was heavy, an I felt I was goin te get sick. I couldn't stop meself from shakin, an I wanted te get up an walk aroun. But Jackser would go mad, so I sat wit me hands clasped together an stared at the floor. More names were called, an new mammies arrived, creepin in the door an lookin aroun the room, their eyes wide an starin, holdin the hands of young fellas, some looked aroun eight or nine years old. An then they looked behind them at an empty spot on the bench an sat down slowly an just stared inta nothin, waitin, their lips movin, prayin tha everythin would be all right.

A name was called, an Jackser jumped up, lookin at me. The man came rushin inta the room an called out me name. 'That's us, Sir!' Jackser said, takin off his cap an holdin it in his two hands.

'Follow me,' the man said, lookin at me. Me heart started hammerin in me chest, an I followed behind Jackser, headin up the stairs an inta a big room.

The room was crowded wit men, all detectives an policemen in plain clothes waitin fer their cases te come up. There were no women, an me ma stayed downstairs. Jackser went te the back of the room an sat down. The man brought me along the side an told me te stand against the wall where everyone could see me. I stood up straight, wit me hands joined at me back, an looked up at the judge sittin up on a high bench where he was able te look down on everyone. A detective stood up an read out the charges against me. I couldn't take in wha he was sayin. An the judge nodded at him, an he sat down. Then there was quiet while the judge read papers in front of him. The judge lifted his head an looked down at me. Then a man wit steel-grey hair an a red face wit a big purple nose stood up an said, 'I'm the solicitor acting for the defendant, your honour.' An he looked at a bunch a papers in his hand. 'I'm Mr Murphy, your honour!'

'Ah, yes, Mr Murphy,' the judge said. I don't know if tha was his right name, cos they seem te mumble. But maybe now tha I'm not on me own it will be better an he will talk up fer me.

I waited, lookin up at them, me heart hammerin away. It seems this is goin te go on for ever. I was swayin an tried te get me feet planted, but me legs was like jelly. An I wanted te stand up straight an stop shakin. The judge was sayin somethin an noddin at another man. Then a skinny little man in a black gown came down te me an took me by the arm an brought me up onta the platform. 'Take this book in your right hand,' he said te me, 'and repeat after me.'

I put me right hand on the Holy Bible an repeated after him, 'I swear by Almighty God, tha the evidence I shall give shall be the truth, the whole truth, an nothin but the truth. So help me, God.'

'Now,' said my solicitor, lookin at his papers. 'Can you tell the court why you took so much butter?'

'Eh?'

An he looked down at his papers. 'You are pleading guilty to these charges? Yes! Yes you are. And there's more than one charge here. Hm! Do you like butter?'

'Eh! Yes!' I said, lookin at him, thinkin, he's makin things worse! The judge doesn't usually bring me up here an ask me a lot a awkward questions! I looked aroun the room at all the men laughin when I said I liked butter. An a man was writin away in his notebook wit a pencil, sittin in the back a the courtroom an liftin his head an writin down everythin tha was bein said.

I looked again at me solicitor, an he said. 'Eh! Yes! Hm! Will you tell the court what you do with all the butter and why you take so much?'

I couldn't believe it. The gobshite was really walkin me inta it! I hesimitated, thinkin. Then the solicitor interrupted me thoughts, sayin, 'For example, you have a charge here for stealing twenty pounds of butter.' An all the aul fellas started sniggerin.

The judge banged his stick wit the knob on an said, 'Order, please!' an glared down at them.

I stared at the solicitor, knowin he had really got me hanged. He should a kept quiet an not asked me all these questions. I was definitely better off on me own wit just the judge. I heard the quiet in the courtroom while everyone waited te hear what I was doin robbin so much butter. I lifted me shoulders an took in a big breath an said, 'I took all the butter so tha I could sell it an buy meself sweets wit the money.'

'You mean you earn your own pocket money?'

I thought about this fer a minute. 'Well, me ma gives me pocket money sometimes. But I like sweets, an tha's why I take the butter.'

'Hm! Yes!' the aul solicitor mumbled, thinkin. 'That's a lot of sweets!' An people laughed again. An then he looked up at the judge, an they nodded te each other.

'Stand against the wall!' the skinny man roared at me.

I crept off the stand an stood against the wall again where everyone could see me. I'm lost! Tha solicitor fella didn't help me. The judge is shakin his head an whisperin wit the solicitor. Then he sat back down, an the judge lifted his head after lookin at his papers again. He looked down at me, leanin over his desk, an smiled at me an said, 'I think, Martha, you would benefit from an education!'

I looked at him, his white face round an happy lookin, an he was very gentle. He's always let me off, an I think he's a very kind man. But I have a bad feelin. I don't like the sound of wha he's sayin an the way he's lookin at me. It's like he's made up his mind te do somethin, an tha stupid aul solicitor has helped him.

'What would you like to be when you grow up, Martha?' he asked me, smilin.

I didn't know wha te say, the only thing I knew was tha I wasn't goin te be like me ma! So I said, 'I don't know, yer honour.'

'Would you like to be a teacher?'

How could I be tha? I thought. I've never been te school! 'No, yer honour.'

'A Bean Gardai?'

I thought about tha, after all the times I was arrested. Me, a lady policeman? 'No, yer honour!'

'A nurse, then?' the judge asked me, smilin.

I got a picture of meself goin up an down, shinin me lamp inta the faces of the injured soldiers groanin in pain, an me fixin them up an givin them a peaceful night's sleep. Just like Florence Nightingale

472

in the comics I read. 'Yeah! Yes, yer honour. I'd love te be a nurse.' I shook me head up an down, wishin I could get started straight away.

'Yes, indeed,' the judge said, smilin an shakin his head up an down agreein wit me. 'I think you should be educated. I am going to send you to a convent where you will be educated. And I must stress, this child is not being sent there as a punishment!' He looked up at the people. 'I am not sending her as a punishment. I am sending her there for an education. And I shall make this as part of the order.' He looked aroun at the people te make sure they understood, then he started writin. 'She will remain at this industrial school until she reaches the age of sixteen.'

The room went foggy, an I couldn't hear or take anythin in. There's a roarin in me ears, an everyone seems te be movin aroun. The detective who charged me gets up smilin an pullin up his trousers. An the little man wit the black gown rushes over te me an takes me arm, handin me over te another man who brings me down the stairs, an down more stairs, an opens a door an brings me inta a room wit a winda high up an bars on it. 'Sit down there an wait!' he says.

Jackser an me ma appears in the door, an the man goes out an locks the door behind him. 'Wha's happenin?' me ma asks, lookin at me an then Jackser, her eyes wide an starin.

'She's goin away!' Jackser says, sittin down in front of me.

'Fer how long?' me ma asks, shocked.

'Until she's sixteen!'

Me ma looks at the wall, thinkin, tryin te take this in.

Then Jackser looks at me, then looks at the door te make sure no one is listenin, an leans inta me, sayin, 'Say nothin! Keep yer mouth shut. Don't tell them anythin! An she comes down wit me if ye do! I won't be doin time on me own. Tha aul one is up te her neck in it. Just you remember tha. An I'll be waitin outside them gates fer ye when they release ye at sixteen. An ye know wha will happen te ye. I'd only get two years at the most. An I'd be well out before tha wit time off fer good behaviour. But them kids will be locked up fer years. An prison would kill yer mammy. So remember tha an tell

473

no one nothin. Do ye get tha?' an he poked me in the chest wit his finger.

'Yeah!' I said, not carin any more.

Me ma stared stony-faced at the wall. 'So tha's tha, then!' she kept mutterin.

'Tha's it!' Jackser said, wit a sour face. 'No more fuckin money.'

Me ma gave me a dirty look. She was ragin, as if I had made the judge send me away.

'No! We're fucked now,' Jackser said. 'Tha just leaves the Charlie fella, an he's useless. Good fer nothin. No, we can't depend on him.'

I sat starin. I'm goin te be locked up! Put away! An me ma won't even look at me. She's bothered cos I won't be bringin her things, or doin everythin she wants me te do fer her. I feel like I'm completely on me own. I'm only good fer doin things fer them. Now I'm no use any more, me ma's not bothered about me. I felt meself goin cold, an I stared at them. Somehow, Jackser reminded me of a big young fella tha went aroun robbin the little kids, takin all their stuff. An a big young fella has put a stop te his gallop, an now he has te fend fer himself. An he's feelin lost an disappointed, cos he's not so brave or smart at all. An he can't play the big man any more, cos he's had his little army of one, me, snatched away from him. An now his game is over. An he's afraid of his life he's goin te get found out. He's only a good-fer-nothin waster. An a coward. He's not a man.

I turned away from him in disgust an looked at me ma. She was still starin at the floor an wouldn't even look at me. If she'd only say, 'I'll miss ye, Martha. I'm sorry ye're goin away.' But no! Her eyes are like two marbles, her mouth is clamped tight, an her face could be made a stone. There's no mammy in her. Just some young one tha trails aroun after her friend, hopin she'll get somethin, doin wha she's told an wantin her friend te mind her cos she's too simple-minded te look after herself. An she doesn't give a fuck about anyone else. Well, fuck you, Sally! Ye're on yer own!

It's dawnin on me, I've been robbed! I was believin I had a mammy. An Jackser was a man, an they were in charge. But they're nothin. I've been rearin me fuckin self. An now they're goin home, an I'm goin te be locked up! Well, tha's it! I'm finished wit them. An when I'm sixteen, I'll make me own way in the world, an I won't ask anyone fer anythin. An no one will ever tell me wha te do. I'll take orders from no one. An it would be a very brave man tha would lay a hand on me, cos he's goin te fuckin lose it. I'm no Sally!

I lifted me back up straight, takin a big breath in through me nose, an folded me arms, gettin ready fer whatever was goin te happen te me. Jackser stirred, lookin at the door, an said, 'We'd better get movin. We left tha Charlie fella watchin the kids. Come on, Sally!' an he nodded his head at her an stood up. 'Remember what I said now. Give them no information,' he whispered over at me.

'Ye needn't worry yerself, I'll tell them nothin,' I said, givin him a dirty look.

'Ye better not,' he said, cockin his eyebrow, tryin te make me afraid.

'No, I won't,' I said, lookin away from him, not bothered, only carin he'd take it out on me ma an the poor childre if he couldn't get his hands on me.

Jackser rattled the doorknob an banged on the door. I heard keys rattlin, an the door opened. 'We'll be ready fer ye any minute now,' a man said, puttin his head in the door.

Jackser turned te me, 'Well, goodbye now. It's not long fer ye te wait.' An he looked out, sayin, 'Come on, they're bringin up the other kids now. The Black Maria is here te take ye's.' I could hear shoutin an cryin.

'Come on!' the man said, noddin at me.

Me heart started te pound again, an I followed the crowd a people up the stairs out the door an onta the path. The Black Maria van was pullin up, an people were millin aroun.

'I'll be off so,' Jackser said, wavin at me.

An me ma stopped te look, 'Goodbye, Martha!' she said, tryin te smile.

'Goodbye, Ma!' I said, tryin te get a good look inta her face, wantin te remember wha she looked like, cos I won't be seein her again.

A detective pushed me forward, an I tried te look back. But all I could see was the back of me ma wit her head down walkin te catch up wit Jackser. I turned aroun, an we stopped while the detective rushed te help two men tryin te wrestle wit an old woman in a black shawl, screamin an tryin te hold onta a little young fella who was holdin on te her fer dear life. He had his head buried in her stomach an his arms wrapped aroun her. An she was tryin te hide him in her shawl. 'Please! Please, Sir! Don't take him away from me. He's only eight years old. I promise as God is in his Heaven I'll send him te school. He won't ever miss school again. I'll make sure a tha.'

The detective tried to loosen the woman's grip, an another policeman tried te pull the child, but they wouldn't let go. 'Granny! Don't let them take me,' he screamed as the third man jumped in an wrenched the child's arm, sayin, 'You have to let go!'

The granny lost her grip on the child, an he was hoisted off the ground, kickin an wavin his arms madly, tryin te get a hold of his granny. 'Jesus! Jesus! No! I'm beggin youse, please give him one more chance. He's only a babby.'

'Well! You should have sent him to school,' an aul fella wit a red face said, holdin her back.

'Jimmy!' she screamed, wipin her snots wit the corner of her shawl as she watched him bein hauled in the Black Maria.

'Come on! Up ye's get,' a detective roared, pushin us from behind.

A young fella of about ten or eleven stumbled in front of me, tryin te look back at his mammy screamin, 'Emmet! Emmet! I'll get the money, an I'll come down te see ye!'

'Ma! I want me ma!' roared Emmet.

'Get up! Come on! Keep movin,' a detective roared at him, pushin him inta the van.

Mammies were standin on the footpath, screamin an wavin. An a young fella of about twelve tried te escape. He was behind me, an he suddenly pushed the detective, knockin him off balance, an jumped screamin, 'Let me go! Ma! I won't rob any more.'

The red-faced man caught him an grabbed him by the neck an

the leg. His mammy rushed at the red-faced man, screamin, 'Take yer hands offa my son or I swear te God I'll be hanged fer ye!'

He pushed her back an grabbed hold a the doors, an looked aroun him, shoutin, 'Is that the lot?'

'Yeah!' shouted the policeman. 'I've done the head count. We have seven! That's the lot!'

'Thanks, Mick.' An the doors was slammed shut. The engine started up, an the noise of the mammies was quieter now.

'They're goin! Oh, Jesus Christ, pray fer them,' I heard a woman cryin.

Young fellas were cryin in the van, an the little fella sittin across from me was sobbin his heart out. The policeman yawned an stretched himself out an asked the detective, 'Where are we headin first?'

The other fella looked at him, about te answer, an then suddenly shouted, 'Shut up! Stop that roarin!' An glared aroun at everyone. The cryin slowed down, an the childre sat givin big sobs, their heads an chests jerkin up an down wit the sobs comin out, an they were tryin te get a breath an quieten themselves. But it was hard, cos everyone was very afraid. 'Well, we have three for Dublin, all in different directions, of course. Then there's a run to Daingean. Drop off two of them there. Then we have a long run ahead of us te Letterfrack.'

'Jaysus! It will be next week before I see a bed,' the policeman complained. Then he pulled out a packet a cigarettes an offered the packet te the detective, who helped himself te one, an they lit up an sat back te enjoy their smoke.

I crossed me arms an lowered me head, closin me eyes. An I wondered how I was goin te get through the next four an a half years until I was sixteen.

Afterword

So there you have it. Martha's story in her own words. The voice of that child in my head no longer haunts me; I carry her within me with great pride. I've set her free. I salute her courage and marvel at her determination to survive. She made me laugh. She made me cry. She made me the adult I've become.